Bridges to Statehood

The Alaska-Yugoslav Connection

If you go far enough east, you enter the west,
The Great Land, Alaska.

"At first we were confused. The East thought that we were West, while the West considered us to be East. Some of us misunderstood our place in the clash of currents, so they cried that we belong to neither side, and others that we belong exlusively to one side or the other. But I tell you, Ireneus, we are doomed by fate to be the East in the West and the West in the East, to acknowledge only heavenly Jerusalem beyond us, and here on earth—no."
—St. Sava to Ireneus,
thirteenth century

Voice of Alaska Press
Big Delta, Alaska

Cover design (includes Yugoslav and Alaska flags): Diane Folaron and Timothy Allen Spurek
Maps of Yugoslavia and Alaska: Diane Folaron
Printed by Publikum Printing Company, Belgrade, Serbia
Publisher: Voice of Alaska Press, Box 130, Delta Junction, Alaska 99737, USA; 907-895-4101
E-mail: outpost@wildak.net
Website: http://www.alaska-highway.org/delta/outpost/

First Printing: February 2009

Elmer E. Rasmuson Library Cataloging in Publication Data:
Ferguson, Judy.
Bridges to statehood : the Alaska-Yugoslav connection / Judy Ferguson. Delta Junction, Alaska : Voice of Alaska Press, c2009.
  p. : ill., ports., maps ; cm.
     ISBN 978-0-9716044-9-0
1. Pioneers—Alaska—Biography. 2. Alaska—History. 3. Yugoslav Americans—Alaska.
I. Title.
                 F903.F465 2009

ISBN 978-0-9716044-9-0 (paper)

Totem pole on title page: Boris Chaliapan, courtesy of Mike Stepovich II family.
Front cover photos: (left) Governor Mike Stepovich and (right) Senator John Butrovich. Courtesy of the Stepovich and Butrovich families.
Back cover photos: Seven of Alaska's governors gathered at the Anchorage Museum on May 9, 2008, to sign copies of *Legacy of Alaska*, the Sydney Laurence painting of Denali for the Anchorage Statehood Celebration. Back: Governors Bill Sheffield, Tony Knowles, Steve Cowper, and Frank Murkowski. Front: Governors Sarah Palin, Mike Stepovich, and Keith Miller. Photo by Marc Lester, *Anchorage Daily News*.
Angie Geraghty dances the kolo at her wedding in Montenegro in 1938. Courtesy of Angie Geraghty.
Father of Governor Mike Stepovich, "Wise Mike" Marko Stepovich, with gold pan at Fish Creek, Fairbanks, Alaska, c. 1942, Mostar Bridge. Courtesy of Vuka Stepovich.

❧ Table of Contents ❧

∞ Dedication ∞

For the late Mary Hajdukovich, whose idea this was. For the late Vuka Stepovich as well as Angie Geraghty, great Montenegrin-Alaskan ladies. With great thanks to my husband Rowe Ferguson, Diane Folaron, Sue Mitchell, to Bob Hajdukovich, the Stepovich family, John Miscovich, John and Bill Dapcevich, the Kleinfelds, the Dan Garvey family, and the indispensable Alaskan contributors. Thanks to Branko Hajduković, Dr. Vladimir Stijepović, Gordan Stojović of Montenegro, and my lifelong Belgrade friends, Zorica Petrović, Majda David, and Miroslav and Zora Konstantinović. Always thanks to my first teachers: Miša, Danilo, Paja, Zorica, Mira, and Verica.

Serpentine Hot Springs, Bering Land Bridge National Preserve. The Bering Land Bridge once connected Russia to Alaska: the ancient pathway from East to West. Courtesy of Junior Ranger Suzanne, www.nps. gov/bela/.

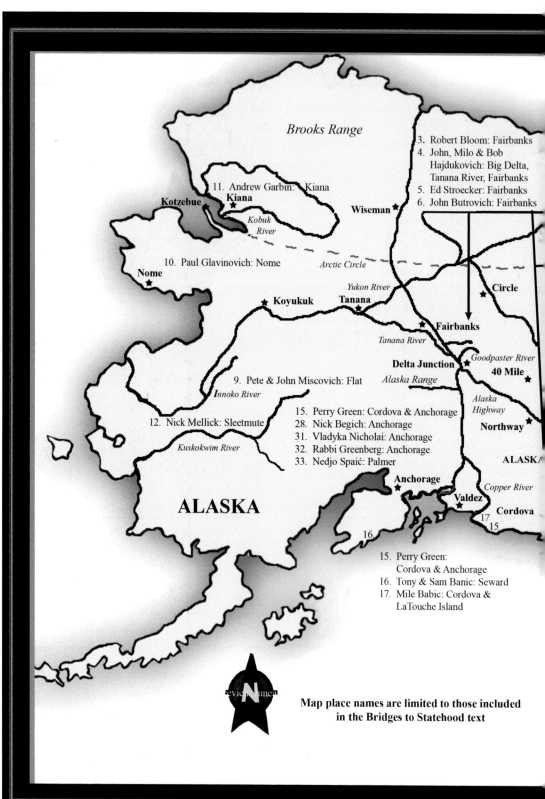

Brooks Range

11. Andrew Garbin: Kiana
Kiana
Kotzebue
Kobuk River

3. Robert Bloom: Fairbanks
4. John, Milo & Bob
   Hajdukovich: Big Delta,
   Tanana River, Fairbanks
5. Ed Stroecker: Fairbanks
6. John Butrovich: Fairbanks

Wiseman

10. Paul Glavinovich: Nome

Nome

Arctic Circle

Yukon River

Koyukuk   Tanana

Circle

Fairbanks

Tanana River

Delta Junction

Goodpaster River
40 Mile

9. Pete & John Miscovich: Flat
Alaska Range

Innoko River

Alaska Highway

15. Perry Green: Cordova & Anchorage
28. Nick Begich: Anchorage
31. Vladyka Nicholai: Anchorage
32. Rabbi Greenberg: Anchorage
33. Nedjo Spaić: Palmer

Northway

12. Nick Mellick: Sleetmute

ALASKA

Kuskokwim River

Anchorage

Copper River

Valdez   Cordova

17
15

ALASKA

16.

15. Perry Green:
    Cordova & Anchorage
16. Tony & Sam Banic: Seward
17. Mile Babic: Cordova &
    LaTouche Island

N

Map place names are limited to those included
in the Bridges to Statehood text

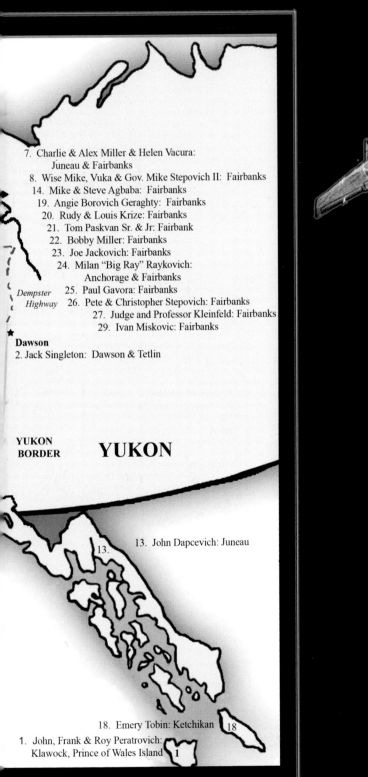

SLOVENIA

22. Kranj
20. *LJUBLJANA

14. Grache-Lika
*ZAGREB

21.   23.

CROATIA

Slavonia

Krajina

Serb Republic

Novi Sad

21. Sunger
23. Mrkopalj
28. Podlapaca
16. Otok
10. Split
6. Brac

28.

Dalmatia

16.

10.

6.

SARAJEVO
Federation
of Bosnia and
Herzegovina

Republic

*

Serb

Montenegro

19. Vinicka
4a.

31.

33.

1.

9.

PODGORICA

8.

7.

13.

24.   4.

12.

*

ALBANI

Adriatic
Sea

31. Ljubinje
33. Trebinje
1. Dubrovnik
9. Imotica
8. Risan
7. Djenovic
13. Ljubotinj
24. Kosijeri
4. Podgor Utrg & 4a. Kolašin
12. Gluhi Do
19. Vinicka

ITALY

ROMANIA

ojvodina

BELGRADE

29. 30.
**Mihajlo Mihajlov,
Miša and Majda David,
Dr. Miroslav Konstantinović,
Ivan Mišković, Zorica
Petrović, Davor Salom,
Spasoje Krunić**

Serbia

Pristina

KOSOVO

*

ŠKOPJE

MACEDONIA

Map
of
former
Yugoslavia

*The numbers on
this map correlate
with the numbers
used on the map of
Alaska.*

We welcome reader response to
Bridges to Statehood: The Alaska-Yugoslav Connection
Your input is valuable.

◦

Books and Materials by Judy Ferguson

Bridges to Statehood: The Alaska-Yugoslav Connection
DVD, *The Shaping of a State*
Blue Hills: Alaska's Promised Land
Parallel Destinies: An Alaskan Odyssey

Children's Books
Alaska's Secret Door
Alaska's Little Chief
Alaska's First People

Signed art prints; lesson plans based on state performance standards on CD
may be ordered through Voice of Alaska Press:
1-907-895-4101
E-mail: outpost@wildak.net
Online store: http://www.alaska-highway.org/delta/outpost/
PO Box 130, Delta Junction, Alaska, 99737, U.S.A.

Thank you for your support.

Judy Ferguson
Voice of Alaska Press
Big Delta, Alaska

Introduction

The Alaska-Yugoslav Connection

Over the Chilkoot Trail's icy steps, these sons of Viches came—Stepovich, Butrovich, Dapcevich, Begich, Paskvan, and Peratrovich—to guide Alaska from a raw land to statehood, from southeast to the arctic, from gold camps to the forty-ninth star! Names so Alaskan that their Slavic stories went untold, they represented the world's former empires and today's Balkan states.

Known in the 1990s as one of the world's hot spots of war and turmoil, former Yugoslavia has a strong link to Alaska's history.

Joe Jackovich, speaking from his office at Jackovich Industrial and Construction Supply, agreed with an old-timer's saying: "If you weren't Yugoslavian during the 1930s to 1950s in Fairbanks, you didn't go far."

A small country that would fit between Fairbanks and Tok, Montenegro has produced many talented people. The Yugoslav names are so identified with Alaska that they are not thought of as Croatian, Slovenian, or Montenegrin. These immigrants contributed greatly to Alaska's development as well as prospering with Alaska's opportunity: Peratrovich, Stepovich, Butrovich, Hajdukovich, Miscovich, Begich, Dapcevich, Yankovich, Paskvan, Agbaba, Franich, Milajich/Miller, Garbin, Bigovich, Mesich, Babic, Banic, Krize, Borovich, Glavinovich, and countless others. Representing today's modern states of former Yugoslavia, these Alaskans were drawn by fishing, mining, and business but always, a new opportunity. Some made gold rings with the emblem of Alaska surrounded by Montenegro's grapes. Like a marriage between the Far North, the place of riches, and impoverished Mediterranean Montenegro, the rings were also an investment for the families back home.

Part of the ancient land bridge connecting North America to Russia, Alaska is a corridor leading from the old into the new world. In the sixth century, Slavs filtered from north of the Danube River southwest down into the Balkans. By the 1700s the Russian Slavs had claimed Alaska. Ruled by the Russian Empire until 1867, Alaska was forever marked by the Slavs. Today many of the Aleut, Alutiiq/Sugpiaq and Yupik peoples have Russian names and worship in the Russian Orthodox Diocese of Alaska church.

In the early twentieth century, Alaska and former Yugoslavia were both young states, both multiethnic, but grown from entirely different root systems with quite different results.

Alaska grew from the Western tradition of law and of democracy. The Balkans grew from a mix of Orthodox Christianity, Catholicism, Islam, and a secular patriarchal figure leading the collective whole. In the villages, the diminution of Slavic family's rocky land holdings historically rendered the people very poor. Living on the coast, peasants, fishermen, tradesmen, and artisans often stowed away on a ship to reach the land of opportunity, America. The mines in America provided an income for the immigrants, and that network led ultimately to the mines of Alaska.

Bridges to Statehood tells the stories of Slavic Alaskans, from Russian days before 1885, through territorial days into statehood and through the Cold War era. It is Alaska from mining to fishing, from fur to bars, from retail to sports, from aviation to politics. *Bridges to Statehood* includes the building of the Alaska Highway, bringing modern communication into the Great Land, and the Alaska state constitutional convention.

It is also the story of an Alaskan in Yugoslavia: a lifelong history with the former Yugoslavia, with its dramatic contrast to the Great Land. It presents my friends, the people of former Yugoslavia. Beginning nineteen years after World War II, including the wars that destroyed Yugoslavia, my story covers the more recent period, while the story of the Alaska Yugoslav immigrants is from the first half of the twentieth century. These are bridges to statehood: here, the Alaska Yugoslavs shaped a state; there, modern states have emerged from the former communist country. Together, the twentieth century is seen both in a new land and in the ancient Mediterranean.

This story of Alaska has never before been told; each person is a door revealing who we are and where we have come from: *Bridges to Statehood: The Alaska-Yugoslav Connection.*

Chapter 1

The First Salmon Cannery in Alaska: John Peratrovich

Before the south Slavs influenced the Alaska interior, John Peratrovich was developing Alaska's first salmon cannery in 1878 in southeast Alaska, two years before gold was discovered in Juneau and six years before the gold rush hit the Interior.

"Because John Peratrovich eventually had three wives and sixteen children, the name Peratrovich in Southeast is almost as common as Smith is elsewhere!" Nettie Peratrovich, the daughter-in-law of Elizabeth Peratrovich, smiled. Among his many children, John Peratrovich

Josie, Mary (Skan) Peratrovich, John, and Mabel Peratrovich, c. 1900, Klawock, Prince of Wales Island. Courtesy of Frank and Nettie Peratrovich.

reared two of Alaska's more notable leaders: Roy, a civil rights activist, five-time grand president of Alaska Native Brotherhood who was married to Elizabeth Peratrovich; and Frank, territorial and state senator, senate president, and first vice president of the Alaska Constitutional Convention in 1955.

Roy and Elizabeth's sons, Roy Peratrovich Jr. and Frank II, remembered the story of his grandfather and his family's milestones in Alaska history.

My grandfather John Peratrovich, a Croatian-Italian fisherman called "Dago John," was born on the Dalmatian coastline about 1859. "Senj" district was noted as his birthplace. He jumped ship from the Dalmatian coast and landed in San Francisco. As an expert seiner, he began looking for work. Word got around the canneries that John Peratrovich knew how to mend seine nets.

In 1868, a trading post and a salmon saltery were opened in Klawock on Prince of Wales Island. [Croatian researcher Mark Eterovich stated that the first salmon cannery in Klawock was established in 1868 and belonged to Sisson, Wallace, and Co. (University of California Berkeley Bancroft Library 602). In 1877, the cannery was incorporated into the North Pacific Packing and Trading Co.] in effect beginning the canned Alaska salmon industry.

The local Tlingits who wintered in Tuxekan used Klawock in the summer as a fishing camp, calling it Klawerak, Tlevak, Clevak, and Klawak.

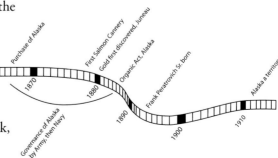

Klawock, Prince of Wales Island, 1885. Courtesy of Frank and Nettie Peratrovich.

In 1876, as North Pacific Trading and Packing Co (NPTPC) was planning on taking over [either the earlier cannery or] the saltery, they were most interested in getting the local Natives in Klawock to make and mend their own seines, rather than sending the nets back and forth to San Francisco. NPTPC hired Grandpa as a net hanger. As the cannery planned its hand-pack system in Alaska, they asked Grandpa to take equipment needed for setup and to establish the cannery. [Family legend has it that on the way to Klawock, the ship wrecked in a storm at the Seal Islands north of Afognak Island. John was rescued by Sugpiaq Eskimos, Alutiiq. A Russian revenue cutter took John to Sitka.]

[Eterovich noted that in the 1901 and 1905 San Francisco City Directories, a "Petrovich Canning Co." was listed.]

When Grandpa arrived in Klawock about 1876, he went across the bay by skiff to the peninsula, called Peratrovich Island, to begin the conversion from saltery [or primitive cannery] to the NPTPC cannery. The local Tlingit chief asked the seventeen-year-old seiner to show the people the art of seine netting. From the beginning Grandpa worked well with the Native people. The chief had a forty-two-year-old daughter, Catherine Snook Skan. From an earlier marriage to John Skan, she had his two teenage stepdaughters, Mary Skan and Nellie Skan. In Tlingit matriarchal culture an older woman traditionally married a younger man. Catherine and Grandpa were married. In 1877, their first son Jack was born, followed by James, Nick, and Robert. The Tlingits in Klawock, unlike subsequent Southeast canneries, were employees in the local cannery. As the cash economy with the gold rush began to invade Alaska, Klawock's cannery employment helped to preserve its people. In other towns, the ethnic tension was so high that miners in Juneau were crying for some form of civil government. Former customs collector M. D. Ball of Sitka was elected by local delegates to travel to Washington, D.C., taking with him a petition asking for formal recognition as Alaska's representative. Congress refused to seat him and would not respond to his plea for Alaska self-government. However, in 1884 the Organic Act made Alaska a district with an appointed governor and officers.

Over the years Klawock took care of itself. As Grandpa worked in the hand-pack cannery, he received shares as well as pay. He often made business trips back and forth to San Francisco. At some point, Libby McNeil and Libby took over the North Pacific Trading and Packing Co. cannery.

As Grandpa traveled, he visited his Slavic friends throughout Southeast, one of whom, Vincent Baranovich, had a still. On trips Outside, some of Grandpa's children accompanied him. [One family story says that John and one of his daughters were once en route back to Croatia when he ran out of money in San Francisco. She said that as they traveled she was designated to sit on "the trunk that was full of money."]

During one trip while Grandpa was gone, Catherine took up with another man, Tecumseh Collins, and she eventually divorced Grandpa. After the divorce, he married his wife's first stepdaughter, Mary Skan (1864–1926) with whom he had nine more children: Josie (portrayed on the early salmon label), Frank (territorial and state senator and vice president of Alaska's constitutional convention), Mabel One (also on the early salmon label), Sarah, Jennie, Ann, Roy (my father), Mabel Two, and Bertha. Uncle Frank and my father Roy were Grandpa and Gramma Mary's only sons. With Catherine's other step-daughter, Nellie, Grandpa also had two more children: Roseanna and George. All of Grandpa's children were born when Natives were not considered citizens. [Citizenship wasn't extended to Alaska Natives until 1924.] Today, Grandpa's progeny number over 680.

Grandpa became the principal person in the salmon cannery. In 1900, a picture of him, my Gramma Mary, and their first two daughters, Josie and Mabel One, was on their Family Brand salmon label. But when Mabel One died, the label was retired. It was too painful a reminder. According to Tlingit customs, as Catherine and Grandpa's first four boys, Jack, James, Nick, and Robert, grew up, they tattooed their family name and an eagle onto their arms. When Grandpa went to San Francisco once a year, he usually took Robert.

Front, seated: Grandma Tecumseh (Catherine Snook Skan Peratrovich Collins); seated w/ baby: Mary Skan Peratrovich with Mabel One; John Peratrovich with Roy (Elizabeth Peratrovich's husband and father of Roy Jr, Loretta and Frank Jr.). Standing behind Grandma Tecumseh, L–R: Georgie; Rosanne holding Evelyn; Josie holding Al. Behind John Peratrovich: Jack's wife; Jack holding Robinson; Nick's wife; Nick holding Alex; Robert holding Helen; James. (Frank Peratrovich Sr was away in the Navy.) Left side: Ann and Jennie and others. Photo is c. 1911–12, Klawock. Courtesy of Frank and Nettie Peratrovich.

Klawock's first cannery's label, show photo of original cannery, 1890s. Courtesy of Frank and Nettie Peratrovich.

Like a second mother, Dad's oldest sister, Josie, grew up taking care of all the kids. Grandpa built a large beautiful home for his wife and children and their mothers, where the children lived until they wed. After marriage, the adult children built homes close to his. [He became a charter member of the Order of Moose in Craig. The spellings for his name found on various records were Petovich, Paratovich (a name found on the Croatian island of Hvar], Peratovich, and ultimately Peratrovich.]

When Uncle Frank was only five, Grandpa's cannery burned. In his desk, he had kept the proof of his company shares; when they burned, he lost control of the cannery. His grandson David did rebuild it and his son Bob ran it.

In November 1915, David was rowing Grandpa in their boat between the cannery and Klawock village when the boat capsized. Although Grandpa was rescued, the exposure triggered a virus in his kidneys. When he was fifty-six, he died. My father, Roy, was only seven and became the man of the house.

Seven of Gramma Mary's daughters went to Chemawa Indian School in the Lower Forty-eight, but few returned. Like his sisters, Uncle Frank went Outside to boarding school at Haskell Institute, Topeka, Kansas. On a sports team tour he met the legendary football hero Jim Thorpe and later, he played against him on the football field. Uncle Frank also served in the Navy.

Uncle Bob's cannery also burned, and after Grandpa died in 1920 he rebuilt it. Bob also had a grocery store, the movie house, and the only power plant in town. At nine p.m. everyone knew Bob had gone to bed because he turned off the diesel run generators and with it, everyone else's power. Bob was quite the gentleman dresser, wearing three-piece suits every day.

Dad told me about the hardships he endured growing up. Uncle Frank was not around after his father died. He was away in school or in the Navy. Dad hunted deer for the family and brought home salmon. He sawed large firewood logs alone, chopped and stacked it. There was no time to play. No one ever helped except one day Uncle Bob saw Dad trying to get the saw to bite into a huge log laying down on the beach. Bob was in his three-piece suit but he jumped down to the beach, took off his jacket and helped Dad saw that log. Dad never forgot that.

In 1924 Demmert's cannery was built. Dad used to wash dishes at that cannery across the bay to make a little money for his fatherless family. He was usually the last one to leave. One weekend when there was a dance at the Alaska Native Brotherhood Hall, he had one more impossible pan to clean. In desperation and when no one was looking, he threw the pot into the woods and rowed to Klawock for the dance. The next day nobody missed the pot!

Filipino employees would work for less than the locals, so the cannery brought them into town. In the bunkhouse at night, the Filipinos jammed on their musical instruments. Dad and his friends really liked the music. They salvaged some instruments the Salvation Army had discarded. The horns had sticky valves, which they fixed with string. From a horse in town, they borrowed some tail hairs. In the bunk house, Dad tied the hair to a steel bunk, anchored them to an upside-down metal tub and voila, he had a bass guitar! The Filipinos taught Dad to play a ukulele as well. I don't know how he could with his huge hands. (He could lift an anvil by the cone with one hand.) Dad's favorite piece was "My Little Grass Shack in Hawaii." No one taught them how to play, they just learned by trying. Once on the Fourth of July, the town's local "marching band" paraded through town. Their bass drummer was deaf and blind but he loved banging on his big patched-up drum. When they got to the "Y" in the road the band went one way and Jumbo the drummer the other way. No one ever had the heart to tell Jumbo he went the wrong way. Dad also played guitar in a small dance band that played on weekends in Craig. He rowed around the coast to get the extra pin money.

When Dad was eighteen, his mother also died. However life had given him training for the battles yet to come. With the advantage of knowing Tlingit and his culture, Dad went on to become a fine speaker and a leader of his people.

San Francisco North Pacific Trading and Packing Company built Alaska's first salmon cannery in 1878 on Klawock Island, locally called Peratrovich Island. It operated until it burned in 1899. Courtesy of Frank and Nettie Peratrovich.

Chapter 2

Alaska's Civil Rights Act: Roy, Elizabeth, and Frank Peratrovich
as told by Frank Peratrovich II

Because we were part Yugoslav, my parents could eat in Montenegrin Mike Pusich's restaurant on Douglas Island—but he only made an exception for my parents. In the windows of restaurants and hotels in Juneau, there were signs, "No Indians or dogs allowed." (However those Slavs didn't care if you were an Indian, a Communist, or whatever, so long as you had that 'vich' in your name.) Through my parents, Roy and Elizabeth Peratrovich, I am both Croat and Tlingit. I was named after my uncle Frank Peratrovich.

Frank Peratrovich running for the Alaska legislature, c. 1944. Courtesy of Frank and Nettie Peratrovich.

Uncle Frank and my father Roy (born thirteen years after Frank) were both active in Alaska Native Brotherhood (ANB). Mother was also very active in the Alaska Native Sisterhood (ANS). One of their goals was to get the right to vote for Natives.

When Uncle Frank was in charge of distribution of food and clothing to widows and children under territorial Governor John W. Troy, Uncle Frank noticed that no Native widows and children came in. When he asked, the governor answered that Natives weren't allowed those benefits. When Uncle Frank replied he would quit, the governor reversed the policy. In 1945, Uncle Frank began serving in the territorial legislature. Later he became first vice president of the Alaska Constitutional Convention, and in the 1960s he was the president of the Senate. A thoughtful man who spoke little, Uncle Frank was deeply respected. He fought to ban national canneries' fish trap monopolies, which caught unfair amounts of salmon and damaged the local seiners' harvest and sales. He included a provision in the new state constitution to outlaw the traps, and he won.

In contrast to the more serious Frank, my father was gregarious, a great jokester, and

Roy Peratrovich, youngest son of John and Mary Peratrovich, 1940, Klawock. Courtesy of Roy Peratrovich Jr.

Native Allotment Act
Alaska Territory two-house legislature; Founding of Alaska Native Brotherhood
Citizenship for all Native Alaskans
Frank Peratrovich Sr./Alaska Territorial Legislature
Anti-discrimination Bill

1910   1920   1930   1940   1950

an excellent speaker. My mother, Elizabeth Jean Wanamaker, was born of the Raven moiety at Petersburg on the Fourth of July. Her parents were Presbyterian lay minister Andrew Wanamaker and his first wife, Jean (a wonderful person who understood English but could only speak Tlingit). The Tlingit name they gave Mother meant "the root of all women." Mother was serious, disciplined, stylish, and beautiful.

Dad went to Chemawa Indian School in Salem, Oregon, where he played guard and was captain of the football team. His senior year in 1930, he left for Ketchikan High School where he met Mom. (Their school annual predicted they would get married.) After graduation in 1931, wanting to teach, they both enrolled at Bellingham Normal (today, Western Washington University) but they ran out of money. Thinking they could better save money, they got married. When that didn't happen, they returned to Klawock, where life for them was less expensive. Dad worked there as a fisherman, laborer, fireman, policeman, postmaster and as mayor. My older brother, Roy, was born in Klawock in 1934 and three years later, I was born in Juneau. In 1937 there were more Natives than whites in Alaska, and the average life expectancy for Natives was about forty-five. We Alaska Natives were at the bottom of the totem pole, on a level with a Third World nation.

Frank II and Roy Jr. Peratrovich, Juneau, c. 1940. Courtesy of Frank Peratrovich.

In 1940, Dad was elected grand president of the Alaska Native Brotherhood (ANB), but he figured he couldn't do much good in Klawock for the Native people. We moved to Juneau in late December 1940. Roy was seven, I was four, and Sis was less than a year old. (Mom used to recall the hair-raising airplane trip coming into Juneau with our pilot Tex Beneke, who later became one of the owners of Alaska Airlines!) Roy was one of the first Native children to go to public school there; previously all the Native children had to attend the Bureau of Indian Affairs school in the village. Renting in Juneau was difficult, but we became the second Native family in a non-Native neighborhood. I always had to wear a white shirt to make sure we didn't appear to be "dirty Indians." We were very poor, so Mom hand-knit and crocheted beautiful dresses to sell. Her passion was reading.

By acclamation Dad was reelected grand president of ANB four more times. (Later in 1945, Mom was elected grand president of Alaska Native Sisterhood.)

In 1941, my parents wrote letters to the vice president and to Gov. Ernest Gruening protesting the racist public signs in Juneau. They noted that Natives paid school taxes even though their children were largely disallowed from public schools.

My parents submitted an antidiscrimination bill to the territorial legislature in 1943, but it failed. A Native American attorney, Bill Curran, began working for them for free, spending long evening hours drafting the civil rights act in our kitchen at 815 Dixon Street, above the governor's mansion. Passage was expected to take years.

At the annual convention in 1944, the ANB prepared Resolution No. Two: Antidiscrimination, to present to the Senate. (While the United States was fighting Hitler's policy of white supremacy in Europe, it looked like Mom was taking on white supremacy in the Alaska territorial legislature.) Sen. Allen Shattuck rose up indignantly and addressed the legislature, "Who are these people, barely out of savagery, who want to associate with us whites with five thousand years of recorded history behind us?"

My mom put her knitting down and came forward. "I would not have expected that I, who am barely out of savagery, would have to remind gentlemen of five thousand years of recorded civilization of our Bill of Rights.

"There are three kinds of people who practice discrimination," she said. "First, the politician to maintain an inferior minority group; second, Mr. and Mrs. Jones, who aren't sure of their social position; and third, the great superman who believes in the superiority of the white race." The Senate and gallery exploded with applause.

After the Antidiscrimination Bill passed on February 8, 1945, my folks went to Percy's Cafe (which catered to Natives) where my Tlingit friend Gus Adams was having a Coke. They were so excited that the bill had just passed that they had to tell someone! Gus never forgot it. On February 16, Gov. Gruening signed the bill into law, nineteen years before the nation's civil rights law. To celebrate passage, Dad and Mom went where Natives had not before been allowed, and they danced beautifully at the Baranof Hotel. People backed up (not out of admiration) and cleared the floor.

The reality was that the civil rights law was good, but its enforcement was never funded. In case of infraction, no one had the money to go to court—and the chances of getting a jury of your peers were poor. It was a moral victory rather than a new litigated way of life. Even with the law passed, Native people returning from World War II and later from Korea had a hard time finding lodging in Juneau. That's how I got to know Cecil Barnes, a former marine in Korea and later, the first chairman of Chugach corporation. A lot of people (including the most decorated Native during World War II) stayed with us for as much as a month.

The biggest difference the civil rights law made was that discrimination could no longer be outright; however, it did become subtle. Hotels just used the excuse, "We don't have any more rooms." However, the law made it possible for Natives to go to public schools.

Mom also fought for the Japanese-Americans who were interned during World War II in camps outside Alaska. My wife Nettie Peratrovich met a young Japanese girl who asked if Nettie had known Mom. The girl said, "Elizabeth Peratrovich was the most wonderful lady in the world. She got so many of us Japanese kids out of the camps. In Alaska, our lands were also not taken from us." As an influential person and big leader in ANS, Mom worked with Governor Gruening to get the Japanese children who had been born in Alaska out of the camps. During the 1950s, Mom helped a Polish marine who jumped ship in Juneau. My folks fed him him and helped him get a job. (During the 1950s, that wasn't popular.) She got

Alaska Native Sisterhood, L, second: Elizabeth Peratrovich, Grand President, 1945, Juneau. Courtesy of Frank and Nettie Peratrovich.

Governor Ernest Gruening signing the Anti-Discrimination bill. L–R: Senator O.D. Cochran (Nome), Mrs. Roy (Elizabeth) Peratrovich (Klawock), Gov. Ernest Gruening, Rep. Anderson (Nome), Senator N.R. Walker (Ketchikan), Roy Peratrovich (Klawock).

a bill passed through Congress that allowed him to stay. When she saw something terribly wrong, she tried to right it.

Nationally, Mom went as the first Alaska representative to the National Congress of American Indians, trying to get support for Alaska civil rights. In 1956, she attended the Institute for Race Relations at Fisk University, where African-American clergy discussed how to integrate the church. Martin Luther King and several others who later became national leaders were also there.

Dad was the first Alaskan to receive a United Nations fellowship; with it, he went to Nova Scotia and studied their fishing industry. In 1952 he got a scholarship to study credit procedure at the Central Bank and Trust Company where he also took a business course at Denver University in Denver, Colorado. I remember Dad and I studying the material together at the dining room table. For the territorial government of Alaska and the Bureau of Indian Affairs, he first served as a special officer, then credit and financing officer, followed as head of the tribal operations program in the state, based in Juneau. In 1955, he became a loan examiner for the Bureau of Indian Affairs (BIA) in the regional office at Anadarko, Oklahoma. In 1968 Governor Gruening announced that Dad was the new BIA superintendent of the Anchorage District, with responsibility in southcentral and in the Aleutian Islands.

Dad was open, very straightforward. Along with Barney Gottstein, he was on the first Alaska Human Rights Commission. When he was the area tribal officer for BIA, he would call up Governor Egan, and let him know what wasn't right. Egan would say, "Roy, you gotta remember you're talking to the governor of Alaska." Dad just said, "Bill, don't pull rank on me now." If politicians ignored Native-related issues, based on the Native vote Dad could negotiate.

In 1958, when Mom died of cancer, few yet knew the name Elizabeth Peratrovich. It was at least twenty years before her name would become widely recognized. In the late 1980s, a university student researching the Alaska civil rights bill kept coming across the name Elizabeth Peratrovich. After he published his research paper, the Alaska Native Brotherhood and Sisterhood pushed the legislature to set aside a day beginning in 1988 to honor my mother, Feb. 16. On Feb. 16, 2003, the Municipality of Anchorage renamed a park at Fourth Avenue and E Street "Elizabeth and Roy Peratrovich Park." June 30, 2008, my brother Roy, a retired engineer and well-known sculptor, presented his sculpture, "Flight of the Raven," dedicated to our parents in Peratrovich Park.

Peratrovich family (fourth in from right, back row: Roy Peratrovich Jr., Loretta Peratrovich Montgomery, Diane Benson, Frank II, and Nettie Peratrovich) at dedication of Flight of the Raven, Peratrovich Park, Anchorage, June 30, 2008. Courtesy of Frank Peratrovich II.

Chapter 3

Jack Singleton, a Story of the Klondike: The Salem, Oregon, "Upper Crust" Youth

In the late 1950s in San Jose, California, a young girl, Roberta Drake, used to visit an elderly woman, "Ol Jenny." An eccentric solitary woman with private memories, Jenny Singleton Reid died in 1961. With no interested relatives, Jenny's burial was taken care of by casual friends, Roberta's parents. Left behind was Jenny's box of unexplained mementos: a pair of beaded baby moccasins, a gold poke, ¼" ivory dominos, the lace collar from her wedding dress, postcards from Jack Singleton, a movie contract with a Hollywood studio, a tiny ivory calendar, Eben Singleton's little red journal, and photos from the Klondike Gold Rush.

Later after they moved to Alaska, Roberta and her husband, Dan Garvey, looked for clues to the story of Ol Jenny and the unknown Eben and John "Jack" Singleton.

Jack Singleton, Dawson City, 1898, cyanotype. Courtesy of Roberta and Dan Garvey.

In 2002, Dan was a manager at Anchorage's Barnes and Noble bookstore. An author had left a new book titled *Parallel Destinies*, the story of John Hajdukovich, on his desk. As he flipped through the book, looking as always for clues, he discovered a chapter on John "Jack" Singleton. With this trail, Dan began to piece together the story of the Singleton brothers— Jack, Harry, and Eben—their cousin Myra Wiggins, and her friend Jenny, young people of Oregon's upper crust who in 1896 followed the gold trail north to Alaska.

John "Jack" Singleton, a lifelong friend of John Hajdukovich, was born in Iowa in 1867. When he was only ten, Jack's father died of a heart attack, leaving behind his wife, Sarah, and their four children. Since she had a wealthy banker brother, John Albert, in Salem, Oregon, Sarah Singleton gathered up her three boys, Jack, Harry, and Eben, and daughter, Bessie, and headed to Oregon from 1880 to 1884. A kind uncle, John Albert sent all three Singleton brothers to Willamette University, where Jack graduated as a civil engineer and then began working as a surveyor for the railroad. Harry and Eben majored in business accounting. John Albert's own daughter, Myra, became deeply interested in photography. On Memorial Day 1890, she gathered the young adults and photographed them, including her Singleton cousins and her friend, Jenny Youmans.

Gold found Fortymile R. 1886 1890 Gold found Klondike R. 1900 Valdez–Fairbanks telegraph built 1910 World War I 1920 1930 1940 1950 World War II

That same year, sixteen-year-old Jenny married Wight "Ike" Frierson, and in about 1893 they had a son, Edwin. At twenty-four, Jack Singleton married Emma Royal, daughter reputedly of a fire and brimstone preacher. Jack moved Emma into Harry's house with him and his younger brothers, Harry and Eben.

By 1893, America's railroads had vastly over-extended, bursting the bubble of a large economic speculation. The nation plunged into a deep economic depression. Jack lost his job. Adding to the stress, Jack and Emma had a daughter, Elizabeth, "Bessie," born in 1895.

At the same time, Jack's cousin Myra married Fred Wiggins. By the late 1890s-early 1900s, Myra was the preeminent female photographer for Eastman Kodak, documented later in *The Witch of Kodakery*.

By 1896, the cry of gold sounded from the Klondike. Dawson City exploded from a town of 500 to 30,000. Claims had to be surveyed and borders drawn, which brought surveyors north. Looking to supply the prospectors, Harry and Eben traveled north on the Topeka alongside famed miner Clarence J. Berry as well as a steward, Belinda Mulrooney, later of Dawson fame.

At the mouth of the Fortymile River on the Yukon, thirty miles from the Alaska border near a large mining camp, a trading post at Cudahy serviced the miners at Fortymile and the new Dawson City. Eben Singleton got merchant work at Cudahy while his brother Harry returned to Seattle and began supplying Eben from the Pacific Northwest. By 1897, Jack had joined Eben and was farther upstream, staking claims at Gold Bottom Creek in the Klondike. Describing the new situation, Eben wrote to Harry of Jack and his partner, Ernest, detailing that first hard winter as thousands of prospectors came north. In passing, Eben also mentioned "Ike," possibly Jenny Frierson's husband. (It's not impossible that Jenny came with her husband, and if so, their son, Edwin, definitely remained behind with Jenny's mother in Idaho.)

Miners Home Bar, Dawson City, 1899 (right fourth: Myra; sixth: Jack). Courtesy of Roberta and Dan Garvey.

Harry published Eben's letter to him in the Oregon Statesman newspaper:

"Fort Cudahy (.5 mile north of the mining camp at the Fortymile River mouth), Northwest Territories [until 1898 the Yukon Territory was a district of the Northwest Territories.]

"October 21st, 1897
Dear Brother,
September 10th: Ernest left No. 74 on Bonanza Creek, and came down to see me. He is as brown as a nut and has a beard. He and Jack are putting up cabins on the claim, and I have made all arrangements for their grub. Ernest thought it was the finest place on the river. Any hour we are looking for a steamer. I have our boys pretty well outfitted with mittens, moccasins, Arctic and German socks, caps and clothing so I don't think they will suffer....

September 18th: Not one of the steamers has arrived.... People are getting quite worried.... The water is very low in the river. Jack and Ernest sent word to me to get all the food possible so I guess they are getting scared....

A fresh strike is reported on the Tanana River, Alaska which is probably true. The strike was made right back of Circle City, the prospector went from Mastodon Creek over the divide to the Tanana.

September 25th:... the faithful old [steamboat] Weare pushed her nose around the point yesterday with about 200 tons of food on board. She is in good condition but for over a month, she was laid up high and dry on a sand bar at Fort Yukon. The miners at Circle City [downstream] held her up and took over forty tons of food from her.... They didn't know they were robbing the miners at Dawson [upstream of Circle and Cudahy] more than the company.... The ship's owner Mr. Weare would not let any passengers come on board since there was not even enough food at Dawson for those who are there. He would not sell any liquor, saying the people needed food more than whiskey even though he could sell whiskey at $40 a gallon.

September 28th: There are 40 men on the Weare working their way down to Fort Yukon (freight free.) They are trying to get Outside this winter but I don't think they will make it.

October 21st: Heading downriver, the steamer Bella arrived here October 1st. She had broken her rudder in the ice and was at Fortymile for repairs.

At Dawson the police had to mount guards while the crew unloaded the Bella. Those miners were then here a week, and sent a committee over. We let them have what food we could spare and then some of them talked of breaking into the store and seizing what remained. When they finally left, we were quite relieved. Due to the shortage of food, the miners were given free passage on the Bella to Fort Yukon. There were 130 on board, many with no caps or mittens, not prepared for winter. They will suffer a lot from the cold weather.

Here, a fellow tried to hold one of my claims. To fight it, I started overland for Dawson with an Indian to pack part of my stuff. When I had gone ten miles upstream, I met a missionary, Rev. Totty, who told me it was impossible to get across the river, especially at Dawson. The Indians with him would not take me across for love or money so I had to go back. Even offering $50 to anyone who would deliver my letter to Dawson, I couldn't get anyone to cross the river. After the river finally cleared, a miner took my letter to Dawson. After a number of delays, I won the case thanks partly to Dr. Wills and Captain Constantine of the Royal Canadian Mounted Police.

Jack and Ernest wrote me that they have all their food okay; they were about to leave for Gold Bottom claim.

It is going to be simply awful in Dawson this winter; unless they get some provisions, the suffering cannot be described.

October 31st: Ike is recovering from bilious fever [stomach flu]; he will be okay in a few days.

November 6th: I got a report from Gold Bottom Creek that the boys are well and hard at work on the claim. Jack staked such a good claim on Sulphur Creek that before he filed in the Commissioner's Office, he was offered $1000 for a half claim.

December 3rd: The river closed for good [November] 9th. It is a very rough [jagged surface]. Traveling will be hard on freighters this winter. On Thanksgiving, the first arrivals over the ice arrived from Circle City; on November 22nd, the first from Dawson arrived. Food will not be as scarce as expected at Dawson; [possibly because] 550 have already left over the ice for Juneau. I bet they will have a tough time of it.

December 11th: The boys wrote that they have a comfortable cabin, plenty of food and are in good health. They won the suit for their claim, 'hands down.'

Captain Ray, USA [Army], has taken charge at Fort Yukon. The rule is the men have to work in the Army's wood yard for their food or go hungry.

After being on the trail from Lake Lindeman for 33 days, a prospector arrived. He said there were a lot of people coming down the trail. He said there was also about 2 tons of mail stuck at Stewart River; the handlers won't bring it down until spring. You bet we were on our ear.

We have 2 large moose hams, each weighing 275 pounds and 35 caribou hams.

Regards to all the boys and the folks. Your brother, Eben Singleton"

Eben enjoyed photography and noted that he would send his "film out to be processed." Eben's photos stored in Ol Jenny's mementos box were cyanotypes, a blue photo on thin paper, an artistic style. In 1899 his cousin, Eastman Kodak's Myra Wiggins, was also developing some cyanotype photos. Probably Eben sent his film to her and she processed them in her darkroom using her cyanotype chemicals.

Intrigued by the Klondike and wanting to photograph the global event, Myra and her husband, Fred Wiggins, took the boat to Skagway, the train to Whitehorse, and a steamboat to Dawson. In an 1899 photo that Myra's husband shot (see page 14), Myra Wiggins is standing near her close cousin Jack Singleton and "Big Alex" MacDonald in front of the Dawson Miners' Home Hotel.

Jenny may have gone north with her husband, but their marriage failed. In Jenny's mementos box were letters from her son, Edwin, writing in a child's hand from "Gramma's chicken farm" in Idaho. In the spring of 1900, Jenny Frierson and Eben Singleton were married at Eagle by Rev. James Kirk, a Presbyterian minister. That winter in their cabin at Dawson, Jenny tacked up photos of her son at home on Gramma's lap along with his baby shoes. During the long midnight sun summer days, Eben tended the Dawson bridge and hauled freight for independent trader and brewery manufacturer Tom O'Brien.

By spring 1901, Jenny was on her way south to get Edwin. The pair returned with Eben's older brother, Harry, up the Inside Passage on the steamer the City of Seattle. Harry, Eben, and Jack were rejoined in the Klondike.

The year of the gold discovery at Pedro Creek in Fairbanks in 1902, Jack's wife, Emma, divorced him. As production dwindled in the Klondike, Eben and Jenny returned stateside in 1904 and soon moved to Jenny's mother's in Idaho. Five years later, Edwin graduated from high school. And by 1910, Jenny and Eben's marriage failed. In 1920, during his third marriage, Eben died. Through good times and bad, Jack kept in touch with Jenny, whom he always called "Little Sister."

Jack and his lifelong friend John Hajdukovich probably first met in the Klondike in 1904. However, Jack remained in the Fortymile and Klondike area through the 1910 census.

In 1904, John Hajdukovich caught the steamboat

Jack, Jenny, Edwin Singleton, c. 1902, Klondike. Courtesy of Roberta and Dan Garvey.

Cudahy, bound for Fairbanks; late in the fall, she went aground in the Chena River. Wet and cold, John walked into Fairbanks. Two years later, John and seventeen prospectors stampeded up to the Goodpaster River strike. John described that arrival:

> We arrived in Big Delta the fall of 1906. During the summer, discovery of placer gold was made on the south fork of the Goodpaster River by Alec Nichol and Tom Hendrick. (You know we landed at Big Delta on September 10, 1906.) We had to be in on the rush. You know the Goodpaster—it can freeze over—couple of cold nights. Now, seventeen prospectors had only four poling boats, and only four men to know how to pole a boat. (So we weren't sitting any too perfect. Now, we have to rush it to pole it up. [There was no outboard motor.] We had to pole the boat and it was bucking the current, 3 and a half mile an hour. ("In the summer, it's 4 to 4 and a half mile an hour, Tanana River.)

By 1912, Jack Singleton had joined John Hajdukovich in the Big Delta and Richardson-Tenderfoot area. John and Jack prospected and trapped the Granite Mountain area near the Alaska Range. They hunted for the Fairbanks meat market and the U.S. Army Signal Corps reservation at Big Delta.

John and his other prospector friends hoped for statehood for Alaska. He said, "In 1915, Judge Wickersham introduced a bill in Congress to provide for statehood for Alaska. And you know," he added, "we expected to get it through that time. The Judge told Congress, 'I don't care what anybody says ... We have a lot of young men there—miners and prospectors—who need statehood.' But when the Judge returned to Alaska from Washington D.C., he said, 'Well, we didn't get the statehood, but we got to work for it. Fight for it until we do get it, get a 'godfather.'"

"Then some of the boys asked him, 'Just how long do you think? We are afraid…?'"

"'I'm afraid,' he says, 'that we will have to wait forty years.'"

In 1918, both Jack and John were basing out of Tanana Crossing, a village served by John Strelic's trading post and the Episcopalian mission, St. Timothy in the Wilderness.

Like John Hajdukovich, Jack Singleton, twelve years his senior, had walked away from his former life, his wife and child. Over the years, both men gradually adopted Alaska's Native people as family. According to Tetlin elder Gaither Paul, Jack "liked the women." Paul said that Jack's adopted son, Teddy, born in 1915, was in reality "Jack's own son."

The *Fairbanks Daily Times* in 1915 mentioned Jack often, calling him, "J. A. Singleton, Tanana Crossing rancher," saying that he had "elicited support from Judge Wickersham regarding his proposal to domesticate a caribou herd with the support of the federal government to supply the Interior with meat."

The *Daily Times* cited Singleton a year later as mushing a load of furs into Fairbanks for Tanana Crossing trader John Strelic and then returning home with the mail. Singleton said, "In the Middle Tanana area, all winter there was a large herd of fat caribou so that Indians have been well supplied with meat. I have only seen one prospector, Capt. Morgan, in the Healy river country."

James Geoghan, Jack Singleton, (front) John Hajdukovich, unknown. Delta's Riley Creek, 1912. Courtesy of Delta Historical Society.

Jack and Teddy Singleton; to the right, with rifle and dog, is Rev. Frederick Drane. Tanana Crossing, 1919. Frederick B. Drane Collection, UAF-1991-46-654.

In Tanana Crossing, Jack Singleton, John Strelic, E. A. McIntosh, and the Natives put up some buildings for the mission. The Fairbanks Daily Times said that when needed, "Mr. Singleton, retired miner, has been looking after things and keeping the Mission going as per schedule." Reverend Drane, the itinerant Episcopalian pastor, took photographs, capturing portraits of Jack's son Teddy and Tanana Crossing and Tetlin's way of life.

After twenty-seven years in the North, Jack made his first trip Outside in 1924 for the Alaska Sourdough convention. In San Francisco, he met his grown daughter, Bessie, as well as "Little Sister" Jenny and her son, Edwin, who by then had adopted his uncle's name, also calling himself Jack Singleton, and was a star of silent films. Jack handed his old friend Jenny a list of his Alaska contacts, including John Hajdukovich and the itinerant nurse at Tanana Crossing, Lucille Wright.

When he returned home to Tetlin, Jack began teaching his son reading, writing, and arithmetic. John Hajdukovich urged Jack to teach the other children as well. The Bureau of Education began paying Jack to teach the village children (but he also taught the adults). In the summer, Jack and the people gardened together. Jack also became the postmaster. When someone was ill, they came to Jack for help.

In 1930, John Hajdukovich mushed Bureau of Education division superintendent Earl J. Beck to Tetlin on an investigative tour. The temperature plummeted to -50° F., forcing Beck to spend two weeks with Chief Peter Joe's people at Tetlin. After such close living with the village and their fourteen school age children, Beck commended John Hajdukovich regarding his trading for "jealously guarding the Natives to see that no harmful influence shall come upon them" and reported that due to the combination of Jack Singleton's care and the Natives' isolation, the village was "a showcase of purity."

The following summer, the director of education in the Office of Indian Affairs, Dr. Carlson Ryan Jr., visited the upper Tanana by boat. He was also very impressed seeing the work Jack Singleton and John Hajdukovich had done with the people.

The Native people, with John and Jack's help, had built their own school and bridge using lumber they had cut themselves. Ryan wrote that the people were clean and healthy whereas Natives elsewhere were infected with tuberculosis and whooping cough. They said that in other places even soap could be a rare commodity. Further, Ryan observed that Jack Singleton had taught the Natives how to use a tractor, and together they had made a garden out of four acres.

However, the *Fairbanks Daily News-Miner* reported on July 29, 1937, "Teddy Singleton, [Jack's son] 22 year old Native from Tetlin, died from acute appendicitis at St. Joseph's hospital last night. Flown Tuesday to Fairbanks by Dick Hawley. Miss L. Wright, Indian Service nurse, accompanied."

That same year, anthropologists were studying the upper Tanana. Jack sheltered many of them, serving as a local hostelry. In the *Fairbanks Daily News-Miner*, anthropologist Ivar Skarland reported that "the natives of the upper Tanana are said to be the 'lost tribe' of the Athapascans, related to the Navajo people of Arizona."

In 1944, Jack made his second and last trip Outside. As reported in the *Fairbanks Daily News Miner*, "June 7, 1944: Jack Singleton, a longtime resident of Alaska and well-known in the upper reaches of the Tanana, Eagle, and Forty Mile country, has just returned from a trip to the States, where he obtained training from the Alaska Fire Control Service to share with those in Tetlin." The article continued, "Jack spent several months in the 'Sunny South' but says there's 'No More Outside' for him but he did really enjoy his extended trip."

In California, Jack visited his "little sister." She'd been divorced a third time. Her husband, the previous chief engineer for the Golden Gate Bridge, had accused her of mental cruelty and won their family property.

Seventy-six-year-old Jack began having health problems. In 1949 before he died, he wrote to "Little Sister, Jenny," poor and alone in San Jose, California, "This cash I am sending you is to put away in case of sickness or any emergency that may come up, as a gift to you. I have plenty for my needs so use it in any way you need with all my kindest wishes to you. Yours, John [Jack]." By Halloween 1949, "Jack" John Singleton, whose life spanned the Victorian era through the Klondike and into World War II, was gone.

In 2002, Roberta, the little girl who had over the many years carefully protected Ol Jenny's mementos from the Klondike, went with her husband, Dan Garvey, to find Jack Singleton's grave. Not far from John Hajdukovich's grave at Fairbanks' Birch Hill cemetery, they laid a packet on Jack's marker. Carefully, they placed a sealed photo of Jack, Jenny, Edwin, and Big Joe MacDonald at Dawson in 1901 on the mound. On Jack's face there was an unmistakable look of great care as he glanced toward his close friend, "Little sis," Jenny Singleton.

Jack Singleton, 1949, Fairbanks. Courtesy of Roberta and Dan Garvey.

Chapter 4

Fairbanks Stampeder, Fur Buyer, and Outfitter: Robert "Bob" Bloom

In the 1850s and 1860s, San Francisco Jewish merchants were heavily involved in Alaska's lucrative seal trade and in the Russian-American Company. When Louis Goldstone, a California fur house agent who knew Alaska's wealth firsthand, reported in 1865 that the Russians wanted to sell Alaska, Goldstone's employers contacted Cornelius Cole, a California senator, who contacted his former classmate U.S. Secretary of State, William H. Seward.

In 1867, after the United States purchased Alaska from Russia, another fur syndicate, chiefly controlled by Lewis Gerstle and Louis Sloss, bought out the Russian America Company, becoming the Alaska Commercial Company.

By 1897 the gold rush was on. Jewish merchants were among those outfitting the prospectors. Robert Bloom, a young Jewish Lithuanian with goods on his back to trade, climbed the Chilkoot Trail for the Klondike.

Robert "Bob" and daughter Meta Bloom, Fairbanks, 1913. Courtesy of Meta Bloom Buttnick.

here was never a better marriage of man and country than Daddy and Alaska," Meta Bloom Buttnick said of her father, Robert "Bob" Bloom, the Fairbanks fur buyer who helped pick the site for the University of Alaska. From her Seattle home, Meta Buttnick remembered her father's story and the development of the Interior:

For generations, the families of both my father and my mother, Jessie Spiro, lived in Shavel (Siauliai), Lithuania. Famines, fire, epidemics, discrimination, no jobs, and little opportunity for education left the people impoverished. However, my father's father was a very learned Jew. He tutored students but he couldn't get enough work. Born in 1878, Daddy had to leave school when he was very young to help support the family.

In the western United States, land was being homesteaded. Promoters for the railroad advertised free land, animals, and tools to anyone in Europe who would come. Daddy's Uncle Shapiro tried to farm but he just couldn't do it, and he settled then in Seattle.

21

Robert "Bob" and Myer Bloom, c. 1916.
Courtesy of Meta Bloom Buttnick.

My parents were distant cousins; their families fled Lithuania together and settled in Dublin. But Daddy wasn't content in Ireland, where to do business Jews had to use assumed names. His older brother Saul left for South Africa. Seventeen and looking for opportunity, Daddy left for America and landed at Ellis Island in 1895. He continued on to his Uncle Shapiro's home in Seattle, where he got a job with the Buttnick family.

Two years later, the Klondike gold rush was on. Daddy quit his job and took a ship to Skagway, where he began packing a load of trade goods up the Chilkoot Pass. He shot the rapids at Lake Bennett and once in Dawson, he rented a cabin, even renting out his extra bed. People said they never saw a man work so hard. He'd load his canvas bags and then go out to the creeks and sell his wares. (Many a multimillionaire Jew—like Gimbel—started out as a peddler.) The shallow gold fields in Dawson played out quickly, but in 1902, Felix Pedro struck gold near the trading post of Fairbanks. The whole world stampeded, and Daddy along with it.

In Fairbanks on Front Street (today's First Avenue), Daddy opened a little hole-in-the-wall store, "R. Bloom Hardware." He bought raw fur and sold to a London firm. He and his friends started Congregation Bikur Cholim, sometimes holding services in their homes. A portion of the Clay Street cemetery was set aside for Jews.

In 1910, he returned to Dublin where he met Mother, Jessie Spiro. She'd been away working in London as well as attending pro-suffrage rallies.

The next year, Daddy's father died and again, he returned to Dublin. His youngest brother, Myer, was still in high school. Daddy's older brother, Saul, took Grandmother Bloom back home to Johannesburg while Daddy brought Myer to Seattle to finish high school. The following year, Daddy and Mother married in Dublin and they returned to Alaska.

After Myer graduated, he ran Daddy's Hardware, Guns and Ammunition store in Ruby.

I was born in 1913 in Fairbanks, one of the first non-Native children. Mother continued as a suffrage advocate and helped lead Fairbanks women as the nation finally won woman's suffrage in 1920.

Daddy's store was sometimes called "The Intellectual Delicatessen." Frequently, the independent types from Graehl stopped in to discuss philosophy and politics. Daddy's stationery logo read, "R. Bloom. Hardware, Guns, Ammunitions, Trappers' and Hunters' Supplies. Raw Fur, Bought and Sold." The Hajdukovich cousins, John and Milo, sold their furs to Daddy who sent them on to the Seattle Fur Exchange. Once after a man shot a wolf, skinned it, and sold it to Daddy, he stretched and nailed the pelt onto the telephone pole in front of the store, where it dried for the next two weeks.

In 1915, Daddy was among those who, with Judge James Wickersham, picked the site for the Alaska Agricultural College and School of Mines; from 1921 to 1925, he served as a charter member of the Board of Regents.

He and Ed Stroecker were the heavier partners in the Fairbanks Airplane Corporation, the corporation for which Ben Eielson, Noel Wien, and Joe Crosson first flew. He and Stroecker also owned a one-hundred-acre farm where Ladd Field was later developed. A Montenegrin, Mike Yankovich (Jankovic) had a farm that is today the University of Alaska Fairbanks Large Animal Research Station. Yankovich, R. K. Lavery, and Daddy used to experiment on Mike's farm with various strains of hardy Siberian wheat.

However, all this business stopped during Jewish New Year, Rosh Hashanah, and Yom Kippur, the Day of Atonement. In Fairbanks, Daddy was satisfied with our education but he wanted us to be around our culture, to have Jewish associates. He couldn't leave the business, so Mama, who still had a father and brother in Dublin, took us four girls there in 1928 for school. I got a degree with honors in modern literature from Trinity College, Dublin University. But when I returned to Fairbanks in 1935, the country was deep in Depression. There was not an English teaching job in sight until one of the teachers decided to get married. (During the Depression, only one job was allowed per family.) I got Mary Benjamin's job when she married Dave Atlin, a book dealer. For three years, I taught English, French,

Meta, Ruth, Jesse, Deborah, Olga, Fairbanks, 1928. Courtesy of Meta Bloom Buttnick.

and Latin. Everyone thought I was terribly lucky, and I was. But again, my dad was chafing at the bit because I wasn't making the associations he felt I needed. I already knew Harry Buttnick, whose family was from Belarus. In 1939, we were married.

The Army began developing Ladd Army Air Field and bought Daddy and Stroecker's farm land for the road into Ladd Field. In 1941, Daddy closed his store and ended an era that had first begun with the Fairbanks gold camp.

During World War II, Daddy was the chairman of Alaska's Jewish Welfare Board. He and Mother served as unofficial chaplains for Jewish servicemen stationed in Alaska. They and others hosted the first public Seder, the Passover meal. By 1943, Jewish army chaplains were officiating as the first rabbis in Alaska.

Daddy, a merchant and the first of the Fairbanks Jewish community, helped shape education, defense, and aviation as well as outfit Alaska miners, trappers, and hunters. He inherited a land that had been secured largely because a Jewish merchant, Goldstone, pressured Secretary of State Seward to buy Alaska. Although Goldstone's motives were for commercial profit, he protected Alaska for us and for those needing the Great Land, a refuge at the top of the world.

Bob Bloom, Fairbanks, c. 1957. Courtesy of Meta Bloom Buttnick.

Chapter 5

The Hajdukovich "Brothers:" Fur Trading and Fairbanks Entrepreneur

The Stepovich, Butrovich, and Hajdukovich families are the longest-surviving Yugoslavian-Alaskan families in the Interior. Only the Peratrovich family of Southeast, and the Mellicks of the Kuskokwim preceded them. These four families are the bridge from the Balkans to Alaska, from the Klondike to the twenty-first century. Politics and business were Stepovich's and Butrovich's interests, while politics and fishing were Peratrovich's; Hajdukovich followed fur trading, property, and aviation. These families represent the thousands of Slavs who shaped Alaska, bridges to statehood, a portrait of who we are.

Milo Hajdukovich, Fairbanks, c. 1935. Courtesy of Bob Hajdukovich.

John Hajdukovich of Rika's Roadhouse was born Jovo Hajduković in Podgor Utrg, Montenegro, in 1879. Montenegro, Crna Gora in Montenegrin, is a mountain fortress, parts of which withstood the Ottoman Empire through its five hundred years of Balkan occupation. This land of rocks struck a marked parallel to Alaska, its rugged cousin across the sea.

In 1903, at the end of the European Turkish Empire in Serbia, John Hajdukovich crossed the sea to an untouched wilderness. He came to the Great Land in that ephemeral time between a land's sleep and its development.

Populated by small, isolated Athabascan bands, Alaska's Interior was a world of moose, swamp, porcupines, and glaciers. John's life permanently became a part of the Natives of the Tanana River.

At the beginning of the twentieth century, in a frontier one-fifth the size of the United States, John traded for furs from Big Delta to the upper Tanana. He became a father to the Natives, built Rika's Roadhouse, and was a big game guide, a prospector, and a U.S. commissioner. In the era before outboard motors, he pole-boated from the confluence of the Delta and Tanana rivers up the Goodpaster River as he prospected. The development of the middle and upper Tanana River is understood through John's lifetime. Once when asked in a State of Alaska courtroom regarding section lines on a map of the Tanana and Goodpaster rivers, John, then eighty-four, snapped at the lawyer, "Don't ask me about section lines. They're numbered on that map but they're not on the land. Marks there, not on the land."

John wore a little smile; he seemed to hear a melody somewhere beyond the normal range. Trading, hunting, and mining were his excuse to ramble. In 1906, he and other prospectors began following trails that moose and Athabascans had first made up the Tanana and Goodpaster rivers.

Montenegro: Jovo Hajdukovic, 1879

Just across Lake Skadar from today's Albania, high in Montenegro's mountains, tribesmen wailed in Arabic-like monotones and shared their brandy as they intoned their epic stories. They sang their history accompanied by sawing a one-stringed instrument, a gusle, braced against their knee. They told sagas of their Kosovo roots, of tribal warriors, and of their success against the Turks and the Illyrians; they blazed the heavens with their tales. The Hajduks were highwaymen, sentries against the Turks, opportunists to catch strangers in their net.

Nikca Hajduk Strahinjič and his brothers lived in stone homes nestled into the mountain. They raided their enemies while their women in the village of Podgor Utrg planted gardens, carried water, and gathered firewood. From their mountains they could see Lake Skadar; on the far side were the Illyrians, henchmen often for the Turks.

The Hajduks kept boulders poised in the mountain passes to roll down on invaders coming from the lake or the coast. Near the highland trail on a plateau, several severed Turkish heads were usually on display at Džafer and Mušina Glavica. Skadar, the largest lake in the Balkans, stretched across two countries' borders. During the night, Turks and Illyrians often slid into Montenegro. Although it appeared peaceful, the lake sat on a cauldron separating two cultures: East and West, Muslim and Byzantine Christian.

In 1878 the Treaty of Berlin officially liberated Serbia and the occupied parts of Montenegro from the Ottoman Empire. A year later, Jovo, known later as John Hajdukovich, was born.

John Hajdukovich, c. 1912, Donnelly Roadhouse, Alaska. Courtesy Alaska and Polar Regions Archives, Rasmuson Library, University of Alaska Fairbanks, James T. Geoghegan Collection, #73-137-43.

On a crude bed made of spruce poles, in a one-room stone house, a woman labored with her second child while Krsto, her husband, drank grape brandy in the yard near the animal stall under the home. With the good news—"a son is born!"—Krsto shot his gun into the air crying, *Ziveli*! ["To life!"] From across the trail, the Vukmanović family responded with congratulatory shots welcoming Jovo's birth.

During Jovo's childhood, his father and he would hike down the long valley, over the hills to the ancient Montenegrin capital of Cetinje, where they visited their cousin, Rade Hajduković, an archpriest and a consulate in the court of King Nikola. Cetinje was surrounded by hills that were dominated by Mount Lovčen, Montenegro's sentinel mountain; foreign embassies lined the boulevard. As Jovo walked the streets, his ears tingled with the sounds around him of people speaking French, German, and Russian.

When Jovo was twenty-five, against the will of both their families, he married pretty, dark-eyed Milica Vukmanović. In 1998, seventy-two-year-old Jovan Hajduković remembered an incident following the marriage. Milica was pregnant, possibly prematurely. As Jovo carried rocks from their family plot, he felt suddenly overwhelmed with the futility of the centuries-old lifestyle

Laco Radojica Bugarin, Montenegro's national guslar, Bijelo Polje, Montenegro, 1999. Judy Ferguson photo.

of digging rocks and planting a meager garden. He threw down his hoe in disgust and cried, "I am leaving, and I am never coming back!" As he packed his clothes, he said, "I am leaving, and I won't be back…until I have as much gold…as there are rocks in this valley!" In 1903, he followed the trail from Utrg and hiked to the Bay of Kotor. Unseen at the harbor, he slid onto a ship bound for Constantinople. As the ship pulled out, Jovo watched the land of his ancestors disappear: his church, his family, his wife, and their unborn child. He traveled around Greece to Constantinople to see his cousin, Archpriest Rade Hajduković. From there, he caught freighters to Egypt, and then on to France. From Le Havre, he boarded the S.S. *La Savoie* direct to New York.

When Jovo arrived, he continued to Seattle where he got work on a railroad tunnel. He went on to Juneau-Douglas, visited friends at the Treadwell Mine, and continued to Dawson. From there, he caught the steamboat the *Cudahy* for Fairbanks, which went aground in the Chena. He got work in the new Fairbanks gold camp. A few months later, his cousin Milo Hajduković from Kolašin, Montenegro, and his friend, Ilija Milajić, later known as Charlie Miller, arrived in the States. Charlie got work in the Montana mines but Milo continued to Fairbanks. Milo began cutting trail for the Washington–Alaska Military Cable and Telegraph System (WAM-CATS). John took off prospecting, striking out for the head of the Wood River. In 1906 with seventeen other prospectors, he stampeded past McCarty's at Big Delta to a strike up the Goodpaster River. When he wasn't upriver, McCarty's roadhouse became John's base.

Unlike the shallow gold of the Klondike, the gold of the Alaska interior was buried under heavy permafrost (there was one hundred feet of overburden at Ester). The prospectors of the Interior worked hard, but the easy gold was quickly exhausted. The years of 1902 to 1914 were the golden era for the prospectors. Heavy equipment for the deeper gold would require steam pumps to thaw the ground, hydraulic pressure to bring the pay to the surface for sluicing, and deep drilling through hard rock. The prospectors worked like dogs, hoped for a supportive industry, and waited for word of the next strike.

In a 1963 State of Alaska Court System recording, Pinkerton v. Yates, John Hajdukovich remembered the prospectors' annual spring rendezvous. "Now every spring," he said, "as soon as the ice was out of the river, the prospectors floated down the river on the rafts or in the boats. They all waited until everybody got there. That was the only couple of days of vacation we had. We had only three cabins, and stayed a couple of days. Now each cabin was lined up with bunks: three high, lots of room for everybody. Only we couldn't cook inside of the cabin. Had to cook outside. After that, the prospectors scattered, everyone in his own direction. Most of them went to Fairbanks to work for the summer. I stayed at Big Delta. In the fall of the year, they got back together and followed the Goodpaster Trail. All of them were poling their boats up the Tanana. They made discoveries on the upper Tanana...from Richardson Highway to the border: two hundred

Archpriest Rade Hajuković, 1899, Belgrade. Courtesy of Anica Hajduković and Miroslav Konstantinović.

miles—all the drainages from the Yukon River to the Alaska Range. In the 1913 stampede of fifty to sixty people from Big Delta to Canyon Creek, I moved a steamin' Jenny, a steam boiler, by horse and sled. I did a little mining in a big way. Each one of the prospectors brought a dog sled and outfit. Every year, I got enough for a grubstake."

In 1923 with the completion of the Alaska Railroad, the Fairbanks Exploration Company (F. E. Co.) could bring in dredges and hydraulic equipment to begin mining on a large and technical level.

John went on, "[In the last international gold rush, the Chisana,] I bought Al Maxey's roadhouse in Big Delta in 1913. In 1914 I built a new roadhouse. Part of that house is there now.... I ran it until 1918." The two-story building became Rika's Roadhouse and in 1909 began to be serviced by an Alaska Road Commission ferry.

By World War I, John's wife Milica was thirty-four, and the daughter he'd never seen, Andje, was eleven. Andje was crippled but still tended the village's goat herd. They were supported, in part, by the family who surrounded them, the Hajduković and Milica's Vukmanović families.

During the war in Montenegro, a Hapsburg Austrian headquarters was in the neighboring village. Those not considered loyal to the Austro-Hungarian occupiers were sent to concentration camps in Bosnia. After the war, surviving Montenegrins struggled with famine, disease, and deep poverty. Weakened and disunited, the tiny kingdom of Montenegro was swept into the Kingdom of Serbs, Croats, and Slovenes, resulting in the "first Yugoslavia."

In 1932, John wrote to his daughter, Andje, on the back of a photo of the roadhouse: "This is the house where I wanted to bring you and live together as a family." [Apparently, Milica, John's wife, refused to come.] Years later in court, John said in a ponderously heavy tone, "I sold that roadhouse, yes . . . to Rika Wallen."

When John described his years of trading up the Tanana River, he began, "After I sold the roadhouse to Rika Wallen, I made a trip upriver in 1919 to 1920. I started in a small way, just got started. I got the trading post in both places: Tanana Crossing and Tetlin. I hauled lots of freight, quite a few tons over the Goodpaster Trail. Finally I had three trading posts: Tanana Crossing (they call it Tanacross); Tetlin; Nabesna, that's Northway now. We took supplies up the Tanana. Pretty rough going: Tanana River. I had two gas boats, and could haul four or five tons each. Took five, six, seven, sometimes eight days from Big Delta to Tanacross." On the way, John stocked a small store at Healy River and a series of caches all the way to the Canadian border, a distance of up to eleven days.

His expenses were high. He bought the best rifles, traps, and clothes, planned logistics carefully, and employed the most competent Natives.

As soon as the river was navigable in the spring, John launched his boat and began stocking for the new season. He and several Native deckhands pushed out from McCarty's. They hauled

John remembered the prospectors' desire for statehood: "In 1916, Judge Wickersham was a forced to introduce a bill in Congress to provide for statehood for Alaska. And you know, we expected to get it through that time. In 1916, the judge [Wickersham] was for statehood. He said, 'I don't care what anybody says. . . . We have a lot of young men here: miners and prospectors, with a great interest in mining and prospecting.' When the judge returned from Washington, D.C., he said, 'Well, we didn't get the statehood, but we got to work for it. Fight for it until we do get it, get a 'godfather.' [In Serbia and Montenegro, a godfather or a kum is a guardian, a blood brother.] Then some of the boys asked him, 'Just how long do you think? We are afraid?' 'I'm afraid,' he says, 'that we will have to wait forty years.' We waited forty-five. Then some of the prospectors in 1915 said, 'What's the use to wait? Forty years from now, we old man. What is good to me?' Okay, then . . . they left. Some joined English Army, and some joined Canadian Army. You know, they went to old country to fight the Kaiser: First World War. And the rest left Alaska for higher wages. Then . . . our country got into war. They joined our army. A good many got killed. Those who left—they didn't return. That was a great financial loss. All our mineral prospects laying there, been laying there for forty years right now. After the war, we considered the situation again. . . . Every few years, we reviewed what can be done. . . . But it remained just the same, with no change."

cable, axes, and food upriver and often returned with passengers. As they approached the few cabins at Tanana Crossing, John's friend, Jack Singleton, came to greet them. They unloaded the *White Elephant*, John's gas-powered launch. When snow covered the muskeg, John hitched a horse to a double-ender sled to ferry his cached supplies to the Healy and Tetlin rivers. For big loads, John used the horses. During the dead of winter, and for smaller loads, he relied on dogs. Whether he freighted by horse or by dog teams, several Natives worked for him.

As Native trappers handed John pelts, he calculated goods in exchange. If they could not pay, John simply skewered another IOU note on the counter's spindle. By 1930, John's habit of never denying a customer was drowning him. Hoping that if someone else were handling the business, profits might increase, John sold the business to Ted Lowell.

Ted later said he spent the winter up the river to protect John from his tendency "to give it all away." But even with John safely in Big Delta, if a Native needed something, John sent notes to Ted to "be sure and give" a needed item to the customer. The tall spindle of IOUs on the counter became a pyramid by spring. Not able to pay John for the stores, and ready to return downriver, Ted turned the business back over to John.

John's supplies were purchased on credit from Northern Commercial Company and from Bob Bloom, the Fairbanks outfitter. John's books, according to Ted Lowell, showed a debt of thirty thousand dollars of merchandise entrusted to his friends.

In 1924 when a Nabesna man shot a Canadian Athabascan at Last Tetling, the U.S. commissioner could not get free to investigate. In an unusual move, Judge Cecil H. Clegg appointed John Hajdukovich U.S. commissioner without power to preside at the inquest and the hearing of the murderer. As a result, John became the law from Big Delta to the border until 1936. By 1920, he was noted in the *Fairbanks Daily News-Miner* as "the well known roadhouse man and freighter." Also, he was in process of becoming a big game guide. Horses

"McCarty's Roadhouse, c. 1922," courtesy Guy Cameron Collection, Accession number 72-38-445, Alaska and Polar Regions Archives, Rasmuson Library, University of Alaska Fairbanks.

John Hajdukovich freighting with his dog team, upper Tanana, c. 1925, Courtesy of Delta Historical Society.

had to be imported and wall tent platforms and cabins built for wealthy clientele. In 1922, feeling overwhelmed, John asked his cousin Milo to join him trading on the upper Tanana. "John's name was a real help to Milo," Carl Tweiten said, "and Milo knew how to use it." John had important stipulations, however. Milo was not to own his own store, gas boat, or do business for longer than two years.

Milo, whose mind was strictly a businessman's, soon had not only three stores but a gas boat as well. Several times, when John told Milo the stipulated two years were up, Milo retorted that too many people still owed him money. He felt it was necessary to keep going until everything due him was repaid.

Milo was competing with his cousin John, Herman Kessler at Nabesna, Ole Fredrickson at Tanana Crossing, Emil Hammer at Healy, and C. D. Flannigan at Tetlin.

Apparently Milo and John continued to work together because in 1925 the *Fairbanks Daily News-Miner* reported "the Hajdukovich brothers just brought in two large truckloads of furs." [The word for *cousin* in Montenegrin is the same as the word for *brother*. This led to confusion as Serbs and Montenegrins used the word *brother* in English meaning either brother or cousin.] When Rika became the roadhouse postmistress, John and Milo could finally mail furs directly from Big Delta. Annually, they mailed sixty thousand dollars worth of furs from McCarty's. Before each sale was made, and before every shipment went out, John first telegraphed the Seattle Fur Exchange to check current fur prices.

About 1903, a Lithuanian Jewish immigrant, Robert Bloom, had arrived in Fairbanks from Dawson. He starting loaning money to the prospectors: grubstaking them. When they could not repay their loan, Bloom might inherit their assets. With the claims he collected, he invested in a store on Second Avenue in Fairbanks, naming it R. Bloom. It quickly became the outfitting headquarters for the Bush. Bloom was also a main supplier to John Hajdukovich. Not only were Bloom and John both from Eastern Europe, but as Bloom once told his daughter, Meta, "John and I understand each other. We are both traders."

Meta Bloom Buttnick added, "John maintained a mailing address at Dad's store. He was often in our home and was always a handsome and respected guest, the consummate gentleman, a cut above everyone else."

Back East, Bloom had extensive contacts with wealthy sportsmen interested in Alaska big game hunting, known as the Campfire Club. They asked Bloom to find them a quality hunt. Bloom knew John Hajdukovich had the class, the endurance, and the eye to do a first-class safari. Bloom backed Hajdukovich in buying twenty-four horses and put him in touch with wealthy industrialists. In February 1924 to begin the business, John drove eight head of horses at sixty-eight below into Tanana Crossing.

Master big game guide John Hajdukovich, 1927. Courtesy Wendell Endicott, Adventures in Alaska and Along the Trail.

Beal's Cache, a roadhouse near Donnelly Dome, was the jumping-off point for John's hunts. Located in good hunting country at an elevation of 1,600 feet, Beal's was a single-story, unpeeled log building on the east side of the road. Like the stage horses and the bison, John's twenty-four horses foraged on the protein-rich vetch of the Delta River.

Both Butch Stock and Jack Ray took care of John's horses at Beal's and at the Little Gerstle River. John mapped out blue ribbon hunts for his millionaire clients. He even included oranges and eggs for breakfast before they went out to stalk sheep, caribou, moose, and grizzly in the hills. Throughout the 1920s and early 1930s, the *Fairbanks Daily News-Miner* described John as "bringing much wealth to Alaska." In 1924, John was heralded as "the recognized guide of the Interior." The *News-Miner* added, "Each year, John gets more and more hunters."

In 1927, the aviation age came to the Bush when A. A. Bennett flew a plane to Tetlin Lake.

In 1931, after John and Milo stocked most of their stores for the season, they invited Fairbanks high society women Helen Franklin Heath, Helen MacDonald Straiger, Mrs. Julian Hurley, and Alaska Stewart (Linck) for an outing upriver to Tanana Crossing. The women brought a Victrola phonograph to the potlatch held in their honor. They demonstrated the most recent dance steps. Even in 1998, Martha Isaac of Tanacross remembered the display with great amusement.

With East Coast hunters Wendell Endicott and Edward Mallinckrodt, John planned "the noblest of solutions," according to Tanana Chiefs Conference president Jerry Isaac. In 1930, they planned the Tetlin Reserve. John longed to see his Athabascan friends protected as well as trained and equipped for assimilation into the modern world. He felt that a federal reserve, implemented by governmental resources and under governmental control, was the answer. Around the campfire, John and his hunters envisioned a school, a clinic, and a post office, all sustained by a village economy. They drew up plans and petitioned to have 625 square miles of public land at Tetlin withdrawn from public domain. The acreage would be a federal reserve managed by the Office of Indian Affairs. The Tetlin Reserve would be developed by the Natives with guidance from the federal government. Edward Mallinckrodt of St. Louis, Wendell Endicott of Boston, and John Hajdukovich imagined a fur ranch, sustained with a farming crop in the village. They worked with Chief Peter Joe of Tetlin, who fully supported the ideas.

In 1930, for the first time in twenty-seven years, John traveled Outside to see his influential friends, Mallinckrodt and H. Wendell Endicott, to discuss the Tetlin Reserve. Endicott had written a letter to President Hoover, which was delivered to the president just as he was considering the reserve. Everything fell perfectly into place, and an executive order was signed on June 10, 1930. Consequently, four hundred thousand acres was withdrawn from the public domain. Earnest Walker Sawyer, a special representative for the Alaska Railroad, announced that in five years, he expected Natives to be trained in fur farming. Further, Natives were encouraged to form more reserves.

Mallinckdrodt donated five thousand dollars for a tractor, sawmill, farming equipment, and seed potatoes. However, both the Office of Indian Affairs and the Bureau of Education claimed they were not authorized to oversee the operation. Depressed fur prices and the onset of the Great Depression doomed the success of the Tetlin fur farm from its inception. Also, John was distracted when he had to repossess his trading business from Ted Lowell and resume trading. Worse, Dr. Carlson Ryan Jr., the director of education in the Office of Indian Affairs, never really supported the Tetlin vision. He was pessimistic regarding the Natives' ability to carry off the utopian ideas. (His posture may have been fueled by Tanana Crossing mission pastor E. A. McIntosh's opposition to the reserve.)

In further sabotage, Ryan refused to give John a salary to supervise the fur farm. The industrial school, which was to be a fur farm, was dead before it began. The tractor and sawmill they had gotten were sometimes rented for local construction, but the cottage industry never developed. John had to turn from the interests of the Tetlin Reserve just to keep himself financially afloat.

In the early 1930s, Milo Hajdukovich left his fur trade in the middle and upper Tanana. Following financial advice from First National Bank's Ed Stroecker, Milo invested in downtown Fairbanks properties. In 1932, he bought the Vance McDonald building on Second Avenue and the Walter Jewell

(Back:) Jelena (Ellen), Kristina, Djurdjina Lesperović, Milo Hajdukovich, 1935. Kolašin, Montenegro. Courtesy of Ruzica Lesperović Joković.

residence on Fifth and Dunkle. Since Milo was becoming well situated, John encouraged his cousin to marry. Milo was sixty and could finally offer a bride a comfortable life. Montenegrin culture assumed Milo would return home for a bride. An old friend of Milo's, Jovan Lesperović, was the father of eight beautiful girls in Kolašin, Montenegro.

On July 21, 1935, John put Milo and his friends Marco Vuyovich and Steve Angelich on a Lockheed Electra airplane. For thirty-two years, Milo had not seen his father, Marko, his brothers, Stanko, Mirko, Drago, Mico, and Filip, his mother, Miloslava, or his four sisters, Milica, Stanica, Katarina, and Ljubica. After much crying and hugging, Milo went down to the village to watch *korzo*, the afternoon promenade when young men and women parade up and down the street, visiting each other. At once Milo noticed the beautiful Kristina and Jelena, two of Jovan Lesperović's daughters. He sent word to Jovan that he wanted to meet with him at the local *kafana*, a bar, where men's business was transacted. After a few hospitable brandies, Jovan's oldest daughter, Kristina, was promised to Milo. However, Kristina had other ideas. Although she was only fifteen but at her father's urging, Jelena volunteered to marry Milo.

While the wedding was prepared, Milo took the train to Virpazar near Lake Skadar to see John's wife Milica and daughter Andje in the mountains of Podgor-Utrg. Milica and Andje

were dressed all in black and lived in the tiny rock room where John had been born, above the goat stall. Sustained by family, they eked out a living. Cousins Jovan and Ilinka Hajduković looked after the women, got their mail, and brought them groceries. The women agreed to attend Milo's wedding in Kolašin.

At a lavish Montenegrin wedding, Milo and Jelena were married. Milo wired Steve Bojanich of the Tavern Cafe: "She is an American-born girl, blue-eyed, sixteen years old and very attractive. As a baby, she accompanied her parents when they returned to the old country. Her father is a businessman. [This was only four years before World War II ripped Yugoslavia apart.] Conditions here in Yugoslavia are very good. I like it very much. We have visited most of the large cities of Europe and we will arrive in Fairbanks in March. However travel documents could delay us."

A year later on a luxurious steamship on their way home to Alaska, they mailed sophisticated photos of themselves back to Fairbanks. On arrival, they were immediately welcomed into high society. The *Fairbanks Daily News-Miner* wrote that "Mrs. D. S. Nickolich sent invitations for a dinner party for Mr. and Mrs. Milo Hajdukovich. He is

Jelena (Ellen) and Milo Hajdukovich, 1935, Belgrade. Courtesy of Nada (Lesperović) Stojković.

34

Mary (baby) and Ellen Hajdukovich, 1936, Fairbanks. Courtesy of Sonja (Lesperović) Slobodenka.

a Fairbanks resident and a property holder. He and his wife will reside at 709 Third Ave. Guests will include John Hajdukovich, Mr. and Mrs. Steve Bojanich, Mark Vuyovich, Mellia Vukovich, and Mrs. S. Canther."

In October, the *News-Miner* wrote again, "Milo Hajdukovich, former owner of upper Tanana trading posts, now has a large financial stake in Fairbanks real estate. Work started in building seven apartments on the second floor of a two-story frame building on the southwest corner of Fourth and Cushman, a $12,000 expense."

November 19, 1936, the *Fairbanks Daily News-Miner* wrote, "Mr. and Mrs. Milo Hajdukovich have a daughter, Mary, born yesterday."

With a critical university housing shortage in Fairbanks, Milo was expanding further. On January 25, 1937, the *News-Miner* wrote, "Milo Hajdukovich has seven apartments on the second floor of the Hajdukovich building on the southwest corner of Fourth and Cushman. It will open February 1 if furniture arrives on SS *Gorgas*. The total investment including the building will amount to sixteen thousand dollars. Milo is heavily invested in Fairbanks real estate and owns several residences as well as other business buildings."

That April, the *Fairbanks Daily News-Miner* announced, "Milo Hajdukovich buys half interest in the Model Cafe from Joseph Raats yesterday afternoon. Peter Despot continues as half owner and manager of the Cafe, one of the oldest institutions of its kind in Fairbanks. Milo will not be actively interested in the management. The cafe was originally built in 1905, after which it burned, was rebuilt, and then burned a second time in 1907 and again—in 1917. The present building was built and the business reopened in June 1919. The cafe employs nine men and women." In Fairbanks, Jelena became known as Ellen and attended school with first grade children so that she might learn English.

Miscoviches and Hajdukovich, Up the Goodpaster

John did nothing small. His hunting adventures in the 1920s catered first-class service to the wealthiest of America's new tourists. His trading employed "half the Natives in the Tanana valley," and boosted the interior Alaska economy.

In mining, John was no different. For years he had prospected the Goodpaster River. Throughout the summer of 1937, the *Fairbanks Daily News-Miner* wrote,

> May 10, John Hajdukovich tractor took 30 tons of freight, cached at lower end of Summit Creek, below Blue Lead Extension project. Freight includes sawmill, prospect drill and supplies for summer. As soon as snow melts, John Hajdukovich's

crew will go there to work next summer. Cat is already there. Ted Lowell, Tom Radovich, and George Bojanich returned to Fairbanks yesterday. In the Goodpaster, the snow is still shoulder deep. John Hajdukovich and Ted Lowell plan to fly to Tetlin tomorrow, where Ted Lowell will work at the Hajdukovich trading post until the Goodpaster is open. Lowell will then go and join John Hajdukovich's prospect drilling. Doc Cripes accompanied the caravan to Summit Creek and will spend the summer prospecting up the Goodpaster. Miner Paul Drazenovich left Fairbanks for the Goodpaster. He and John Hajdukovich are placer drilling their ground on Central Creek.

In late August the *News-Miner* reported,

> John Hajdukovich, upper Tanana trader and a man of many progressive enterprises, has crew stripping overburden and open quartz mineral veins in Goodpaster camp sixty miles southeast of Fairbanks, the first operation of its kind. Louis D. Colbert reported that he thinks Hajdukovich has found an effective way of trenching and locating quartz veins and digging into surface prospects. Hajdukovich has cut several such veins on a number of properties.

In November, Ellen, baby Mary, and Milo flew to Tetlin, the area of Milo's former trading. Throughout midwinter, Milo continued to fly back and forth, buying fur again in the upper Tanana. The *Fairbanks Daily News-Miner* wrote,

> Milo Hajdukovich, who works for his 'brother' John, [the Serbian word for cousin is brother] reports that Tanacross, Tetlin, and Nabesna trappers have taken more than 200 wolves and mostly coyotes which are increasing in numbers. John Hajdukovich has posts at Tanacross, Tetlin, and Nabesna. Wolves are about evenly divided between the blacks and the grays. The latter bring a higher price. Rabbit and fox are plentiful but fox prices are low. Because of a higher rabbit cycle, lynx are coming back. Outside, there is a good demand for lynx; they pay as high as $40 for a No. 1 prime pelt. Hajdukovich reported that back in 1928, he bought more than 1,000 lynx pelts. After that, the rabbit and lynx cycle declined. He said that the peak of the current cycle may be next winter. He observed that native trappers brought in quite a few young animal pelts, a sign that the lynx are 'breeding up.' Milo estimated that there are 25 native trappers at Tanacross, 12 at Tetlin, and 15 at Nabesna. The Hajdukovich brothers sell their furs through several places: Seattle Fur Exchange, John Schwegler, buyer for Jacobson, Goldberg & Co. in Seattle, and others. Next week Milo will leave on another trading trip. His home is 412 Dunkle St.

By February, Milo had sewed up a deal for the Model Cafe, as reported in the *News-Miner*: "One of the most important business deals of the year in Fairbanks took place today when Tom Youle, Steve Bojanich, and Milo Hajdukovich took over the ownership and management of the Model Cafe, one of the oldest restaurants, fronting on First and Second Avenues, in the heart of the city. The building will be enlarged to include a second floor at a cost of $50,000."

By spring it was reported,

> Work on one of the most important building projects for Fairbanks for the season of 1939 started this week when carpenters began erecting a structure at Fourth and Cushman streets, three stories, not counting the basement. The main floor is assigned for store spaces. The second and third stories will be apartments, 36 feet by 96 feet. The outer walls will have fireproof shingles. Fairbanks Lumber Supply will furnish the lumber and other supplies. L. P. Cysewski is the construction contractor. The cost will be $65,000. Milo Hajdukovich hoped to have his first story completed for occupancy by mid May.

In early 1941, there were reports of Milo gambling. He began having health problems and planned a trip to Mayo Clinic. In the fall, the *News-Miner* reported, "Milo Hajdukovich has extended the back of his Silver Dollar Bar to First Avenue. Bar will occupy the first floor but Milo may install apartments on the second floor." (Later his daughter Mary would remember that when her father went into one of his bars to do business, that as in Montenegro where daily dressing includes a man sticking a gun into his waistband, Milo would lay his pistol on the bar, and then proceed.) Slavs pretty much owned Second Avenue.

By 1940, John felt confident of his mining prospects up the Goodpaster River and asked Pete Miscovich if he might invest up the Goodpaster River. He also tapped Senator John Butrovich for support. Later John remembered very somberly of his Goodpaster mining venture, "I made a trip Outside. I got around twenty-five to thirty thousand dollars in freight, which included a complete outfit for six men for six months. Another thirty thousand dollars cash was set aside to pay those men."

John Hajdukovich's Cat train to the Goodpaster, 1940. Courtesy of Delta Historical Society.

In 1940, with a grubstake from Pete, John bought a top-of-the-line Caterpillar. Then with loaded metal sleds, go-devils, and wagons, John skidded his mining outfit to Central Creek up the Goodpaster River. With a cat train, Silas Solomon of Kechumstuk freighted twenty-four tons of goods overland. Natives Kenny Thomas and Abraham Luke drove fifty-foot riverboats eighty miles up the Goodpaster River loaded with seven thousand feet of hydraulic pipe. Where Lawrence and Walter Johnson had once discovered coarse gold, John began open-cut, hydraulic mining. There they worked until the money was exhausted, but the color never showed. After two such seasons, prospects looked grim. Pete Miscovich was stuck with the bill, and John with a crushing debt. John later summed it up, "Now, all I have left is a D-6 cat and," he added heavily, "my experience."

John summed up the first fifty years of the prospectors' work in the Interior: "They discovered metals in hard rock: copper, nickel, antimony, mica, gold, tungsten, and even discovered platinum in a hard rock. Not very many places they discovered that peridot, but it's there. And even if only part of that was developed into mining, there is plenty there to support between thirty-five and forty thousand people. Sometime in the future," John prophesied, "the Goodpaster Trail and the branches leading out of the Goodpaster Trail, someday…will lead our younger generation to find natural success. Now, our main interest is not dead by a long way…but at a standstill due to obstacles."

John was right. The gold was far too deep for him to reach. In the late 1990s, the Pogo mine was developed up the Goodpaster: gold veins in hard rock at a depth only attainable by modern mining equipment. John knew where the gold was.

Trading and the Office of Indian Affairs

John claimed the trader Herman Kessler had broken the 1932 traders' agreement and that he had begun shipping in liquor. First, he shipped in three tons, and then, in 1938, he brought in fifty tons. The liquor came first to Nabesna; from there, he traded to all the villages. When John was sure all the traders were selling liquor, he tried boycotting. He quit his post in protest, resigning as U.S. commissioner in 1936. However, this resulting lack of authority only removed the fear of him, deleting his stick. The door for liquor swung further open.

John asked Mallinckrodt to help. Mallinckrodt wanted a second opinion, and paid an investigator, Moris Burge of the American Association on Indian Affairs Inc., to check into the situation. Burge reconnoitered the upper Tanana with John in 1938. He said,

> The Tetlin area in which John does his trading and offers his hospitality is somewhat a paradise. In his business with the Indians, John has made it his constant effort to keep sobriety and industry at the highest possible point among the Indian Alaskans. Largely as a result of his insistent efforts, the Tetlin Indians have maintained a clean, straight thinking, and nobility of character that speaks well. Their genuine, wholesome way of living has given them a share of pride not often found among the more discouraged Alaskan Indians of other areas. The Indians relied on him for matters of all importance, and had it not been for his influence, the picture would have been entirely different. But one day, Hajdukovich will be gone and the Indians can not rely on one man always.

Burge suggested more governmental involvement in the area and pushed for a larger game reserve. John was bankrupt, and he was forced to sell his business to Herman Kessler, the man who had brought in the liquor. In 1942, John went to Washington,

Milo Hajdukovich's brother, Filip Hajduković (shot by Tito's Partisans, c. 1943), 1935, Kolašin, Montenegro. Courtesy of Ruzica Lesperović Joković.

D.C., to the Office of Indian Affairs, seeking reimbursement for the money owed him from his stores. They promised him they would pay him at the end of World War II. In 1947, however, the OIA disavowed ever having promised to help.

After the Alcan Highway was built in 1942, the river traders and their stores became an anachronism. John's life's work was turning out, like his trading boat's name, to be a white elephant.

As Hitler began to march across Sweden and into Norway, John and Rika listened intently to the radio, catching the European news. When Serbia refused to cooperate with the occupying Nazis, all of Yugoslavia dissolved into flames and chaos. To punish the Serbian impudence, Hitler carpet-bombed Belgrade. The devastation was followed by civil war as Utaše, Croatian nationalists and Axis sympathizers, killed Serbs, Jews, Roma (Gypsies), and some Croatians. As the chaos escalated, thousands were transported to the infamous Jasenovac Concentration Camp, "Croatia's final solution." In Belgrade, across the Sava River at their fairgrounds, the Third Reich dumped their truckloads

Johnny Jonathan of Tanana Crossing and John Hajdukovich with a WWII weapons carrier, Big Delta, c. 1943. Courtesy of Rika's Roadhouse.

of corpses from south Serbia. Marshall Josif Broz Tito's communist Partisans promoted themselves as the country's only hope; they fought not only the Utaše but also the Serbian monarchist government who cooperated with the Nazis. Royalists and property owners like Milo's brothers lost their land and were shot. In 1946, the country became the Socialist Federal Republic of Yugoslavia, dedicated to "brotherhood and unity."

At Fairbanks' Model Cafe, Chicago's *Serbian Unity* newspaper helped inform the Alaska Yugoslavs; personal communication with Yugoslavia was impossible.

Greater than all the previous gold rushes, World War II ushered a billion dollars into the territory. Alaska's ice-box isolation was converted overnight into a G.I. camp. During the summer of 1940, tons of construction materials were freighted to the Interior as military airfields and bases were built. For the construction of the highway, thirteen sawmills began operating from the Alaska-Canada border to Big Delta.

The new Alcan trail connected Alaska, through Canada, with the Lower Forty-eight states. John owned three of the thirteen mills. To obtain 50,000 board feet of Gerstle River timber, John deposited fifty dollars for a grant and installed a mill at the Gerstle. With a contract for 250,000 board feet, he put a second mill at the Tok River. Army engineers rented his sawmills, tractor, poling boat, and outboard. The soldiers floated the felled logs downstream, using John's boat to nudge them along to the sawmill. To collect his money from the military, John's men were supposed to tabulate all the board feet that they sold to the Army. When he was later asked about his sawmills' records, John simply responded, "Oh, I don't know. I never kept track of that." Without the appropriate documentation at the project's end, the Army refused to pay John. For the last time, John lost a small fortune.

In 1939, John predicted that a large military base would be built near Nabesna. Two years later, the village of Nabesna had relocated as the new highway community of Northway near its airfield. Tanana Crossing and Tetlin were eclipsed by the highway junction town of Tok.

In three years, the Alaska Highway was transformed from a dogsled trail to a graded corridor. Anyone with a little gas money, a vehicle, and permission from the military could travel. Overnight, traders had become an anachronism.

Ellen Hajdukovich learned enough English so that when her children, Mary and John, were seven and five, she landed a job at the new Ladd Airfield. Although Ellen was young, she was not completely well, and she neglected to see a doctor. According to her close friend, Vuka Stepovich, Ellen's problems should have been tended sooner.

In 1944, the beautiful young Ellen was dead. Milo asked his boyhood friend Charlie Miller, born Ilija Milajić, to move from Juneau to Fairbanks to care for Mary and John.

One morning in 1945 while visiting his friend George Bojanich, and while waiting for coffee, Milo quietly died in Bojanich's living room. After Milo was buried at Birch Hill cemetery in an Elks' plot, John left for the Kuskokwim River. Some of the Hajdukovich kinsmen were fur traders and merchants in the lower Kuskokwim. Montenegrin Nikola Mihaljevic, known as Nick Mellick, was a fur trader and store owner at Sleetmute. Concerned about Milo's death and his will, John and Nick traveled to Napaimute to see Pete Mihailovich, and to Aniak to visit Sam Voich.

Milo had created a trust; he appointed Ed Stroecker's First National Bank of Fairbanks as a trustee. He gave the bank the authority to decide where his children would live and to see to their care. The Stroeckers asked the Miller family to continue their care of Mary and John.

For years after World War II, communication between Yugoslavia and the United States was difficult. Yugoslavia had been decimated and converted to a Stalinist-aligned communist state until 1948 when Tito broke with Stalin. Partnering with Truman in the early 1950s, Yugoslavia began to rebuild as it spanned the chasm between the Western and Warsaw Pact nations. During the Cold War era, Yugoslavia was still somewhat perceived as being behind the Iron Curtain.

In Alaska as military bases were established, construction boomed. The established Allen Army "Big Delta" Air Field and the Alcan Highway gave rise to Delta Junction, nine miles south of Big Delta. As the Big Delta airfield grew, John worked for Lytle and Green Construction Company. On an errand for the company once, John gazed at the hundreds of army tents pitched on either side of his old trading route. He murmured to himself, "I don't want to see any more." Later in 1946, John rode a military bus from the Big Delta Airfield. Following his old trail to Tanana Crossing, he arrived in mere hours.

When John was out of gas money, his shoulders rounded in despair and he simply walked. "Until his last two years, he could walk young men into the ground,"

John Hajdukovich, c. 1964.
Courtesy of Pioneers' Museum.

Milo's son, John, remembered. "Gold was not a big thing to 'Uncle' John," he said. "Coal was more interesting to him; it had more of a future."

Maury Smith, a former *Jensens' Daily* reporter, recalled John: "He was a philosopher; a gentle soul who said a lot with his eyes. He loved the out-of-doors. People in Fairbanks didn't really know him. I'll never forget the sight of his dogs running on the sparkling, hard-packed snow ridge from Northway in 1939."

John never found as much gold as there were rocks in this valley, his 1903 stated prereq-uisite for returning home, and so he never returned home. When statehood finally arrived on John's eightieth birthday, Rika offered John the money to return home. He said, "It's not enough," and he refused to go.

In the early 1950s, Montenegrin friend Vaso Kentura discovered John's two women liv-ing in destitution in Podgor-Utrg, and he wrote to John. When John heard the description of them living in the tiny house devoid of any facilities, he borrowed money to send home. With it, the women built a two-story addition. They could then step from the upstairs kitchen into a new upstairs bedroom and living space. On the ground floor, they had a larger animal stall under the added bedroom. A Hajduković cousin in Montenegro bragged that Milica and Andje's new room became the social gathering spot. Many a night, there was singing and storytelling in the room. By 1964, John's wife, Milica, was gone. John, too, was not feeling well. Maury Smith visited John in the hospital, "You'll be out of here, John, in a few days," he lied. John said quietly, "I'm not going anywhere." The next day, July 18, 1965, Milo's son, twenty-seven-year-old John Hajdukovich, left the hospital alone. The prospector of 1903 was gone.

In 1974, Andje's neighbor, Miodrag Mijać, found her lying dead next to the family tree where she had been feeding her chickens. Her body was laid next to her mother's, in the vault of their wealthier relatives in the church cemetery, nestled into the mountain. The view was equal to John's on Birch Hill in Fairbanks.

John's estate was valued at two thousand dollars, only a token of the twenty-three thou-sand dollars he owed his creditors. The life insurance he had retained for his daughter never arrived in Yugoslavia.

One day in 1999, I looked for John's grave. I was sure I would find it on the summit of Birch Hill in the sunshine. There it was, next to a solitary tree. Flying with the sunlight reflecting on its wings, a yellow butterfly did peaceful loops, landed on a lilac bush near John's grave, and then on to an evergreen tree.

Pronunciation Key

Jovo Hajduković=Yo'-voh Hi´-doo-koh-vich	Bay of Kotor=Koh´-tuhr	Utaše=Oo'-stah-shee
Crna Gora=Sir'-nuh Gor'-uh	Kolasin=Koh´lashen	Nikola Mihaljevic=Mee'-halye-vich
Podgor Utrg=Pohd´-gor Oo'-trg	Milo=Mee´low	Napaimute=Nuh-'pie-myut
Gusle=goose'-lay	Ilija Milajic=Ee´-leeyuh Mee´lye-ich	Mihailovich=Mee-'hy-loh-vich
Živeli!=Zhee´vuhlee	Lesperovič=Les´pehrovich	Voich =Voy'-eech
Cetinje=Sehteen´-yeh	Ljubica=Loo'-beet-za	Vaso Kentura=Vah´-so Ken´-tooruh
Rade=Rahd´-ay	Korzo=Kor'-zoh	Mijac=Mee' yach
Lovcen=Lohv´-chen	Jelena=Yel'-enuh	Nikca Hajduka Strahinjiča=Neek´tzuh Hi´-dookha
Milica=Mee´-leetzuh	Kafana=kuh-'fah-na	Stra´heenneechah

Chapter 6

Trail-hardened President of Alaska's Oldest Bank: Ed Stroecker as told by Bill Stroecker

Before 1896–1898, access into Alaska and to the Klondike was a challenge. Men took a schooner to Nome, caught an infrequent steamer around the coast and up the Yukon River, or hazarded the Chilkoot or Valdez trail. To go by steamboat from Seattle to Dawson was over five thousand miles, while access from the Chilkoot was close to five hundred miles. With thousands of men stampeding to stake claims, timing was critical. Retired president of Key Bank Bill Stroecker's family had not one but two ancestors who hiked the Chilkoot and Valdez trails. Stroecker's grandfather, Charlie Creamer Sr., freighted the Chilkoot and his father, Ed Stroecker Sr., scaled the Valdez trail. He stampeded out past the Kuskokwim Delta and then came to Fairbanks and helped lay its financial foundation. As president of the First National Bank of Fairbanks, he advised Tanana River fur trader Milo Hajdukovich on how to invest, and Milo in turn was very successful. However, when

Ed Stroecker Sr. on trail to Bristol Bay, 1910. Courtesy of Bill Stroecker.

Milo and his wife Ellen suddenly died, Stroecker's First National Bank became the appointed guardians of their children, John and Mary Hajdukovich. After sixty years with the bank in 2008, and fifty years since statehood, Bill Stroecker remembered his grandfather Charlie Creamer and his father Ed Stroecker, who helped build the fish camp on the Chena.

My maternal grandfather, Charles N. Creamer, ran the Wells Fargo Express from Weaverville to Redding, California, in the late 1800s. As soon as he heard about the Klondike, he headed north. He arrived in Dyea in 1897, set up a tent, and began freighting with horses from there to Sheep Camp. The following spring, when his family moved up, they got a cow and built a cabin, barn, and corrals. Son Charles A. Creamer (later the owner of Creamer's Dairy that is today a state wildlife refuge) began by selling cups of milk from a bucket to the prospectors.

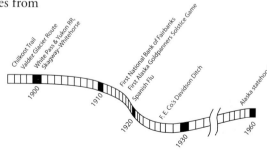

The Scales, a gulch filled with men crawling to the summit like ants, was overshadowed one day in 1898 with precipitous, hanging snow. Suddenly, a strange "wind" roared down the Scales; anyone on that section of the trail was buried in an avalanche. For two weeks, Dyea residents freighted stiff, frozen bodies to Granddad's barn. In the spring, graves were dug in a special "Slide Cemetery."

When the railroad was built, our family's freighting business closed in 1899. The family had to scatter and find jobs wherever possible.

In 1903 on the first boat to Fairbanks, Granddad and Fred Noyes moved to the new gold camp on the Chena River. "Uncle" Fred Noyes installed a small sawmill on Granddad's lot near today's Wendell Street bridge. When the family later joined Granddad, Uncle Charlie (Charles A.) began wrangling cattle for the Waechter family from Circle to Fairbanks and delivered meat to local homes.

Back in the Lower Forty-eight, my father, Edward H. Stroecker, born in 1877 to German immigrant parents, had grown up on the Barbary Coast, the streets of San Francisco. After losing his father when he was in fifth grade, Dad quit school to support his mother. He took a three-month business course that later enabled him to become a bookkeeper. At twenty-one, he was interested in baseball (considered a rough sport then), so his mother urged him instead to see the world.

In 1900, Dad and eleven others left the Golden Gate on a sixty-two-foot schooner. They explored along the Aleutians and up to Bethel on the Kuskokwim River. In the fall, they returned home, but Dad liked Alaska. He wanted to return immediately. He and his friend Oscar Hultburg left for Valdez in January 1901.

Valdez Glacier Route, 1898 to 1899. Courtesy of Candy Waugaman.

The main gold trails into the north then were the Chilkoot, the White Pass, and the glaciated Valdez Trail. Valdez offered not only an ice-free port but a direct "all-American route," but the massive icefield of the Valdez Glacier obstructed access to the Copper River and the Interior. It was a more difficult trail because they had to carry firewood up four benches and across the immense glacier.

Stampeders in Skolai Pass, c. 1899. Courtesy of Candy Waugaman.

In March, Dad and Hultburg walked with four dogs pulling a sled of provisions up the four benches of the steep glacier face, using a series of pulley, block, and tackle. While looking back on their last vista of Valdez, a shrieking spring blizzard whited out their last link with the port camp. Hurriedly, they anchored their five-by-seven-foot tent with bull rock, huddling on the last bench wearing only wool clothes while several tedious, cold days passed. When the sky cleared, they discovered they were not only five miles distant from the summit, but before them a huge wall stretched straight up to the peaks. After double-tripping [breaking one segment of the trail ahead, then returning the next day to bring the supplies forward] for days to reach the top, they rode the sled downhill to the Klutina River, which they floated.

They traveled up the Copper and Chistochina rivers to Slate Creek, where prospectors in that valley of copper had found some gold. After sluicing dirt for the summer, the partners felled a few spruce in the fall, lashed them together, loaded their provisions, and were riding toward the Tazlina River when the Copper capsized them, spilling everything into its roiling waves.

Dad and Hultburg landed near Lt. George Burnell's crews, who were cutting a telegraph line out of Valdez. The sodden pair shared the soldiers' rations and returned on the government trail to Valdez. Hultburg headed home, while Dad got a job at the Montana Saloon serving the Fort Liscum soldiers.

44

Tessie LeRoy, a madam, was entertaining in September 1901. After her customer left, she noticed her gold dust and an English sovereign in its silver box were missing. At the saloon, a soldier cashed the unusual English sovereign, which Dad duly noted and reported. The burglar was arrested, and out of gratitude, Miss LeRoy gave the coin to Dad, which I have to this day.

Each spring, Dad packed out across the Valdez Glacier before the Klutina melted and prospected on Slack and Chititu creeks. Among the prospectors, he met Lee B. "Ike" Loomis (originator of Loomis, Fargo, and Co.), who was freighting for the military on the government trail. Dad, Loomis and several other prospectors formed a partnership.

Planning on wintering near the White River, Dad and his new partners freighted provisions to the Canadian border. They double-tripped, leading a pack string of nine horses and mules up the Nizina River. They fought through a storm on the Nizina Glacier, lost a horse in a creek in Skolai Pass, and then continued over the Frederika Glacier to the White and its tributary, the Snag River.

With a plan to winter over, prospect and trap, the partners built a cabin. They smeared bacon grease on the window's canvas to make it both translucent and waterproof.

Trapping was good, but one spring night, one of the partners quietly woke and mushed the only dog team out over the hills and headed for Dawson. He left the others stranded with the fur and provisions. An old gunslinger and famous guide, Shorty Guinn, rescued them, and after the summer's work, Dad and his friends decided to leave the Copper Valley for the new diggings at Fairbanks.

Six men with three horses had just enough supplies to cross Skolai Pass in late September, down the White River, and up the North Fork, following tributaries to the Chisana River. The Indians warned them it was too late to float down the Chisana and the Tanana into Fairbanks. With no choice, Dad and his partners whipsawed lumber and loaded all they had into the crude boat. Two days downstream, they lost everything. Able to save only waterlogged flour, bedding, and caribou, they didn't even have any cooking utensils until they reached Tanana Crossing.

People call that era the "good ol' days," but when my dad landed in the freezing temperatures on the banks of the Chena in October 1904, he had nothing. If Dad had written a book, everyone would have said, "So, what? It's normal." The ones who returned Outside were the ones who wrote the books, and all of those ended with "Finally, back to civilization!"

He pitched a tent and, for work, he began digging the foundation for the California

Ed Stroecker Sr. at a Fairbanks dog race, c. 1930s. Courtesy of Candy Waugaman.

45

Ed Stroecker Sr., Cashier Albert Visca, Bill Stroecker, Eddie Stroecker, 1947, First National Bank of Fairbanks. Courtesy of Bill Stroecker.

Saloon: today, the Key Bank parking lot. That winter, he worked for "Swiftwater" Bill Gates on Discovery Bench at Cleary Creek.

In spring 1905, Dad's friend Ike Loomis got the Alaska Road Commission contract to cut a ten-foot-wide swath from Fairbanks to McCarty at Big Delta (later called Rika's Roadhouse). He, Dad, and six others packed five horses and cut trail while mosquitoes swarmed twenty-four hours a day.

The September chill finally cleared the air. Again Loomis referred Dad for another job. He and his partner Fred Date switched from horses to canoe to run the mail down the Tanana River, trying to keep to schedule. They poled their boat through soft slush ice, carrying dogs and a sled to Fort Gibbon. Twenty-five miles above the village of Tanana, the ice locked up. The men and their dogs crossed on foot, six hours after freeze-up, still delivering the mail on time.

Throughout the winter, Dad and two partners with a crew of nine men cut two thousand cords of wood five miles from Fairbanks for the Northern Commercial Co. boilers. When he was twenty-eight in the spring of 1907, Dad went to see E.R. Peoples Inc. on Second Avenue. Peoples supplied the miners out on the creeks. Dad was quickly hired as their bill collector. He got to know every prospector, his solvency, his eccentricities, every claim, and its value. In the winter, he was the dog mushing bookkeeper and in the summer, he collected on horseback. He also scheduled his trips so that he returned to town in time to play for the first Midnight Sun ballgames. Even though it had no cars, planes, trains, or roadways, Fairbanks did have baseball!

As the bill-collecting season for 1910 eased, Ike Loomis secretly sent a letter from the Iditarod to Dad: "Come quickly, and keep it quiet!" he said. Getting leave from Peoples, Dad grabbed his buddy Bill McLean, harnessed his team, and in November they quietly left town. They mushed down the Tanana and the Yukon rivers, and to the bewilderment of onlookers, they didn't take the usual turn at Kaltag to the Iditarod Trail. People began to wonder what Dad knew that they did not. McLean and Dad kept right on going to the coast, past the mouth of the Kuskokwim, south to sixty miles short of Goodnews Bay. What Loomis' note to Dad had said was that Frank Waskey was digging up $1.25 to $1.50 per square foot of bedrock. Waskey was digging gold next to a claim that in the first twelve hours had taken out $2,500. Dad staked claims, but the round trip required so much time that he had to return to Fairbanks. He told his partner Bill McLean to record the claims at Bethel, but somehow McLean never did. However, there were Fairbanksans who caught on and gave chase. The *Fairbanks Weekly Times* wrote, "Stroecker Put Fairbanks Wise: Two Tons of Quartz Shipped to San Francisco." In May when Dad pulled into Fairbanks, reporters noted his strawberry-colored beard and trail-hardened appearance.

By the time Dad was thirty-eight, he was taking his meals at Mattie Creamer Anderson's boardinghouse on Third Avenue. Her sister, Marian, was married to R. C. Wood, the manager of E. T. Barnette's Washington-Alaska, Fairbanks' first bank. With a plan to start a second bank, Square Sam Bonnifield, an honest gambler, tapped Frank Manley, who had the richest claim on Cleary Creek, to put up half the capital for what became First National Bank of Fairbanks. In 1908 to 1909, Barnette knew there was an opportunity to buy up the new bank. He told Wood about the option to buy First National. Wood and his attorney, John McGinn, purchased the controlling interest in the bank. As manager and president of First National, he kept the bank stable, even though in 1911 Barnette had just embezzled a million dollars from the Washington-Alaska and left town permanently in the middle of the night.

In 1915, Dad married Mattie Creamer Anderson, and I was born in 1920. By the end of World War I, the creeks of Fairbanks had played out for the prospectors, the Spanish flu hit, jobs were hard to find, and men were leaving. Peoples sold to the Northern Commercial Co., and Dad went to his brother-in-law, R. C. Wood, looking for a job. In 1918, at age forty-one, Dad became a teller, but the bank was in bad shape. Loans had been extended and not repaid. Because Dad knew firsthand the value of all the claims, he knew precisely if a loan was truly warranted. He spoke the language of the men and was savvy. He became a cashier very quickly and began effectively running the bank. Realizing that the Fairbanks Exploration Co. was considering local development, my father and the bank's cashier George Wesch bought out Wood and McGinn in 1926. In 1927, the construction of the huge Davidson Ditch (the engineering feat of its day) began, and new dredges were assembled. The impact of the F. E. Co. doubled the size of Fairbanks.

With a fifth-grade education, a three-month business course, street- and trail-toughened, Dad's vision and grit became fully productive when he also began a family. Until his death in 1952 at age seventy-five, Dad was bank president. He was succeeded as president by my older brother, Edward F., who served until 1965.

When Dad was sixty-seven, I graduated from the University of Alaska with a degree in business administration. I enlisted in 1942 and served until the end of World War II. In 1947, I became a bookkeeper at First National Bank. In 1965, I became chairman and president of the bank until First National, then the oldest bank in the state, was sold to Alaska Pacific Bank in 1977. Twelve years later, Key Bank purchased the bank founded in 1905, over a century ago. To celebrate the anniversary, I had "horse blanket bills" printed, so called because they were large: 7 ⅜ inches wide by 3 ⅛ inches.

For sixty years, I have walked to my office at Key Bank on First and Cushman. From the days of handwritten ledgers to digital banking, the bank has changed with Fairbanks. A frequent reminder of my dad's friendship with Ike Loomis is the Loomis, Fargo, and Co. armored car that routinely picks up our funds.

In 1997, one hundred years after my grandfather Creamer started at Dyea, to commemorate the history on both sides, at age seventy-seven I hiked the Chilkoot Trail.

As president for forty-two years of the Alaska Goldpanners, I follow Dad, who played in the first Midnight Sun game in 1906. In 2006, one hundred years later, ESPN picked up the Midnight Sun baseball game, where on June 21 we play with no artificial lights. Before the game began, our three-piece band, the Frigidaires, whose cumulative sourdough time is two hundred years, got the atmosphere rolling.

Dad always said of Fairbanks, the gold camp on the Chena: "I think she's going to stick."

Bill Stroecker at seventy-seven, climbing Chilkoot Pass, 1997. Courtesy of Bill Stroecker.

Chapter 7

John Butrovich, Alaska's Statesman

John Butrovich was possibly one of Alaska's finest and certainly the longest serving territorial and state senator. He was not self-serving, he helped the needy, he avoided accolades, and he called things as they were. A son of a miner who came over the Chilkoot Trail, John Butrovich Jr. was born on Fairbanks Creek in 1910 to John Butrovich Sr. and Zada Kepart Butrovich. Like many of Alaska's most influential pioneers, his father came from Croatia, former Yugoslavia. Butrovich's father, "Poppa John," ("Butorovich") was born in 1867 on Brac, an island near Hvar, the same island heritage of former Alaska First Lady Matilda Baricevich Stepovich. The Dalmatian coastline was a jumping off spot for those seeking opportunity in the new world.

Senator John Butrovich, c. 1970. Territorial and state senator, 1944–78. Courtesy of Nick Stepovich.

By 1896, Poppa John had immigrated to Placerville, California, and had married Zada. When news of the Klondike hit, he and Montenegrin Marko ("Wise Mike") Stepovich packed over the Chilkoot Trail, seeking fortune and adventure.

The two eventually staked claims at the new Fairbanks gold camp. Near today's Fort Knox gold mine, Poppa John and Wise Mike Stepovich prospected on Fish and Fairbanks creeks. Poppa John soon brought his wife, Zada, to Alaska.

When Ester Creek struck, many prospectors including Poppa John took off, leaving their claims untended. In those days, the modus operandi was, "To the fittest go the spoils." Reportedly, Wise Mike moved onto many of those unguarded claims. When the angry prospectors returned, they planned to surprise Wise Mike. One night, feigning a phone call for Wise Mike, Poppa John and two friends threw open Wise Mike's door and fired a couple of shots. Wise Mike grabbed a pistol hanging on his bedpost and shot four times, scattering Poppa John and the seventeen men hiding just outside his door.

Zada and Poppa John had three sons, including John's older brother, George, born in 1906. Throughout the following years, Poppa John was frequently gone, prospecting up the

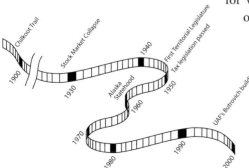

49

John Butrovich (Butor'ović), c. 1894,
Brac, Dalmatia, Austro-Hungarian
Empire. Courtesy of Lesley Sims.

Koyukuk River at Nolan Creek near Wiseman. In 1916, following a strike up Michigan Creek off the Goodpaster River, Poppa John met two prospector brothers, Lawrence and Walter Johnson, who became lifelong family friends. Poppa John was rarely around Fairbanks, although for a time he did work for the Alaska Road Commission.

Bill Stroecker, retired president of Key Bank, remembered John Butrovich who was known as "Deny," "Johnny," or when he was older as "Butro." Deny grew up hunting, supplying his mother with game. As a child, he took the newspapers to the ladies of the Line (the red light district) who in turn gave him candies. As a teenager, he delivered fuel for Standard Oil on Illinois Street and freight for the Northern Commercial Company. Deny's older brother George went to work for the Fairbanks Exploration Co. (F. E. Co.), but after he and his wife had John III and George Jr., George Sr. moved the family to California.

"Buster Anderson, my half brother," Bill Stroecker continued, "had one of the few boats in town. Often he and Deny would go duck hunting. Deny never got cold," Stroecker recalled. "He had a spot at Hidden Lake where he'd sit and watch for hours and hours.

"He loved basketball. Goodpaster River prospector and trapper, Lawrence Johnson—who lived full time at the forks up the 'Goodie'—was a sports expert. Due partly to their mutual interest, Lawrence took Butro up the Goodpaster once for a week. If their motor quit, Lawrence could pole upstream as he had in his pioneer days."

A well-respected gentleman in Fairbanks, Major Albright, who owned the local insurance company, greatly influenced John. Where Albright came from basketball was a way of life. He asked John to put together a local Fairbanks team. Once after John had played, worked up a sweat, followed by a hot shower, he'd run home with no hat in the sub-zero temperatures. Butrovich told Stroecker that was the beginning of his lifelong battle with asthma.

Nonetheless in the late 1920s, "Johnny" Butrovich became the top high-school player in Alaska. His friends included early aviator Noel Wien. In 1929 John graduated in a class of thirteen. As remote as Alaska was then, amazingly, Butrovich got a basketball scholarship to Washington State College. "However, after the stock market crash, the funds for his scholarship dried up. He wanted to stay after his first year but he couldn't afford it," Lesley Sims, John's granddaughter, said.

Fairbanks High School basketball team. Back row, L–R: John O'Shea, Coach Budnick, Bud Boyd, Jim Vernetti; Middle: John Butrovich, Don MacDonald (III), Edson Moody; "Front" man: Leonard King. 1925–26. Courtesy of John Almquist / Butrovich Family and Donald and May MacDonald III.

In 1936, John returned to Fairbanks where he married Grace, the granddaughter of Paxson roadhouse owner Dan C. Whiteford. In 1939, he and Grace had a daughter, Sylvia Jan Butrovich. He and Grace began selling insurance for Major Albright. Later they bought Albright's Alaska Insurance Agency in the Nordale Building on Second Avenue. "Really that was the only street in town cause the town was so small then," Stroecker added.

Alaska Territorial Senate, Three of the four senatorial "viches": Front back to right: Ralph Rivers, Mike Stepovich, John Butrovich, Frank Barr, George Miscovich, 1955, Juneau. Courtesy of John Almquist.

When he was only forty-two, John's brother George Butrovich suddenly died, leaving two young sons, John Butrovich III and his younger brother, George Jr. John and Grace raised young John until he was sixteen. Later they brought up the younger brother George and put him through college in Fairbanks.

The Fairbanks district attorney was Julian Hurley, who was also prominent in the Republican Party. The word was that Hurley had never lost a case. Hurley mentored Butrovich and in 1933, he realized the possibilities Butrovich had as a politician. Hurley wrote Butro's first political speech. Bill Stroecker added, "Hurley had a great influence on both Johnny and Mike Stepovich."

In 1944, Butrovich was one of two Republicans elected to the first sixteen-man Territorial Legislature. During his first years, he co-authored the Alaska Tuberculosis Act and the Veterans Act; both passed and performed well.

"'Grandy' lost money, though, going down to Juneau," his granddaughter, Lesley Sims, said of Butrovich. "At first, 'Geegee' [Grace] had to run the business while Grandy went down and had to rent an efficiency at the Baranof Hotel. (Later Geegee joined him during the sessions.)"

"Grandy always spoke constructively. He was salty but he always called things as they were," added grandson John Almquist.

In 1945 and for the next two years, the legislature budgeted expenses totaling ten million dollars but only provided $5,631,000 for revenue. Governor Ernest Gruening said, "[This action] in my view, came close to a collapse of responsible government." In 1948, Democratic Alaskans only re-elected one of eight senators: a Republican, John Butrovich, because they could trust him to balance the budget. Even in the 1949 Democratic-dominated legislature, Butrovich was chosen as the head of the powerful Senate Finance Committee, a post he held for eight years. Thanks partly to Butrovich, by the session's close Alaska had an income tax, a uniform business-license tax, a tobacco tax, augmented fish trap license tax, and increased fisherman's license taxes, demonstrating Alaska's ability to support itself and govern. Butrovich liked to say, "Democrats can spend," so he kept a close eye on the budget.

In the late 1940s, Butrovich noticed that two government audits were never presented to the legislature as required by law. Further research indicated many discrepancies. He discovered an under-the-table operation within the government that had been illegally wheeling and dealing alcohol in the state. Some $27,000 worth of federally issued liquor stamps were unaccounted for.

Twelve years before the 1964 earthquake and the 1967 flood, Butrovich tried to create a disaster fund, but his "Nest Egg Bill" was defeated.

Impoverished, unable to organize and create revenue, Alaska chafed over territorial constraints. Without statehood, Alaska could not control its own natural resources, develop its infrastructure, or provide adequate health care, and it had no effective representation in far-off Washington, D.C. Frustrated over poor airfields, meager tuberculosis hospitals, undependable shipping, and minimal national defense and security, Alaskans pushed to have two senators and a representative, each with a vote in Washington, D.C.

In his State of the Union address in 1954, President Eisenhower favored statehood for Republican-leaning Hawaii but not for Democrat-leaning Alaska. With nothing to lose, Alaskans formed Operation Statehood with Victor Fischer, Thomas B. Stewart, Niilo Koponen, and John Butrovich. The group chartered a plane and flew to Washington, D.C., to speak with President Eisenhower.

"En route, there was tension regarding who would actually speak to the president," Sims recalled, "but with only twenty minutes to spare, the group turned to Grandy and said, 'Butrovich will talk to the president.'"

Eisenhower was perched on his desk when Butrovich entered the room. Reportedly, Butrovich began, "President Eisenhower, we think you are a great American. But we are shocked to come down here and find that a bill which concerns the rights of American citizens is bottled up in a committee when you have the power to bring it out on the House floor." Eisenhower flushed as Butrovich banged his fist on the chief executive's desk for emphasis.

The president denied that any partisanship politics played a role in the Alaska statehood issue. However, with some concern about impending civil rights legislation, a national coali-

Mike Stepovich, Frank Barr, John Butrovich, Ralph Rivers, 1955, Juneau. Courtesy of John Almquist.

tion of Republicans and "Dixiecrats" kept blocking the passage of any Alaska statehood bill. Most likely, Eisenhower was concerned with maintaining the narrow Republican margin in Congress. Still, there was also the question whether Alaska could support itself or would be a burden on the federal government.

Needing a strong (territorial) governor in the fight for statehood, Butrovich wrote to Secretary of the Interior Fred A. Seaton in 1957, recommending a new appointee. He began "the important role the new Governor will have is mainly with the building of a strong party system in Alaska. [Among the options] our choice is pretty limited to Senator Mike Stepovich of Fairbanks. Mike is a terrific vote-getter. He is thirty-eight years old, active, intelligent, and more important, a man of high principles. He will make plenty of mistakes but he will make plenty of friends. He has always been able to get elected from our Interior Division and as near as I can tell, he would be acceptable in Southeast Alaska by both Republican and Democratic Parties."

"Eisenhower had first offered Grandy the governorship," Sims explained, "but he had a battle with asthma, often sleeping upright in his chair. Grandy felt Stepovich, nine years younger, was better for the job."

However, when Congress passed the Alaska statehood bill on June 30, 1958, Stepovich, then the last (nonacting) territorial governor, resigned so he could run as Alaska's first U.S. senator. Similarly, Butrovich resigned as territorial senator to run as the state of Alaska's first governor.

The two men, whose fathers had both walked the Chilkoot Trail, flew across the state campaigning. In September before the election, Butrovich was quoted in the *Fairbanks Daily News-Miner* as saying, "Unscrupulous promoters who look to Alaska as a good place to make a killing may have to look elsewhere. Protection of Alaskans against come-ons and modern

John Butrovich, dean of Senate, retirement; Senate presidents John Rader, Chancy Croft, Terry Miller, John Butrovich, James Nolan, Frank Peratrovich. Juneau, 1978. Courtesy of John Almquist/Butrovich family.

shell games of the get-rich-quick boys should be one of the first obligations of officials in the new state of Alaska." However, Butrovich was defeated by William Egan, and Stepovich lost to Ernest Gruening.

In 1962, after Butrovich was elected to the state Senate, he served on every committee. He was vice-chairman of two and from 1967 to 1968, he was president of the senate. "In thirty years, he said he never traded a vote and made no compromises," Stroecker said. "He was firm and everyone knew it; he was well respected by both parties." Dedicated to education, Butrovich helped win support for the formation of the University of Alaska Fairbanks.

By 1978, Butrovich retired both from his business and from the Senate. A lot of people moaned when he left the legislature. That same year he served as honorary chairman of Terry Miller's gubernatorial campaign. He was elected an honorary member of the House of Representatives by the Congress. In 1980, he was named Alaskan of the Year and awarded an honorary degree by the University of Alaska. In 1995, a UAF administration building costing twelve million dollars was dedicated as the Butrovich Building; today it houses a super computer.

In the early 1960s John, who was pretty nonmechanical, bought an outboard motor. He loved going up the Goodpaster River but like many old-time Alaskans was apprehensive of the glacially cold water. People joked that Butro was also the oldest student pilot in Alaska. He had bought a Super Cub in 1958 but he had never registered as a pilot. He had taken the pilot test twice and failed both times. Grandson John Almquist laughed, saying, "Grandy was so nonmechanical that once when professional photographer Ruel Griffin bought him a camera, he presented it by saying, 'This type is the least troublesome, John.' But he could walk my legs off," his grandson added, remembering a hunting trip when he followed Grandy across Minto Flats.

Before his death in 1997, Butrovich enjoyed the peace of his Goodpaster River cabin. He was not averse to offering what he called "unsolicited" political advice on relevant issues. Butrovich admitted missing the "rowdy dowdy" business of politics and commented in the 1982 *Fairbanks Daily News-Miner*, "If a guy serves [in the legislature] thirty years, and doesn't have any respect left, he should go out and cut his throat." Senator Bill Ray added, "Butrovich could make you see the trees through the forest." Indeed the Butrovichs had blazed the trail from Dalmatia, over the Chilkoot, and through thirty years of Alaska's most formative period. A statesman, Butrovich had learned to pole his boat upstream, believing if something was good for Alaska, he was for it.

John Butrovich sharpening a knife, Goodpaster River, c. 1973. Courtesy of John Almquist.

Chapter 8

Charlie, Alex, and Helen Miller Vacura: Serbian Juneau Society

In the heart of Montenegro, Kolašin was home to some of Alaska's leading pioneers: Milo Hajduković, father of John Hajdukovich of Frontier AlaskA, (formerly Frontier Flying Service and Hageland Aviation Services); Mike Janković of today's University of Alaska Fairbanks Large Animal Research Station; and Branka Pekić and Ilija Milajić, father of one of Alaska's most powerful lobbyists, Alex Miller. In 1998 as a guest of Branko, Danica, and Dr. Dragan Hajduković, I stood in Kolašin's alpine cemetery at the grave of Milo and Filip Hajdukovich's father Marco. Clear mountain streams ran off the hills, funneled through a pipe available for public use.

Charlie and Mary Miller, wedding, 1922, Juneau. Courtesy of Helen Vacura.

Following the gold rush John (Jovo) Hajduković of Podgor Utrg came first to Alaska. His cousin Milo came a few months later, followed by Ilija who in Montana became Charlie Miller.

In 2005 in Fairbanks, I spoke with Charlie's daughter Helen Vacura. Helen began telling the story of her family and of early Alaska.

My father, Ilija Milajić, Charlie Miller, was born in 1889 in Rečine-Ko´lašin, Montenegro. My mother, Marica Pusić, Mary Miller, was born fourteen years later in Djenović near the beautiful Bay of Kotor, "Boka."

Former Yugoslavia was ruled for centuries by both the Ottoman and the Austro-Hungarian Empires. To survive, Montenegrin men migrated west for work to support their families at home.

About 1909, my father left Montenegro for the United States. He joined friends working in Montana's copper mines. His childhood friend, Milo Hajdukovich, went to Alaska. Daddy heard about the Alaska-Juneau (A-J) Mine and in 1911, he went to Juneau for work. Juneau had the largest and longest running red light district in the territory. Daddy began driving a cab hauling its clientele as well as local residents.

My mother came from a well-known family, a village that was half Serbian Orthodox and half Roman Catholic, Djenović, in the hills. Our family was Roman Catholic. My friend, Vuka Stepovich, grew up in nearby Risan on the Bay of Kotor.

After Mother's father died in Djenović, she and her mother were left alone with the other six children. Hearing about Juneau's A-J Mine, mother's oldest brother, Mike Pusich, left to find work in Juneau-Douglas. (He later became known for his restaurant, Mike's Place, on Douglas.)

In Juneau in 1920, many Serbian men worked in the mines that ran three nine-hour shifts, 363 days of the year. Workers were paid four dollars a day with no sick, death, medical or hospital benefits and often fell to their deaths in the glory holes. Such common conditions greatly influenced my father and, later, my brother's political stand for labor.

In 1921 when my Uncle Mike had gotten some money, he invited his younger sisters, my mother and Darinka, to join him.

When Mother and her sister arrived in Douglas, Uncle Mike gave them a party, inviting eligible bachelors. My father was fourteen years older than mother. Having already done his time in the Montana mines, his usual attire then was a three-piece suit, white shirt, and silk tie: a real dandy. A man about town, he had the gift of gab and knew business. That evening he arrived in riding breeches. Afterward, Uncle Mike asked my mother, "Which of the men did you like?" Mother replied, "The one in the jodhpurs." Uncle Mike wasn't exactly thrilled

Serbian Flag Society's drama, "Osveta/Revenge," Middle left: Charlie and Mary Miller, 1928, Juneau. Courtesy of Bill Dapcevich.

Serbian Society Flag Number Sixty-Five, celebrating Saint Sava's Day. Second row, right: Mary and Charlie Miller. Lap: possibly Bobby Dapcevich. Floor: Helen, Millie, Nellie, Rosemary, Sam, and Violet Dapcevich. Back, right of flag: Bill and John Dapcevich. Left, cupboard: possibly Alex Miller. Juneau, 1933. Courtesy of Bill Dapcevich.

since Daddy was more sophisticated. Only a month later, however, Mother and Daddy were married. Barely twenty-one, Mother was a very sheltered girl. Throughout her life, she was the nearest thing to the Holy Mother.

Daddy had a line of cabs (which included delivering customers to the red-light district, which controlled the bootlegging-speakeasy network). His most famous customer was President Harding on his 1923 tour of Alaska; he rode in one of Daddy's taxis out to the Mendenhall Glacier.

During Prohibition in 1922, my brother, Alex, was born ten months after my parents married. Daddy said to Mother, "You know, I can't run a cab company now that I am a family man." So Daddy purchased a pool hall business. (I never quite understood how that was such an improvement but ...)

The second child of five, I was born in 1924, followed by Millie, Nellie, and Rosemary. We lived in a house on the unstable slopes of Mount Roberts. One night when Daddy was at work in 1928 (I was only four), I awakened because the rain was so loud. My brother, sisters, and I were sleeping on the second floor. Mother and the baby were on the first floor. Suddenly I noticed that my ceiling light and my room were really tilted! We yelled but mother hollered back that she could not get to us. We didn't know that the staircase had broken off and that our house had slid down the side of Mount Roberts, only stopping at a bridge. She screamed, "I've gone to get help!" After what seemed like an eternity, our neighbors waded in through the kitchen, somehow got to us, and carried us out through the rushing water, dodging bushes and trees as we went. Fortunately my parents didn't rebuild there because ten years later, it happened all over again. That time, people died when the landslide engulfed an apartment building.

For social gatherings, we attended the Serbian Society Flag Number Sixty-Five, our local organization. Sometimes at holidays, our parents put on the theatrical production *Osveta*, a drama depicting the Montenegrin style of law, "blood revenge," or "an eye for an eye." In January, we gathered for Savedan, St. Sava's Day, in honor of the first bishop who in 1235 brought Christianity to Serbia. The Yugoslav men, most of whom were bachelors, would give us kids a dollar for the movies when it cost only fifteen cents. When our countrymen died, it was too expensive to ship their bodies back to Montenegro. Because we had no Serbian Orthodox church in Juneau, the bodies were shipped to the Orthodox church cemetery in Seattle. However the Seattle bishop bought a plot for the Serbs and Montenegrins in the Juneau Evergreen Cemetery. When people died, we inscribed their names on headstones like those in Montenegro.

With Prohibition repealed in 1933, Daddy bought a tavern. We didn't feel the Depression because Daddy could pay the bills. Probably we were living on credit, but Mother had a Maytag wringer washer in our comfortable home. Daddy built the Capitol Cafe and Bar, which boasted the biggest dance floor in all Alaska. Its other trademark was the big round table next to the snack bar. After 4 p.m., it was filled with local politicians talking and solving the world's problems.

Typically Slavs have a passion for politics, and Daddy was no exception. A staunch Democrat, a strong labor advocate, he thought the sun rose and set on Franklin Delano Roosevelt. An informal lobbyist, Daddy influenced a lot of people. If there were undesirable people in Juneau, the local businessmen just gave them a "blue ticket" and dropped them down the road out of town. (I never understood who decided who was undesirable.)

Helen Miller (Vacura), high school, 1941, Juneau. Courtesy of Helen Vacura.

Daddy thought Bob Bartlett and Anthony Dimond walked on water. When Tony came over, he wrestled with us kids on the floor. The day we turned eighteen, my father expected us to vote and to become politically active. He was a Democrat, but, of course, he voted for (Republican) Mike Stepovich, whom he loved.

My father spoke with a heavy accent. Once during the war on the radio, he was promoting war bonds. To our astonishment, we could hardly understand him.

Juneau was a melting pot of seven thousand people. The Slavs and Norwegians worked in the mines. The Finns ran the steam baths. The Swedes fished. The Filipinos ran restaurants on South Franklin Street. But I am ashamed to say that the Indians weren't part of our lives. For example, when my girlfriend's sister married a handsome educated Native man, it made no difference. He was still an Indian, and the marriage ended in divorce. Intermarriage was not acceptable.

When I graduated, there were only forty students. Our valedictorian, a Japanese-American,

John Tanaka, was interned shortly after Pearl Harbor. Today this is recognized by all as a terrible injustice, but in May 1942, our class knew it firsthand as we looked at our valedictorian's empty chair.

In 1942, I went to work as the secretary for the territory's public welfare director. Once, annoyed by her clientele's accents, one of the social workers whined, "Why can't these people speak English without those heavy accents?" I replied gently, "Hazel, if you lived in their country, you might well still be learning."

The war began scattering our family. My brother Alex joined the Navy. While he was stationed in Juneau with the Corps of Engineers, I met Al Vacura.

Daddy's lifelong friend Milo Hajdukovich, a real estate entrepreneur, was the father of two young children, Mary and John. His wife, Ellen, had just died. Milo asked Daddy and Mother to move into his home in Fairbanks to take care of his children.

Alex Miller, 1998, in memoriam photo. Courtesy of Helen Vacura.

When my parents arrived in Fairbanks, Milo offered Daddy the lease on one of his buildings. On First Street, Daddy built the Dreamland Bar, and on Fourteenth and South Cushman, he made a nightclub, the Talk of the Town, with live entertainment.

While Al was finishing his service, I followed my family to Fairbanks.

Milo had added a wing on for our family, but the fracas we girls made in playing our music and cavorting was too much for Milo. With a good understanding, we moved from Milo's at Fourth and Dunkel into a house on Noble Street. Every afternoon after school, Milo visited his children. However, in 1945 while visiting at George Bojanich's house, he suddenly died of a heart attack. Ed Stroecker's bank, First National, became the children's guardian, and my parents were appointed their permanent home.

As usual, Daddy was active in the community and local politics. Even though he didn't golf, he donated to the Fairbanks Golf Club who made him a charter member.

I worked for George Louden of the welfare department in the office complex above the Co-op Drug on Second Avenue, where once the wealthy and eccentric Mrs. Ford had lived. On my first day, I whipped off my typewriter cover and a cockroach came flying out! I screamed: not the best way to impress my new boss.

When Al returned, he and I married in 1946. He went to work for Daddy. (Later he, Daddy, and John Hajdukovich began a flooring business: today's Florcraft.)

Being away from the sea was a difficult adjustment for Mother. She had grown up on the breathtaking Bay of Kotor and raised us children by the sea in Juneau. She always spoke of going home to Yugoslavia, but during wartime it was impossible.

Mother developed a serious heart condition. She and Daddy went to Oakland, California, for help. One day, we got a call to come on down. In 1948 when mother died at forty-four,

I was pregnant with my second child. With Mother gone, Goldie Radunovich briefly took care of Mary and John Hajdukovich, who were then in sixth and fourth grades. Rather than go to boarding school, the children preferred to be with Al, me, and two of our soon-to-be eight children. Two years after we lost Mother, Daddy died also in 1950.

My brother, Alex Miller, born in 1922, eventually followed in my father's footsteps but to a much larger degree. In 1952, he was an alternate delegate from the Alaska Territory to the Democratic National Convention; in 1955, he was the Alaska Territory Democratic Party chair, a member of Alaska's Democratic National Committee in 1963, and for years, he served as the administrative assistant to Governor Egan. He became a powerful state lobbyist. He was known for his position on labor and his battle for statehood.

In the 1970s, I returned to my parents' Montenegro home with my uncle Mike Pusich and his friends Petar Postak and Boyle Gervich. Petar's relatives lived up in the hills, accessible only by trail. In his eighties on that very hot summer day, Mike climbed those mountains. We passed several loaded donkeys. I was exhausted. On arrival, the woman of the house kindly invited me under her grape arbor. Although she had little, she presented me with just what I needed: cold water—in a crystal glass covered with a linen napkin. It was the highlight of my trip. It embodied the dignity of this impoverished people, able to produce a silk purse from a sow's ear.

On the other hand, my extended family was in the metropolis of Herceg Novi and its environs. Petar dryly commented, "Wouldn't you know my family would be remote while yours would be in the city." (Like many of Yugoslavia's divided families, some of Petar's relatives were staunch communists, working in a Titoist munitions factory.)

My brother died at seventy-five in Alaska in 1998. He was named "One of the Forty Most Influential People in Alaska." A federal judge once commented, remembering, "You didn't go anywhere in Alaska politics if you weren't okay with Alex Miller." In Juneau, a legislative hall was named in his honor. To remind us of his quiet, omnipresent negotiations, there is a bronze cast of his ashtray and cigar in the legislature. A senator once commented, "Alex never asked me how I intended to vote as long as I was consistent—just so there were no surprises." John Dapcevich, former mayor of Sitka, remembered that Alex never crowded him on political preferences but simply wanted to know how things stood.

My brother knew the playing field. He was generous and interested in people. He pushed for busing for private schools like Monroe Catholic. Alex fought for those who had no large retirement and pushed for the Permanent Fund dividend. Sure, he handled more important things, but he didn't talk about those. Today his son, Charlie Miller, named after our father, is a successful lobbyist in the capitol.

Fifteen years ago, I finally put an end to missing my old life in Juneau. I returned for a Pusich family reunion during a siege of typically rainy weather. With a greater appreciation, I returned to the Interior's sunshine. These days, Al and I enjoy wintering in Palm Springs, California.

While we were growing up in our Serbian community, Daddy would routinely bring home any "Vich" who needed a place to stay. Accustomed to being poor and from a small country, we Viches always clustered together. Once, while traveling to a Serbian Flag convention in the Lower Forty-eight, my parents' train broke down. Daddy told Mother, "Don't worry." Although it was the middle of the night, he thumbed through the local phone book looking for a Vich. Some third- or fourth-generation Vich answered Daddy's phone call. "What?!" he cried. "Are you crazy? I don't know you! It's midnight. Leave us alone!" Daddy could not believe such a thing could happen.

Both my parents are buried in the old Serbian cemetery in Juneau. With Cyrillic lettering on many of the weathering stones, the graveyard could easily be in Montenegro. My parents' monuments have angelic wings spread like a protection over the plot. The community's stones are huddled around the base of a large, protective tree: huddled together in death as they were in life, immigrants in a new and opportunity-filled land.

Pronunciation Key

Š="sh," Y=J (e.g., Jugoslavija/Yugoslavia), č=(tongue down) ch; ć=ch; c=ts; Ilija=Ee´leeuh

Governors of Alaska Territory

The District of Alaska was organized into Alaska Territory on August 24, 1912. Governors continued to be appointed by the President of the United States.

Governor	Held Office
John Franklin Alexander Strong	April 18, 1913–April 12, 1918
Thomas Christmas Riggs, Jr.	April 12, 1918–June 16, 1921
Scott Cordelle Bone, appointed by Warren G. Harding	June 16, 1921–August 16, 1925
George Alexander Parks, appointed by Calvin Coolidge	August 16, 1925–April 19, 1933
John Weir Troy, appointed by Franklin Delano Roosevelt	April 19, 1933–December 6, 1939
Ernest Gruening, appointed by Franklin Delano Roosevelt	December 6, 1939–April 10, 1953
Benjamin Franklin Heintzleman, appointed by Dwight D. Eisenhower	April 10, 1953–January 3, 1957
Waino Edward Hendrickson, acting	January 3, 1957–April 8, 1957
Michael Anthony Stepovich, appointed by Dwight D. Eisenhower	April 8, 1957–August 9, 1958
Waino Edward Hendrickson, Acting	August 9, 1958–January 3, 1959

Governors of the State of Alaska after admittance to the Union January 3, 1959.

Governor	Held Office
William A. Egan, Democrat	Jan. 3, 1959–Dec. 5, 1966
Walter J. Hickel, Republican	Dec. 5, 1966–Jan. 29, 1969
Keith Miller, Republican	Jan. 29, 1969–Dec. 7, 1970
William A. Egan, Democrat	Dec. 7, 1970–Dec. 2, 1974
Jay Hammond, Republican	Dec. 2, 1974–Dec. 6, 1982
Bill Sheffield, Democrat	Dec. 6, 1982–Dec. 1, 1986
Steve Cowper, Democrat	Dec. 1, 1986–Dec. 3, 1990
Walter J. Hickel, Alaskan Independence	Dec. 3, 1990–Dec. 3, 1994
Tony Knowles, Democrat	Dec. 5, 1994–Dec. 2, 2002
Frank Murkowski, Republican	Dec. 2, 2002–Dec. 4, 2006
Sarah Palin, Republican	Dec. 4, 2006–incumbent

Chapter 9

Bridges to Statehood: Vuka and Governor Mike Stepovich

I first met Vuka Stepovich in 1998 while researching the story of Rika's Roadhouse builder John Hajdukovich. Vuka, was the wife of Marko, "Wise Mike," Stepovich and the step mother of the last territorial governor, Mike Stepovich. During World War II, the Stijepović family in Vuka's home town of Risan were almost annihilated. Hitler's Third Reich had the policy that if one of his soldiers were killed then one hundred of the local inhabitants would pay with their lives for that one German soldier. In Risan, the streets ran blood when sixteen Stijepovićs (Stepovichs) and eighty-four others, man, woman, and child, were murdered in their school and homes. In the 1960s, a Communist monument was constructed in Risan to honor the dead. Luka Stijepović, cousin to the Fairbanks Stepovich family, read the dedication.

Vuka Stepovich, 1993, Ninetieth birthday. Photo by Judy Worrall. Courtesy of Stepovich family.

When Vuka left Risan in 1928, she thought she'd be back. But as in many Yugoslavian families, some became Communists while others were adamantly opposed. The resulting bitter division was not something Vuka wanted to experience; she never returned home.

In 1999 when NATO bombed the Federal Republic of Yugoslavia, Serbia, Montenegro, and Kosovo, Vuka Stepovich once again suffered. A year before she died, she said, "During the wars of 1912–13, my brother was killed and his bones were left in Albania. I have lived through five wars in my lifetime: the Balkan Wars, World Wars I and II, the 1990s breakup of Yugoslavia, and now the bombing of my country. It is enough." With the new Millennium, Vuka went to her reward.

Had there not been a Vuka, Mike Stepovich II, the last territorial governor, might not have made Alaska his home. Vuka left behind many who called her Mother, Nana, and friend.

In 1998, before I went to Vuka's country, she advised, "You must ride the train around the tops of the Montenegrin mountains with its breakneck views of the Lim River. Before it was built, they said that such a train could never be built, but they did it!"

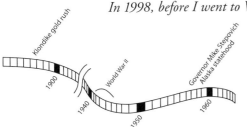

Klondike gold rush 1900 1940 World War II 1950 Governor Mike Stepovich Alaska statehood 1960

Vuka's younger brother, Nikola Radovich, described the background of the Mediterranean town of Risan and its Bay of Kotor in *Reflections of the Past*, published in 1993. He painted a picture and described its ancient and very colorful past.

The Bay of Kotor is divided into four smaller bays, including the Bay of Risan. The Stepovich (Stijepović) and Radović families came from the oldest town on the bay, Risan, which was originally a fortified Illyrian settlement, dating back to the third century BC. The Romans left a perfectly preserved mosaic of the reclining god, Hypnos. In ancient times, the Venetians spanned the narrow mouth leading into the inner Bay of Kotor, Verige, with chains to prevent incoming warships. The Bay of Kotor is framed by steep mountains; residents simply call it "Boka."

From 1397 to 1797, the Republic of Venice ruled the Dalmatian coast. The local Dalmatian Slavs worked with the Venetian Navy to keep the Turks away from the coast. Inland, the Ottoman Turks occupied much of Croatia, Bosnia and Serbia.

In 1600 the Turks controlled Risan from a stone tower, *kula*, an artillery depot, high on a hill overlooking the bay. Vuka's ancestor with other Montenegrin men began building a cannon of cherry wood. They called for the men of Herzegovina to come over the hills and help. Vuka's ancestor lit the cannon aimed at the Turkish fortress. For months Montenegrins and Herzegovinans stormed the fortress until they finally took the high ground that commanded the Bay of Kotor. As a reward, the Turkish tower and its grounds, quite a high prize, were awarded to Vuka's family.

Even throughout four hundred years of Venetians and Dalmatians fighting the Turks, the Venetians never opened a school in the native language, Serbo-Croatian.

In Bosnia and Serbia for centuries, the Turkish ruling Pashas humiliated the Serbs by taking their lands and giving great opportunity to the poor peasants if they accepted their Islamic religion and culture. Every year they stole young boys and made them part of the Janissaries, the elite army that controlled the Balkan Peninsula. The girls were taken to amuse the sultan in Istanbul/Constantinople.

Vuka's two-story home, the 1600 Turkish kula, arsenal tower, Risan, Montenegro. Photos by Judy Ferguson.

In 1797, Napoleon invaded Dalmatia and abolished the Venetian Republic. Although Napoleon didn't remain, his presence fanned the Slavs' hope for freedom. But those hopes were dashed when in 1814, the Austrians took control of Dalmatia from Venice.

For five hundred years, the Ottoman Turks had made Serbia, Bosnia, parts of Croatia, and some of Montenegro European Turkey. Finally in 1878 with the Treaty of Berlin, Serbia and Montenegro gained complete independence, only to have Austria illegally annex Bosnia and Herzegovina thirty years later in 1908. An underground movement, the "Young Bosnians" gathered strength in Sarajevo. The rumor was that Austria wanted to make Yugoslavia another province.

For the Germans and Austrians, the Balkans were the battleground for retaining a bridge through Turkey to Arabian oil. Sandžak, the Ottoman military land belt from Bosnia-Herzegovina through Montenegro to Kosovo-Metohia, was that Balkan corridor to the oil.

Vuka's Bay of Kotor had been settled by Montenegrins, Serbs from Herzegovina and a few Croatians. Before World War I, many Slavs were shouting for unity, a pan Slavic movement while others preferred the opportunities Austria could afford them.

Trieste was the economic center for the coast while Risan and Kotor, both cosmopolitan towns were the transit hubs to Montenegro. A local butcher, Mijo Stijepović, had a small hillside farm, Pelinica. He reared several sons including Gojko, Daniel and born in 1880, Marko, Vuka's future husband.

Pelim (Pelinica), or sage, covered the surrounding hills along with many other medicinal herbs. Herb collecting and meat smoking (*kastradina*) was one of the main businesses of the Stijepović family. Before Christmas when the island Dalmatians came to trade, the herbs were in great demand.

However, the economy was poor. The local soil was rocky and it was hard to raise a cash crop. Tired of depending on the sale of herbs and with little hope of independence and prosperity, many of the young men wanted to find opportunity elsewhere, including Marko Stijepović.

View of the Bay of Kotor from Vuka's window, Risan, Montenegro, 2003. Judy Ferguson photo.

Mike Stepovich I, "Wise Mike," c. 1943, Fish Creek at Slippery Gulch. Courtesy of Nick Stepovich.

The Bay of Kotor offered an automatic springboard to the world. Every time an overseas boat arrived for loading, young Slavs frequently jumped aboard and hid until the ship was on the open seas. Many young men became stowaways to avoid serving in the Austrian (foreign) army. In 1895, Marko Stijepović jumped on the ship for the United States.

On top of the hill where Vuka's ancestor had been awarded the old Turkish tower and its land, the family had built a large two-story stone house with an open well. The well, built against the house like a small pond, supplied fresh water and refrigerated the family's cheese and butter. From the front door, there were terraced pastures where their sheep grazed. A sanctuary, the home had a breathtaking view overlooking the Bay of Kotor. Vuka's parents, Simo and Sava had four boys: Savo, Filip, Aleksije, and Nikola, and four girls: Vukosava, Jovanka, Vidosava, and Zorka. Born in 1903, Vuka, a nickname for Vukosava, was number seven of eight children. Her father, Simo Radović, owned the store on the first corner by the bay. On weekends, villagers packed their vegetables, berries, buttermilk, cream, goat and smoked cheeses, sausages, and animals to trade at Radović's store or in the open market. In Risan on the sea, oranges, grapefruits, pomegranates, and figs grew in abundance. Up in the colder alpine areas, the villagers could not grow these tropical fruits. They traded their own goods for dried fruit, coffee, sugar, salt, and olive oil that came from Trieste. The peasants bought on credit. If they had a good season, Simo Radović was paid at harvest. If not, he suffered. Frequently the peasants overnighted on the floor of Simo Radović's store before returning to their village.

During the Balkan Wars of 1912–1913, as Serbs and Montenegrins pushed the Turks out, Vuka's oldest brother, Savo, "the most beautiful," she called him, died on the far side of Lake Skadar in Albania in 1913. The family had no way to bring his body home. Even at age ninety-six, she mourned, "His bones stayed on Albanian soil!" His loss was devastating to Vuka's mother.

The next year when Gavrilo Princip, a Bosnian Serb of the Young Bosnians, assassinated Austrian Archduke Franz Ferdinand, the Austrian rulers in Risan rang the church bells, calling everyone to mourn the duke's death. Each home was required to hang a black flag of mourning. Vuka's father resisted the order. He was arrested, but after a warning to change his politics he was released.

The Austrian naval artillery in the Bay of Tivat bombarded the Montenegrin mountain Lovčen. Food became scarce during the war. Because Vuka's family had a small farm, they avoided famine during the last two years of World War I. She and her family subsisted on cornbread and polenta. Their cow and chickens saved their lives.

With the end of the war in 1918, Serbia and Montenegro united in the new Kingdom of Serbs, Croats, and Slovenes. This union meant that Germany and Austria had lost their corridor, Sandžak, to Arabian oil. With the loss of that access, Austria's ambitions for the Balkans subsided.

Vuka's mother, Stana, caught the Spanish Flu and died in 1918. With her death, Vuka said, "nothing remained the same. Everything went downhill." For the next ten years, Vuka took care of her father.

Eight years before Vuka was born, Marko Stijepović, only sixteen was on his way to America. Speaking no English, he was discovered in Baltimore as a stowaway. He was put on a train and tagged for delivery to Fresno, California, where there was a large Serb community. He got a job buying and selling calves from ranchers; it was the only eleven days in this country that Marko ever worked for someone besides himself. He also gathered figs, hired Serbian ladies who knew how to dry them, and he sold them to merchants in Colorado.

When news of the Alaska Gold Rush hit in 1896 to 1897, he purchased supplies and headed north. He left word with a friend from back home to tell his father he'd gone on to the Klondike. He hired packers and they freighted through Dyea and over the Chilkoot Trail. Soapy Smith policed the trail and at each stop, his gang extorted toll money from the prospectors. A stubborn Montenegrin, Marko and his men broke trail around the outlaws which forever gave him the name "Wise Mike."

At Bennett Lake, Wise Mike built a raft and a cabin and wintered over. The next spring after he rafted to Dawson, he loaded his freight onto a steamboat. However it was breakup and the ice was going out. Apparently the deckhands didn't tie the boat well. During the night the cracking ice tore the boat from the bank; it and all its cargo were lost. Wise Mike picked up three teams of horses; that winter in Dawson, he freighted for the miners. With his profit, he grubstaked a prospector. Shortly before breakup, he rented a Canadian government warehouse, bought a bunch of salmon, and hired someone to cut the ice to pack the fish, but after two to three days, the ice melted, the salmon spoiled, and the Canadians fined Mike. He went over to a strike on the Stewart River, and continued freighting there with his horses. Unfortunately, all but one got Hobb's Disease and died. When Fairbanks struck gold in 1902, Mike took his remaining horse and packed cross-country to the Alaska interior. Fairbanks was just Barnette's Cache, the Northern Commercial Company and a lot of prospectors.

Mike Stepovich II and his mother, Olga Barta Stepovich, c. 1921, Portland. Courtesy of Nick Stepovich.

With a Canadian partner in 1902 to 1903, Mike staked Graehl but due to a citizenship issue, the partner lost it. Mike claimed the land from today's Gavora's Liquor and Fine Wines store to Denali State Bank on Garden Island. When the nuns of St. Joseph's Hospital needed a pasture for their cow, he sold them two acres. Near today's Fort Knox gold mine, Mike staked many claims on Fairbanks and Fish creeks. When gold was discovered in Ester, prospectors including "Poppa" John Butrovich left their claims untended. Wise Mike claimed what was left behind. After the Ester strike subsided, the prospectors, including Butrovich, returned. Disgruntled at their lost claims, they sneaked into Wise Mike's cabin and took all his guns. That night, while Mike was in bed, the prospectors burst into his cabin. However, they had forgotten the gun that any Montenegrin caches in his boot. Mike fired over their heads, and they took off into the trees.

Mike's brother Dan arrived, and got work at the Ester mine. However, in those days there were a lot of accidents. In 1913, Dan was killed in a cave-in; today he is buried at Clay Street cemetery.

Mike began prospecting for gold on Gilmore Trail but discovered quartz. His friend Freddy Johnson told him there was not only quartz there but also tungsten, which was in demand for light bulbs. Mike dug a deep shaft, loaded the ore into boxes, and skidded them onto a steamboat for Seattle. From that, he earned a lot of money. Well-heeled then, he asked a stylish Croatian woman from Portland's Balkan community, Olga Barta, to marry him in 1918. When she moved into Wise Mike's isolated, primitive cabin at Fairbanks Creek, the lifestyle did not agree with her. After Mike II was born at the cabin in 1919, she took him with her to visit her family in Oregon and never returned. She divorced Wise Mike and later remarried.

Over the next ten years, Wise Mike wrote his mother in Risan but she could neither read nor write. Vuka Radović, whose older sister Zorka had married Mike's older brother, Gojko, came often to visit. She read Mike's letters to his mother. Vuka was intrigued by the Alaska adventures she read on every page.

Vuka tells her story in her own words:

In 1928, forty-eight-year-old Mike returned to Risan for six weeks. He mentioned to me, "How would you like to come back to Alaska with me?" At first I thought he was out of his mind. But the more I got to know him, I thought he was smart and interesting, and he talked me into it. He was twenty-three years older but at twenty-five, I was ready to begin a family; I knew he would take care of me. I packed some of my mother's jewelry and clothes. Mike promised the family that we'd be back.

After a long journey by ship, we caught the train for Seattle. Once in

Vuka arriving at Fairbanks Creek, 1928, Courtesy of Mike Stepovich III.

a while, I had seen snow on the mountains back home. Traveling through the mountains in Oregon, I saw snow up past the top of the train. I wondered, "*Where* am I going?!" Only two weeks after my twenty-sixth birthday, we arrived by train in Alaska. There was lots of snow, and smoke coming from the Northern Commercial Company's powerhouse. Friendly people met us at the train station and took us to the Pioneer Hotel where there were more people to greet us. To me, English sounded strange: loud and noisy. I didn't know anything, and I had to depend on an interpreter. I had no home and felt disoriented and uncomfortable. After a few days, I had an idea: "Mike, why don't we go out to your cabin!" With no way on our own to get there and no broken trail to the cabin, it wasn't a simple move.

Freddy Johnson loaded up our baggage in his car and took us out to Gilmore Trail to meet Pete Bojanich, who was waiting there with his horse team and a sleigh. I was wear-

Back: Mrs. Jack Eagan, unknown, Mrs. Martin Sather (Nellie Eagan), Mrs. Dan (Isabelle) Eagan, Vuka Stepovich. Front: Martin Sather Jr., Paul Sather, Pat Eagan, Doris Eagan (Jack Eagan's daughter), Margaret Eagan (Dan Eagan's daughter), Fairbanks Creek, 1929. Courtesy of Mrs. Pat Sather Franklin.

ing a coonskin coat, and Mike wrapped a wolf robe around me. Pete drove us out to Twenty Mile. At the roadhouse, all the mailmen from the creeks were there. The roadhouse owner, Mr. Birch, made us a delicious dinner and offered me a very nice room. I met my neighbor, the Fairbanks Creek postman, Dan Eagan. He called his wife and told her, "I'm bringing Mike Stepovich's bride home!" The trail narrowed and the next day, they had to drive two sleighs in single file. I rode with Dan Eagan in his mail delivery sleigh while Mike rode in Pete's. But we came to a one-thousand-foot chasm, and the horse took off fast downhill. Terrified, I threw myself off into the snowbank. Mike waded back in the snow to get me. I was shaking. He said, "You disappoint me. Dan is really a pretty responsible driver." As we pulled up to the Fairbanks Creek schoolhouse, five children were on the steps waiting to greet us. As soon as I saw the children, I felt much better. It was evening, and we decided to overnight at the post office. The next morning after Mrs. Eagan made us

L–R: Vuka, Ellen, Mike I and Nada, Miso, Alex Stepovich, c. 1944, California. Courtesy of Radović Family, Risan, Montenegro.

a delicious breakfast, we began breaking trail three miles to the cabin. Over the next three days, Dan's oldest son Jack mushed our baggage in.

Almost every day, Jack and Martin Sather would ski over to see us. They were very curious. One time as Jack was ready to go, I got brave and said in English, "Go back!" He took his skis off and explained to me for the first of many times the difference between saying, "Go back!" and "Come back!"

As the children studied in school, I joined them. They became my English teachers. In the summer, Mike Yankovich brought me whole milk from his cows so I could make *kajmac* cream to top off my moose meat soups. In a truck in the fall, Mike brought our groceries (including eggs) in for the winter. I had a garden. During the winter, we root-cellared our vegetables, including celery that lasted until New Year's. Throughout the winter we had to rotate our eggs, and by spring they could be used only for baking, not for breakfast.

Living out at the creek made me a very strong person. I wasn't afraid of anything. The Fairbanks Creek community was a couple of dozen men and two women. Winter was hard but I was busy with the house and later on, with boiling diapers.

Mike's son, Mike Stepovich II, began writing letters to us. Miso was born in 1929, followed by Alex and then Nada. The children had no other family, and letters from their big brother became a very big event. They were all excited in 1936 when for the first time, young Mike visited. He fell in love with three-year-old Nada. Three days after he arrived, our youngest child, Ellen, was born.

Mike Stepovich II tells his story in his own words:

Vuka became the cement for both sides of my father's Stepovich family.

In 1936 when I was seventeen, I visited Alaska for the first time since I was small. Alaska was altogether different from Portland.

The June 9, 1958, issue of *Time* magazine described my father: "Wise Mike was rugged and sometimes mean tempered, and there were those who say he won his nickname with wise-guy answers to everything. His breakfast appetizer was four or five coffee royals—a couple of slugs of bourbon sweetened with a dash of coffee—and his hobby later was seven-deck 'pan-ginney' dealt out at the Pastime Cafe."

Every summer, I began working for my father. He had eleven people working for him: seven Italians, two Slavs, and two Norwegians. I drove the truck into town every week for supplies, where I played baseball. I met outstanding people in Fairbanks: both lawyers and Jesuit priests. Julian Hurley, the finest of trial lawyers, became one of my mentors. At the creek, Vuka treated me better than her own children. I began to think of making Alaska my home.

When Vuka's four children were school age, she moved her family into a house on Cushman between Seventh and Eighth. My father was usually out at the mine and came to town once in a while. He had been advised by a lawyer to invest in downtown real estate. He already owned the Cushman Street house and a building at Fourth and Cushman. He bought the Shields restaurant with apartments upstairs on the corner at Second and Lacey across from the Savoy bar. (After he sold it, the new owner had the Savoy bar.)

Vuka resumes her story:

In 1942 when Miso was recovering from typhoid fever, Mike was down at the Pioneer Hotel, waiting to see who might come in on the afternoon train. I left Miso and Alex with our neighbor the mother of Mrs. Reeves and I went with Tillie Reeves and the girls to Badger's Greenhouse on Front Street to get some flowers for a funeral Mike was going to attend. As we walked, we heard the whistle on the Northern Commercial power plant signaling a fire. We saw the smoke but thought it was coming from a block one over from ours. As I came out of the greenhouse, I saw a neighbor and asked to use his phone. The operator, Florence, recognized my voice and said, "Vuka! It's *your* home!" I asked, "Can you get me a taxi?" She said, "I can't! They're all down at the train station waiting for the arriving tourists!" I threw my flowers at Mrs. Reeves, said, "It's *my* house!" and caught a ride home with the N. C. Co. delivery truck. I circled the house; there were four-foot flames coming out of every window! As I stood by the fence, I fainted. As people carried me into our neighbor's Bob Driscoll's, Mike came around the corner and saw us. In the hustle and bustle, I saw Alex but I couldn't see Miso! As I laid on the Driscolls' bed I could hear the fire roaring and the grass crackling. Then out the window, I saw my boy! He was helping the Reeves get their furniture out of their house. I thought, "Let the house burn! I have my boy!" The rest of the summer we lived out at the creek; it was very hard.

Since the war had begun, Mike couldn't mine any longer. His equipment was taken for defense. Mike, sixty-two, thought it would be more economical to rebuild back in California where he had first arrived. We moved to Los Gatos and two years later when Miso was thirteen and Ellen was only five, Mike had a stroke and died at sixty-five. I was left with four young children to raise.

Governor Mike Stepovich continues his story:

My father had sold the Fairbanks Creek claim with the house still on it to the Fairbanks Exploration Company. After the war, we moved the house to Fish Creek. Unfortunately Fairbanks Claim was never dredged because World War II brought a halt to mining. However tungsten was needed for the manufacture of light bulbs and bullets so that mine continued to be worked.

In Oregon where I was raised, all we Slavs lived in Portland on the north side. As I grew up, I saw Matilda Baricevich at family parties. I noticed her before she did me. I spent a lot of my extra time playing baseball and was eventually asked to play for the Boston Red Sox. However, my mother felt strongly about education. I enrolled at Gonzaga University where I graduated in 1941. I continued, and entered Notre Dame's law school where I had excellent professors and studied both contract and criminal law. My grades continued to improve.

Just after Pearl Harbor, I enlisted. When the military realized I was in law school, they allowed me to continue until I got my LLB, Bachelor of Laws degree, in 1943. Then they retained me for domestic legal work.

The Navy stationed me at Fleet City, only forty miles from Los Gatos, my father's new home. However before I was able to visit, my father died when he was sixty-five in1944. My step-brothers and sisters were still young so I visited Vuka and the kids often. To be near them, and also to prepare for the bar exam in Fairbanks, I audited a post-graduate law class at Santa Clara in 1946.

When I was twenty-eight, I approached Matilda Barecevich who was twenty-four. We had similar personalities and shared the same faith and everyday lifestyle. I knew she was what I wanted and in 1947, we were married. A strong personality, her affectionate nickname for me was "Mali," Little One. Her thinking was clear and she believed in following her husband. Although she had never been to Alaska, we moved to Fairbanks in February, moving into my father's apartment building at Second and Lacey in the middle of winter.

In early Fairbanks, it was said that if you weren't Slav, you didn't go anywhere. There were a lot of so-called "sons of viches"; many were bachelors who came and went with the wind while others were the merchants, politicians, miners, inventors, and farmers of the Interior. From Croatia, Montenegro, Serbia and Slovenia, they had an amazing impact on the shaping of Alaska. Their names are so intertwined with Alaska history they seem to be merely

Governor Mike Stepovich, Time *magazine cover, 1958. Courtesy of Nick Stepovich.*

73

Alaskans. When they left the Balkans, they were free as I, the son of immigrants, to expand their talents.

At Second and Lacey streets in 1948, I started practicing law with E. B. Collins and Charles Clasby in Fairbanks. When our first child, Antonia, was born, I left the hospital thinking, "Now I have a child, it's about time to go into my own private practice and buy a home." I went to work and told my friend, Clasby, that I was going to open my own law office. He offered me a raise, I declined, and soon my own shingle, "Mike Stepovich, Attorney-at-Law" was hanging at the corner of Fourth and Cushman. Besides taking cases, I also took care of my stepmother, Vuka's, real estate; collected rent; did her legal work; and went out to the creek to do the assessment work on my father's claims. For the first six months, I had no secretary.

Time magazine quoted Matilda describing this period, "When we were living in Fairbanks and Mali was practicing law, the jacket pocket on every one of his suits used to be torn from getting caught on the parking meter where he was leaning while talking with the boys." The article continued, "Mat stayed home and cared for an increasing crop of children—now the famous 'eight little itches' (nine years to five months old) who are part of a Step-by-Step plan that calls for an even dozen children."

Mike continued: Early Fairbanks was great. If there were a murder case involving indigents, I'd be appointed by a judge and get paid fifty dollars a day. I was in the courtroom a lot, handling all types of cases: embezzlement, rape, gambling, prostitution, personal injuries, and some civil cases. I got experience quickly.

With the Cold War era, there was a build-up of military bases and a lot of huckledy-buck went on in town. In a de facto legality, the Line was tolerated, but on the books, prostitution was illegal. The girls paid the city clerk weekly and were routinely examined by doctors.

I tried my second murder with a great trial lawyer, my mentor Julian Hurley. He used the law of evidence, protecting the client and was excellent in picking juries. I would put him up against any trial lawyer in the world.

I remember a prostitute in Nenana went on trial for murder. After an episode with a customer, he paid her and left. An hour later, the big, powerful guy returned and banged on the door, wanting his money back. She barred the door but as he pushed it ajar, she shot him.

As was customary when Julian and I finished trying the case, we left our respective phone numbers with the court clerk. He would call us when the verdict came in.

Later as I sat at my desk, a guy walked by and hollered, "Congratulations!" "What for?" I asked. "Hurley's down at the Mecca,"

Governor Stepovich pinning the forty-ninth star, Alaska, on new American flag, 1958. Courtesy of Stepovich family.

he responded, "spending money like a fool: buying drinks for the house." So I hurried over. I walked in, sat down on the bar stool, got a drink, and asked Hurley, "Did we win?" Smiling broadly, he fanned $800 like a deck of cards. Then laying the bills on the counter, we divvied it up. I bought a round for the house and left.

Had I started my practice in Seattle, I would never have seen a courtroom for six years. In Fairbanks, there were only seven lawyers. If you couldn't make it in Fairbanks, you couldn't make it anywhere. I was in the right place at the right time.

During the 1940s, my friend and mentor, John Butrovich, started in politics on the City Council and became a territorial senator in 1944. He was nine years my senior and the finest man I ever knew. The son of a Croatian prospector, "Poppa" John Butrovich, John was a very knowledgeable statesman. I watched and listened to him carefully. In 1950, I was city attorney and in 1951, I was in the Territorial House of Representatives for three years. By 1953, I had joined John in the senate. We always felt if our point of view didn't win, who cares? Everyone has good ideas; nobody's perfect. If good resulted from a decision, that was the important thing.

Because I was in private law practice, I had to close my office during each of the sessions. I bought a building at 310 First Avenue from Mr. Swift. I added onto it. (Sometimes I did renovation work.) We asked the priest to bless it and called it the Matilda Building. We rented it to the United States Geological Survey. After my friend "Big Ray" began running Big Ray's in 1951 he bought the old Waechter's meat market complete with an elevator at 543 Second Avenue. Raykovich leased the building and the lessee operated the Crystal Room bar. In 1957 when oil was discovered in the Kenai Peninsula on the Swanson River, Big Ray sold me the old Waechter building. However there was a fire; even the cash register melted. The building stood vacant for awhile until I took out a loan and refurbished the building. Across the street Melo Jackovich's Fairbanks Bar also burned. My building was in better condition. He leased from me and ran his bar out of my building for a while.

In 1956 to 1957, the drumbeat for statehood was increasing. Delegates E. L. "Bob" Bartlett and Tony Dimond were good delegates. But to the federal government, the territory was like a step-child; we had to beg Washington for everything we needed. Congress felt sorry for us and generally gave us what we asked. But it was time for us to have equal footing over our own destiny. From Milwaukee to San Francisco, through newspapers, and congressmen, Governor Gruening pushed for statehood. Eisenhower was lukewarm; as a soldier, he wanted to keep the state open for federal defense. But Fred Seaton, secretary of the interior, strongly supported statehood and convinced Eisenhower. The *Time* article said, "Fred Seaton flew to Alaska in 1957, looking for a new governor. There were seventeen candidates and a dozen others being urged by individuals or groups. I saw this young lawyer in Fairbanks. Just thirty-seven at the time. He never applied for the job. The more I saw him, the more I knew I was going to recommend him. Steering Mike Stepovich from behind were two powerful Republicans: Territorial Senator Butrovich and Fairbanks Publisher (*Daily News-Miner*) Bill Snedden."

In 1957, the longest serving senator and chair for the Finance Committee, respected by both parties, John Butrovich, recommended me to Eisenhower for governor. Matilda, my seven children, and I flew to Juneau and moved into the governor's mansion.

Since the territory was controlled by the federal government, there were only certain things I could do: the oversight of the National Guard and of local affairs. Congress met only every two years. *Time* magazine wrote, "Alaska's first native-born governor...Mike Stepovich...deals with the forty-seven appointive territorial boards and commissions, oversees emergency work projects, orders examination of fiscal programs that will help Alaska's ability to stand alone, confers with Washington and territorial officials, studies his mail, e.g. 'We the undersigned students have been recently examined by Dr. Brownlee, and sixty having been found with defective teeth, do humbly petition our Governor, Mike Stepovich, to send us a dentist.'" Alaska was a vast wilderness with a few cities. We were given a big Lincoln, a large house, a maid—all paid for by the federal government. It was the easiest job I ever had. There is a big difference between being territorial and state governor. Speaking of the push for statehood, *Time* quoted Governor Stepovich, "It wasn't until I got into office that I really began to appreciate, with our resources potential, how much we could have accomplished even by now, if only we had the freedom and responsibility [as a state] to operate."

Reflecting upon his political work, Stepovich told *Time* magazine, "When I was governor, it was mostly a sales job, going around the country selling statehood. I was a new face, energetic, and enthusiastic. When I traveled around the country, I just talked to people and sold Alaskan statehood. It was a good job." In Congress, arguments against granting statehood had to be overcome. First, it had to be resolved that the noncontiguity of Alaska with the lower U.S. would not be a burden on the Union. "Secondly, there was the question of whether the small population of Alaska—then only 127,000," reported Dan Whipple in the *Portland Magazine,* "deserved two senators in Congress. Moreover, the Seattle fishing industry was determined to see that a new state did not make major changes in the fishing regulations off the Alaska coast. The Alaska Salmon Industry, Inc., of Seattle had lobbied successfully against statehood for years. But Stepovich, supported by Fred Seaton and steered

L–R, Back: Jim, Pete, Nick, Matilda, Governor Mike, Mike III, Chris, Dominic, Ted; Front, L–R: Nada, Laura, Andrea, Melissa, Toni, Maria, Vuka's funeral, Fairbanks, 2000. Courtesy of Stepovich family.

by John Butrovich and Bill Snedden, built up the campaign like never before. The discovery of oil on the Kenai Peninsula, along with the promise of the virtually untapped mineral deposits, showed Alaska was filled with potential." In 1958, statehood passed in the U.S. Senate sixty-four to twenty and was signed by presidential proclamation in January 1959. Afterward I ran for the Senate but Gruening defeated me by nine hundred votes. (In those days, Alaska was predominately Democratic.)

Whipple's *Portland Magazine* article continued, "Later in 1962 on the fourth anniversary of Alaska statehood, Stepovich—a man known for his open-faced friendliness and earnest warmth—recalled his last meeting with President Eisenhower with simple satisfaction: 'It was at the White House again. Eisenhower told me that he'd made a lot of appointments that day, but he thought that I was one of his better ones. That made me feel pretty good.

I returned to private practice. The priest blessed my 543 Second Avenue property, the old Waechter Building, and named it for my first-born, the Antonia Building. We leased the basement and second floor to Lois and Gene Tapp's Mukluk Shop. On the ground floor, we leased to the Star of the North Bakery. Behind the bakery, on the Third Avenue entrance side, I set up my law office. I put a freezer upstairs for the bakery. The district court rented the third floor for a while. The bakery needed more space so in 1971, I bought an empty lot belonging to Harry Avakoff the jeweler between us and the Mecca bar. With the lot, I added on to the bakery.

By 1978 to 1980, I was in retirement. My oldest son, Mike, took over my law practice on Second Avenue in Fairbanks. When I was seventy-five, Mike and my younger son, Ted, an Anchorage attorney, called me to help on a couple of cases; those were was my last trials.

The *Portland Magazine* quoted Matilda about our years in Alaska: "'It has always been important to our family that we were a part of a significant occasion in history—in short, a part of history.' What is more, history and life in Alaska contributed to the endeavors of Matilda and Mike in raising their family. Mrs. Stepovich elaborated, 'Certainly, the Territory—and later the State of Alaska—was conducive to that end.'"

As I look back, I know marriage was the most important thing in my life. When we were young, I thought bringing in the meat and potatoes was enough but it wasn't. My wife was the backbone of our family until 2003 when she passed away, a woman who was nurse and teacher for fifty-six years to our thirteen children.

My wife and I were both children of immigrants. The people of former Yugoslavia—Butrovich, Milajić/Miller, Peratrovich, Begich, Dapcevich, Hajdukovich, Miscovich, Jackovich, Glavinovich, Yankovich, Bigovich, Pekich—have been involved in every 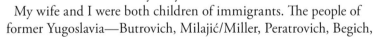level in Alaska, with a profound influence on the Great Land.

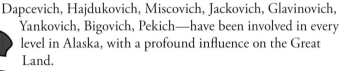

MONTENEGRO

Longest Owned Family Gold Mine: John Miscovich, One Hundred Years, Flat/Iditarod Strike

In 1908, John Beaton and his partner, Frank Dikeman, left the Ophir district, went down the Innoko River, up the Iditarod River, and began exploring east from the mouth of Otter Creek. In December, they sank a prospect hole where ten feet of overburden lay over six feet of gravel. By Christmas, they had struck gold at Discovery Claim on Otter Creek.

Throughout 1909, prospectors came down the Yukon River to Holy Cross, up the Innoko and Iditarod rivers to the mouth of Otter Creek, to the newly formed Otter City at Discovery.

As prospect holes were sunk to bedrock, the prospectors' pay streak expanded to the east, south, and west of the original Discovery Claim.

By the spring of 1910, thousands, including my father, Pete Miscovich, were heading on steamboats to Otter City. At the deeper port of Iditarod, the prospectors unloaded and then poled six miles upstream to Otter City.

John Miscovich in Poorman, 1952 with 750 oz. of gold. Courtesy of John Miscovich.

Overnight Iditarod became a tent city with a sawmill, Northern Commercial Company, and saloons. The third largest gold rush in early Alaska was on.—John Miscovich, Flat, Alaska, 2008, one-hundred-year anniversary of the gold rush at Otter, Flat, and Iditarod.

Before the use of heavy equipment and high-pressure water hoses, my father, Peter Miscovich, a prospector, began his mining career in Flat/Iditarod.

He was born Pero Miscović on June 29, 1885, in the village of Imotica, twenty-seven miles north of Dubrovnik on the Adriatic Coast. The village was so small that its mail was delivered at the nearby larger town of Ston. Imotica, with its population of three hundred in 1885, was poor. For over a thousand years, peasant families had divided and subdivided their small stony plots of land among their heirs. Dominated by first one empire and then another, the peasants were also heavily taxed. To farm, the Slavs dug up rocks and stacked them into walls, then piled dirt between,

78

where they raised cabbage and potatoes; tobacco was their cash crop. In each family, someone herded the family's sheep and goats to upland pastures.

Balkan villages were traditionally tribal strongholds. Imotica was the village of the Miscovich family as well as my wife's family, the Stankovich. A half-mile valley separated the families. If you wanted to call your neighbor, you stood on your hillside and hollered across to him.

Village protocol had changed little over hundreds of years. There was no public schooling; every family member worked to survive. Dalmatian men fished but could also become a priest or serve in the Austro-Hungarian army. Consequently, on Sunday after church when my father talked about his dreams of going to North America, people thought he wasn't quite right in the head. However, in 1903 at the age of eighteen, he caught a ship to LeHavre, France, where he boarded *La Gascone* and sailed on to Ellis Island, New York, where he stayed briefly.

He followed friends to the Anaconda copper mine in Butte, Montana, where he got on with a six-year apprenticeship program. But the work was both toxic and dangerous. Next he tried Angels Camp, California, followed by coal mining in Wilkensen, Washington, which was even worse. The mines were tough, miserable work. There was no thought for conditions, health insurance, or safety for the miners. The men worked twelve hours a day in hot conditions. My dad said, "If you didn't like it, there was someone on top waiting to take your job."

He was against Communism but was for improving the working man's conditions. Slowly he began to doubt his American Dream, but when he heard about the gold strike at Flat/ Iditarod in 1910, he packed to leave. He cashed his last paycheck and booked steerage as far as he could pay to St. Michael's on the Yukon River. From there, he worked for passage up the Yukon, Innoko, and Iditarod rivers.

Iditarod Traction Company with mule drawn tram leaving from Iditarod to Flat City, May 30, 1912. Courtesy of John Miscovich.

By 1910, Iditarod was a large city with three newspapers, a bank, sixteen saloons, and regular dogsled mail delivery. The deeper port of Iditarod supplied gold mines on Otter and Flat creeks. However, they needed a road. Jake Mutchler, a Flat teamster, built a wooden tramway to connect Iditarod to Flat in 1911, enabling Flat to supply the nearby creeks. Jake used a team of eight horses and a Model T Ford. Guggenheim's Number Seven dredge at Dawson was dismantled, loaded on barges, shipped to Iditarod, and tramed to upper Flat Creek where it was reassembled on Marietta Claim.

When my father arrived, the good paystreaks on Otter and Flat Creeks were already taken by the big operators: Guggenheim, Riley, and John Beaton. My father cut wood for the Otter Creek boilers to thaw shafts in underground drift mining. At six dollars a cord, he got a few bucks ahead for the long winters of 1910–11. Along with his Slavic, he knew some Italian and had a grasp of English. A fair carpenter, he became a section foreman building the tramway, which got him into the field where he looked for a claim. He watched for claims abandoned by those discouraged by the deep permafrost. Fortunately in 1912, he caught part of one: fifteen acres of Hensley's

Assay office, American Bank of Alaska, Iditarod, $125,000 in gold bricks, c. 1911. L–R: Mrs. F. W. (Emily) Herms, Dr. F. W. Herms, Sr., and unknown. Courtesy of Fred Herms Jr. Collection, UAF-1974-42-4.

available for staking. He jumped at this three-quarter placer claim. With his brother, Andrew, and countryman John Popovich, he began a small underground drift mining operation. Through the winter in the wood-burning boiler house, steam was generated and shot through three-quarter-inch pipe into an underground eight-by-eight-foot trench to thaw the paydirt. By pulley on a cable from the shaft to a tall tripod, the paydirt was ferried in buckets and dumped on a dirt mountain, the winter dump. In the spring, the dump was sluiced.

However, the ground in Flat was so level it was necessary to push the dirt up to the sloping sluice through hydraulic lifts. To gain the needed pressure to push the paydirt up, miners went upstream to a higher elevation, where they dug a ditch from the creek down to the sluice. One hundred feet of gravity drop generated thirty-five pounds of pressure. The miner then fed that pressurized water into a hose that forced the paydirt up into the hydraulic lift. Due to the constriction in the stovepipe-like hydraulic lift, the velocity of water and gravel increased. The soaked gravel shot thirty feet up the pipe into the sluice box. In the high, low-angle slope sluice boxes, tailings were run out over long distances. It was inefficient but it worked.

Another Dalmatian Croatian who followed the Iditarod stampede, John Bagoy and his wife, Marie, showed my twenty-seven-year-old father a photo of his beautiful sister, Stana,

Andrew (brother), Nick Miich, boiler house, photographer Clemons, Peter and Stana Miscovich, drift mine (underground) at Discovery Claim at Otter Creek, 1914. Steam generated in boiler house shot through ¾" pipe into 8' x 8' trench/shaft to thaw the paydirt. Partners in the trench/shaft dug paydirt and loaded into bucket, pulled up by boilerman via hoist/pulley, and levied over onto winter dump/mountain of dirt. Dump was sluiced in spring. (Flume in background belongs to another miner.) Courtesy of John Miscovich.

in Dunave, Croatia. He said she might consider coming to Alaska. Realizing that a letter from Flat to St. Michael, to Seattle, by train across the States, to Dubrovnik by boat would never get to her soon enough to get her in Flat before freeze-up, Pete Miscovich hustled to Iditarod's U.S. Army Signal Corps telegraph station and wired his message to Dubrovnik!

From the time of Alexander the Great in the Balkans, gold, *zlato*, was highly valued. With it, Dubrovnik had bought its freedom from the Ottoman Turk Empire. Under the following Austro-Hungarian Empire, gold had been a dependable currency.

Stana Bagoy accepted Father's invitation. She arrived in Canada and took a train to Seattle where she caught a steamer to St. Mary's and got on the last boat up the Yukon, Innoko, and Iditarod rivers, arriving in mid-October just as the winter snows began.

Mother moved in with her brother John and Marie. My father walked eleven miles from his claim at Discovery on Otter Creek to Bagoys' cabin. Mother was glad to finally meet the man for whom she'd traveled all the way from Dubrovnik. The engagement was sealed and plans for a wedding got underway. However, the local ladies advised Mother that Pete Miscovich had no money and could not properly take care of her. The wife of the president of the Miners and Merchants Bank whispered that Peter Miscovich didn't even have an account there. Through the grapevine, Father got wind of the conspiracy. He promptly deposited $15.00 and presented Stana with his new bank account book with his name embossed on it. Although she couldn't read or write English, Mother was satisfied that Father was a wealthy man. The wedding was set for December 24, 1912, in Iditarod. Father found a cheap gold band with a small diamond. Mother never knew what it was worth; it was a ring!

After the wedding, the couple left by dogsled to his small frame house at Discovery on Otter Creek. There was an outhouse and water was packed from a creek. Mother's honeymoon morning began by cooking breakfast for my father, his brother, and John Popovich. Life was a far cry from the warm breezes of beautiful Dubrovnik on the Adriatic Sea! "Discovery City" had 1,500 people scattered in the valley and across the river on the hillside. Mother began making many good friends who helped her get through those early years.

Mother pitched in with Father getting firewood for the home and boiler house. The first two winters at Discovery, Mother miscarried twice. But in 1914, she was able to deliver George, followed by Eva.

On Saturday nights, Father and Mother never missed a local dance. Dad was learning the fox trot, the two-step, and square dance. Just after my older sister Eva was born, the Arctic Brotherhood (AB) hosted their last big dance of the season eleven miles away in Iditarod.

Mother gave Father permission to go. In the afternoon, he hitched up his three big dogs but at 5 p.m. he returned home. He'd forgotten his dancing shoes. Four hours later with shoes in sled bag, he arrived in Iditarod to trip the light fantastic.

When my arrival was close, Dad mushed his team to Flat to pick up the registered nurse, Mrs. McDowell. By 3 a.m. in 1918, I arrived in the little house at Discovery on a stormy spring morning, the third of seven children.

Pete with dog team: three miles east of Flat at Discovery on Otter Creek, April 1920: Peter, George, Ann, Eva, John. Courtesy of John Miscovich.

Besides the Guggenheim dredge, John Beaton and Alec Matherson had a second dredge. In 1914, George Riley brought in a wooden-hull dredge to Flat. In twenty-four hours, it could dig 2,500 cubic yards, working eighteen feet below the water level: quite an efficient plant. A dredge required a lot of land. In those days, if miners weren't occupying their claim, their land was unprotected. Riley took advantage, and in 1921, he began dredging the absentee drift miners' claims. A Montenegrin miner, Milo Segura, was out cutting wood for the dredge and wasn't on his claim. When he returned he was told he might not be paid compensation for his claim. While the dredge staff was eating lunch, Segura shot Riley in the back of his head. He threw his gun away, gave himself up, and later was hung behind the wooden courthouse in Fairbanks, the only hanging in Alaska. The dredge then went into a state of limbo.

For years at $6.00 a day, Guggenheim employed four hundred laborers and also kept local woodcutters and teamsters in work as well. The men grumbled about hours, pay, and conditions. Some were for organized labor while others were outright Communist sympathizers who read *The Daily Worker*.

In 1921, the price of gold went down to $20 an ounce. When Father saw that his underground mining couldn't support them as well as pay his partners, he shut down his operation. It was rumored Guggenheim might also shut down. A good friend and a Guggenheim representative, Cap Osborne, offered Father ten percent royalty of gross if he leased all of Guggenheim's holdings on Flat Creek. A deal was signed. Father hurried to raise the money for a hydraulic plant to remove overburden and worked with Dave Strandberg to use his Fox Gulch water ditch. Father figured if he could make a hydraulic lift that would get the gravel up to a fifteen-foot-high sluice, he'd have adequate slope downhill. A year later, Guggenheim suddenly laid off its workers and shut down its large dredge. Worse, a couple of lawyers, Taylor and Albright of Fairbanks, negotiated a package deal two years later. With no thought for Father's lease, the sale for the dredge and all the Guggenheim's holdings on Flat Creek was negotiated with Dave E. Browne for $10,000, a huge blow to my father and mother. My father's decision to give up on the underground mining was a great disappointment to Mother but her faith in God kept her going. That year, Father moved us into Flat where there was a little city with stores and a hospital. Dr. Moore and a dentist, Dr. Behla, practiced in the upper story of a two-story log building.

Using horses and a dog team on frozen Flat Creek, Father skidded his hydraulic plant and blacksmith shop four miles to his original claim to begin open pit mining in 1923. In the spring when school closed and other kids were vacationing, we moved back to Discovery Claim. To survive we all had to work with wheelbarrow, pick, and shovel six days a week to buy groceries for the long winter months ahead.

Lawrence Walker, George Miscovich, John Miscovich, Mike Demientieff, Pete Miscovich, Discovery, 1928. Courtesy of John Miscovich.

Water was essential for mining. Slate Creek, a tributary to Otter Creek, was critical on Discovery. George and I began hand-digging a downhill, two and a half mile ditch so we could capture one hundred feet of gravity fall and gain thirty-five pounds of pressure.

In his blacksmith shop, my father made his lift. Skeptical onlookers scratched their heads. My father had no money, no credit, just faith. We dug the ditch, set up the hydraulic plant, and made wooden boxes and riffles for recovery. By mid-1924, ditch, pipeline, and hydraulic lift were in place.

However, the claim owners below us, Bill and Jack Richardson, built a dam to keep Dad from discharging his tailing water through their claims. Dad started for his twelve-gauge shotgun, but Mother convinced him to contact the U.S. marshal in Iditarod. A peaceful settlement was reached but forgiveness, never. [In the Balkans the *modus operandi* tends to be "An eye for an eye" and is called "blood revenge."]

However, God was with my parents and in the fall of 1924, Dad cleaned up $8,000 in the nick of time, just before creditor Sam Applebaum closed his plant and claim.

Under these pressures, Mother fed three small children, managed in a cabin with beds even in the loft, and deflected local gossip that Father wanted to be the second Guggenheim but without the money.

In search of a human-interest gold mining story, Alastair McBain and Corey Ford of the *Saturday Evening Post* magazine arrived in Flat. They were quite surprised to find a large family living among the tailing piles, and they did an story on us. But we couldn't have cared less. What mattered to us was when Father found us a larger house.

The Miscovich family in 1924 in Flat, by Alastair McBain and Corey Ford of the Saturday Evening Post *magazine. Courtesy of John Miscovich.*

All of Flat was built on federally owned ground; local merchants and homeowners had only squatters' rights. In 1926 Mutchler, the freighter who owned the tramway, decided to sell his outfit and his large house. At $500, Father was the only bidder. However, what Dad didn't know was that the Matheson Beaton dredge manager had leased all of Guggenheim's ground and planned to dig up all of Flat. After moving into our beautiful large home, we woke to a note on our door telling us to move. It was thirty below and we had no way to move our house. Mother farmed us kids out. Matheson gave Father a three-hundred–by-three-hundred-foot lot a quarter of a mile east composed of leveled tailing piles. Father borrowed a team of horses and some forty-foot planks, slid the lumber under the house, and hoisted it with borrowed screw jacks onto six of Guggenheim's sleds. He got some six part dredge blocks with cable running through each one. He inserted the nearer blocks under the sleds and then spaced the subsequent blocks one hundred feet apart, then anchored the far end of the cable to a "dead man" in the ice. He hooked the cable to Frank Manley's Best Thirty little tractor. The city of Flat turned out to see what they were sure would be a disaster. As the tractor started pulling the slack through the six-part line in the blocks, a screeching noise started and the big house started to tremble and then to move. The big house was now on the river ice that Father had prepped by first snow-shoeing and hosing. Next in four segments he had to turn the sleds together twenty-five de-grees. That done, the house had to come up a birch and ice ramp onto the tailings platform of our lot. Later, Father decided to jack the house up again and dig a basement to heat the house. Once again, he jacked up the house. As an eight-year-old boy under the house, I had to oil the jacks as one by one Father elevated the house, easing up the corners. In the new basement he installed not only a stove that burned four-foot tramway timbers but also a cooler-type boiler for steam.

With number four child Annie en route, laundry was really increasing. My father bought a washing machine whose wringer levers were too hard for Mother to keep shifting. My father figured since by means of a pulley his steam engine could bring up pay dirt, it could also pulley the washing machine lever. He bolted the steam engine on a mounting near the washing machine and connected a pulley to the handle of the washing machine. Mother thought it'd be nice to also have a shower. Dad had picked up a building in Flat which he converted into a bathhouse complete with a boiler with circulating hot water system for a shower and steam bath. Mother was ecstatic how well the system worked. From drift mining, she knew how to inject water into the boiler and monitor the valve. Laundry was coming out cleaner; bedding was washed more often, but the greatest benefit was in washing all those flannel diapers.

At first, Mother invited a few guests for a steam and shower. Then, badly needing a cash income, she realized she could open a bathhouse and charge $1.00 a head as well as take in laundry. My father only had to get the wood in. The water was pumped from a creek via a steam-operated water siphon and stored in an elevated storage tank to ensure gravity feed to the washing machine and shower. On Saturday nights for over ten years, Mother operated the bathhouse for both men and women. It became a hub, a place to chew over local gossip as Mother served coffee and a sweet roll. Many of the good women of Flat-Discovery ostracized the girls of "the Line," but Mother set aside early Saturday evening for them to allow them a steam bath and conversation.

My father was a strict disciplinarian. We ate what we were served. Every evening after school, we brought firewood and water to the kitchen. We fed the sled dogs and shoveled snow for their water. Twice a year, spring and fall, we ordered new clothes and boots from the Sears and Roebuck catalog. My father's favorite expression was "Rac[h]unat," meaning "bill," a reminder that there is a price to pay for every action. Father wasn't a dictator, but you'd better have a good reason if you said, "No." He didn't rely on words to express his love but it was evident in his actions.

Each spring for Easter, the Catholic priest from Holy Cross Mission came and served Mass in our home. All of us were baptized by the priest in Flat, to whom Father always gave generously. The rest of the year, Mother was our religious teacher. Her faith in God was a continual support and inspiration to all of us.

Water rights on Slate Creek were further complicated when the J. E. Riley Company bought Beaton's original claim and installed its three-and-one-half-foot dredge using water from Slate Creek. The Richardson brothers had the second claim and we became the third water right on Slate. For us to get one hundred feet of gravity drop, we had dug our gated ditch from the three hundred foot elevation. If Riley wanted more water, he just closed the gate to our ditch. When the weather was dry for sixty days, we could be without water. Riley's superintendent, Silas McCanaugy, hated to see my Father make it; for years he caused us hardship.

Eva, Olga, Stana, Howard, Pete, Ann, George, and John Miscovich in front of hydraulic lift at Discovery on Otter Creek, 1930. Courtesy of John Miscovich.

George Miscovich operating diesel 50 Caterpillar, Discovery, first in Alaska, 1935. Courtesy of John Miscovich.

However, a silver lining came when the Richardson brothers sold their first claim water rights to Martin Roslyn, a Danish old-timer who was very supportive of us. During the dry season when water was low, Rosyln overflowed water from his ditch into my father's ditch. Riley's superintendent went nuts with jealousy and anger.

Roslyn was suffering with rheumatism. Keeping it mum from the Riley staff and the local banker, Roslyn sold his plant to my father. For $2,500 cash, my father got Roslyn's plant, pipe, monitors, boxes, riffles, water rights, and mining claims! Several others had been eyeing Roslyn's claim and were dumbfounded how quietly the deal was made. We were then holding several hundred acres.

Also, John Beaton, the original discoverer, was selling 136 acres for $12,000 on a pay-as-you-produce basis. This addition along with his acquired claims from disgruntled miners gave my father a key position on Otter Creek near Discovery. However, the local general consensus was that the ground had been drift mined, scraped with drag-line Bagley scrapers, and then dredged, sometimes more than once.

My father didn't accidentally fall into the age of heavy equipment. Instead of indulging in the common winter pastime of gambling and drinking as did most of his fellow miners, my father was burning his gas lamp until late reading magazines about the construction of modern roads, of the Grand Coulee and Hoover dams. He wrote many letters inquiring about cost and performance of contrasting equipment. He figured that the coarse nuggets and richest ground on Discovery lay below the digging depth of Riley's small wooden-hulled dredge and the drag-line scrapers. Perplexed over his seriousness, his neighbors called him "unsociable."

I had my own concerns. Working ten hours a day on the Monitor hydraulic giant, a very cumbersome, heavy and hard-to-handle tool, I began to think there had to be a better invention. Over the years, I pondered the solution.

While Father was saving every dime for his new dozer, Mother was secretly saving her bathhouse money. Mother's brother, John Bagoy, and his wife, Marie, had moved to

Miscovich Family Mine: Bob Miller, Harry Leov, Leonard Weltzin, Eddie Barge, George Miscovich, Harry Binden, Juro Miscovich (younger brother of Pete, arrived 1931), Andrew Miscovich (brother), Andy Miscovich (son), Annie Miscovich, Olga Miscovich, J. L. McCarrey, John Popovich, Pete Miscovich, Flat 1935. Courtesy of John Miscovich.

Anchorage to put their oldest son Peter in school. My folks sent George to live with them to attend high school. Eva was due next, followed by me. Mother began to worry how her seven children could get an education beyond eighth grade. My father vetoed our moving to town because he didn't want to lose his mining crew. He tried to get a high school in Flat but it didn't fly with the Department of Education in Juneau. Boarding all of us was too expensive. Father needed to buy a tractor but Mother's mind was on education. She'd never gone to school and could neither read nor write English, but she would give her children the tools needed for life. Her sister tried to advise her.

In 1929, a Mr. Spencer came upstream selling water jugs at $60 each. Mother trusted him enough to ask politely if he might consider looking in Fairbanks for a house for us and gave him part of her bathhouse money. Committing Spencer to the secret and without discussing it with Father, she gave him $1,700. Two weeks later Spencer sent a telegram to Mother saying that he'd found a log cabin with three bedrooms on Seventh and Barnett near the high school. Mother wired back to buy it. The fall of 1930, Mother sent George and Eva to go to high school in Fairbanks and (unbeknownst to Father) live in Mother's house. Since that worked, she prepared the following year for her, Eva, and the youngest children to leave Flat in September on the last boat out to Holy Cross. Mother's plans had to work flawlessly because she was determined not to spend another winter in Flat. (George and I would stay as long as possible and help father.) Glen Day Navigation's last boat had to be on time to meet the Alaska Railroad boat bound for Nenana to catch the last trip of the season.

On a windy, rainy Saturday in early September, a Model A Ford truck pulled up to our big house. Mother had all the bags and sacks ready to go. Father was so surprised he was spellbound. He said goodbye and returned to the house where a few customers were finishing their Saturday night scrub. Mother never faltered. She said goodbye to a few dumb-founded friends. There wasn't enough gold in all Discovery to prevent Mother from getting her children on that Danaco No. 1 model boat.

When the truck arrived in Iditarod, Glen Day was anxiously waiting. He quickly un-loaded the baggage. The children boarded, followed by Eva and then Mother. Twenty years before she had arrived there to meet Peter Miscovich. Now she had seven children and a memory of hard work, suffering, and hardship behind her. Mother felt the pressure of such a decision coupled with leaving me and George, but she knew God was carrying her. Making a record-breaking trip to Holy Cross, Glen Day opened up the throttles on the twin diesel engines and caught the steamer by minutes. And he didn't even charge Mother for the trip.

Pacific Airways had just begun operating out of Anchorage. Two weeks later PA pilot Bob Ellis flew in to Holy Cross to pick George and me up in a small biplane, the New Standard. I'll never forget riding in front of the pilot's open cockpit to McGrath and through Rainy Pass to Anchorage and then on to Fairbanks. The weather was bad so we flew low, following the railroad tracks into Fairbanks with us squeezed in behind the passenger seats. We landed in the slough alongside Buzby's Ranch where Fort Wainwright is today. Mother was glad to see us but that winter I knew would be lonely for Father.

Mother's three-bedroom log cabin had no well or inside toilet facilities. It was far from what she wanted. Before winter froze the ground, she hired two men to dig a cesspool and a fourteen-foot shallow well that afforded us a toilet, bathtub/shower, and kitchen sink water. We installed an electric water heater and a filter softener for the mineral-hard water. In the partial basement, there was a good fifty-gallon drum stove funneling heat through air ducts into the three bedrooms. Through the winters of 1931 into 1934, we managed quite comfortably while returning each summer to Flat.

In 1931, my mother wanted to go in to Fish Creek and see Vuka Stepovich. Paul Drazenovich had a 1926 Dodge, an old clunker pickup to drive us in, but the road was nothing but a mudhole. The last hour we had to walk in.

By 1934, my father had the down payment for a Caterpillar Diesel Fifty tractor with an Isaacson bulldozer, the first to be used in Alaska. He paid Northern Commercial Company,

Eva, John, Olga, George, Ann. Front: Andrew, Pete, Stana, Howard Miscovich, Fairbanks, 1933. Courtesy of John Miscovich.

AFL CIO Local 444 F. E. Co. strike, c. 1935, Fairbanks. Courtesy of Alaska S. Linck.

Caterpillar's agents. The tractor came by rail from Seward to Nenana by boat, down the Tanana and Yukon, up the Innoko to Iditarod, and was walked over the road to Discovery Claim where we put it to work on our land. That season of 1935, the bulldozer increased our production from $8,000 a season to $60,000 while gold jumped to $35.00 an ounce.

Throughout the years, my father treated all our hired help well but demanded a full ten-hour day's work in return for $7.00 a day along with room and board. The dredges didn't hire Natives but as long as a man showed up for work, my father did. All his employees learned to weld, operate, and repair machinery. If a family needed help, Dad advanced pay. One spring, two black men arrived in Flat looking for work in order to fly out. They tried every camp but only my father would hire them. One of them, "Black George," had a crippled walk. He asked for two twelve-inch planks and as he pushed a wheelbarrow full of rocks, he used them like skis. That night when George was soaking his feet in the bunkhouse, we saw that he had no toes; his feet were stubs! He'd frozen his feet.

In town, Mother decided our new log cabin was too small. The three girls needed their own rooms as did the boys, and Father could use an office. Unbeknownst to my father, Mother raised the house three feet, excavated a full basement, lined it with creosoted planks, and elevated the roof to add a second story, including three bedrooms and Father's office. A new eighty-foot well was dug. The water was hard but drinkable. A second bath and shower were installed upstairs. The basement would accommodate an Iron Fireman stoker furnace as well as a room for ten tons of coal, filled through the outside coal chute. In each room, there was a thermostatically controlled hot water radiator. It was my job to calculate the bills. When Father arrived in the fall, Mother presented him with the bills for lumber, plumbing, windows, and carpenters who were still outside finishing up. The total was $25,000. For awhile, I thought Father might return to Flat, but as I pointed out to him the convenience of his big office, he began writing checks for the bills. If winter had come early, our home would've been a disaster. But Mother, who attended the old Immaculate Conception church by the Chena River, had good connections with the Almighty, and we had a very late fall that year. Mother was a natural organizer and construction engineer, and her work crew loved her cooking.

When we moved to Fairbanks, it was the first time I had ever seen a moving picture show. Over the years, a friend of mine from Main School, Bill Stroecker, liked to say, "When those seven Miscovich kids hit town, Fairbanks was never the same!"

In those days, the derisive term for Slavs was Bohunks. Some Slavs called themselves Austrians. (Before the Kingdom of Serbs, Croats, and Slovenes, Slovenia, Croatia, and Bosnia were under the Austro-Hungarian Empire. So before 1918, they were Austrian Slavs.) When I started school, someone made the mistake of calling me, "Hunky." Weighing in at 212 pounds, I let him know that was not a good idea.

However, the stereotype did have a true ring because a lot of the Slavs indulged in shady behavior. Many were involved in bootlegging, gambling, and some in prostitution. Because of the long winters of no wages and low pay in the summer, many of the immigrants made and sold moonshine. They had stills up and down the river. Everyone played cards (*pan gingy*) through the long winter days to pass the time, hence the Pastime Card Room. All over town, there were private poker games where card sharks playing for high stakes waited for some guy who'd worked all summer. In a matter of hours, they'd be cleaned out.

Around the red light district, the Line, there was a fence. It was common knowledge who frequented the Line. Locals owned the small houses rented to the girls, and anyone entering by the back alley was noticed. But it was part of Fairbanks, part of Flat, part of the Iditarod. When Fairbanks shut the Line down, the business was no longer corralled but it became dispersed all over town.

Fairbanks was a pretty dusty place with no paved sidewalks. A big event was the arrival and departure of the trains. Out in the Chatanika and Goldstream valleys, the Fairbanks Exploration Company dredges (U.S. Smelting and Refining Company) were digging, sup-

George, Howard, Andrew, and John Miscovich, Fairbanks, c. 1942. Courtesy of John Miscovich.

*Pete Miscovich's fifty-third birthday: John Miscovich, Paul Wabnig, Jerry Autumn, Glen
Barnett, Fred Patterson, Evelyn Awe, Pete, Ann and Howard Miscovich, Jim Allison, Whitley
Ray, Rasmus Nielsen, Justice Johnson, John Popovich, Olga Miscovich. Miscovich camp. Courtesy
of John Miscovich.*

plied with water by the Davidson Ditch. Once I went with my buddy Leonard Weltzin to
see his father on one of those monsters, churning away. During the summer, some of the
students at the Alaska Agricultural School of Mines worked for the F.E. Company.

During the winter holidays, we Slavs celebrated our two Christmases, Roman Catholic and
Orthodox, going from house to house. We had smoked sausages, homemade cheese, and even
during Prohibition wine and *rakija* (a "brandy" similar to vodka) made from the grape wine
dregs. George Bojanich, who was a wonderful cook and baker, and his wife, Mary, put on a big
spread on Orthodox *Badnjak* (Christmas) in their modest home. Everyone in town came.

Politics were discussed in Serbo-Croat, Georgian, and Russian at Charlie Phillips' Cigar
Store. Many couldn't read or write and had no education. Among the Slavs, there were
opposing opinions regarding Josef Stalin's new Five Year Plans, a series of three stringent
programs to take Russia from a peasant agricultural-based society to a modern industrial-
ized, competitive country. Some of the Slavs read *The Daily Worker*, a Socialist paper. The
movement was a very active, underground one. The locals who were Communists were well
known, but they were here in America and free to believe as they wanted. Many of the Slavs
worked for the F. E. Co. and resented the company. They worked hard for $7.00 a day. Every
spring, they'd line up on Garden Island in front of the F. E. Co. (today, a Golden Valley
Electric Association building) waiting to get back to work on the ditches, hydraulicking, and
driving thaw points. Roy Early, who was in charge of the F.E. Co., never sympathized at all
with the hard work these people were doing, day in and day out for years. There were two big
employers in the Fairbanks area, the F.E. Co. and Cap [Austin] Lathrop, a tough employer,
who supplied Fairbanks and later Ladd Field with coal from his Healy and Lignite coal
mines. The F. E. Co. worked right up until Christmas when they shut their dredges down.
They'd take the parts off the dredge then and all winter repair them with their crew in the
machine shop. The working men were not too organized because they had to keep their jobs.

However, in the 1930s, the AFL-CIO Local 444 did strike. An accountant for the F. E.
Company, James Edson Moody, his wife, Alaska, and son, Jim, lived close to the F. E. compound. J. E. Moody was in charge of all the F. E. camps' cleanups and wrote all the checks
for the employees. The F. E. Company compound and its generator were surrounded by a

fence. As the workers struck, young Jim remembered his father saying that some men were packing shotguns. Unruffled, Moody said he'd just bring the man in charge of the strike an extra cigar. Due to Fairbanks' small size, its boom and bust economy, and the transient population, the organized labor movement never gained much leverage.

World War II not only shut down mining but swept away any talk of Socialism as well. My father and many other immigrants believed strongly in the opportunities and freedom in this country and in the capitalistic incentive.

Every summer we returned to Flat. In 1936, the tool my father had dreamed of to dig that rocky bedrock arrived: a sixty-five-ton, one-and-a-half-yard P & H backhoe, the first in the northwest states and in Alaska!

To harness the power of Otter Creek, in the late 1930s Dad began studying water turbines and Pelton wheels. Other miners depended on diesel-driven pumps. Dad and I found a low head, water-driven, high-volume turbine to run a pump and generator for only $500. We called it the "White Elephant" and had it shipped in 1937.

To divert Otter Creek, my father cut a two-and-a-half-mile ditch and a five-thousand-foot drain with his new backhoe, and installed a steel penstock and fish elevator with a revolving screen. By the end of 1938, the turbine was supplying 210 horsepower, all the electrical power needed for the Miscovich camp and shop.

Hydraulic elevators were mechanically inefficient; with his new dozer, Dad could push the pay gravel to the elevator. With all these innovations, my Father increased efficiency twenty percent; the family's gold production increased into the thousands of ounces per season. After twenty-five years of struggle, hard work, and overcoming impossible obstacles, Peter and Stana Miscovich were finally realizing success.

The years from 1936 to World War II were the glory years for the Miscovich family.

Miscovich Brothers Mining Operation, Poorman Creek, Ruby Mining District, 1958. Courtesy of John Miscovich.

By 1940, my father and we four sons had formed Peter Miscovich and Sons. My father always felt, "I made it in Alaska; I'll spend it in Alaska." We branched out to the Manley Hot Springs area on Amelia Creek, in the Circle District on Butte Creek, off Birch Creek, on Fairbanks Creek with the Sathers, up the Goodpaster River from Big Delta with John Hajdukovich, on Goodnews Bay on Watermouse Creek, and out of Ruby on Poorman and Flat creeks. We had quite an extended family operation. Later we bought the infamous Riley three-and-one–half-cubic-foot dredge and ran it for a number of years.

I knew additional improvements could convert the conventional Monitor hydraulic giant to automatic. I talked to old-timer operators about the possibility of a fully automatic water-controlled giant, but they'd roll their eyes at each other and walk away. But I kept thinking about that as well as how to perfect the hydraulic elevator.

During World War II when other miners who were dependent on the diesel-driven L-208 pump had to shut down, my father could keep operating because of his water turbine. My father's turbine was the first water power plant used for placer mining in Alaska; for years, it impressed visitors.

Even when my father could afford Italian silk suits, he never went beyond bib overalls and shoe packs. After my parents left Flat, they liked to tell jokes on each other. When we were growing up, they didn't fight but they sure had some heated discussions regarding mining and the education of us kids.

I never saw my father cry. When a close friend died, he absorbed it internally. His determination to mine kept him through long winters and summers of ferocious mosquitoes, gnats, and no-seeums. During the six months my father lay dying of kidney stones and cancer, he accepted it.

After Father's passing in 1950, we began working a claim outside of Ruby with sixty feet of overburden. To stay in business we had to reduce our crew and cut our costs. I went to the States where with engineers I developed my fully automatic, preset pattern control, water cannon patented Intelligiant. Although it was too late for it to be used in Alaska, a design based on mine has been used globally by firefighting companies and mines.

As the years went by, my brothers, Andy, Howard, and George, operated heavy equipment in the Operating Engineers 302. George, along with other Republican territorial representatives John Butrovich, Jack Coghill, and Mike Stepovich, served in a Democratically dominated Senate from 1949 to 1954. He became speaker of the House and was responsible for balancing the budget in 1953. George often criticized Governor Gruening for his one-party manner of governing Alaska. He stood his ground for increased taxation on the Lower 48 industries draining Alaska's resources. Four years after I married Mary Stankovich, George married her sister, Kate. Both Kate and George were buried back "home" in Imotica, Croatia.

Our big house at Seventh and Barnette streets was sold to the City of Fairbanks where they built a large state building. Mother moved to Seattle where in 1968 she passed away.

In 1969 I bought the lode structure the Golden Horn from Bob Lyman. At the head of the played-out Otter Valley placer deposit, I moved the water turbine to the ditch off Otter Creek to the Golden Horn. After we bought the Riley dredge, I ran it for six years, developing the Golden Horn as a hard rock and residual-lode property. However, I was not able to keep up with the environmental requirements and closed down in 1993. Today, Doug Tweet has the only operating dredge in the state, near the mouth of the Kougarok River near Nome.

In 2002 at the Anchorage Sheraton, my father was inducted into the Alaska Mining Hall of Fame. Chuck Hawley said, "Overcoming language barriers and the challenges of living in remote territorial Alaska, Miscovich built a placer mining dynasty known for technological innovation and organizational excellence enduring from the late 1920s to statehood."

In 2008, as I do every summer, my wife Mary and I returned to Flat. On the Fourth of July we celebrated one hundred years since John Beaton and Frank Dikeman first struck gold at Discovery on Otter Creek. Every summer I keep guard over the land that shaped my life; what else is there?

Memories of the Slavs

A Croatian Paul Drazenovich, who later became just Paul Drezon, was well educated, mined on Fish Creek, worked for the F. E. Co., and used to go back to the old country every year. He advanced himself up through the F. E. Co. ranks and became a lead person on the dredging crew. Some of his relatives still live in Fairbanks.

John and Marie Bagoy raised gardens and greenhouses and sold from their three floral outlets in Anchorage. John Bagoy identified all the grave markers in downtown Anchorage, and was memorialized for this large effort with a plaque.

The Pioneer Hotel was near the Masonic building on First Avenue. Nearby there was a Merchant Café. In both the Pioneer and Nordale hotels, pioneers often sat in chairs and watched the river traffic.

Close to Samson's Hardware, the International Hotel was built by Emil Pazzo who came to Alaska in 1897 and died Sept 30, 1968. Pazzo opened the hotel August 3, 1920. In 1927 he sold to John Vukmir, formerly of Lika, Croatia, and Chris Radovich, formerly of Montenegro. Lots of Montenegrins lived in the hotel upstairs, gambled in the back rooms downstairs and the pool tables out front. Big men Chris Benanich, John Lekich, Mike Merkaich, Bob Bigovich, and Tom Radovich were proud Montenegrins who loved to talk about their history of fighting the Turks. Tom Radovich was married to a colored lady and lived on Eighth Avenue near where George Bojanich lived.

Billy Vick owned the Eagle Liquor Store. My sister Eva worked for him. He loved to gamble and would come rob the till to keep his game going.

Steve Bojanich had the popular Tavern Inn, which became the Mecca Bar with a night-club dance floor in the back. In a second marriage, he married a young Roma woman, a dancer for his nightclub act, who also spoke four lan-guages. She and her son took Bojanich for a ride.

In their early years, Steve's brother George and his wife Mary Bojanich, both Montenegrins, mined up the Koyukuk River and then moved to Fairbanks. Nick Mandich and John Jurich were wonderful old miners at Livengood.

CROATIA

A Casual Remembrance of the Fairbanks Bars

Note: Property and business owners of Fairbanks lots and their bars changed continuously. The bar list below is an incomplete sketch and is by no means exhaustive.

California Bar: Milo Hajdukovich and Rudy and Louis Krize
Silver Dollar: Krize brothers; initially property owner Milo Hajdukovich
Savoy: Melo Jackovich
Cottage: John Vukmir and Bob Bigovich
Arctic Hotel: Pete Mesich
Nevada Bar: John Vukmir; part owner Bob Bigovich
Miner's Home: Frank Miller
Tavern Inn/Mecca Bar: Steve Bojanich
Pastime Cardroom and Bar: Chuck Pasco and Bob Portman
International Hotel/Nevada Bar/Big I: Emil Pazzo, Chris Radovich and John Vukmir, Tom Paskvan Sr., Pete
    Mesich, John Butrovich and Bob Bigovich, Jack Sexton, John Jackovich
Fairbanks Bar: Melo Jackovich
Diamond Horseshoe: Joe Jackovich
Dreamland Bar and Talk of the Town, 13th
    Avenue: Charlie Miller
Tommy's Elbow Room: Tom Paskvan Jr.
Horseshoe Cigar Store
Elks Club
Eagles Hall
Chena Bar

Mecca bar, Fairbanks. With thanks to Stephen Cysewski.

Chapter 11

The Dredges of Nome: Carl and Paul Glavinovich

In the summer of 1898, "Three Lucky Swedes"—Lindeberg, Lindblom, and Brynteson—discovered gold on Anvil Creek on the Seward Peninsula. By 1899, ten thousand people stampeded to the new Nome Mining District. For miles along the coast, gold was found in the beach sands, which further ignited the rush. In the spring of 1900, thousands more came by steamship. For thirty miles up the beach, a tent city stretched from Cape Rodney to Cape Nome. Between

1900 and 1909, Nome's recorded population was 12,488, but more likely it was almost double that. Nome was the largest city in the Alaska Territory. Every fall the U.S. Army removed anyone who didn't have shelter before the onslaught of winter. Total gold production for the Nome district was at least 3.6 million ounces.

In 1906, Carl Glavinovich was born in Split, Dalmatia, Austro-Hungarian Empire. His father was a commercial fisherman. Paul Glavinović was in the [Austrian] Army Reserves, and he could see the rebellion brewing before World War I among the south Slavs. He packed up his family and left for the United States. They settled in the Slavic enclave of the Ballard area near Lake Union in Seattle. When Carl was only fifteen, he graduated from high school and began pre-med studies at the University of Washington. A lot of Yugoslavs were working up north with the Nome gold dredges. In 1925, needing a job to pay for school, Carl went north. He liked what
he saw, and he returned to
Nome the following summer
with his brother Walter. The
Glavinovich brothers began by
driving point in the Nome gold
fields, working with the monsters
that dug up the wealth of the
ancient beaches. Today, with gold hovering
at eight hundred fifty to one thousand dollars an
ounce, Paul Glavinovich, son of the former manager
of Nome's gold dredges, remembered his father, Carl's,
historic treasure-scooping boats:

Carl Glavinovich, holding gold pans of sized gold, Nome, c. 1978. Courtesy of Paul Glavinovich.

96

The flood plain of Nome was built on a ten-thousand-year-old ocean erosion surface. Nome's gold was concentrated along the perimeter of its ancient, buried beaches, located within twenty feet of bedrock. The closer you got to shore, the steeper and the deeper the gravel gold-bearing strata became. The gold was most concentrated where the waves impinged upon either bedrock sources or contributory gold-bearing streams.

In the Nome gold rush of 1899–1909, drift miners randomly sank deep shafts into the sand. Amazingly, they sometimes hit the gold-bearing layer! In a ripple effect, once one person struck gold the others nearby dug feverishly. (In 1908, Frank Waskey Alaska's first delegate to Washington, D.C., became known as the king of Nome's Third Beach line.)

By the early 1900s, small steam-powered dredges were mining the coastal plain. Water was supplied from the headwaters of the Nome River. Men with horse-drawn scrapers had dug the fifty-mile Miocene, Seward, and Pioneer ditches, which funneled water downhill to the Nome dredges. The water thawed the large frozen areas of ground before the dredges (called *boats*) could operate. Cold water thawing technology was just developing.

As my father and his brother swung their ten-pound sledge hammers onto the "thaw points" of the Nome pipe, they analyzed the process. With the water above freezing, it thawed the ground, circulated the warmth, came back to the surface where it warmed, and was then pumped back into the ground. They pondered, "What was the ideal water temperature for thawing the Nome ground, how long to circulate the water, how to improve the method?" Soon they developed techniques for drill field thawing that endured for the next forty years.

Thaw point field, four men preparing ground for dredges to dig, c. 1924. Courtesy of Paul Glavinovich.

Very low pressure water (about five pounds), continually circulated through a main pipe that fed into many smaller pipes. The water was forced into the frozen ground all the way to bedrock. Two "doctors," laborers, watched to be sure the points didn't get plugged. If a point got plugged, the doctor jimmied it, being careful not to pull the pipe out, to get it off the bottom and create a cavity below so the point would flush itself clear. After the ground field was thawed, all the pipes and points had to be removed.

The "boat" moved on its own

Three Friends Mining Company Dredge No. 1, Solomon River, c. 1924. Courtesy of Paul Glavinovich.

pond, digging continually as it went. A conveyor belt with buckets carried the pay dirt into the dredge's hopper and thence the trommel, where pressurized water cleaned and separated the pay within a big revolving screen filled with holes. The undersized material fell into the boil box below and then into the active sluice boxes where it washed down over riffles. The heavier gold was caught. The finer tailing material shot out the dredge's stern and sealed off the pond. The coarser materials went out the stacker, piled on top of the tailings, and finished damming the lake.

In the summer of 1926 when Dad returned with his brother to Nome, the famous diphtheria epidemic had just happened. In February when diphtheria started running rampant through the Native people, the territorial governor authorized delivery of antitoxin serum on a train from Anchorage to Nenana. Dog mushers met the train. In a record-breaking five and a half days, twenty mushers with 150 sled dogs covered 674 miles and brought the serum safely to Nome. However, the persons who had already died were buried in mass graves out on Belmont Point. Once Dad took me there to make sure I knew the location of those graves.

When Dad was twenty-two, a fire broke out in Nome. The only way to stop the raging blaze was to create a fire break by taking out some houses. Some of the founding fathers went out to the U.S. Smelting and Refining and Mining headquarters (Hammon) and asked them to level some houses with dynamite. Of course the mine had the powder as well as the men who knew how to use it; my Dad was one of them. My mother, a small Swedish-American teacher, and several of her teaching partners were renting one of those cottages. The women had twenty minutes to gather their personal belongings, and then Dad blew their house up. So my father met my mother by blowing up her house, and they were married in 1935. I was born in 1939, and fourteen months later, my sister came along.

During my childhood, I was the only Caucasian in my high school graduation class. In the spring, the King Islanders loaded up their families, their worldly possessions, ivory they'd been carving all winter, and dogs and paddled in their skin boats across to the beach at Nome. All summer, they lived out on the east end. There were two wells in town; each home had a water storage unit capable of holding about a one-week supply. Starting with each fall, water was hauled to our homes to last throughout the week. Nome had honey buckets as well; periodically a horse-drawn wagon picked them up from each home. The lidded containers were then set out on the frozen ocean ice till they went out with the spring thaw. Anytime you have unsanitary conditions like that, you create a breeding ground for hepatitis. That's how my mother died.

Nome was a town I have no regrets about growing up in. I had opportunities that most American boys would never experience, such as seal hunting, trapping fox, ermine, and a lot of muskrat from the tundra ponds. I also ran a dog team.

Dredge in background. Paul's parents: Marguerite in Hup Mobile Ford, predecessor to the snow machine. Carl Glavinovich. c. 1937, Nome. Courtesy of Paul Glavinovich.

We needed the entire high school to field a basketball team; we took the state championship twice during my four years. We played our entire season within the Nome community; our competitors were the grown men in the city teams: a pretty rough and tumble league. State was our only tournament, and it was either in Anchorage or Fairbanks. What got us was how close the referees called the games. We had our *own* rules at home. Because of that we usually lost the first game until we got used to the outside world's rules.

In the summers I'd tag along with Dad out to the dredges. In 1952, Dad became the manager of USSR&M Nome operations. He oversaw four dredges, capable of seven to ten thousand cubic yards per day, as well as the construction of a new dredge, Number Six.

From 1958 until the early 1960s, I worked on the Nome dredges. Later I worked with the same company in Fairbanks where I was involved in the operation of the six cubic foot bucket dredge at Hog River in the Upper Koyukuk and peripherally with the small dredge at

Chicken. A dredge's size is described by the size of its buckets. For example, the largest boat in the state, near Ester, has ten cubic foot buckets.

When I first started working boats, I was involved in the cleanups and weekly production monitoring. I'd creep up ahead of the dredge with surveying equipment and measure the edge of the cut as the boat was digging under the bank. The trick was how close I could get to the edge and not fall into the dredge pond.

In 1961, I graduated as a geologist from the University of Alaska School of Mines. I became involved in exploration and new recovery techniques for the dredges. I continued to work cleanups with a select crew in a controlled, very short amount of time in which we had to pull the riffles, collect the gold, replace the riffles, and get off the boat! For five hours, a big boat like Number Five took no breaks! No lunch, no coffee, no smokes, no nothing. Dredges were incredibly efficient but in 1962 when the price of gold was fixed at $35 an ounce, and against rising operating costs, the dredges had to shut down. Of the high gold concentration of Nome's paleo-beaches, only about 16 to 17 percent has been mined. On a base of 1,000, the fineness of that gold is about 905 to 906. But it's necessary to move multiple yards of dirt to recover 1/100th of an ounce of gold. By contrast, at Pogo mine up the Goodpaster River, the initial reserve was estimated at .5 to .55 ounces of gold per metric ton. Also at Pogo, the gold is concentrated in a vein, not scattered over buried paleo-beaches.

In 1985, working with the U.N. and through a fellowship with the Colorado School of Mines, I visited two formerly premier mines in Yugoslavia: the Bor copper mine in eastern Serbia on the Danube River and an underground lead and zinc mine, Stari Trg in Trepca, Kosovoska Mitrovica. We were there to discuss new mining methods and mine-level exploration techniques; the visit was a real eye-opener. At Bor the smelter waste products were dumped right into the Danube River. Conditions were so toxic in the smelter that men could only work a week and then they had to rest and flush their systems for ten days. The ecological and safety protections were almost nonexistent and the management ethic to fix it was equally absent. In the 1990s, because of the Balkan wars, the mines stopped completely.

Today I work as an independent mineral consultant, primarily with NANA Regional Corporation, the owner of the Red Dog mine, the largest producer of zinc concentrate in the world.

Through attrition, there are only a few of us left in engineering and geology who have placer gold experience. However, from my father's early development of cold water thawing to today's multinational owned, high-tech mining, our family has been inextricably intertwined with Alaska mining. And who knows, maybe someday the big boats will return.

Paul Glavinovich, Anchorage, 2003. Judy Ferguson photo.

Chapter 12

Andrew Garbin, the Kiana Prospector Who Never Smiled

South Slavs penetrated every corner of Alaska. A prospector to the Nome and Kobuk River gold rushes (1898–1909), Andrew Garbin, a Croatian and father of Pauline Garbin Schuerch and grandfather of Tony and Lorry Schuerch, helped found Kiana.

Andrew Garbin, c. 1910. Courtesy of Lorry Schuerch.

n 1977 before the 8.5-million-acre Gates of the Arctic National Park was formed, my husband Reb and I kayaked the Kobuk River. "Kiana, Kiana, Kiana," my husband Reb repeated as we paddled toward the intersection of the Kobuk and Squirrel rivers. He remembered the words transmitted on his firefighter's radio once when he was on a Kobuk River fire. However, he did not know that the Inupiaq word *qayaana* meant the point across from the village, or that the original village was Katyaak, "where three rivers meet," a traditional meeting spot for the Kowagmiut Inupiaq Eskimos. (Prospectors like Andrew Garbin asked the locals where a village might be and were told, "*qayanna*," "there," or "there's a point.")

During the gold rush, Qayaana/Kiana was briefly called Garbintown after Andrew Garbin, a miner, settled there. In 1977 Garbin's daughter, Pauline Schuerch, lived in Kiana, where she owned a store.

When we landed in Kiana, Pauline's store was bustling with the arrival of a celebrity in town. California Senator S. I. Hayakawa was researching the proposed federal parks in the Kobuk area. A person who never met a stranger, Pauline thoroughly charmed the California senator at her store counter. After he left, Pauline and her two sons, Tony and Lorry, invited us upstairs for coffee, where they told us the story of the immigrant prospector. Pauline showed us a photo of her father, Andrew Garbin, whose gold strike transformed Kiana into a permanent settlement. Lorry told his grandfather's story:

Ironically because my mom always smiles, Grandpa was called "the man who never smiled." A street-wise peasant and a man who trusted no one, Grandpa was born about 1860 off the Dalmatian coast in Croatia, an Italian-influenced seacoast. In the Austro-Hungarian Empire of Croatia, he jumped a ship that took him to South America where he knocked around a few years. Later he continued to San Francisco. In 1900, the Nome gold strike electrified Seattle

101

Andrew Garbin and unidentified, Klery Creek, c. 1908. Courtesy of Lorry Schuerch.

and San Francisco. Disliking crowds, Grandpa didn't hurry. He wound up sailing to Nome but only after the good ground had been claimed. Dissatisfied prospectors were looking for boats to get to the Kobuk River.

Grandpa had no Arctic experience, yet he loaded his sled with rice, dried beans, and tea and crossed the Seward Peninsula, alone, in midwinter. For weeks he ate rabbits he shot along the way, and finally he arrived at a little Inupiaq campsite just upstream from today's Kiana on the Kobuk River. He asked the Natives if any white men had passed. "Yes," they gestured, "many." "Where did they go?" Grandpa asked. They pointed up the Kobuk. "Did anyone go up that river? [the Squirrel River]" Grandpa asked. "No," they replied. "Then that's where I'm going," he said. When asked, Inupiaq Loren Black agreed to guide him upstream.

After ascending the Kobuk, they turned east at Klery Creek, where Grandpa soon struck it big. Loren said that after they'd filled up his pack, it was almost impossible to climb the valley wall out of Klery with fifty to one hundred pounds of Grandpa's gold on his back. They walked downstream to the Kobuk, boarded a steamship for Kotzebue, and then sailed south for Nome.

Unlike the Kobuk gold, the Nome ore was known to be fine grained. When Grandpa deposited his coarse gold nuggets at the banker's window, the teller immediately became suspicious. For some reason, he was sure Grandpa had raided a sluice box. After an assay, the banker believed Grandpa as to the origin of the nuggets, bought them, and displayed them in his showcase window.

Miners gathered around the glass case, stung with jealousy at the sight of the gold nuggets. Seeking Grandpa, the men embraced him as a fellow miner, escorted him to the nearest bar, and began plying him with drinks, congratulating the hero. Soon, Grandpa's mouth got loose, and he told them everything. In days, three hundred miners were on their way to Klery Creek. By the time Grandpa arrived, it was too late. He had ruined it for himself. Worse, there were claim jumpers who intimidated Grandpa, saying he could not own a claim because he was not an American citizen. He never fought it. He was already forty-five years old. He moved down the creek, figuring he could always find more gold at another spot. After a while, he got too old. He stayed in Garbintown/Kiana, which sprang up around his gold strike.

However Grandpa didn't stay too long with my grandmother. They were culturally too different. The Eskimo culture was to give everything away. That went completely against Grandpa's grain, but he did take up with several other Native women.

As if to underscore the point of generosity, Pauline laid out exotic treats: boiled whitefish stomachs dipped in seal oil with blueberries, bear fat, raw, frozen grayling, dried white fish, muktuk rolled in oil, and salmonberries.

Kuspuk-clad ladies lined a Kobuk sandbar that night as villagers seined for sheefish. Lorry loaded our packed folding canoes, Folbots, into an airplane. We prepared to leave the Inupiaq camp that had, in 1905, been forever changed by one hermit who just wanted to be left alone. As we flew over the village once known as Garbintown, the Arctic fell behind us and we entered the Alaska interior, bathed in the midnight sun.

Pauline and Lorry Schuerch wearing seal oiled waterproof caribou boots, Frank Gooden's cabin. c. 1950. Courtesy of Lorry Schuerch.

Chapter 13

The Trader of the Kuskokwim: Nick Mellick

In 1998 while researching the story of John Hajdukovich, I encountered the names Mihaljevich and Mihajlovich on the Kuskokwim River. A year later while visiting the Hajdukovichs in Montenegro in 1999, a relative of Danica Hajduković, Nikola Mihaljević, asked me to coffee. At the time, I spoke no Serbian and Danica and Nikola spoke no English. Nikola began drawing a map of Alaska, including river drainages, on a napkin. He pointed to a spidery line and wrote, "Kuskokwim." When his adult children, Aleksandra and her brother arrived, they explained in English that their cousin, Nick Mellick, had lived in Alaska before his passing. He was a well-known trader, and he was a kinsman of John Hajdukovich and a friend of the Stepovich family.

When I returned to Alaska, I happened to get a job working for the 2000 U.S. Census. I was supposed to be sent to Lake Iliamna, but instead I was sent to the Kuskokwim River. In McGrath I remembered my Montenegrin errand, looked up the number, and called Nick Mellick's son Nixe Mellick. We hit it off and spoke many times over the next three years until his untimely death in 2003. Since then, his younger brother Pete calls periodically to discuss trapping, politics, or the family in Montenegro.

Nick Mellick, Sleetmute, 1957. Courtesy of Pete Mellick.

In 2006 and 2007 when I visited the Stepovichs in Risan, Montenegro, I met neurological surgeon Dr. Milo Mihaljević, the Mellick's cousin, and also met the family of former Fairbanksan Bob Bigovich. Risan, the home of three Alaska-related families, felt like a microcosm of Fairbanks.

The trader Nick Mellick was born Nikola Mihaljević, in Gluhi Do, not far from John Hajdukovich's village of Podgor Utrg in Montenegro. Both born about 1879, they shared the original Hajduković family name, Strahinjič. Nikola crossed the ocean before John Hajdukovich and went to the mines of Arizona, where he became Nick Mellick.

Nikola Mihaljevic, 1999, Podgorica, Montenegro. Judy Ferguson photo.

Mining is a network, and when the Nome gold strike began in 1899, Mellick

Nome gold rush

1900

1910

Kuskokwim Georgetown mercury mine

1920

1970

Alaska Native Claims Settlement Act (ANCSA)

1980

Alaska National Interest Lands Conservation Act (ANILCA)

stampeded to the Seward Peninsula. By mid-life, he was living up the Kuskokwim River where he and his countryman, Sam Voich, became the major traders who controlled the Kuskokwim drainage from the 1930s through the 1950s.

Nick's daughter "Ana" in Montenegrin, Annie Vanderpool, remembered her family:

My father came from a thin strip of rocky mountains in former Yugoslavia between the Adriatic Sea and a lake bordering Albania. My older brother Nixe said that Daddy had been a part of a failed revolution to push the Austrians out of the Dalmatian and Montenegrin coast. So just before the turn of the twentieth century, my father and his cousin borrowed money for a ticket to America. Following leads, he went to the copper mines and worked in Bisbee, Arizona, and in New Mexico. In what is now downtown Seattle, he helped clear land by dynamiting stumps. He said the mine bosses treated mules better.

In Seattle he heard about the Nome gold rush. He could only afford a ticket on a schooner from Seattle to Unalakleet. From there he walked with his dog to the Nome gold strike. He continued to Ophir, where he mined for several years and made big money but something happened with that.

He heard about the strike in Takotna. When that didn't pan out, he made a raft and floated the Takotna River to the Kuskokwim to the big Georgetown mercury claims. In that community of three hundred cabins, he became the U.S. marshal for several years. He went over to the gold strike at Flat and joined the crew of Croats and Slovenes working at Pete Miscovich's mine. Every year after freeze-up, the prospectors along the Kuskokwim cut firewood for the steamboats and got five dollars a cord. By winter, Daddy was trapping up the Holitna River.

Front, L–R: Blashia, Anna Mellick, Sammy Mellick, Katherine Mellick; Back: Auntie Natalja, Mary Lou (a cousin) and Mary Mellick, c. 1940, Sleetmute, Courtesy of Anna Vanderpool.

While cutting wood between Georgetown and Parks when he was past fifty, Daddy met my mother, Katherine, a Yup'ik, born in nomadic times from the village of Nogamut near Sleetmute. They married in 1930 and had eight children. The six of the eight who survived to adulthood were Mary, Nixe, me, Sam, Kathryn, and Pete. Nixe was born in 1932, me in 1934, and Pete in 1941. In the evenings, Daddy loved to play the accordion and dance the *kola*.

The mercury/cinnabar mining drew many prospectors to the lower Kuskokwim. Our area, Sleetmute, means village of sandstone, which is native to that region. The area is about twenty miles long and is a traditional intersection where five languages are spoken within a fifty-mile radius: Yup'ik, Russian, English, and several Indian dialects.

My parents built a home near the Holitna River mouth on the Kuskokwim. Daddy was trapping the Holitna to Itulilik Creek near Nogamut and would stay there the majority of the time until he returned Fourth of July. At that time, everyone went to fish camp to catch the big salmon runs to dry fish for the winter. By September, Daddy would pull his boat back up the creeks to his trapline.

At Sleetmute Daddy built a store at a vital crossroads for the Natives and the Kuskokwim and Flat/Iditarod prospectors. He wasn't the first. Behind our house were the log remains of the old Russian Sleetmute trading post. It had once connected with other Russian trading posts up the Holitna and down the Nushagak River to the coast.

Daddy used to trade with Henry Jung at his trading post at Napakiak on the Kuskokwim River delta. Daddy's partner was Jack Smeaton, who ran the post office on our side of the river. When Daddy mushed his team to buy fur from the trappers, Jack watched Daddy's store.

Daddy and his countryman, Sam Voich, (born Vojvodić), with his stores downstream at Napaimiut and nearby Aniak, controlled the lower Kuskokwim from the 1920s to the 1950s. John Miscovich of the Miscovich family mine at Flat remembered, "From the Kuskokwim's

mouth, Sam Voich was a general in command while Nick Mellick, a trader and a miner, developed the middle and upper Kuskokwim. Nick and Sam were on the Kuskokwim from the beginning and kept law and order. They bought furs, employed the Natives, and were great disciplinarians."

My brother Nixe used to say, "Slavs had an opportunity here in Alaska and they worked like hell."

Twice a year, Daddy made a trip to Seattle for orders, which arrived later in huge boxes by mail—beads and everything! We had no local doctor, but in a glass case in the store we had aspirin, liniment, and band-aids. A doctor's office in Bethel called the school two times a day on VHF radio to see if anyone needed medical attention. If so, a plane could fly in, weather permitting.

Anna Vanderpool, 2004, Anchorage. Judy Ferguson photo.

Daddy spoke some Tanaina, Ingalik, and Yup'ik along with English and his native Serbian. As a transit hub on the Kuskokwim, he hosted salesmen, game wardens, mail carriers, and fur buyers such as Leo Koslosky, Bob Henning, Norm Goldberg, and Sam Applebaum. When they were staying with us, we brought out canned goods from the store to serve and put away our subsistence foods.

I grew up canning moose meat, fish, and sauerkraut. We had a big garden and greenhouse. When she first married, Mother felt a little isolated because at first, villagers didn't like her marrying a *kass'aq* ["Cossack," a white person]. She had to balance both worlds.

Once when some missionaries were visiting, she dressed nicely, came over and introduced herself, "I'm Mrs. Mellick's wife." As the conversation progressed, the missionary asked, "Do you believe in God?" Confusing her verb tenses, Mother answered, "I did."

When the steamboat arrived, people from the villages came to help unload the cargo at our store. My girlfriend and I heated a big spike nail on the wood stove to curl our hair and—I scorched my hair! After the groceries were put away, Daddy handed out oranges to everyone, especially the children. He was really good to kids.

Once when Hans Halverson's family along with Mother and Mary were picking berries, they found big chunks of cinnabar, the red mineral that contains mercury. Daddy and Hans leased the claim and Daddy made a lot of money. In 1931, he sent seven thousand dollars back to his family in Montenegro, twelve years before World War II and the onset of the Communist regime. With the money, the family in Montenegro left their village of Gluhi Do and built a new home in the coastal, more cosmopolitan town of Bar. After Montenegro became one of the six republics in the Socialist Federal Republic of Yugoslavia, Daddy was afraid to send more money back home because he thought the Communists might steal it.

Daddy was an avid reader, and despite the weather he made sure my brothers, sisters, and I went to school. We got used to walking downriver a mile and a half in sub-zero temps and in the blowing snow.

In the summer of 1941 when he was nine, my big brother Nixe went downstream to Napaimiut to clerk for Pete Mihajlovich and Sam Voich. He said it felt like he was going to the moon! When he was ten the next summer, he went back and earned twenty dollars! Voich's best store, he said, was downstream in Aniak. In 1945 when Nixe was thirteen, John Hajdukovich came to see our Dad. By then, John was a bent-over old man. He had one of the first semiautomatic pistols, a Mauzer, and he gave it to Daddy. In the wintertime, I remember, Daddy would sometimes go see the Bojanich brothers, George, Pete, and Steve, in Fairbanks.

Nixe Mellick, c. 1933. Courtesy of Pete Mellick.

When I was eleven, I went away to school with my older sister and brother, Mary and Nixe, to Seward boarding school and then to Old Eklutna. It was a real culture shock, but I loved learning. For high school, we went to Mt. Edgecumbe, but Mary quit so she could help Daddy run the store. Over the years, Pete, our youngest brother, and Mary took turns running the store while Nixe was away studying business at Bowling Green University in Ohio. By then, I was married.

Even though he only had one seeing eye, Nixe decided he wanted to fly. People called him "One-Eyed Nixe," and they said he never would. Like Daddy, Nixe loved to read. He read about Wiley Post, a one-eyed pilot. Nixe said that Noel Wien also only had one eye but that he didn't let people know. If Nixe wore a patch like Post had, people would know his problem. He went to a flight instructor who had Nixe wear a patch and point out objects. He told him if he could see an object and get to it, he could fly. The patch over his eye really got Nixe going. When he was twenty-one, he started Nixe's Flying Service and like Daddy, he began buying fur.

In the early 1960s, as interior Natives organized to fight for Native land claims, Nixe represented our Kuskokwim people. He was committed to protect our land. He joined our voice with Tanana Chiefs Conference and the Alaska Federation of Natives based in Anchorage. He later became chairman of our Kuskokwim Corporation.

In his spare time, he tape-recorded many of the Tanaina, Ingalik, and Yup'ik elders and documented some of the Russian Orthodox history in the Yukon-Kuskokwim Delta.

In his travels, he met Bud Brannon, nicknamed the Sourdough Swahili, who had an exclusive hunting lodge in Rainy Pass. He mentored Nixe on how to entertain the wealthy in style.

In 1968, Nixe dug his own septic system and built a private fishing lodge with a wine cellar with four hundred wines for his client fishermen and hunters. He installed a four-thousand-foot lighted runway and began catering to millionaires. Pete helped guide the clients and cooked for them. In the early 1970s, Nixe logged twenty thousand flying hours with oil companies and researchers for the Alaska Native Claims Settlement Act and the Alaska National Interest Lands Conservation Act. He was busy flying ten hours a day.

Today only three of us eight children are living: Mary, me, and Pete, who is our recently retired tribal council president. In 2003, we lost Nixe.

In 1999, Nixe's friend Dick Bishop of Fairbanks sent him a copy of Judy Ferguson's *Fairbanks Daily News-Miner* March feature, "The Montenegrin Connection." That same fall, Judy met with our Montenegrin family in Podogorica, Montenegro. Our cousin, another Nikola Mihaljević, said that with Daddy's gift in 1931, they had bought property on the Adriatic coast where they had built the family home in Bar. Because we know so little of Daddy's family, this bridge back to the Alaska-Balkan immigrants who shaped much of the Great Land meant so much to us. We plan to visit someday and bring the bridge full circle. Until then, as we say in Yup'ik, "Some day when the sun rises again, we shall one day see each other."

Katherine (Nick's wife) and her youngest son, Pete Mellick, c. 2000, Anchorage. Courtesy of Colleen Mellick Bolerjack.

Chapter 14

John Dapcevich: Son of the Mine, a Bohunk's Great Alaska Snow Job

Juneau was the portal through which many Yugoslavs first entered Alaska. Because of the large Serbian community in Juneau, they had fraternal orders and a dedicated section of the cemetery.

I first met the Dapcevich family of Juneau in 1998 as I researched John Hajdukovich, the builder of Rika's Roadhouse.

In 2007 in Belgrade, I was interviewed by the historic Politika newspaper regarding the Alaska-Yugoslavs. After the story was published, the Belgrade Dapcević family called me. They were hosting one of their first family reunions in Belgrade since the passing of their kinsmen Peko Dapcević in 1999 and Vlado Dapcević in 2001.

From 1948 to 2001, the family had suffered deep divisions. Three years after World War II when Tito broke away from Stalin, Vlado remained loyal to Stalin while his brother, Peko, became a great general under Tito. During the next fifty years, family members who were even suspected of supporting Vlado were sent to Tito's gulag, Goli Otok, while others were poor, and some were turned out on the street. All suffered confusion and heartbreak. With the passing of both brothers in 1999 and 2001, the family could begin to heal.

Stana and Savo (Sam) Dapcević, c. 1920, Montenegro. Courtesy of Bill Dapcevich.

In February 2007, Dapcevićs from as far away as Belgium gathered in Belgrade for the reunion. Spontaneously invited after the Politika story, I shared with them my published stories in the Anchorage Daily News about the Alaska Dapcevichs. When I returned home, I shared with John Dapcevich of Juneau the story of his Belgrade relatives and their journey to becoming a family.

Born in 1926, I am one of the many Alaska-Yugoslavs who shaped the Great Land. Mayor of Sitka for six two-year terms, my life spanned the days of immigrants working underground in the Alaska-Juneau Mine as well as eighty-two years of Juneau's growth. As mayor of the former capital of Russian-America, Sitka, as well as in other public offices, I have served six of Alaska's governors.

Because Alaska seemed so remote in Montenegro, a Serb there once referred to Alaska as, "You mean, 'the land behind God's back?'"

However, at the turn of the century, many Montenegrins followed the gold rush to Alaska. The miners bought gold rings that they sent home to

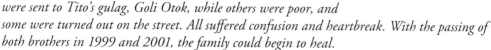

their families both as a pledge to return and as an investment for their future. Made of gold and zinc, the word "Alaska" or "Yukon" was emblazoned on the rings, surrounded by grape leaves and roses. Today, those rings are hard to find. During World War II when Yugoslavia was devastated, many people had to sell their rings just to survive.

The Alaska-Montenegrin rings owned by many Alaska Montenegrins, also shown on back cover. Jeweler: Tom Grapengeter; Diane Folaron photo.

World War II and its consequences cut my Dapcevich family in half. Two of my cousins, Peko and Vlado, fought initially with Tito. After Tito's 1948 split with Stalin, Vlado remained loyal to proletarian internationalism based on Marxist-Leninism while Peko supported the Titoist interpretation of Communism. Those not supporting Tito were sent to Yugoslavia's gulag, Goli Otok, Naked Island, described as worse than Hitler's concentration camps. In the Balkans where the continental plates of the world's empires have met for centuries, tensions grind out the struggle between east and west.

General Peko Dapcević greeting Mile Salom (father Davor Salom & Majda David) before leaving for USSR, September 1945, Ljubljana, Slovenia, Yugoslavia. Courtesy of Davor Salom and Majda David.

Miners, Alaska-Juneau Mine, c. 1915, Courtesy of John Dapcevich.

Not long after "the war to end all wars," 1914 to 1918, my parents, Sam (Savo) and Stana arrived in Pennsylvania in 1923 from the Dapcević village of Ljubotinj, Montenegro. At first my father worked in the coal mines in Hazelton where Bill was born and in Pottsville where Paul and I were born. Our family went on to Butte, Montana. However, as the Great Depression deepened, my father decided to join his brother, Pete, and cousin, Marko, who were working in Juneau's Alaska-Juneau (A-J) Mine. They warned Dad that he would have to wait in line but eventually he would get work. We arrived in Juneau in 1928.

Juneau was built on the A-J Mine's tailing piles, and its society was comprised of business-men, the immigrant poor, and the Juneau Indian village. There was no middle class. In the Lower 48, the Depression was raging, but its effects in Juneau were offset by the mine.

The A-J had very low grade ore valued at only $1.50 a ton. The only way they could afford to stay in business was to work their men under terrible conditions. There were a number of glory holes where it was rich, but the blasting had to be done inside the hole. To prevent large blasted boulders from going down the mine's chute, they were blocked by a log grizzly. When boulders hit the grizzly, it rolled, and the men had to jump quickly. Sometimes, the men weren't fast enough, and many died. In 1913 when the A-J Mine began, drillers pushed to create a tunnel that stretched 6,500 feet from the Last Chance Basin to the main ore body. Three other tun-nels and a tramway connected the mine's entrance to the company's new mill site just south of town. Dug into the heart of Mt. Roberts (3,819 ft.), the mine honeycombed many stories deep into the earth, emitting foul-smelling gases as my father and his friends worked there for years. The mine ran three nine-hour shifts, 363 days of the year. Workers like us from all over the world arrived to fill the demand for miners to work the three shifts a day. As a result, Juneau's schools were overcrowded and there was a severe housing shortage. Laborers were squeezed into the few available tenement buildings. My mother scrubbed our clothes and that of all our boarders on a scrub board. She tended two diabetic young sons; lost one daughter, Mileva; and every day single-handedly fed and took care of all of us: Bill, Paul, John, Bobby, Don, Natalie, and Violet.

My dad was rarely home and when he was, he arrived dirty and tired. One day he told us a story from Sam Voich's days back in the Montana mines. The Slavs were working

Bill, Paul, John, Stana, Sam, Violet and Bobby Dapcevich, 1935, Juneau. Courtesy of Bill Dapcevich.

underground where they seemed to be at their best—in the dark. Sam, whose name "Voich" meant duke, was deep in the mine working with the usual sooty-black mine face when a countryman asked him, "Well, Sam, how does it feel today to be a duke?" (The first generation really paid the price for us the second generation to become established in this country.)

In 1932 when I first went to school, I spoke only one word of English: "Hello." Many of the immigrant children were no better, but no help was given. My teacher understood my malcontent for her, and routinely she put me in the closet. Throughout third grade, I made U's (Unsatisfactory, F) and spent a lot of time in the closet. In the "Chicken yard" at the bottom of Starr Hill where I played basketball with the local kids, I began learning English. After school, my siblings and I picked berries and sold newspapers to help out. The family grew a garden, and we subsisted on undersized fish from the dock. We raised chickens and goats, and purchased half a beef to smoke and make sausages. We managed to make our own wine. We had no refrigeration except coolers. To heat our home, we carried coal and wood seventy-two steps up Starr Hill. But the ascent had its rewards. During the winter, we made skis from barrel staves, cut up inner tubes for bindings, and then sledded down Sixth to Franklin Street at the bottom.

As I grew up, my family, friends, and I were called "Bohunks." But a consolation was that we had a close Serbian community, the Serb National Federation and the Circle of Serbian Sisters. When my father built our house on Starr Hill, it cost only $1,200 because everyone in our Serbian community helped each other. Many of the bachelors came over to share a drink, be with our family, and help my dad. Together we took care of the community's graves, celebrated Saint John's Slava (our family's patron saint), and enjoyed everyone's open house on Orthodox Christmas. The Saint Nicholas Russian Church was very close. A special section in the city cemetery was set aside for the Serbs. Some gravestones were written in Cyrillic alphabet and are of the same weathered, lichen-eaten stone as is common in Serbia and Montenegro.

Our cousin and many other families lived on the soft side of Mt. Roberts' slope. Ten years earlier, there was a mudslide that destroyed our countrymen's homes. But one night during a terrific rainstorm in 1936, when our cousin was at our house having dinner, houses slid, broke open, and buried people inside their crushed homes.

The A-J, which employed one thousand men, was the largest mine of its type and produced eighty million dollars in gold. During its fifty-eight years, my father and the others got four dollars a day with no sick, death, medical, or hospital benefits. Anytime we heard the whistle blow, we stopped because that was the signal that someone had been injured or killed. If a man got hurt, he kept on working. If he couldn't work, he healed up and then had to stand in line again—"rush"—for his job.

In 1935 as both gold prices and profits rose for the company, the company cut even the bonuses that had previously been given. Frustrated workers organized by John Čovich in the Alaska Mine Workers Union asked for a wage increase, a forty-eight-hour work week, hospitalization insurance, and a hiring preference for Alaska workers. When talks stalled, a strike began. The miners formed a picket line on South Franklin Street in front of the Juneau Cold Storage to block the onslaught of armed scabs, men after their jobs. Angry over the strike, local businessmen armed themselves. Eight years old and standing on top of a building, I watched local merchant Percy Reynolds and others pick up hoses and clubs. A scab hit

Serbian school, Juneau, c. 1931, Front, L–R: second: John Dapcevich; fourth: Bill Dapcevich. Courtesy of Bill Dapcevich.

a huge Finn on the head. He turned and slammed the scab against the wall, and the would-be strike-breaker slid down like a cold mackerel. Nine hundred went on a strike that lasted forty days. After the strike, wages increased to five dollars a day.

Due to the miners, loggers, and fishermen, men outnumbered women five to one in Juneau. Speakeasies, cigar stores with their poker games, and brothels comprised Alaska's largest and longest-running red-light district. At that time, I drove a cab for Red Holloway. The women on the line paid us drivers a dollar for every customer we delivered to their doors. As teenagers, my older brother, Bill, and I helped our parents pay off the house mortgage and buy appliances.

Rooftop view of Alaska-Juneau Mine Strike, Juneau, 1935. Courtesy of John Dapcevich.

Signs stating, "No Natives allowed" were common throughout Juneau. One day, a Tlingit friend and I went to a movie. "Hey, let's sit here," I said. He pointed to the seats near the screen and said, "I have to sit there."

As long as the A-J Mill kept dumping its tailings along the tidal edge, downtown Juneau could expand. The land mass from Willoughby Avenue to Egan Drive is nothing but tailings. When the A-J Mine asked the city administration, they were told not to dump rock along the tidal beach any more. Then Juneau was forced to build down the Mendenhall Valley, unable to expand its central downtown area.

During World War II, the military supervised Juneau's dock and built a sub-dock of embarkation. Men were shipped up to Fort Chilkoot Barracks at Haines, a training area for men going to the Aleutians.

As men enlisted, the price of labor at the mine rose. Gold was held at a pegged price and A-J's low-grade ore was no longer profitable. In 1944, the A-J closed, my father lost his job, and he got hired as a custodial superintendent in the federal building.

As a result of the mine's closure, many of Juneau's Serbian families relocated, some to Anchorage and others to the Slavic community in Fairbanks.

At the onset of World War II, my dad said I couldn't enlist. I had almost flunked the first semester of my senior year. "You don't go anywhere," he said, "until you finish school." That last semester, I made the honor roll.

My dad, who'd worked hard all his life, said, "If you do something, do it well or don't do it at all." Success is very important for a Montenegrin.

Both Bill and I enlisted. When I returned from the Navy, the GI Bill of Rights offered free college to returning soldiers. I wasn't confident I could do college, but figures came easily for me. Congress' GI Bill had given the Veterans Administration basically a blank check. Many former soldiers had taken advantage of the bill and gone to college. As a result the VA had reams of accounting, few executive personnel, and lots of opportunity for a new employee. I was hired and the VA sent me to school under their operations manager for ninety days in Seattle. I was hungry; every time an employee went on vacation, I subbed for them. I did a stint in finance and in supply. My supervisor wrote me up saying what a good job I had done. At nineteen, I got brave and became a deputy supply officer. As my peers returned to the work force, I was already their supervisor. When someone asked if I had the skills to fulfill a particular position, I would say, "Sure," and then work hard to teach myself. Alaska is like that: if you have talent and work hard, you can achieve.

I became the auditor for the Alaska Road Commission. Raised poor, I could spot fat in a budget immediately. I sliced it and could then show a profit. This paved my way in life. In 1950, I became the auditor for the Treasury Department in Juneau. In 1951, I became the head of accounting for the territorial Department of Education. I approved the submitted budgets. There was no inflation then. I figured in projected growth, items like fuel for the coming year.

In the 1950s, when the Anchorage School District submitted a budget for six million dollars, I cut that in half, saying they needed only $3.8 million. When the commissioner of education asked about my figures, I told him the local district was way out of line with their projection. He said, "You stick with your figures and I'll back you all the way." At the end of that school year, the district had a $240,000 surplus.

Laws were vague in those days. When the Education Department had a question, we asked the attorney general who consulted the Territorial Court. He often asked us how we felt an opinion should be written. In effect, we wrote the laws relevant to our departmental needs until statehood.

We had the supervision of twenty-eight school districts and seventy-two rural schools, not including those operated by the Bureau of Indian Affairs. Following the 1950 addition to the Johnson-O'Malley Act, the Bureau of Indian Affairs transferred twenty-two schools to the territory. We also began running eight schools on military bases. We told BIA to upgrade their schools, give us the operating money, and then we'd run them.

We trained our new teachers in the Native Bush culture while the BIA did not. As a result, our students were two years ahead of those in the BIA schools.

Bill and John Dapcevich, home from the Army and Navy, Starr Hill home, Juneau, 1946. Courtesy of John Dapcevich.

In 1953, BIA allowed six southeast Native communities to run their own schools: Kake, Hydaburg, Craig, Angoon, Hoonah, and Klawock. These communities asked us to help them set up their school board, elections, and taxes to pay their share. Out of appreciation, a Tlingit clan gave me the name "Cog dah,'" meaning "sharp" as an ulu. Gov. Egan, Jim Harrigan, and I became the first Caucasians to be brought into the Alaska Native Brotherhood.

With statehood, the data from the territorial hand-written and typed files all had to be put into the computer-based system. (Under the territory, there were few standards and the resulting files were not orderly.)

I became the first territorial budget analyst and after statehood, the first state budget analyst. I had to approve the budgets submitted from all departments.

At the same time, my brother, Bob, was seriously injured at the new pulp mill in Sitka. My family and I alternated visiting Bob in the Sitka hospital for weeks. With my frequent visits, I decided to move to Sitka. I educated myself on tax law and set up Dapcevich Accounting there.

There was not a lot to do in Sitka, so I became the district chairman of the Democratic party. As I considered running for the city council, I had, at that point, been married four times, was a single parent, and was known to gamble and party. I was advised, "The public will crucify you." But I won. Throughout my subsequent nineteen years in politics, the Native vote often elected me. Possibly this would be better understood from an introduction given by Superintendent Gil Truitt, a Native Alaskan at a Mt. Edgecumbe graduation ceremony in 1986: "John Dapcevich, a man whom I have known all my life—who spoke to our people when it wasn't fashionable to do so."

John Dapcevich, mayor of Sitka, presenting a Tlingit paddle to the Russian commander of the Soviet research ship the Odyssey, *Sitka, c. 1970. Courtesy of John Dapcevich.*

I also undertook to save Sitka money in novel ways. In 1970, I served on the charter commission studying whether to unify Sitka's city and borough government, something not done before. After the subsequent consolidation, I became the first mayor of that more cost-effective government.

In 1966–67, we received a federal grant for $600,000 to build a centennial hall and a community center to celebrate

Alaska's Centennial, 1867 to 1967. We also received federal monies for the Thompson Boat Harbor. As the harbor was dredged that dirt was dumped near the shoreline to create new land for the centennial building. Essentially by using common sense, we got a two-million-dollar centennial building for free.

Between 1974 to 1975, there was a lot of oil money but I knew that revenue would progressively dwindle. I slowly spaced the many projects we projected and then put the balance of the money in certificates of deposit. When a CD reached a million dollars, the interest went up twenty percent. This way we earned ten million dollars in interest on capital that was supposed to have already been spent. When the Legislature found out, they said they would withhold future monies until we actually did the projects. Maintaining our goal, we just switched our method. We took that ten million dollars and made a permanent fund for Sitka. Any money from the sale of city property now goes into that fund. The fund is now up to twenty-some million. But it's also necessary to inflation-proof savings, so rather than spend the total, we kept investing a residual amount to keep the nest egg growing. It's worked beautifully; no other city has done it. I wanted to make Sitka better for cheaper.

Under Governor Knowles, I was on the Statewide Economic Recovery committee. Wanting some of that recovery monies pie for Sitka's projected two-million-dollar cold storage building, I realized how to meet the required matching funds. A piece of Sitka property was appraised at one and a half million dollars; we put that land up for our half of the matching funds. In the end we essentially got a free cold storage building.

As mayor of the former capital of Alaska and its fifth-largest city, I have met with the governors and leaders of Alaska. Before Perestroika, I greeted the Russian commander of the

(Podium) Sitka mayor John Dapcevich, (center) Senator Mike Gravel, Bishop Gregori on Alaska Day, celebrating the sale of Alaska to the United States, Sitka, October, 18 1972. Courtesy of John Dapcevich.

Soviet research ship, the *Odyssey*, when it landed in Sitka. As a Montenegrin and the mayor, I greeted Alexander Solzhenitsyn when he appeared unexpectedly in Sitka. I also received James Michener, the author of *Alaska*. When the Tongass Timber Reform Act was fought under the George H. W. Bush administration, I testified for the ecological harvest of timber in Sitka before the subcommittee on agriculture in the U.S. House of Representatives. In 1976 when a capital move was considered, *The New Yorker* magazine quoted my two-billion-dollar estimate of the cost of the projected move. It was decided later that my figure was the most accurate. On the Alaska Statehood Commission under Governor Jay Hammond, we investigated other forms—besides statehood—of government and their progress. I helped plan Sitka's annual celebration of the sale of Alaska from Russia to the United States on Alaska Day, October 18.

From statehood to present, I have served Governors Egan, Hammond, Hickel, Sheffield, Knowles, and Murkowski on committees, projects, and boards.

The position of mayor paid very little but to do a good job, I had to put in many hours. In the meantime my two oldest sons, Dick and David, ran our accounting business.

My son David, who served as deputy mayor of Sitka in 1984, said, "Anyone who has been mayor five times should be immortalized. When I filed for a sixth term, he said, "Anyone who has served six times should be institutionalized!" And he was right. However, today our son Marko, yet another Dapcevich, is mayor of Sitka.

Some people feel that my vocation, taxes and accounting, is not interesting, but they are tools that help other people save money. Helping others is one of the greatest feelings in life.

In 2002, Gov. Tony Knowles presented me with a lifetime achievement award. He wrote, "Your commitment to the Great Land is truly remarkable." The Great Land also did a lot for me, a bohunk who pulled off quite an Alaskan snow job.

Bill Dapcevich in the Serbian section of Evergreen Cemetery, Juneau, 1998. Judy Ferguson photo.

Chapter 15

Agbabas, Father and Son, Founder of the Alaska Dog Mushers Association and the Voice of the Goldpanners

There was not a sports announcer in Fairbanks who could match the color and spice of Steve Agbaba, son of Croatian immigrant and champion dog musher "Mike" (Milan) Agbaba.

Agbaba's daughter, Mary Eberhart, told the story of her colorful father, Mike Agbaba, and brother, Steve Agbaba. "Dad was born in 1898 in northeast Croatia, Grache-Lika, two and a half hours from Zagreb. When he was only sixteen and spoke very little English, my father arrived in the United States alone in 1914."

"Initially," Mary said, "he worked in the Hibbing, Minnesota, mines, but by 1918, he was in Juneau as a laborer at the Treadwell and Perseverance Mines." Mike then began working

Mike, Mary, Milan, Daniel, Steve Agbaba, Fairbanks, 1935. Courtesy of Mary Eberhart.

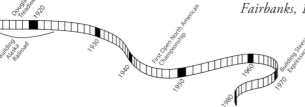

on the Hurricane Gulch section of the Alaska Railroad, where he met Joe (Gaetano Iannone) Reno, an Italian merchant from Girdwood. Reno introduced Mike to his daughter, Mary Iannone, and in 1921, they married.

Their first two sons, Milan and Daniel, were born in 1922 and 1923. The following year, they moved to Fairbanks where they bought a one-room cabin on Fifth Avenue between Wickersham and Cowles. They grew a large garden and raised chickens. Throughout the summer and fall, Mary Agbaba canned and stored vegetables in a root cellar.

Theodore Van Bibber, a lean Dutchman from the Klondike, was a dog racing legend at the time. Van Bibber sold his Clay Street kennel to the strong-willed immigrant from Yugoslavia. Mike raised his own dogs and boarded others for extra income. On the banks of the Chena, he worked at Independent's lumber mill, followed by eleven years as a jail guard.

In 1927, Fairbanks' future Goldpanners sportscaster, Steve Agbaba was born, followed by Mary (later Eberhart) in 1936 and younger sister, Jeanne, in 1944.

The family's eighty-five malemutes lived on "Rabbit Island" near the river at Third and Clay Street (today the David Salmon Tribal Hall). Mike raised eighty-pound sprint dogs and supplied racers Steve and Rosie Losonsky, Bob and Libby Westcott, and Jim and Hazel Brown. Next door to Mike Agbaba's dog lot, Jeff Studdart kept his own kennel.

To feed his dogs and chickens Mike kept slop buckets to collect waste food both at the Model Café and the Piggly Wiggly grocery. Unfortunately to Steve, his job was to daily collect the filled slop buckets. Remembering the chagrin he felt as a kid, he wrote in the July 1977 All Alaska Weekly his particular memories of pioneer life. After each anecdote, he refrained, "Little did I know. . . ." He recalled hooking up one dog to a short sled and heading out on his daily dog food run to retrieve the buckets. On the way he was more embarrassed when he passed his immigrant father and countryman Martin Klaich down in a ditch replacing sewer pipes. Once again, he chorused, "Little did I know."

During the summer, the three Agbaba boys watered and fed the eighty-five dogs; in fall, they cut wild grass for the dogs' houses. For income, the family sold pups and boarded dogs. Like many other Slavs, Mike had a still on the banks of the Chena. In his spare time, with the other "viches," he played cards at the Pastime Card Room, owned by his good friends Chuck Pasco and Bob Portman. He managed to always send money home to his family in Yugoslavia.

Steve and his two brothers delivered newspapers and shined shoes and gave the pennies to their mother for grocery money.

In 1939, Mike raced but did not place in three contests: the Livengood dog race; in 1946, the Anchorage Fur Rendezvous World Championship Sled Dog Race, and the first Open North American

Mike Agbaba. Studio portrait for North American Championship, 1947, Fairbanks. Courtesy of Mary Eberhart.

Mike Agbaba, North American Championship, 1947, Fairbanks. Courtesy of Mary Eberhart.

Championship. However, two years later when Mike was fifty, he won the Yukon and Alaska Territorial Championship in Whitehorse, competing against clever Jake Butler and a young superstar, Gareth Wright. That year, the Alaska Dog Mushers Association (ADMA) was founded partly through the leadership of Mike Agbaba and Jake Butler to promote humane dog care, racing, and the North American Championships.

Just before retiring, Mike Agbaba began Checker cab with Steve Agbaba. When he did retire, Mike began dealing cards at the Pastime Card Room at First and Cushman. When Mary Agbaba needed grocery money, she sent her daughter, Mary Eberhart, down to the Pastime. "Gee," Mary remembered, "there were so many Yugoslavs there! And they'd always give me some silver dollars!"

"My dad was very strict," she continued, "domineering, and hard working. He never accepted welfare; he sold his garden produce and eggs."

Mary continued, "Steve loved sports and practically lived at the baseball park. In high school, he played on the 1945–46 first string of the Malemutes high school basketball team. Following school, he played semi-pro baseball in Iowa. In 1955, he began sportscasting in Juneau. He announced the Anchorage Glacier Pilots, and in Fairbanks, he was the voice of the Goldpanners. At KFAR, he hosted his own morning show."

After his marriage to Delphene in 1977, Steve began announcing games out of Seattle's King Dome. In the 1970s and 1980s, he published *The Agbaba Gazette*. In that newsletter he noted when his pioneer father, Mike Agbaba, returned to his native Yugoslavia for a visit in 1970 eight years before his death. The visit was not long before the sale of the Agbaba and Studdart kennels, which were sold during the construction of the Steese Expressway.

When Steve Agbaba died in 1992, the Alaska Legislature "In Memoriam" observed in 1993, "He allowed listeners to live the game via radio. His statistical chatter and enthusiastic presentation added the special Agbaba color to each game." That same year, Fairbanks North Star Borough Mayor Jim Sampson named and dedicated the Chena Lake Recreation Area twelve-mile winter trail "The Lake Park Mike Agbaba Trail."

Mary remembered, "My father was really glad to be in this country. He always told his children and grandchildren, 'Honor your mother, your flag, and this country.'"

Steve Agbaba, about forty-eight years old, c. 1975, Fairbanks. Courtesy of Mary Eberhart.

Chapter 16

First Family of Fur: Perry Green

In the 1700s, when the fur sources for the Russian Empire were critically dwindling, explorers reported that at the eastern edge of the empire there was a wilderness with abundant fur-bearing animals. Merchant companies on the frontier were among the few open to Jewish participation. As a consequence, the fur trade became increasingly international as well as Jewish. With the purchase of Alaska, Jews dealing with the Russian-American Company took over the Alaska Commercial Company and established large supply houses in San Francisco and Seattle. Seattle became the supply hub for the Alaska frontier.

David Green, 1937, Seattle. Courtesy of Perry Green.

Alaska's first family of fur today is the David Green Master Furrier family. The Greens originated from an historically Jewish area, Galicia, part of which evolved into Poland. Before the Holocaust that later destroyed the Lvov ghetto in Poland, the Green family had long since left for New York. Perry Green tells the story of his family and of David Green, master furrier.

My father, David Green, was born under the Austro-Hungarian Empire about 1900 in the cultural center of Galicia. He and six of his seven brothers became furriers. Sons were expected to carry on the family trade. A boy apprenticed to a master in the guilds and thereby learned that master's trade secrets. An apprentice's purpose was to glean something that his own family didn't know and to qualify as a master furrier. But in return, an apprentice had to be at the beck and call of his master. He was a houseboy who slept at the foot of his master's bed to ensure that the room was always warm and water was available. An indentured servant, he went to the shop daily with his master and worked alongside him. When the apprentice's period was over, he had to pass the tests of the guild. As master furriers, my grandfather and his brothers traveled to Leipzig, a fur center of Europe, where they traded for skins. Seeking freedom and opportunity in the late 1800s, my great-uncles immigrated to New York, where they began one of the largest fur manufacturing outlets in New York City, Green Brothers and Goldstein (a cousin to the Juneau Goldsteins). In 1904, my grandfather and their eight children, including my four-year-old father, David Green, followed. When he was ten, my father apprenticed to a master furrier in Philadelphia, which was a twenty-four/seven job. When he wasn't working, he read Jack London's *Call of the*

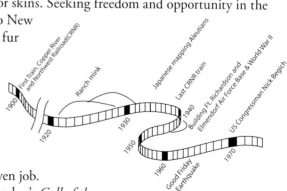

Wild. As he read the northern adventures, he saw himself in it. He knew that with his background he could make a living as a furrier, fur buyer, or fur trapper in the North. It was adventure and opportunity, and he would do it. Once he had achieved master furrier, he was on his way to Seattle.

When Dad, a very young man, reached Seattle in 1921, he saw a sign in a window that read, "Help Wanted, Master Furrier." When he walked into the Baker Fur Co., introducing

Cordova, 1920s. Courtesy of Perry Green.

himself as a master furrier, they couldn't believe that such a youth could be a master of his craft. But they said, "Okay, we'll give you a try." After six months, they didn't want to let him go. In his free time he climbed Mount Rainier, which only whet his appetite more for Alaska. After establishing a Seattle base, he left for the North.

Because of the Copper River and Northwest Railroad terminus that connected to the Kennecott copper mine, Cordova was a critical port. Dad opened a shop and hung out a furrier shingle. In those days, a merchant could be open only half a week and enjoy Prince William Sound the other three days. Dad didn't come to Alaska to make money but to ply his trade and enjoy the frontier. In those days, people traded and sometimes sold for cash. They didn't need much. When a furrier traded in skins, he made coats. A master furrier like my father could do everything: design, match, stretch, nail, cut, and sew fur. The only thing he wouldn't do (because it was beneath the dignity of a furrier) was to sew in the lining of the garment. This chore was done by a finisher. (As the assembly line developed later, duties were assigned to specialists who did only those jobs: design, match, cut.) But my father could do every phase of the business (except process furs) and did. On occasion, he would work with a needle and thread if there was no finisher available. In those days, a customer didn't buy a ready-made coat. He brought his own furs or he selected hides from those in the store. Dad sent a customer's furs off to be tanned, matched the furs, and created the coat. Then he only charged for his labor.

In those days, every Alaskan, especially along the coast, had at least one fur coat. That was a standard. They'd trap and save for years. The ultimate garment was otter. With the tanning method of the day (tanning chemicals today are for speed), an otter coat would last fifty years and was called a lifetime coat.

When my father began, there was only wild mink. Ranch mink only started about the 1920s and then it was in only one color. When my father began in Cordova, he was the only master furrier in Alaska. There were fur collectors who made coats, but unquestionably, my dad was the most knowledgeable. The president of the Seattle Fur Exchange, Michael Dederer, referred those looking for coats to David Green. My father could make two or three coats a week.

While in Cordova, a friend suggested to my dad that he meet Ruth Grad, a Latvian immigrant who kept a traditional home and was the daughter of the first Hebrew teacher in Vancouver, British Columbia. (Vancouver was off the beaten path for immigrants.) Mother was a beautiful and intelligent woman who liked the North; my father felt lucky to find such an Orthodox woman. In 1926, my parents married. Dad didn't think Cordova would continue to be viable for both of them, and he closed his shop. He began a store in Seattle but just in time for the Great Depression.

Customers in Ketchikan encouraged him to set up shop there. He always had a helper, but by the 1930s, he had a staff. Ketchikan was a good trapping area, and he did well. Living on the coast, he had a boat and was an accomplished seaman. If a man didn't go to the bar, he went fishing to relax.

Natives on the coast began to report that the Japanese had been seen and appeared to be mapping. The government realized that something was up and dispatched forward observation posts. However, the newly assigned troops were ill-prepared for the weather in the Aleutians and on the coast. They needed cold weather

U.S. Marshall Fourth Judicial District Lynn Smith, Tommy Wright, and George Preston wearing typical Alaska fur coats at a Fairbanks dog mushing race, c. 1933. Courtesy of Candy Waugaman.

clothing right away. Dad had a small shop in the Harper Building in Seattle. In the 1930s, my father began making full-length muskrat parka liners with a camouflaged outer shell for the troops. Shortly after Pearl Harbor, and the subsequent battles in Attu and Kiska, Dad was busy twenty-four hours a day. He slept at the factory and got up and worked eighteen-to twenty-hour shifts. Mother brought him food to the factory and she fed all the workers. During this period, Jerry was born in 1934, and I was born in 1936.

In the 1940s, he began working with his brother Jacob who had a factory in New York. Dad opened a third shop in Juneau. He was always on the road.

During our free time after school and on Sundays, my father ordered my brother Jerry and me to the shop where we were treated as less than workers! A boss could be tough on his workers in those days. If a worker did the wrong thing, he got his hands slapped and was scolded continuously until he was respected as a craftsperson. My father was a hard worker. Once he said, "You sew another seam like that, I'll kiss your hands and then, cut 'em off!" (Of course, he never did.) You can't say that to your workers now.

The stores in Ketchikan and Juneau did okay but he soon realized that Anchorage

would be the center for the developing Alaska. The Alaska Highway had just been built and via the Glenn Highway, it came into town on Fifth. Fourth Avenue was Anchorage: the City Hall, the courthouse, the federal building, the bars, everything. From D Street down to B, it was "the longest bar in the world," with bars on both sides. It was a way of life. In 1950 Dad bought on Fourth Avenue thinking the city would grow from there but it didn't. It grew up toward the bluff, toward Fifth Avenue. Dad opened the company's headquarters, with a down-stairs shop and an upstairs family apartment.

The stores in Ketchikan and Juneau did okay, but he soon realized that Anchorage would be the center for developing Alaska. The Alaska Highway had just been built and via

David Green with three-year-old Jerry Green, Miriam Green (cousin), Seattle, 1937. Courtesy of Perry and Jerry Green.

the Glenn Highway, it came into town on Fifth. Fourth Avenue was Anchorage: the City Hall, the courthouse, the federal building, the bars, everything. From D Street down to B, it was "the longest bar in the world," with bars on both sides. It was a way of life. In 1950 Dad bought a building on Fourth Avenue, thinking the city would grow from there, but it didn't. It grew up toward the bluff, toward Fifth Avenue. Dad opened the company's headquarters with a downstairs shop and an upstairs family apartment.

When I graduated from high school in 1954, my mother moved permanently to Anchorage. The summer of 1953, I worked on the Alaska Railroad as a gandy dancer, the crew that used to straighten track with a rod that looked like a long crowbar. I'd order, "Heave!" and we tried to straighten track and sometimes moved it a sixteenth of an inch. I worked all the rail stops to Hurricane Gulch; now all that is done by machine. My brother Jerry went to college and I tried it for six months. Then in Seattle, I volunteered for the Army's Alaska Communications System for three and a half years.

In 1956, I married seventeen-year-old Gloria Dolgoff in Seattle and moved her to "faraway" Alaska.

Dad had the retail business. All I knew was fur, so I got into the business of buying skins. Alaska has a long history of Jewish fur buyers, beginning with the Russian-American Company and extending through generations including Reuben and Charlie Goldstein of Juneau: 1883–1959. Charlie could speak Tlingit, which brought him a lot of success and respect. (Jewish fur buyers and traders are pretty adept at learning languages, which has been a big help to them.) Jewish fur traders in Alaska were not big names. Each one worked out of one small store throughout the Bush: Louis Rotman in Kotzebue; Samuel Applebaum in Nikolai (who lived the whole winter on sardines,

Fur buyer Sam Applebaum of Applebaum and Seligman in Seattle, Sleetmute, 1957. Courtesy of Pete Mellick.

earning the moniker "Sardine Sam"). Applebaum partnered with Milton Seligman, who ran their company Applebaum and Seligman in Seattle. In Fairbanks, John Swagler, "Johnny Muskrat," freelanced for a number of fur houses. Fred Hamburg was in Juneau. Sam Applebaum employed Oscar Samuelson in Bethel. Oscar had a large family who became pilots and traders locally, in Bristol Bay and in the Kuskokwim. Since 1919, H. E. Goldberg has operated out of Seattle. Until the early 1980's, Norman, the brother of CEO Irwin Goldberg, traveled to Alaska to buy the company's fur. About 1963, I started Perry Green's Anchorage Fur Trading Co. At first, I would load my car up and drive the highway buying furs. There were a lot of trappers, both white and Indian.

In the 1970s, there had been reports of missing persons. As I was driving down the Dot Lake Road once, my radiator burst. I walked toward a really big log house for help. A woman holding a kerosene lantern opened the door. I asked, "Do you have a telephone?"

She asked, "Who are you?" I said, "Perry Green." She said, "My husband will be right up." All of a sudden, I was amazed to see the floor opening up, like a surrealistic scene from "Arsenic and Old Lace": a man emerged from underneath the floor through a trap door. He returned into the hole and climbed back up a ladder. "What are you doing here?" "Well, I'm a fur buyer and my car broke down." "You're a fur buyer?!" "Yeh." "How much you paying? You buying or are you cheatin?" He asked me every question in the book. I said, "No, I'll give you a good price." (In the past three days on the road, I'd only bought 110 lynx and the selling price of lynx then was hot.) He asked, "How much will you pay for a good lynx?" (Lynx were not yet worth eight hundred dollars apiece because the lynx population cycle was still high.) I quoted my top price—about $125. He said, "I got one." He went back in that hole. Didn't tell me nothing. I just wanted to use the phone; I didn't know if he might be digging a grave in that hole! He

Perry Green with his father, David, at Fur Rendezvous, 1960. Courtesy of Perry Green.

comes back up with a cat. "How much you give me for this one?" I said, "Ninety-five." He said, "Give me one hundred and you got it." I agreed; I wanted to use the telephone. As we were waiting for the tow truck to come get me, he said, "I got some more." He went back down into the root cellar [cool for storing furs] and came back with an armload on a wire. He must've had thirty lynx. I went through them and they averaged about eighty dollars each. We made a deal but then he said, "Wait a minute." He went downstairs and brought up thirty more! We dealt over those; I paid him. He said, "Wait a minute." He went back down. Then he said, "If the market goes up, you better give me a better price." I ended up buying between ninety and a hundred lynx just from him. I bought nine hundred lynx total that year. The market did go up, and I paid him a good price: $110 to $120. I figured I'd get $150 net, but I got $175–$225. I never try to make too much. You always want to be able to go back and buy. I'd been taught you milk the cow but you don't butcher the cow. I bought from him the next year and paid him a little more that year, but he didn't have as many. Buying fur was a great, great, huge business.

I bought a lot of wolves up in that country. Paul Kirsteatter was probably the most famous in that area. I bought from the grocers from Tok Junction to Northway, and I went across the border. There were a lot of Natives on both sides. (It was a little easier to go back and forth then.) With Warbelow's Air Service, I flew into Tetlin. I wrapped the furs in bedsheets and slid them into canvas bags. When I got back to Tok, I'd mail them back to Anchorage.

We had a store for a short time in Fairbanks. I used to put on a sale with Lois and Gene Tapp at the Mukluk Shop. Oh, yes, I knew all those old Yugoslavs in Fairbanks: Alex Miller, the Bigovichs, and the Bojanichs who owned the Model Café. Those Slavs were fun, tough, and fair: very much old Alaska. At Tommy's Elbow Room and the Pastime Bar, I'd play poker with another fur buyer, Koyukuk trading post owner Dominick Vernetti, who came from a great fur area. Dominick prided himself (justifiably) on speaking Koyukon Athabascan and on his poker and pinochle skills.

Each year I traveled four months, buying ivory and furs. Over time, I visited over three hundred villages: Nikolski in the Chain, Mekoryuk on Nunivak Island, Dillingham, Chevak, St. Lawrence Island, up the Yukon River, north to Point Barrow, upriver, downriver, and in between. In those days, there were still women who wore facial tattoos and men adept at survival skills who signed their name with an "X." I'd issue a check to village trappers, who then circulated it like cash. Six months later, the check with six or seven endorsements on the back would hit the bank in Anchorage.

Being put up in the villages was never a problem. The Eskimos and Indians are the most gracious of hosts. I also meant something economically to the village. They'd get excited when I came to town: "Perry Green's in town!" I'd say I'll be buying furs at so and so's house. If I went down to Bethel, I'd be at Mendel's. Wherever I stayed, I would even leave my black bag with $20,000 cash in it on my bed or under it. Not one person ever thought of taking that money. It wasn't in their methodology to steal that much money. They respected a guest's presence in the village and treated a person wonderfully. I have a particular fondness for the indigenous people of Alaska. If anything changed village life, it was TV and the incursion of the government creating so many government-help programs that didn't help. They were poor but they helped one another. If a family had no children and a neighbor had six children, they'd just give that childless family one of their children. Whenever they walked by that house, they wouldn't say, "Oh, that's my son that I gave you." They'd say, "What a lovely child you have." They were protective, loving, and understanding of each other. They were very traditional and respected their elders. Children were always loved and important; the old people were revered. (Alcohol was a small problem, but when drugs came in, I retired.) I thought life would always be the same. Children were important, old people

Perry Green, St. Lawrence Island, c. 1991. Courtesy of Perry Green.

were revered, and there was a tranquility. Those who still live the more subsistence lifestyle have a measure of that happiness and tranquility.

A buyer can't be afraid when buying fur. I never really lost any money buying furs. I did come across some tough trappers to do business with, though. I never tried to steal a skin and I always tried to pay value. But I knew they needed money for gas and food, to be able to go back on the trail again. When they had a big family, I paid a little bit extra. I was a fair buyer and was always welcomed back. Once I could get the market to come to me, I did. I can name on all my fingers bush pilots who had an accident or two. At least eight pilots I flew with died later. (Alaska Bush pilots get pressed into high risk flying trying to get a sick villager to medical help; frequently they die in service for others.) Trappers began mailing skins to me and I mailed the checks to them. But I had started to buy more and more fur outside of Alaska, too. Since I wasn't traveling, the competition within the villages was getting tougher. I was getting fewer skins. If a buyer comes to a trapper's door, he'll take $620 instead of waiting, shipping, and maybe getting $35 more. I was sorta phasing out except for going to my favorite places like Mekoryuk on Nunivak Island, St Lawrence, Gambell, and Savoonga, Kotzebue, Kivalina, and Point Hope.

I also enjoyed the Interior: Gakona, Chistochina, and the Indians in the Copper Basin. I knew all the Ewans and Ben Neely as well as Cy Neely, a white family. I enjoyed going along the Yukon to Ruby and Grayling and along the Kuskokwim and the Takotna rivers. Out of nostalgia I'd go back to the villages. People in the cities think they live in Alaska but they don't know Alaska until they have seen the Bush. The Natives who didn't speak English but knew how to survive had my deep respect. Traveling to the villages was my favorite time in life.

I traded wholesale wherever the best prices were. I sold to the Montreal Auction, to the Seattle Fur Exchange, directly to Germany, and to Norway. I sent them all over the world. I knew that the best prices for otter were in Montreal; for beaver, in Seattle; for marten, in Vancouver; for lynx, in Europe. My only competition in those days was Chris Brusilus out of Anchorage, and he was getting old.

Downtown Anchorage, Good Friday earthquake, 1964. Courtesy of Perry Green.

In 1964, we had two Anchorage stores: David Green Furs as well as Arctic Fur and Leather, also on Fourth Avenue between D and E streets. Friday, March 27, that year was both Passover and Good Friday. At 5:36 p.m., I had just taken my three-and-a-half-year-old son to get his very first hair cut. I pointed to the barber's chair and said, "Get up there, Alan." He started shaking his head and as soon as he did, the building began to shake because it was Dykes old wooden building; then the window busted out. Just as the barber grabbed my daughter by the hand a shard of glass flew at him and cut him. He said, "I think we better get out." We just stood outside, swaying back and forth. The earth began opening and closing three to four inches every fifteen yards, increasing then to twelve to fourteen inches, and then, with a large BANG! the earth closed tight. Thirty feet from us, the buildings across the street fell one story for three blocks down Fourth Avenue. Registering 9.2 on the Richter scale, the earthquake released ten million times more energy than the Hiroshima atomic bomb. It was the strongest earthquake in North America and the second strongest in the world in recorded history.

I had a kid on each hand. I saw the grizzly bear on a pedestal on rollers in our store sliding across our linoleum floor. Every time the earth rolled, the bear went back and forth. My wife and the clerk were hovering over the bear. Before the quake, my father had gone down to the athletic club for a massage. Leaving our children with my wife, I went looking for him. All the bodybuilders in towels had come pouring out of the club. Downstairs the lockers were fallen in on them-selves. I started calling, "Dad, Dad!" My father was still sitting on the massage table, mutter-ing, "Well, the damned fools did it. The damned fools did it." What are you talking about?" I asked. "The Russians dropped an atomic bomb," he said. "No, it was an earthquake," I explained. "How's Mother?" he asked. "I don't know," I said, "but there's a lot of damage." He was just so lucky because everything else in that club was in shambles. He said, "Go down and tell me how Mother is." On the north side all along the street, the buildings were all down. But on my side of the street where our store was, there was no problem. It was like the Passover Death Angel went over. I ran upstairs; Mother was in the back of her apart-ment above the store. She was rocking and lamenting, "Oh, my Passover dishes, all broken!" [Orthodox Jewish families have three sets of Passover dishes: one for meat, one for milk,

Brothers Jerry, left, and Perry Green, Anchorage, 1990s. Courtesy of Perry Green.

and another for the holiday of Passover. The family cooks and eats with those dishes only.] I said, "Mother, come out here." (One of the fluorescent lights in our home was down but otherwise, there was no damage to our building.) She looked out the window where all the destruction was, and said, "Oh, we better go out and help somebody." I said, "No, people are already doing it."

Our home was untouched. Since it happened at 5:36 PM on a Friday of a holiday week-end, the loss of life was very minimal. All Mother's cooking was in the oven. The electricity was off; the water was suspect. My father said, "Finally, I get to brush my teeth with whiskey."

Dad was slowing down. He tried a manager at the Seattle store but that didn't work. He realized it was too hard to manage two factories. In the mid-1960s, he reluctantly closed the store in Seattle.

Dad never got over his fantasy with Jack London's *Call of the Wild*. He still dreamed of the massive huskies, their power and magnificent appearance. He bought two Mackenzie River malamutes and had them shipped to Anchorage. It cost a ton to feed them; he ordered, "No dog food for those dogs!"

Dad spoke several languages, but even I was stunned in 1970 when Nick Begich took office as U.S. senator and my father publicly addressed him in Serbo-Croatian. I'd had no idea, nor did anyone else, that he spoke that language as well.

When my father got sick, I still had my business but I had returned to Anchorage. Since the late 1960s, Jerry had been there. Dad's heart was bad and we knew what was coming. When my cousin in New York died, I began running the New York factory in 1970. Both Jerry and I began to take over David Green Furs. In 1971, Dad was gone. Jerry and I have run David Green Furs together ever since. He took the inside: the accounting, taxes, the pensions, the personnel. I took the outside: the fur buying, the retail, the advertising, the designing, and being the out-in-front person. My brother and I bought the lot next door to David Green's for a parking lot.

Since the construction of Ft. Richardson and Elmendorf Air Force Base, we've had a wonderful relationship with the military, including General Simon Bolivar Buckner Jr., who protected Alaska as commander of the Army's Alaska Defense Command during the Aleutian campaign, and Air Force Brigadier General Frank A. Armstrong, deputy commanding general of the Alaska Air Command at Richardson in 1948, about whom the movie *Twelve O'Clock High* was written. We used to make thousands of military ruffs and special furs for the generals until the Army decided to go synthetic. [A ruff is the fur that rims a parka hood and protects the face.] We made fur coats for Mary Martin, customer Cincinnati Reds baseball player Johnny Bench, and Lyndon Johnson's daughters. When Hubert Humphrey fished in Seward, he always stopped in. (A fur coat was all that his wife Muriel bought during her husband's campaign, and she wore it for the inauguration.) Over the years, my father built a superb reputation, and we have maintained the quality and price. The wife of the chairman of GCI said she saved $26,000 getting a coat here. We'd rather sell a fur coat and have a happy customer. We tell people, "If you don't know furs, know your furrier." You can't please everyone but we've come as close as anybody. Our best customer is someone who has bought from us. We have sold them quality, style, and a great price.

From years of experience, we know which farms excel in which animals and colors. It's very privileged information. Fur ranches harvest two peltings per year; we only buy at the prime time. We buy sixty percent ranch furs and forty percent wild because that makes a more uniform blend. We only buy mink and fox from ranches, and fitch [a marbled polecat] but fitch is not a big item. We go to the Calgary and Edmonton Fur Auctions both for selling and purchasing.

Jerry's son David apprenticed at two or three of our New York factories. His wife Shani graduated from the New York Fashion Institute of Technology. She designs our patterns. It's a military secret but I'd say the best places for marten are the upper Yukon, the Canadian interior and of course, the Bargusian Sable of Russia. If Fort Yukon with their temperatures bred and raised sable, they'd get as good a price as the Russians. They get a heavier furred lynx at Ft. Yukon than is in the Yukon Territory.

In 2000, our children took over. David now manages David Green Furs. His wife, Shani, is our fashion manager. My daughter, Deborah Grashin, takes care of the accounting -- the "inside." My oldest son, Alan, runs the store in Ketchikan. Jerry's daughter, Sarah Green, runs Sarah's Specialty Shop, and my son Jay Green has three gift shops, Polar Bear Gifts. We are a history of Alaska, where it has been my great joy to know its real people.

Perry Green with a painting of his father, 2007, Anchorage. Judy Ferguson photo.

Chapter 17

The Banic Brothers, Seward Pioneer Entrepreneurs

"Come to Seward, Gateway to the Interior, the 'Keyhole' through which all traffic flows to western and Interior Alaska.—December 5, 1925, Prosperity Edition

An exuberant and powerful little lady, Ivanka Banic and her mother, Anka Banic, of Seward, remembered their family's origins in Croatia and early Alaska. They described the impact of both Prohibition and the 1980s movement Mothers Against Drunk Drivers on the bar trade in Alaska.

"In the old days, it was really comforting to meet other Yugoslav families in Alaska, no matter from what republic," Ivanka Banic began, "just to speak the language." The niece of two pioneer uncles, Tony and Sam Banic, Ivanka explained that there were originally three brothers: Tony, born in 1889; Sam, born in 1892; and Stipan Banic, born in 1898 in Otok, Croatia, near the Dalmatian seacoast. In a two-story home, the family had slept upstairs while on the ground floor, the animals were safely corralled from thieves. By day, a child herded the livestock up to alpine pastures.

Tony and Sam Banic, c. 1945, Seward, Courtesy of Anka and Ivanka Banic.

In 1907 when Tony Banic left Croatia for the United States, it was ruled by the Austro-Hungarian Empire. Three years later, Sam Banic jumped a German ship and followed his brother. Neither brother ever saw the 1918 Kingdom of Serbs, Croats, and Slovenes that followed the Austro-Hungarian Empire.

In 1910, Sam arrived in the United States. Because he lacked the proper documents, as he neared the dock in Pennsylvania he slid into the water and swam to shore. He continued to Chicago where he looked for his older brother, Tony.

"In Chicago," Anka Banic remembered, "the brothers helped run a club where customers brought their own bottles. Who knows if it was a speakeasy."

Tony and Sam went on to work for the railroad and arrived finally in Portland where they met local Dalmatian families, including Olga Barta Stepovich.

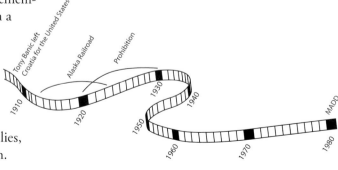

In Portland in about 1920, the brothers bought a bar and restaurant. Needing alcohol for their customers but constrained by Prohibition, they made their own home brew. On an island chicken farm, they made sour corn mash. (Traditionally in Croatia each family had their own wine and brandy stored in barrels in the cellar.) Tony and Sam Banic later loved to tell their family about when "even the chickens got drunk on the sour mash!" In those days, Sam kept a boat tied and hidden in the trees in case of a raid. Once, hearing approaching revenuers, the brothers rolled full barrels into the boat and cast off. The revenuers demanded of the remaining hired man, "Who is responsible for this?!" "Tony Parish [Tony Banic]," the man replied, "and Sam Romack" [Sam Banic].

The brothers continued north with their moonshine, fishing as they went. However, an informer called the Coast Guard. "Hey," he said, "that Sam Romack gotta moonshine ina boat!" Anka recalled the story. But someone else called Sam and warned him: "Coast Guard is looking for you!" Sam tied up his boat, unloaded the booze and hid it carefully in the trees, and began fishing. When the Coast Guard approached, the Banic brothers responded, "We no gotta nothing." Anka smiled, remembering the story. After the Coast Guard left, the brothers loaded up and continued on north.

In Alaska, they based out of Seward, the "Gateway to the Interior." By rail, the port city connected to the new railroad terminus at Ship Creek Landing, the origin of Anchorage. Over the years, the brothers fished in Bristol Bay and in the Bering Sea. Tony worked on the railroad, and in winter they both fished the Kenai Lake. Once they netted $3,000 worth of fish. They shipped the catch with the Alaska Steamship Company to Seattle. With their profit, Sam bought the Pioneer Bar on Fourth Avenue in Seward, and next door he built the Portland Hotel. One door down, Tony built Tony's bar. Behind the buildings, the ladies of the red light district purchased Tony's retail goods, camouflaged in Coca Cola bottles.

At Mile Six, a creek just outside of town, the brothers had one still. "Nobody today knows where the other still was," Anka smiled. The two brothers made whiskey and delivered it to fishing villages up and down the coast. Boots Henderson, who liked the merchandise too much, often accompanied Sam selling booze to the Bering Sea fishing villages.

Once on a premonition, Sam suggested, "Let's skip this next one!" But Boots wanted to go in. He agreed that if he didn't return in two hours, Sam should go on. Sure enough, Boots didn't return. Sam continued his deliveries up the coast. He found a dependable friend and gave him some money and his boat to return and bail Boots out. On the way, the police spotted the familiar boat and said to its skipper, "This is Sam Romack's boat." Anka laughed: "The dependable friend said,

Gateway to the Interior

The "Keyhole" through which traffic flows to western and Interior Alaska

"Prosperity Edition, Seward, Alaska, 1925."
Courtesy of Kathy and Steve Miller.

Andja, Anka, Ivanka and Sammy Banic, April 1, 1968, leaving Otok, Croatia, for Alaska. Courtesy of Anka and Ivanka Banic.

'I don't know thisa guy,'" then continued to town, bailed Boots out, and returned both Boots and boat to Sam. "Oh, boy, those guys had alotta stories."

Although the brothers had a strong network of friends, neither of them ever married.

In the newly created Yugoslavia of 1929, Tony and Sam's younger brother, Stipan, had a new son, Johann Banic. Five years before Hitler marched into Poland, Anka Klajajo was born in Otok.

Anka remembered her childhood growing up during World War II, seeing burning villages, blocked bridges, and condemned prisoners forced to dig their own graves. Not long after the 1944 Soviet Russia liberation of Belgrade from the Nazis, Tony Banic died in Seward in 1947.

Following Josip Broz Tito's split from Joseph Stalin, when life in Yugoslavia was hard and precarious, Anka Klajajo married Johann Banic, Tony and Sam's nephew. With the communist takeover, private property was seized and dissidents were shot or sent to Tito's own gulag, Goli Otok. Under President Truman's administration, food staples were sent to the Yugoslav people.

However, the routine of pastoral life continued as it had for centuries; Anka's five-year-old son, Sammy, herded the family's goats up the mountain as generations before him had done. In the early 1960s, Yugoslav passports and the new ability to leave with very minimal money permitted Johann to begin working in Germany. At the same time, he kept in touch with his Uncle Sam in far off Seward, Alaska.

For years, the Banic brothers used sleds and horses to freight to remote Alaska villages and trade with the Natives. In town when necessary, Sam Banic gave freezer space to Natives to store their fish. "'The most merciful' was Uncle Sam's nickname," his nephew, Sam Banic, recalled. "After fifty years in Alaska, Uncle Sam had many powerful friends. January 1965, he was even invited to Washington, D.C., for the inauguration of President Lyndon Baines Johnson."

Tony and Sam never had any children. Seventy-two years old, Sam Banic wrote his nephew Johann in Frankfurt, asking him to come to Seward and take over the business. In his free time for the next four years, Johann flew to Seward while his family in Croatia strove to get their travel documents.

Finally in 1968, having never gone more than fifty miles from home and alone with

Mira Banic (Sammy's wife), Tony's Bar, Seward, May 2003. Judy Ferguson photo.

three young children, Anka Banic left on the train to catch a plane in Frankfurt. In Salzburg with no explanation, the train abruptly unloaded. Speaking no German, but figuring the conductor would put them on a train for Germany, Anka and her frightened family waited on a train station bench. "Luckily," Ivanka grinned, "a man in the railroad office noticed us, spoke Croatian, and helped Mother get our German visas. He said, 'It's lucky for you you ran into me or they'd have sent you back.'"

A week late to catch their plane in Frankfurt, the family finally flew to Anchorage for a reunion with their father and uncle. "Uncle Sam's good friend in immigration," Ivanka remembered, "smoothed our entry into the United States. All summer," she went on, "we studied English to begin school in the fall.

"In Seward, a town of 2,500," Ivanka remarked, "we, the only foreign family, including me, a 'little'

person, really stood out!
But like a huge family, they
took us in." For the next six
years," she continued, "my
father and brother, Sammy,
worked closely with Uncle
Sam until he died in 1974."

After graduation, young
Sammy lived with Governor
Stepovich, his Croatian wife,
Matilda, and their thirteen
children while attending
the University of Alaska
Fairbanks. Three years
before the family obtained
American citizenship, their
youngest son, Tony Banic
Jr., was born in 1973. The
uncles never had their own
children, but to honor them

Johann, Anka, Andja, Tony, and Ivanka Banic, American citizenship, November 1975. Courtesy of Anka and Ivanka Banic.

Johann and Anka gave each of them a namesake in their sons.

Ivanka said, "The 1990s wars in former Yugoslavia were horrible. My mother's nephew was critically injured; today, he is still paralyzed."

From 1968 to 2005, the Banic family lived above Tony's Bar on Fourth Avenue. "It was impossible to take family vacations together," Ivanka said, "We were tethered, twenty-four/seven for thirty-seven years to the business. But the bar was a warm, friendly place. After fishermen returned from an opener, where they'd made $2,000, the first place they hit was Tony's! They'd bring us fish and treat their friends to rounds for the house. By the end of three days, however, they were broke again!

"In those days," Ivanka continued, "customers could have drinks lined up next to them on the bar, but not now. The new alcohol-related laws [an effect of MADD, Mothers Against Drunk Drivers] protect the public but they have also greatly changed the bar business. And too," she added, "today society is different. These days, the possibility for a truly dangerous customer is much greater.

"Tony's afforded us a good life in this new country," Ivanka explained, "but it was time to get out of the business.

"Every few years," she smiled, "I try to go home to Croatia; it's an ancient and a beautiful land, but to live…it's better to be here in the United States, here in the Last Frontier."

Chapter 18

Mike Babic, Copper River Powder Monkey

n 2007 as I visited the fishing town of Cordova, I met Mary Babic at the Ilanka Cultural Center. Recognizing a Croatian-Alaskan name, I asked about her family. She directed me to Heidi and Jack Babic Jr., the grandson of Croatian immigrant, "Mike" Mile [Mill′ay] Babić [Bah′bich]. Each of the Alaskan Slavs is a window into Alaska's history, geography, and culture.

The Babics remembered Guggenheim and J. P. Morgan's Kennecott Copper Corporation mines at Kennecott with their Copper River and Northwestern Railway (CRNW) that extracted copper ore by 1911, as well as their LaTouche Island copper mine in Prince William Sound. The Kennecott Copper Corporation was a large Outside industry in territorial Alaska.

L–R: (Baby) Jack M. Babic Sr., unknown, Mike Babic, Leona Babic, LaTouche Island, 1930, Courtesy of Heidi and Jack Babic Jr.

Born in 1896 in the small fishing village of Lukovo south of Sv. Juraj, Senj, Croatia, Mile Babic lived on the idyllic coastline of the clear Adriatic Sea. Just across from his village, he could see the island Goli Otok, which later became a communist prison camp. However, at the turn of the century, Croatia was Austro-Hungary. With the end of the Ottoman Empire, avaricious Austrian and Russian expansionism were making the Balkans a pressure point. Sensing war was coming and that her son would be drafted by the Austrian army, Mile Babic's mother, Mica Adzic, put her fourteen-year-old son on a ship bound for the United States. He could join family friends in Minnesota's Iron Range mines.

Once in the Iron Range, he became known as Mike and worked as a powder monkey. He was light and quick and became clever with igniting the dynamite. Following the trade, he worked in Washington where he met and married his wife, Leona. Together, they went to Kennecott's booming copper mine, Beatson, on LaTouche Island in Prince William Sound in 1929 where Jack Babic was born. Three hundred people worked at the mine. However, Beatson closed a year after Mike's arrival when copper prices hit five cents a pound. Beatson had produced a total of 182,600,000 pounds of copper ore.

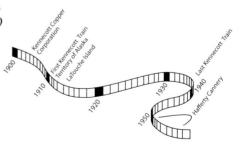

Mike Babic, thirty-two, U.S. citizenship, 1928. Courtesy of Heidi and Jack Babic Jr.

A powder monkey in demand, Mike got a job at Kennecott's McCarthy operation. Kennecott had five mines: Bonanza, Jumbo, Mother Lode, Erie, and Glacier. The Mother Lode mine was located on the east side of the ridge from Kennecott. The Bonanza, Jumbo, Mother Lode, and Erie mines were connected by tunnels. Ore was hoisted to Kennecott by trams that ended at Bonanza and Jumbo. From Kennecott the ore was hauled mostly in one-hundred-forty-pound sacks on steel flatcars to Cordova, 196 rail miles away.

Just after Mike Babic began work, geologists said the highest grades of ore were gone. The Mother Lode closed in July 1938. Erie, Jumbo, and Bonanza closed in September. The last train left Kennecott on November 10, 1938, leaving it a ghost town. In its twenty-seven years of operation, Kennecott produced almost five million tons of thirteen percent copper ore at an estimated profit of one hundred million dollars.

After being laid off, Mike, a skilled Croatian fisherman, worked out of Cordova and for years, harvested sockeye salmon in Prince William Sound.

Commercial canneries operated near river mouths where salmon schooled before going up the river to spawn. Across the river mouths they placed barricades, efficient fish traps that prevented most salmon from escaping upstream. In the 1950s, one of the Cordova canneries was Hafferty Fish Cannery, which later became the Alaska Packers Cannery. Mike, who was well liked, worked at Hafferty and as a fisherman, he sold Copper River salmon to the cannery.

In 1964, as travel for Yugoslavs opened in the Socialist Federal Republic of Yugoslavia, Mike returned to his birthplace. There were stories of the many political prisoners President Tito sent across the water from Mike's village of Lukova to Tito's gulag, Goli Otok or Naked Island. Mike's grandson, Jack Jr., remembered his grandfather's stories, told in his heavy musical accent. When Mike was eighty-three in 1969, he died at home, leaving behind his son, Jack, a fisherman, and grandson, Jack Jr., a third-generation Cordova Copper River fisherman.

Chapter 19

From Gold to Ink: The Alaska Sportsman and Doris Bordine

Immigrants from many nationalities went to the Klondike, including Swedish immigrant August Tobin. Tobin's son Emery followed his father to Alaska. In the early years, newspapers and the Alaska Sportsman *helped preserve Alaska's history. At a time when Southeast was Alaska's hub, Emery Tobin began the magazine that became the voice of the Great Land. Interestingly, in the era before oil discovery, Emery Tobin was against statehood. In 2006, Doris Bordine, Emery Tobin's daughter, remembered the magazine that ultimately became* Alaska *magazine.*

My father grew up without his father, August Tobin, who had gone North during the Klondike "for just a few months." The months evolved into sixteen years. In Massachusetts, my dad, Emery Tobin, grew up listening to his father's letters. Dad loved to read, preferring the stories of Horatio Alger, the boy who did right, worked hard, and rose from rags to riches. Pursuing that lifelong philosophy, he became a reporter for the *Quincy Ledger*. During World War I while in France, he sent articles featuring the soldiers back to the newspaper.

When Dad returned home, Grampa also arrived there from Alaska. Of course he was a stranger, was

Top: The Alaska Sportsman *logo, Courtesy of Doris Bordine.*
Above: Doris was featured on the Tobin family Christmas card in 1935. The card read, "I may not be able to type so well, but my wishes are true." Ketchikan. Courtesy of Doris Bordine.

short in covering his debts, and was an alcoholic, so fairly soon he returned to Wiseman, knowing this time "just where to strike it rich." However, on arrival the price of gold had plummeted while the cost of a grubstake had risen. He began walking, returning on 470 miles of new railroad tracks from Fairbanks to Seward. He worked for passage to Ketchikan, intending to return home. However, Dad wrote Grampa saying, "Don't come. I'll meet you there to see what's so wonderful in that country."

Dad and Grampa met in Ketchikan, where they both got jobs at a fish-packing company. They lived in a tent that first winter to save money to bring Gramma and my aunt there in 1922.

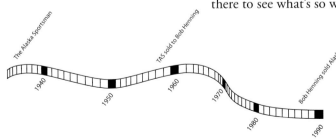

In Washington in 1925, my mother, Clara Willard, had just graduated as a school teacher. Some of her Alaska classmates directed her to a teaching job in Seldovia and also encouraged her to meet Dad in Ketchikan on her way to Seldovia. Smitten with each other immediately, Mom and Dad corresponded for the next two years and married in 1927. They made their home in Ketchikan.

Even during the Depression, fishing and timber were healthy. Just after I was born in 1930, Dad switched jobs from the fish-packing company to the *Ketchikan Chronicle*.

Civically active, Dad listened when the local sportsman's club pressed him to begin a magazine. It was not the best economic time to begin a periodical in a territory whose population equaled that of a city in the Lower Forty-eight, but still Dad liked the idea. In 1935, Dad began publishing the *Alaska Sportsman*, printed first at the *Ketchikan Chronicle* and then at the *Ketchikan Daily News*. He and the local sportsmen intended to have an Alaska version of the national hunting and fishing magazines that arrived late in the territory on the steam ships. However, supplies were expensive and they were slow in arriving. Income was not offsetting cost. Dad soon realized he had to purchase a press and do it himself. In an old hospital, we set up both a bindery and print shop; upstairs, we had an apartment. Every night, I went to sleep to the sound of the press. An artist passing through, Bill Gabler, created the *Alaska Sportsman* banner. Far in advance of each issue, paper had to be ordered from back East.

An only child, I grew up learning how to do everything except run the press. I did layout, linotype, and (hot) type set. We had to send the photo negatives by boat, taking two and half days to Seattle, where a copper imprint was cut and attached to a woodblock for printing each photo. (If there was a delay from a storm at sea, we were in trouble.) Printing four pages at a time, it took all month, with two to three pressmen running the Kelly press twenty-four hours a day, seven days a week. Dad made a Lazy Susan table that we turned, collating by hand. Paid under a dollar an hour, women cut, collated, and ran the stitching machine, pumping it with their feet.

Ranging between thirty-six and forty-eight pages with two pictures on every page, the magazine included classifieds, often from singles looking for mates. The latter brought Dad a lot of criticism from the conservative sector, who might comment on the result, "Oh, she came up on the boat." Each magazine cost twenty-five cents.

Doris Tobin, Clara Tobin, Mrs Way, Emery Tobin, Ketchikan, 1947. Courtesy of Doris Bordine.

The magazine was southeastern in scope, focusing on big-game hunting and written in the words of the hunter or the fisherman himself, a magazine of the people and for the people. When Dad was financially desperate, which was most of the time, the bank or his sister loaned him money. When it was worse, Mom sold off much of her family inheritance, including acres of timberland in Washington state.

Dad never missed an issue. We had a local souvenir store featuring a huge rain gauge. The store prospered and fed the magazine.

Dad wrote the "Main Trails" section and the editorial page. He always waited until the last minute, usually holding up the presses. Using a distributor, he circulated all over the state as well as throughout the Lower Forty-eight.

He so believed that one man can make a difference that when he realized the depth of

Emery Tobin, protector of Native artwork, conservationist and publisher at the Alaska Sportsman *headquarters, Ketchikan, 1953. Courtesy of Doris Bordine.*

the corruption in Ketchikan he testified before a federal grand jury in 1953, telling all he knew. The chief of police and the police captain were both indicted and the district attorney resigned. In the next year and a half, only one body was found floating in Thomas Basin.

One of my father's young employees was Gordon Bordine, whom I married. He soon became a Lutheran pastor.

Before oil discovery, Dad was against statehood, believing that only the federal government could support the state. He also supported big business, believing that fish traps were the most efficient way to catch fish for the commercial canneries. He always favored making money, although he never had any.

After twenty-three years, Dad sold the magazine in 1958 to Juneau journalist Robert A. Henning. At the time Dad sold the magazine *Alaska Sportsman* had a circulation of sixty-five thousand and was "the largest outdoor sports publication west of the Mississippi," according to the *Ketchikan Daily News.* My husband and I could've taken it, but I knew what a struggle it had been and I wanted no part of it. Bob Henning, a lifelong Alaskan, was perfect. He eventually dropped "Sportsman" from the title, slickened the publication, edited it in Anchorage, had production offices in Edmonds, and published it in Seattle. He had a savvy blend of public relations and environmentalism. In the 1980s Bob's health forced him to sell. *Alaska* magazine now belongs to Morris Communications, based in Georgia.

When Dad retired to Vancouver, Washington, he got an electronic typewriter and frequently wrote letters to the editor.

Since Grampa's wandering across the Arctic, we have had five generations of Tobins in Alaska. Entrepreneurs in soul, we found that a good idea along with a lot of sacrifice can leave a legacy worth having: the *Alaska Sportsman.*

Chapter 20

Montenegrin-Alaskan Lady Angelina Saičić Geraghty

In the book *Montenegro: Ecological Country,* the land is described: "Centuries of outside aggression have not changed the sublime beauty of Montenegro. Its karst mountains are bordered by the Adriatic Sea, hemmed in by a series of tiny beaches. Home to the world's second largest canyon, Montenegro also boasts the Balkans' largest inland body of water, Lake Skadar.

"Many of its rivers flow off its mountain range into eastern Europe while the Morača River drains to the west. Montenegrins say, 'Even the water imprints a destiny on our people, a flow of east and west.'"

An eloquent people with a love for language, Montenegro developed the first printing press in the south Slav regions in 1494. "No other country," according to John Hajdukovich's cousin, physicist Dr. Dragan Hajdukovic, "has produced, for its size, such a large number of creative minds.

"Even ruled by poets, Montenegro's unique 'prince-bishops,' a blend of church and state, have imparted a servant's humility, fighting alongside their war-

Morača River, Montenegro. Judy Ferguson photo.

riors, keeping their mountains free through five hundred years of the Ottoman Empire. Montenegro has long stood for independence and freedom of the common man."

When I first met Angie Saičić Borovich Geraghty, she began, "Montenegrins have such a heart," she said. "You will never find anywhere else. They give even after being hurt repeatedly. They trust without caution and treat visitors like royalty."

She turned to a 1910 photograph hanging in her vestibule of Montenegro's King Nikola I and the royal family. Savoring the memory, she said, "My father used to dance with the king's daughter, Elena." The poet/prince-bishop, Njegoš, whose portrait hung in her hallway, once told his people, "Defend yourself from attack, but protect the vulnerable, even from yourself. Your only nationality is man and his dignity. Your real heritage is never to submit to evil or to betray faith."

Over the last ten years, including the 1999 NATO bombing of the Federal Republic of Yugoslavia, Angie, a hostess of great grace and a beautiful lady, has been my friend. Over the years, she has told the story of her people and of her own ninety years:

1930   F. E. Co. Ester dredge   1940   Ladd Field Built/World War II   Socialist Federal Republic of Yugoslavia   1950   1960   1970   (E. L. Patton) Yukon River Bridge built   Bush schools built   1980   1990   NATO bombing of Federal Republic of Yugoslavia   2000

Nick and Angie Borovich and her brother Milos Saičić, law student, Belgrade, 1938. Courtesy of Angie Geraghty.

I was born in 1919 in Vinicka near Berane, Montenegro, one year after the beginning of the Kingdom of Serbs, Croats, and Slovenes. Muslims call my area Sandžak, an Ottoman Bosnian military province that stretched from Bosnia-Herzegovina to Kosovo-Metohia, 5,397 square miles. To Serbs it is Raška, which along with Kosovo comprised the heart of the medieval Serbian state.

Montenegrins were mountainous tribesmen with varying autonomy from the thirteenth to the mid-nineteenth centuries. Each tribe had its own chief. Following the Ottoman occupation that was the dissolution of the Serbian Empire, these old Montenegrin tribes governed until the Kingdom of Serbs, Croats, and Slovenes. Our tribe was the Vasojeviči and our area was Brda.

Beginning under the House of Petrović-Njegoš in 1853, a gradual coalescing of the highland tribes, "old Montenegro," the coast, and more recently former Austrian Herzegovina began to give birth to modern Montenegro.

In 1905, Prince Nikola Petrović held tribal assemblies, the General Montenegrin Assembly, that mediated between the people and the Ottoman authorities. In 1910 King Nikola Petrović took the throne. Many of his daughters were married to European princes and kings, earning him the nickname "the father-in-law of Europe." Our family was a friend of King Nikola, who fought for Montenegrin-Serbian sovereignty.

Montenegro was an ally of Russia. During the 1904 to 1905 Russo-Japanese War, to start the battle when the Russian and Japanese armies confronted each other in Manchuria, they each offered their biggest heroes: a flying Samurai and my uncle, Aleksandar Lekso Saičić.

145

The Russians were terrified of the flying Samurai. As the two horsemen charged each other with sabers, Uncle Aleksander quickly swung under his horse's belly and then snapped upright to deliver a killing blow to the Samurai. A hero, Aleksandar was made the general of the Russian Army and is sung about to this day.

Throughout the centuries of the Ottoman Empire, countries under the empire's dominion annually lost some of their children at a very young age. The children were sent away for years of training in the sultan's schools; some returned as Ottoman administrators. In fact, the empire had the only viable schools. The Serbian serfs farmed to survive and pay Ottoman taxes. What schools Montenegro had were under-financed and poorly attended. However, later in the era when the Ottoman Czar and King Nikola *were* friends, my father, Milovan, was privileged to be selected to attend those Ottoman schools. At a very young age, he was among one hundred children selected for education in Turkey. As a student in Istanbul, my father wore a white tunic with "Students of the Czar" [Turkish] on his collar. He studied French, Greek, Turkish, Italian, Russian, ballroom dancing, and all that related to courtly life. However, when he did return home to Montenegro, he'd forgotten his own native language. King Nikola made my father secretary of defense and as such, my father and mother lived near embassy row in the ancient capitol of Cetinje. An excellent dancer, he was often at the palace where he frequently danced with Princess Elena. Father fought in both the Balkan Wars [1912–1913] and in World War I.

I never had a suit with the name of the czar across it. When I was growing up, I studied five years at our school in Vinicka. In 1906, a neighbor from nearby Andrijevica, Nikola Borovich, left for the United States when he was twenty-two. Working first on the Panama Canal, he moved to Fairbanks and began mining on Ester Creek.

It is not uncommon for Yugoslav men to marry when they are older to better provide for a young lady, and to begin their new family. In 1929, Nick's Fairbanks friend from Risan, Mike Stepovich, had returned home to Montenegro for his bride, Vuka Radovich, a wonderful lady. Six years later, Milo Hajdukovich returned to his home of Kolasin for his beautiful wife, Ellen Lesperović. When he was fifty-three in 1937, Nick decided to also return home and find a bride as well.

In Montenegro on Saturdays when people went to the market, the youngsters strolled in a social promenade called *korzo*. Nick knew my father, who was the chief of police. As Nick watched *korzo*, he saw me walking with my brother. Interested, well-dressed, and carrying an attache case, he asked if he could meet my father and brother at an espresso and brandy bar, a *kafana*. After a few greetings, he immediately asked for my hand. (Can you imagine?) My father agreed, and at home, he told me the arrangement.

Angie Saičić Borovich Geraghty dancing the kolo at her wedding in Vinicka, Montenegro 1938. Courtesy of Angie Geraghty.

Only nineteen, I ran upstairs crying. Nick Borovich was fifty-four and a stranger! However, my father, who'd served in the First World War, knew another war was coming. In 1938, Hitler was talking invasion. My father came into my room and gently took my hand, saying, "Gina, Nick Borovich will take care of you. You are going to the greatest country in the world. However, when you go there," he advised me, "mix with Americans—not with your own kind. Find out what makes that country great." He explained, "A big war is coming. You may be the only one of our family to survive." It meant nothing to me, but I would not go against my father's promise.

Leaving my four brothers and five sisters on our mountainous farm, I married Nick in Vinicka and traveled to Belgrade, where we waited two months for my documents. We went by train then to Austria and to LeHavre, France. We sailed on the *Queen Mary* but already pregnant, I got very sick. The boat was loaded with Jews from Germany, Austria, and Czechoslovakia (they'd read Hitler's *Mein Kampf*, published in 1925, and they knew what was coming.) The Czechs and Slovenes and I could understand each other. They saved chairs up on deck in the fresh air for me. After we arrived in New York, we caught the train for Washington state.

When we arrived in Seattle, I awoke and pulled the drapes back. There were fields of beautiful pink rhododendrons. I thought, "Oh my gosh! I am in heaven!" All of Nick's Montenegrin friends met us, including Petar and Zorka Raykovich. Two years earlier, Nick had brought the Raykovichs' son, Milan, "Big Ray" to the university in Fairbanks where he played basketball as the tallest guy on the team. Since I wasn't feeling good and to help me adjust to the language and new country, we stayed with them for two to three weeks. In the afternoons, I took naps.

That fall, we rode the mail boat to Alaska. On board, Alaskans circled around, teaching me English. I remembered my father: "Mix with Americans; learn what makes that country great."

When we arrived in Fairbanks, I was so disappointed. It wasn't "beautiful America" at all but only broken-down old cabins everywhere. While we stayed in town the first year, out at Ester Creek Nick put two of his cabins together for us. I cried the whole first year, but I never told my family my reality. My husband wanted to send me back, but I was expecting a child. Vuka (Radovich) Stepovich from the beautiful Bay of Kotor just off the Adriatic understood how I felt. She was twenty years older than I and she was my friend.

Nick was proud of his new bride and took me to meet Dr. Bunnell, the president of the

Slavic Fairbanks Ladies, Back, fourth: Ellen Hajdukovich; Front, second: Angie Borovich, Fairbanks, c. 1943. Courtesy of Sonja Lesperović, Belgrade.

Alaska Agricultural College and School of Mines (University of Alaska) who strongly supported miners.

When I was pregnant, the doctor said, "If it's a girl, what will you name her?" Thinking then what I'd call her, I said, "Virginia." He told Nick to tell me that was the state he came from, but I understood the doctor's English; I learned very fast.

Only months after our first child, named Vera, was born, again I didn't feel so good. Vuka took me to the doctor, who said

Johnny Hajdukovich, Olga Miscovich, Nicky Borovich, Martin and Andrew Slisko, Vera and Olga Borovich, Donna Slisko, Mary Hajdukovich, c. 1944, Ester Creek, Courtesy of Angie Geraghty..

that once again I was pregnant. "It can't be!" I protested. "My mother had a baby every three years!" With each birth, I stayed in town with some Croatian friends and when I was ready I went to St Joseph's hospital. By 1941, when I was twenty-two, I had three children.

As World War II heated up, news filtered through our Fairbanks-Balkan community. I thought my family, monarchists—called *chetniks* at home—must be caught up in the battle between the Ustaše (Croatians working with the Nazis) and Tito's Communist partisans, the war within the greater war. On the creek, there was no one to talk to me, to cheer me up.

We lived in cabins on a little hill half a mile past today's Malemute Saloon. A huge Fairbanks Exploration Co. dredge was digging down in the valley. The F. E. Co. community, mostly families, had dances at the community hall; sometimes I went. To get to Fairbanks I took a bus.

One day in the Goldstream Valley, a Montenegrin, Jabuka, killed a miner then murdered the man's wife and daughter. As Jabuka walked on the railroad tracks to town with a list of men he intended to kill, the news of the murders was broadcast throughout Fairbanks. A man in town was shaving and in his mirror he saw Jabuka behind him, but the man escaped. Nick was scared but I wasn't. I didn't know anything. That night, there was a loud knock at our door in Ester: "Nick, Nick!" It was the U.S. marshal. "He's after you, Nick." Nick went down the tunnel with his gun to tell "Moose John," another Montenegrin. He crawled through the woods to John's house where he saw him cooking breakfast for Jabuka. John saw Nick but pretended not to and gestured for him to leave. Soaking wet with sweat, Nick returned home. That night the police heard shooting from inside the tunnel and smoked the guy out and killed him. Not so unusual, because these bachelors living alone frequently went crazy. But I was scared then. The deputy from town also said the children had to go to school.

The war was bringing mining to an end but Nick assured me he'd get $1,000 that season from his claim. When I was in town once visiting Ellen Hajdukovich, her cousin John Hajdukovich, a miner from Big Delta, was there visiting. He said, "$1,000, mining?

Back: John Lekich, Billy Vuicich, (behind Novack) Nick Borovich, (far back) Harry Leov, (moustache) John Popovich, (back) Mary Bojanich. (far back) Bob Bigovich, Ann Miscovich, (far back) Tom Radovich, unknown, (wall) Stana Miscovich, Angie Borovich, (glasses) Steve Bojanich, (leaning) John Miscovich, (children) John & Mary Hajdukovich, (back) Pete Miscovich, Eva Miscovich, (print dress) Aurora Leov, (far corner) Howard Miscovich, (near right) Olga Miscovich Front: Bertha Novak and son on lap of Nick Novack, Charlie Miller, Mrs. Raganovich, (near front) Helen Miller (Vacura), Mary Miller, Fairbanks, 1949. Courtesy of Angie Geraghty.

Dreams!" Even though I was born into a patriarchal society, I was beginning to understand the difference between talk, dreams, and reality. I told Nick to get a job at Ladd Field and I said, "I am moving into town." I wanted the children to go to school. Nick said I could teach them at home, but I said, "I don't know anything myself!" It was time to learn the new country and a new era.

In 1943, through my husband, I became an American citizen. In Fairbanks, I borrowed $1,000 from my Finnish girlfriend, Sali Benson, and got a log cabin on Second Avenue with no running water, no toilet. Our family moved there in 1944. I put the girls in school. Vera wasn't used to English or being with other children, so the next year the school held her back and Olga and she were then in the same grade. Due to our family's difference, Olga felt self-conscious. I enrolled the girls in Sunday school at St. Matthew's Episcopal Church and joined the women's group where I knitted with the ladies and even learned to bead. During the war, we invited the Russian Orthodox priest at Sitka to come and baptize my daughters.

My girls loved the Native children. After church, they'd come over and give me a kiss. Nick was working at Ladd Field.

In those days, we were all afraid of tuberculosis. In 1943, Nick got sick. For three and a half years, he was bedfast. I began taking children in for fifty cents an hour. For months, Nick stared out the window, worried about our future. After twelve years of marriage, when Nick was sixty-five, he died in 1950 with no social security pension, insurance, and not having title to his own gold claim.

The Butrovichs and others in the community helped me. One New Year's Eve through mutual friends, I met Alaska-born Clyde Geraghty. Handsome and smart, Clyde was nonetheless very shy. In those days, freight arrived at the port of Valdez. He and his friend, Bob Mitchell, had a trucking company and hauled freight out of Valdez to Fairbanks.

Clyde asked me to marry him. In those days, people were pretty clannish. Americans frequently called Slavs "bohunks," and on occasion Slavs called Americans *furesti*, "foreigners." When I married outside the Slavic "tribe," many of my community cried that I was marrying a *furest*.

I ignored them; I knew what was important. At first, it was hard for my girls, but Clyde treated them with the greatest of love and care.

During that impoverished era, we were also concerned about polio. We were told not to have public gatherings. Despite that I was a struggling widow, I planned a nice wedding. My girls—Vera, eleven; Olga, ten; and Nicky, eight—were my junior bridesmaids. John Butrovich gave me away and, despite health concerns, the church was packed.

A few years after my marriage, I flew home for a visit, taking money to my mother. I never told my parents how hard my life had been; when I had an extra dollar I sent it to my mother. During the war when the Communists began taking over, they had shot my father on the street. My mother hadn't been allowed to bring him home. One brother paid a Partisan to be able to watch over his grave until Mother could bring his body home. Another brother, also a monarchist, fled to Italy, but the British (who supported Tito) sent him on to Egypt where his children were born. Finally Australia opened their doors to him and his family. During the war by day, my mother hid another of my brothers in the closet; at night, he came out.

Bob and Mary Mitchell, Vera Borovich, Clyde Geraghty, Olga & Nicky Borovich, Angie Geraghty, John Butrovich, Geraghty wedding, Fairbanks, 1950. Courtesy of Angie Geraghty.

In the 1950s on my trip home, I found out that my brother was a judge. One of my sisters was married to an admiral. As in every Yugoslavian family, some members were now Communists, and that was hard on every politically divided family. Also, people were leaving the traditional village life for the city. With an atheistic government in charge, few people went to church. The Communists had killed many intellectuals, taken property, and were making changes too fast. People were brainwashed that the socialist dream was the answer to people's problems but in reality Communism deeply wounded our people.

Back in Alaska, with the new aviation age, less cargo was arriving by water at Valdez. My husband and his partner sold their trucks and bought an old Army bulldozer. During the day, they worked for the Alaska Road Commission, and in the evenings they dug basements. They began with nothing as they started general contracting but the economy was picking up.

In 1952, Clyde and his friends Carl Heflinger, Carl Erickson, Harvey Marlin, and Robert Mitchell incorporated GHEMM Co. Very soon Heflinger sold his share to Conrad Frank, the only engineer. GHEMM hired other experts as needed.

In 1952, our son Mike was born, followed by Steve in 1956. My girls were busy watching their new brothers. They also used to babysit for Ted Stevens' kids. As my boys grew up, they worked with their father.

After the 1976 Tobeluk v. Lind Consent Decree (Molly Hootch Act), the state built schools in the villages, contracting frequently with GHEMM Co. During the pipeline construction, GHEMM, along with the Seattle-based Manson-Osberg Construction Co., built the $33.5 million Yukon River Bridge.

During the late 1970s, Clyde and I visited Montenegro together. We had a second honeymoon there; it was beautiful showing him my country, and he loved it.

In 1987, while visiting my brother in Australia, we were in a car accident in Perth. Clyde was paralyzed, and his hands and lungs were also weak. A doctor flew home with us. For years night and day, I took care of him. We bought a house in Palm Desert and split our time between the two homes. In 1994 however he died from the paralysis in his lungs.

Five years later, during the 1999 NATO bombing of the Federal Republic of Yugoslavia, I suffered again along with my longtime Montenegrin friend Vuka Stepovich. Between the Turks, Communism, and today's nationalism, my country has been badly damaged. My brother, who lives near Belgrade today, says life there is very tough. "When someone gets up to help," he said, "he gets knocked back down again." That is my country, always torn between East and West. Many good, beautiful, and talented people have come from Montenegro and enriched the world, especially in Alaska.

In the 1970s, my middle daughter, Olga, and her husband, Ken Carson, went to my village, Vinicka. My people sang a folk song for her about the beautiful Montenegrin girl who left to marry an American millionaire, apparently pointing to me. The people loved Olga and Ken.

I am an active member today of the Alaska-Yukon Pioneers. The land that so greatly disappointed me in 1938 has made me proud and grateful for seventy-one years. An invisible bridge seems to connect the Balkans to Alaska, the home of many Montenegrins, including my fourteen grandchildren, seventeen great-grandchildren, and two great-great-grandchildren— five generations of Alaskan-Montenegrins! It has been good to honor my father's wishes to "learn what makes that country great."

Angie, Olga Carson, Pamela Wendt, Stephanie and Clara Newton, Arizona, 2005. Courtesy of Olga Carson.

Chapter 21

The Krize Brothers, Owners of Second Avenue

Geron Krize and Katherine Petic Krize, Minnesota, 1900. Courtesy of Geron Krize.

Parts of Fairbanks' Second Avenue were owned for many years by the son of a Slovenian immigrant, Rudy Krize. His brothers Frank, Ted, and Louis owned many of the downtown businesses.

In the late 1800s, Geron Kriše came to this country; in 1900, he married Katherine Petić. Like many, he worked in the iron ore mines of Minnesota. Together Goran and Katherine raised ten children: sons Rudy, Louis, Frank, Hank, Ted, Eddie, and daughters Mary, Rose, Angie, and Julie. In 1907, when Rudy started school, the family name was changed to Krize. The children grew up with their Croatian friend, Tom Paskvan Jr., whose father, Tom Sr., was a longtime friend of Geron Krize. As the boys became young men, to survive the Great Depression, they played gigs in Rudy's Minnesota Vagabonds swing band. Louis' son Bob said, "Rudy, Frank, and Dad were all excellent musicians. In Judy Garland's first audition, she was accompanied by Dad."

In 1938 to 1939, family friend Tom Paskvan Sr. went north to survive the Depression by trapping in the Fortymile River country. By mid-winter, he had arrived in Fairbanks where he lived at Pete Mesich's log Arctic Hotel on the Chena River. Working with Mesich, a wealthy miner from Ophir, Paskvan invested in the Owl Cigar store and in 1939, in the International Hotel on Garden Island across from the train depot. Paskvan needed a bartender and asked Rudy Krize to work for him. In 1939, Rudy arrived and began bartending for Paskvan Sr. at the International and at the Wagon Wheel outside of town, on Thirteenth Avenue. Brother Ted Krize arrived not long after Rudy and began working for Fairbanks Lumber and Supply.

Ted's son Geron remembered "Rudy, the oldest, and my dad spearheaded all the Krize brothers' endeavors. Like Milo Hajdukovich, Uncle Rudy invested in downtown properties." Frank's son Dennis Krize recalled, "At home in Gilbert, Minnesota, Louis and my dad, Frank, were operating the High Hat Club, but by the end of 1943 my dad had retired from it. In early 1944, Rudy returned to Minnesota to get married. He and my dad returned to Alaska together; in October, my mother, Sophie D. Krize, and I joined Dad in Alaska."

Milo Hajdukovich owned the California bar property. Buying in with Milo, Rudy and Ted eventually bought the

152

California bar business, located on Cushman between Second and Third avenues. With their profits and with a ten-thousand-dollar loan from Hajdukovich, the Krize brothers leased another Hajdukovich property across from Cap Lathrop's Empress Theatre (generally today's Co Op Plaza area) where they built the Silver Dollar bar. (At some point, the California bar burned down.) The Krize Brothers, Ted, Louis, and Frank, ran the bar that got its name from the rows of silver dollars embedded into the wall. Dennis continued, "Uncle Rudy bought from Cap Lathrop at Second and Lacey, south toward Third and west up Second Avenue. In a partnership with a Yugoslavian family from Minnesota, the Koschalk brothers, Rudy built and opened a restaurant, the Café Aurel. One of the Minnesota partners became the chef. Frank managed Aurel's and bartended at the Silver Dollar. "In 1941," Dennis said, "Ted was stationed at Ladd Field." He continued, "In 1948 when the dishwasher didn't show up, I began washing dishes down in the basement for Uncle Rudy and the Koschalks. But there just wasn't any money in town so they closed the restaurant." Rudy knew the Raykovich brothers, Milan "Big Ray" and Phil, down by the river, were running a military surplus store out of a Quonset hut (near today's Morris Thompson building). Rudy asked the Raykovich brothers if they'd like to lease his new building on Second Avenue. In 1951, Big

(Back) Frank, Ted, Louis; (Front) Hank, Rudy and Eddie Krize, c. 1946. Courtesy of Sophie and Bob Krize.

153

Louis Krize, Fairbanks' Second Avenue,
c. 1962. Courtesy Sophie and Bob Krize.

Ray's Surplus Store moved to its current location on Second Avenue.

By then, the younger Krize brothers, Hank and Eddie, were out of the military and were looking for work. Older brothers Rudy, Ted, and Louis urged them to come up to Fairbanks. The older brothers had begun gold mining as well with Krize Brothers Mining Company at Manley Hot Springs in 1946. Hank and Eddie went to work for them until the brothers sold in 1948. The younger brothers bartended at the Silver Dollar and the Flame Room. In those days, the older brothers, Krize Brothers Distributing Company, also distributed Royal Bohemian Beer. They had the bar business, coming and going.

Rudy owned the building that housed the Top O' the World clothing at Third and Lacey streets but the business itself was owned by Alfred "Happy" Holter and Gene Clayton. Frank managed the business. When Holter was ready to sell, Ted, Louis, and Frank bought the Top O' the World clothing. The Krize Brothers opened the Flame Lounge above Big Ray's Surplus Store. During the mid-1950s, younger brother Eddie, a bartender and a jazz clarinetist on a level with Benny Goodman, played at the Flame as well as other spots around town.

In 1950, Rudy Krize retired to California and Ted left for Minnesota. Rudy and Ted often returned home to Alaska to hunt and fish, but in 1956 on a fishing trip, Ted drowned in Minto Flats. After the tragic accident, Frank and Louis bought out Ted's interests.

During Alaska oil exploration in the mid-1950s, the Raykovich brothers and Big Ray's partner Glenn Miller bought leases in the Kenai Peninsula Swanson River oil speculation. In 1957, Swanson River became Alaska's first commercial oil discovery. In 1961, Frank's son Dennis graduated in business administration and marketing from the University of Alaska. When Glenn Miller and Big Ray Raykovich began receiving their Swanson River oil checks, they decided to sell Big Ray's Surplus Clothing. The business was sold back to Krize Brothers Louis and Frank. Under the umbrella of the Krize Brothers, Rudy maintained ownership of the building. Louis took over managing Big Ray's business while Frank bought wholesale clothing for both Top O' the World and for Big Ray's.

As a commissioned Army officer, Dennis Krize went to Europe. During his stint, Frank and Louis asked Dennis to come back and work with them. In 1963, Dennis returned and began working in the store; however, it didn't go well with Uncle Louie. Dennis told his father, "You and Uncle Louie step back and let me manage and or I'll go elsewhere." To Dennis' mild surprise, they stepped back. From 1965 to 1979, Dennis ran Krize Corporation.

During the 1967 Fairbanks flood, Rudy's wooden building, Top O' the World, as well as his property where Lou Kinda ran the Cottage Bar were both badly water damaged. The brothers realized they had to change course.

Rudy owned the Krize Building, where Harold Bittner and Buzz Brazeau had their Sportland Arcade business, café and newsstand. Frank and Louis bought the empty parking lot behind Big Ray's and the Sportland Arcade from Rudy. Dennis built an extension on Big Ray's and extended over to Third Avenue but separate from the Sportland Arcade, on Second Avenue. In 1968, Dennis extended the Sportland which became the new location for Top O' the World clothing. The old wooden building for Top O' the World on Lacey and Second was torn down.

As Dennis ran Top O' the World clothing, Krize Corporation, and Big Ray's, he dropped the handle Big Ray's "Surplus Clothing" because by then, they carried very little surplus.

"Over the years," Bob Krize said, "Not only was Dad a partner in the Silver Dollar, the Krize Building businesses, but in 1950–1952, he was also involved in the Northward Building, Fairbanks' first steel girder 'skyscraper,' eight stories, which was the city's first apartment building and was used as a backdrop in Edna Ferber's *The Ice Palace.*" Bob added, "Dad also sat on the board of directors for Alaska National Bank, which evolved later into National Bank of Alaska and later Wells Fargo. People came to Dad figuring," he smiled, "that he knew how to solve business problems. Dad not only had amazing business acumen but he was also a gentleman's gentleman.

"When I was growing up," he remembered, "Dad had me memorize the Gettysburg Address. He would take me to the Silver Dollar, set me up on the bar, have me recite the Gettysburg for the customers, then he'd reach back and hand me a bag of pistachios.

"When I was eighteen, my mom, Sophie Krize, went with several Fairbanks families—Matilda Stepovich, Franichs, Milos Beconovich, and the Joe Jackovichs—to Croatia in 1967; twenty-one of them rented several cars, and toured Yugoslavia."

By 1999, Louis Krize was gone. In 2006, Dennis' father Frank had also passed away. With their deaths and in 2003 the passing of their friend Tom Paskvan Jr., an era closed. Gone was the time when a man could look down First and Second avenues and note that almost every bar and many businesses were owned by Yugoslav-Alaskans. Those Slavs first came as miners, but made their real grub-stakes with businesses in pioneer Fairbanks.

Bob Krize, 2008. Judy Ferguson photo.

Chapter 22

The International Hotel and Tommy's Elbow Room: Tom Paskvan Sr., Jr., and Joe Paskvan

In November 2008, Joe Paskvan won the election for District E state senator. A Fairbanks lawyer born in the Golden Heart City, Joe Paskvan's grandfather, Tom (Tomislav Paškvan) Paskvan Sr., originally came to Alaska in 1909. After a short stay, he returned to his home in Minnesota. However, in 1939 he returned; in 1940, he brought his son, Tommy Paskvan Jr., along with his friends Rudy and Louis Krize. Senator Joe Paskvan, the family's third generation, described his family's key businessmen and the history of downtown Fairbanks.

Tommy Paskvan Jr. at Tommy's Elbow Room, c. 1958. Courtesy of Joe Paskvan.

My grandfather Tom Paskvan grew up in the isolated and beautiful mountains of northern Croatia, just west of Rijeka in Sunger, under the Austro-Hungarian Empire where life was hard. In 1909, my nineteen-year-old granddad and his sixteen-year-old brother jumped ship in the Rijeka harbor and went to the coal and lead and zinc mines of Iowa. Grandad may have continued on to the Douglas Treadwell Mine, but in 1911, he was on the Fortymile River in the Yukon Territory prospecting for two years. Like many of the Slavs, Grandad went on to the Iron Range mines in Minnesota, where he met Goran Krize and John Begich. In January 1919 he married my grandmother, Catherina Toldo who from an earlier marriage had a daughter Stella who later became a long time clerk at the Fairbanks Co-op Drug. In November, my father, "Tommy" Paskvan Jr., was born. In 1929, Grandad graduated from the William Hood Dunwoody Industrial Institute as a certified welder. Over the years, he blacksmithed and welded out of his own shop and in mines both in Minnesota and Alaska.

As the Great Depression hurt the mine economy, Grandad left the Iron Range to go trapping for a few winter

International Hotel, c. 1939. Courtesy of Candy Waugaman.

months in 1938 and 1939 in Alaska's Fortymile River country. The local Minnesota newspaper wrote: "Tom Paskvan Sr. and Ralph Andrews of Skibo left Tuesday for Alaska on a trapping expedition for two years."

In August through November 1938, Grandad worked for four months at Hirst's Chichagof Mine at Kimshan Cove on Chichagof Island before it closed down. He went on up to Fairbanks and stayed at Pete Mesich's Arctic Hotel, a log hotel on the Chena River. Pete was a kindly illiterate Croatian miner from Ophir who felt a little lost in Fairbanks. He and Grandad invested together, trading labor for investment capital. Grandad bought the Owl Cigar Store, a bar/smoking house [a cigar store offered various tobaccos as well as gambling] in Fairbanks, from Dan Nickolich. In 1939, Grandad bought the International Hotel on Garden Island across from the train depot from John Vukmir, a well-respected businessman. The International was built in 1920 by Emil Pazzo. In 1927, John Vukmir and Chris Radovich bought the International Hotel, which had a bar and cabaret downstairs and inexpensive rooms upstairs, where many bachelor Montenegrins lived. John Miscovich described the International Hotel:

It was a hangout in the winter with the hotel upstairs, gambling in the back end, and pool tables up front. I used to play pool there in the 1930s. I knew Chris Radovich very well. Most of the people were from Montenegro. John Vukmir was from Lika in Croatia, though. There was also Chris Benanich, John Lekich, Mike Merkaich, Bob Bigovich, and Tom Radovich. All those Montenegrins were very proud because they were all big men and had a history of fighting the Turks. They always talked about it.

Joe Paskvan continued: After he bought it, Grandad built the semicircular bar, which became a hallmark of the International Hotel. Grandad applied for and got a job driving thaw points for the Fairbanks Exploration Company. Retired president of Key Bank Bill Stroecker remembered, "Tom Sr. was really proud that when he was almost fifty he could hold his own with the younger men."

Grandad went back and forth between Minnesota and Alaska. In 1940 he, Dad, and the Krize brothers arrived in Fairbanks. Rudy and Louis went to work at the California bar and began investing in downtown Fairbanks. Dad enrolled at the Alaska Agricultural College and School of Mines (UAF) where he played hockey and basketball; he was close to graduating with an engineering degree when World War II broke out. After enlisting in the army, he was assigned to the security of the Richardson Highway, guarding the Interior's artery to the deep-water port of Valdez. He played basketball for the army and was even sent to Canada to play ball.

When the war was over, Dad got a ten thousand dollar G.I. loan. In 1947, he opened Tommy's Elbow Room on Second Avenue between Noble and Lacey streets. Dad wasn't sure if the bar business would succeed, so just in case, he cut a garage door in the building's front wall. He covered the bottom half with boards and above, inserted a plate glass window. If the bar business didn't fly, he'd open a mechanic shop! However, Tommy's did prosper. Grandad made another one of his semicircular bars, emulating the renowned one at the Big I. Tommy's had slot machines, pinball machines, and an ongoing poker game.

There was no TV or live sporting events in Fairbanks then. In Seattle, a Budweiser distributor put films of sporting events and newsreels on the twice-weekly Pan Am flight to Fairbanks. From behind the bar on a sixteen-millimeter projector, Dad would show his clientele the week-old sporting events and news.

Dad and his friends Ken and Mark Ringstad played on a local city league basketball team with Andy Miscovich Sr. and Bill Stroecker. The Ringstad brothers eventually married two of the Potter sisters: Rose and Kate. The third sister, Joyce Potter, my mother, came in 1950 to visit. One day Uncle Mark wanted to drive to Paxson and check out some mining equipment. He asked Aunt Rose and Mother to come along. Once he was there, he needed more help to bring everything back. He called Dad to come help him retrieve the equipment with his A-frame truck that had a winch on the boom. When Dad showed up, Mom snapped a

Tom Paskvan Sr. and Tom Paskvan Jr., Fairbanks, 1940. Courtesy of Joe Paskvan.

photo of him, thinking, "He is so handsome!" On the return trip, Mom rode back with Dad. The following January, they were married. The oldest of their nine children, I was born in 1952. My grandparents lived right behind us at 1106 Fourth Avenue; we were on Third. We had a smaller house, and in 1955 after the third child, Margie, was born, Dad built the new house.

My father planned to expand Tommy's with a cabaret, but the Korean war stopped that because the country required the steel.

In the mid-1950s, construction began on the Distant Early Warning System, the DEW Line, a three-thousand-mile virtual electronic wall of defense across Alaska and Canada. Later my father said that when contrasting Alaska's post-war economy and the impact of the lucrative

DEW Line boom with the later effect of the Trans-Alaska Pipeline on the early 1970s economy, that the former had a more dramatic impact on Fairbanks than the latter.

My father was strongly pro-statehood. There was no infrastructure in place then for an entrepreneur. The Democratic Party, his party, was interested in good business practices, responsible capitalism, not predatory. He was a big advocate of hydroelectric power and was in favor of the Rampart Dam construction. At Tommy's he'd hung a sign saying, "Electricity Powers Progress."

I was six when the U.S. Congress passed the Alaska statehood bill on June 30, 1958. I went into Tommy's and the Coop Drug to see my Aunt Stella Wallace as I delivered newspapers that headlined, "We're In!" Up and down the street, everywhere, people were celebrating in the bars and with bonfires on the street.

Finally in the late 1950s to early 1960s, the extension to Tommy's with its big fireplace and increased seating was built. Tommy's was a working man's bar, but the clientele also included professors, businessmen, UAF students, local teachers, and journalists from the *Fairbanks Daily News-Miner*.

On Father's Day 1965, the *News-Miner* honored Dad and photographed him with his wife and eight of his eventual nine children as "Father of the Year."

In 1968, my father, a supporter of the working man, campaigned for Hubert Humphrey for president.

In late 1970 to 1973, we began construction next to Tommy's on the long-dreamed-of addition. My dad had six sons and taught us all to work hard: building, bartending, cleaning. (I used to bicycle in early every morning and mop the floors.) We did everything from

Margie (hidden), Joe, Frank, Gloria, Tommy, Charles, George, Joyce pregnant with Ted; Front: Steve, Bonnie, 1965. Courtesy of Joyce Paskvan.

welding and hauling concrete bricks to mixing and pouring cement. However, Dad felt that education was the answer. He said, "Without an education, hard work is rewarded only with a bigger shovel."

Sam and Sharon Nault (who owned Sourdough Sam's) leased from us. On the ground floor of the new addition, they ran the Firelight restaurant. Just in time for the pipeline in 1974, we rented office space on the second floor of the addition to Morris-Knudsen and Alyeska Pipeline. Later we rented that space to Howard Rock of the *Tundra Times*.

L–R: Tom Paskvan Sr., Catherine Paskvan, Tommy Paskvan Jr., Joyce Paskvan, Rose Ringstad, Beverly Ringstad, Sylvia Ringstad, Bing Ringstad, c. 1958. Courtesy of Joe Paskvan.

From 1971 to 1978, I tended bar. During my junior year at UAF, I was actually running Tommy's and was responsible for the hiring, firing, ordering, and banking. After the pipeline construction was in full swing, we'd open at 11:30 a.m. with thirty people waiting outside the door. Daily, thousands of transients were passing through with incredible amounts of money.

In May 1975, I graduated from UAF with a degree in political science and a minor in history. I worked full time tending bar on the weekends and nights for three and a half years. It was an exciting time. In 1978 at Tommy's, we converted the Firelight into a nightclub and opened it as the Cabaret featuring a disc jockey with a state-of-the-art sound system synchronized with strobe lights: a high-class disco.

I had kept in good contact with my UAF advisor, so when pipeline construction was over, he told me that if I made a good LSAT score, Seattle University Law School would take me. I studied and was accepted. In August I married Barbara Tritt. For our honeymoon, we drove down the Alcan Highway to enroll me in law school. The year I graduated, we returned to Fairbanks.

For the first six months in 1981, I worked at the newly formed State of Alaska Court of Appeals for Chief Justice Bryner. Then I went into private practice with Lloyd Hoppner. In 1997, I formed my own law firm with my first cousin, Ken Ringstad Jr.: Paskvan-Ringstad PC.

Toastmasters at Tommy's semicircular bar, c. 1962. Courtesy of Joyce Paskvan.

Between my mother, Joyce, and her two sisters, Rose and Kate, the three ladies have produced twenty-five first cousins born in Fairbanks from the late 1940s to the 1960s: quite a concentration.

In 1971 when I was first began bartending, one of the old-timers remembered a story. In 1950 my grandfather was tending bar; some newcomer walked in and ordered an old fashioned. My grandad promptly poured him a shot of liquor backed with beer and answered, "That's about as old fashioned as you get!"

When my father died in 2003, the state Alcoholic Beverage Control Board remarked that he was the longest single-owner liquor license in the history of the state. Tommy's Elbow Room spanned six decades of Fairbanks history, 1947 to 1993. Dad was one of the last of the Yugoslav early Fairbanks saloon owners; the end of an era.

Joe Paskvan, 2004. Courtesy of Joe Paskvan.

161

Chapter 23

Intersecting the North: The Alaska Highway and the Modern Age

Before World War II, Alaska had few roads. Traders, miners, trappers, loggers, fishermen, gold rush immigrants, and Natives made up Alaska's society. Bulldozers were not yet common. Communication with the Outside was limited to letter or telegraph.

The upper Tanana River, known intimately to fur traders like John Hajdukovich and to the local Natives, was accessible only by dogsled, boat, or airplane. There were 4,900 people in the Yukon Territory and 74,000 in Alaska, living mostly on the coast.

Chief John Healy on John Hajdukovich's riverboat, using the historic river highway before the construction of the Alaska Highway, c. 1917.

Alaska's connection to the Outside was limited to sea and some air travel. The Yukon Territory had no sea outlet or road to southern Canada. In the 1930s, British and Canadian officials had begun an efficient air corridor between the North and the Orient, the Great Circle Route. To improve safety, the Canadian government upgraded airports at Grande Prairie in Alberta, Fort St. John and Fort Nelson in British Columbia, and Watson Lake and Whitehorse in the Yukon, calling the linkage the Northwest Staging Route.

In 1940, with Japanese aggression accelerating, the Permanent Joint Board on Defense, made up of Canadians and Americans, began studying how to improve their air corridor for mutual defense.

With the Axis pounding Great Britain, President Franklin D. Roosevelt authorized the Lend-Lease act, entitled "An Act to Promote the Defense of the United States," to help the Allies in early 1941. To supply airplanes to the Allies, the United States noted the Bering Strait was the shortest route for ferrying airplanes to the Soviet Union. However, there was not yet a road linking the United States with Alaska.

In June, Hitler invaded the Soviet Union. Six months later, the Japanese bombed Pearl Harbor. Tensions soared, particularly in the Pacific Northwest. The Japanese were jumping from island to island. Alaska's Aleutian Chain,

Northwest Staging Route

1930

1940

Lend-Lease; Japanese bombed Pearl Harbor
President Roosevelt authorized building of Alaska Highway
Telegraph & telephone connection to "America"
CANOL oil to Whitehorse

1950

162

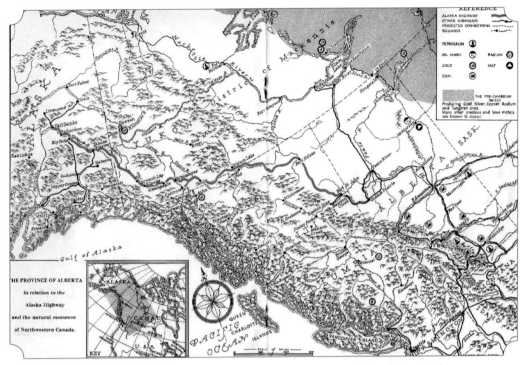

An old Canadian travel bureau map from 1943 shows the route of the Alaska Highway.

750 miles from Japan, was a land corridor leading into the United States. While Alaska had a few, albeit indefensible, military outposts, the Yukon Territory had not a single soldier. Europe was overwhelmed; Canada and the United States feared they might have to face the Axis powers alone. Further concerned the Japanese might seize American shipping lanes, General B. Sommervell, commander of the U.S. Army Service Forces, commissioned Colonel J. H. Graham to study how best to defend North America by sea or by land. The colonel decided on a highway running from Edmondton to Fairbanks, following the Northwest Staging Route.

On February 11, 1942, President Roosevelt authorized the construction of the Alaska Highway. The road, passing through over twelve hundred miles of Canadian territory, would connect with Edmonton at Dawson Creek and continue on to Big Delta, where it would join the Richardson Highway to Fairbanks.

Surveyors and vast amounts of road building supplies began heading north. Workers signed up en masse with the Public Roads Administration, the civilian agency that would subcontract to twenty other companies.

With most U.S. troops committed overseas, the Army experimented by sending black—mostly Southern—soldiers to help build the new highway. More than a third of the 10,607 troops who built the highway belonged to the three all-black regiments, the 93rd, 95th, and 97th, and the African-American 388th Battalion. Black troops were given inferior provisions and required to work with shovels before eventually being given road-building equipment.

Then-Colonel William M. Hoge, commander of the U.S. Army Corps of Engineers, had the initial oversight of the highway construction. With little or no scientific equipment and maps, he sought the most accessible route to connect the existing airfields. Surveyors from the Canadian Department of Transport, the United States Army Corps of Engineers, and the Public Roads Administration (PRA) began planning the route for the road. Trail selection and clearing was up to the U.S. Army primarily while civilian contractors under the PRA followed, widening and straightening the road.

On April 11, 1942, eleven thousand men armed with shovels and bulldozers began a road in the wilderness. Big Delta Army Airfield, Edmondton, and Whitehorse served as the centers for the construction. Hoge made his assault in a three-pronged attack: north from Dawson Creek, shipping supplies by train from Skagway to Whitehorse, and heading south from Big Delta down to Whitehorse. Due to the pressure of war, survey crews pushed hard, practically hearing the bulldozers coming behind them. They consulted Natives and old-timers like trail-blazer John Hajdukovich for the best route.

Urgency for the road increased in June 1942 when the Japanese bombed Dutch Harbor and invaded Attu and Kiska in the Aleutian Chain.

From Dawson Creek, the 341st and the 95th General Service worked north to the 93rd General Service Regiment, just south of Whitehorse. From Whitehorse, the 18th Engineers headed north to Alaska to meet the 97th Engineers.

John Hajdukovich, possibly explaining to an Alaska Highway subcontractor at Tok, c. 1943. Courtesy of Judy Ferguson.

Fred Ferrell in rear, Whitehorse barracks, c. 1942. Courtesy of Fred Ferrell.

The seven regiments with their forty officers and up to twelve hundred enlisted men used twenty D-8 tractors and bulldozers, twenty-four D-4 and R-4 tractors and dozers, two half-yard power shovels, fifty to ninety dump trucks, twelve pickup trucks, six tractor-drawn graders, one portable sawmill, one truck crane, six twelve-cubic-yard carryalls, two pile drivers, and assorted small tools. They worked twelve hour shifts, seven days a week.

Spring nighttime temperatures hit −30˚F; the soldiers' clothing, boots, and equipment were inadequate. However, summer's mosquitoes and no-see-ums were a comparable torment. With no bug dope, the men wore campaign hats with double bug nets. In the heat, they kept their sleeves down and gloves on. The crews ran into muskeg, permafrost, mountain passes, and swollen creeks and rivers. Living in tents and often surviving on Spam and pancakes, the men said the isolation just topped off their misery.

Because of the war, cost, environmental impact, and long-term road use were not the engineers' concern. Following the bulldozers and using local timber, the men made temporary bridges and culverts, dug ditches, and laid corduroy road. A following group widened and straightened the road, reduced steep grades, and covered and packed muddy areas with gravel, creating a road eighteen to twenty-four feet wide. Another following group replaced temporary pontoon bridges with stronger materials.

To supply Whitehorse from Skagway, in October the U.S. Army's 770th Railway Operating Battalion leased the White Pass and Yukon Route Railroad, increasing the train's daily tonnage from two hundred to two thousand, which required thirty-four daily train operations.

To connect the airstrips with Outside communication, Fred Ferrell, a soldier with the Alaska Communication System, spent his war years installing cable. "Our goal," he remembered from his Anchorage home in 2006, "was to supply the first pair of cable wires. They were to transmit both Teletype[?] and telephone service to Ladd Air Force Base by September 1, 1943. We worked in sections and connected them through switching systems to circuits in Chicago and Seattle.

"The first winter in Edmonton [Canada] in 1942," Ferrell recalled, "three of us lived in an eight-by-eight tent." Ferrell paused, "September 1943, I arrived in Whitehorse, where we again lived in eight-by-eight tents. By the summer of 1944," he said, "we had Quonset huts for shelters. A highlight for us," he smiled, "was always the arrival of the sternwheeler *Keno*. Once a month it brought liquor. Men lined up with their ration cards, trying to get a thirteen-ounce bottle. In those days," he pointed out, "there were only five civilian cars in Whitehorse. The old 1898 prospectors' tramway of birch logs was still there. The previous year, Whitehorse had gone from a town of a thousand to ten thousand." Ferrell continued, "Between 1942 and 1945, we laid 994 miles of telephone lines."

The defense fuel pipeline, CANOL (Canadian Oil) project, installed 1,647 miles of four- and six-inch pipe. "Standard Oil," Ferrell continued, "dismantled a refinery in Houston and reassembled it in Whitehorse." The new CANOL Road connected the pump stations and wound 231 miles from the Norman Wells oil field across the broad plains of the Mackenzie River valley, through several mountain ranges, over the Continental Divide, and into Whitehorse.

"By 1943," he continued, "I was in Skagway putting in Teletype; I saw the old railroad that used to run down the middle of Broadway during those war years.

"By fall of 1943," he concluded, "we had installed three channels on an open-wire system from Edmonton to Fairbanks. Alaska could talk to America for the first time. Moreover, by April 1944, the first oil had reached Whitehorse."

The booming wartime construction provided work to some Alaska Natives, but the road and its new population forever changed their lives. Previously a remote wilderness, Nabesna/Northway, Mansfield Lake/Tanana Crossing, Tetlin, and Healy Lake lost the isolation of their subsistence-based lives.

Oscar Albert, born in a tent near Nabesna in 1917, remembered in 1998, "I grew up trapping and traded furs with John Hajdukovich at his Nabesna store. Summers," he continued, "I ran his freight boats. About 1927, I worked in the Kennecott copper mine. By 1940, I was working," he said, "on the new Northway airstrip. When the war started, men suddenly showed up to build the new highway. Sure surprised us!" He added, "The old village of Nabesna relocated in 1946 at today's Northway, just off the new highway."

Charlie David, born 1924 in Tetlin, recalled, "Main thing I remember of war was hardship of village: no food. After awhile, we got ration: oatmeals and other nonfreezables. Morrison-Knudsen," he continued, "was supposed to build an airport in Tetlin but when Army found out Tetlin was in [federal] reserve land, they moved the airstrip to Northway." He added quietly, "The highway opened the world to us. But there was a restriction on the [military] highway; you can't drive."

Fred Ewan, born in 1915 near Gulkana said, "During the wartime, I had a cabin at Moose Creek at Glennallen where they ran the highway. When they rerouted the Richardson Highway through our homes, they didn't warn us but pushed rocks right into our tents. As chief," he said, "I was asked in 1942 to sign a document. I thought," he said with chagrin, "it allowed the military to dig gravel for the Richardson Highway, but I had signed off title to the land." Shaking his head, "Hundreds of soldiers camped there to build the Tok Cutoff Road. We should at least have been paid. But," he added, "that's how things were done them days.

"The Army," he added, "brought measles. Boy, we really suffered. We got into a steam bath—we didn't know—and it really spread.

"The military was also at Meier's Lake during the war. We registered, but they never called us," he recalled.

Ken Coates in his book *North to Alaska!* noted that there were men who forced themselves on local women, usually Native. Justified in their minds by racism, these men were remembered in a 1970s study of the Copper River Basin concerning the effects of the Alaska Highway construction. Fred John Jr. of Mentasta recalled, "Older women who had previously kept quiet began to talk of what they had suffered by some of those men building the Alaska Highway."

Kenny Thomas Sr. of Tanacross, after serving in the Aleutians and in Okinawa, returned home in the mid-1940s. In his book, *Crow is My Boss,* he recalled, "I landed in Fairbanks and caught the military bus home. There was a military police gate at our village! Near our airstrip, there was hangars, hospital, store, warehouses, a PX!"

Change was blowing like a chinook wind.

On October 29, seven and a half months after the start of the Alaska Highway, two soldiers, black and white, met on Caterpillars in a forest. Corporal Refines Sims Jr. of the 97th Engineers met Alfred Jalufka of the 18th Engineers north of Kluane Lake, twenty miles east of the Alaska-Yukon border at Beaver Creek.

A month later, on November 20, a ribbon-cutting ceremony for the completion of the 1,619-mile pioneer road was held at Soldier's Summit in the Yukon. The PRA estimated the final total expenditure for the road at $66,160 per mile. Greyhound got the contract for running soldiers from Canada north to Fairbanks. The leisurely winters of Alaska's Natives, traders, and roadhouses began to evaporate like a southerly wind blowing through the forest. The modern age had come to the north.

"Intersecting the North: the Alaska Highway and the Modern Age" was first published in the state's official anniversary publication, Alaska 50: Celebrating Alaska's 50th Anniversary of Statehood 1959–2009.

First Truck, Dawson Creek to Whitehorse, 1942. Courtesy of Paul Kirsteatter.

Chapter 24

Bobby Miller: Miner's Home to Box Stores on Merhar Avenue

Most of the Alaska-Yugoslav families were from Croatia or Montenegro. A few, like Bobby Miller of Miller Salvage and Arctic Circle Hot Springs, were Slovenian. Most of the Slavic immigrants worked first in the mines: in Minnesota's Iron Range, in the mines at Butte, Montana, at the Douglas Treadwell or at the Alaska-Juneau Mine. When they could leave the mines, they frequently went into the more lucrative saloon trade. The men tended to marry late and to a young woman. The next generation might go into the trades or professions.

Frank, Billy, Mary, Josephine, Albina, Bob, Emma Miller, 1921, in today's Fairbanks Daily News-Miner *parking lot. Courtesy of Bobby Miller.*

Bobby Miller, born in 1917, is an epic of Fairbanks-Slavic history. His father, Frank Miller, established a chain of saloons in Alaska's gold rushes: Fairbanks, Flat/Iditarod, and Chisana. Bobby Miller's ninety-one years span from the old train depot to 2008 with his mother's name, Merhar, on the service road to the new box stores, intersecting with Miller Boulevard. Bobby remembered the days when a man's word was considered his bond.

My father, Frank Miller, was born in Kranj near Ljubljana in 1856 under the Austro-Hungarian Empire. In Slovenia about 1880, he married Andje Merhar, the older sister of my mother, Mary Merhar. By 1890, they had six children to support. Hearing of mine work in Montana, my father left for Butte. He sent for his wife and children, who brought her parents and her sister as well. However, a diphtheria epidemic hit and my father lost his wife Andje and four of their six children.

When Fairbanks struck gold, he headed north. Figuring he'd make more serving the prospectors than digging, he built the Miner's Home Hotel and Roadhouse on Garden Island. In 1903, he returned to Butte where he married his twenty-five-year-old sister-in-law, my mother, Mary, who was twenty-six years his junior. In 1906, they returned north by steamer to Skagway, took the Yukon Railway through the White Pass and on to Whitehorse, arriving by steamer in Fairbanks. In

1909, he went west to the boomtown of Iditarod and built a saloon; in 1913 in the last international gold rush, he built one more bar in Chisana.

My parents had eight children: Mary (Burglin Foran), Albina, Pauline, Max, Josephine, Henry (Rear Admiral Miller), Emma (Vasquez, Alaska Office Supply), me in 1917, and then Billy. All of us learned to work by the time we were five. As we attended school, sometimes Mike Yankovich was also there trying to learn to read English.

My parents were pretty smart people but they had no education. As they fought to survive, they learned to speak English; my mother wrote a little.

In Fairbanks, my father picked up mining and farming properties. At the Miner's Home, he and his partner John Susang briefly showed "moving pictures" as well as had a bar, cigar store, and billiards. At that time in the summer, Fairbanks was about six thousand; two hundred children were in school. There was daily train service to the creeks, two banks, two hospitals, and four newspapers, including daily and weekly. A main recreation was watching the trains come in. We lived in the center of the activity, between the train station and the river. At my father's Miner's Home Bar, miners gathered and complained about mine conditions, arguing that they should unionize. Judge Wickersham didn't like the rabble-rousing. He talked about closing my father's bar, but three years after I was born, Prohibition hit in 1920 and my father had to close his business anyway. By the early 1920s, the railroad was expanding so the abandoned Miner's Home had to be moved to make room for the new train terminal. When I was eight in 1925 I remember watching my father take the old saloon apart and skid it log by log to our nearby lot, where today the *Fairbanks Daily News-Miner* parking lot is. There, out of the Miner's Home Bar, he built us a three-story log home. Dr. Romig and

Frank Miller's Miner's Home Hotel, three doors from Samson's hardware, N.C. Co. powerhouse smoke across Chena River. 1913. Courtesy of Candy Waugaman.

Dr. Lundquist lived nearby. Past Yankovich's farm where the University of Alaska Fairbanks' Large Animal Research Station is today, we had a one-hundred-sixty-acre farm. Every spring, we'd go out there by horse and buggy.

Since he couldn't mine himself, my father invested in Joe Chesna's Big Chena mine and another one in the Wood River country, but he was never paid back. My father, dubbed Big Hearted Frank, lost the money he invested in those mines.

We were one of the poorest families in Fairbanks. I always felt sorry for my mother. Our father did a lot of barking. I learned to do what he said the first time because I didn't want him telling me twice. When I was five, I began knocking on doors for little jobs shoveling snow or hauling coal. My father told me, "When you work a job, you work. Don't be sitting on your fanny." It was good training.

Max Miller, 1958, Miller home. Courtesy of Bobby Miller.

As soon as school was out, I'd run over to my brother Max's auto and truck repair shop. When I was ten, I began fixing cars, washing and polishing them so I could drive them! R. K. Lavery, who had Lavery and Bailey grocery store at Second and Cushman, let me drive his sedan around town.

Every summer, I went out to Livengood where my brother, Max, was mining. When Bill McMahon, the local merchant, wanted to ship a car in, my brother said, "Bob can tear a Model T apart and put it back together." So the manager bought it from Northern Commercial Company (N.C. Co.) in Fairbanks, took it apart, strapped the parts all over the outside of an airplane, and flew it into Livengood. I worked with a mechanic. I was the one who carried the job, but I was only given $7 while the head mechanic got $28.00!

Billy Root used to run buses out to the dredges in Goldstream, Fox, Gilmore, and then across the hills to Cleary and Chatanika. I was too young to get a driver's license but no one cared. I could barely see over the steering wheel of the seven-passenger Studebaker sedan, but I drove for Billy Root. When I was fourteen I drove a truck for the Alaska Road Commission. In 1934, my brother Max began the first big trucking outfit in Fairbanks, General Transportation Company, where Alfred Ghezzi, later of Alaska Freight Lines, got his start.

For a month I borrowed Gene Rogge's truck and after school, with a number two size shovel, I'd dig gravel from the gravel pit and into the truck bed. I dug until the tires went half flat. I knew that would be about six tons. I went around to my neighbors and offered to spread it on their driveway for a buck and a half. I paid Rogge with a battery for his truck.

I graduated from high school in June 1935. The day after I graduated, I went out to Pete Miscovich's mine in Flat. Miscovich was known as a slave driver. He had a tough life raising seven kids over there in Flat. He had to go out and cut wood with a Swede saw and shoot rabbits for his family because during the winter the store there wouldn't give him credit. He drove all his employees; I admired him. He also had the foresight before others to see what heavy equipment could do. In the fall of 1934, Pete bought the first diesel bulldozer in Alaska from the N.C. Co. and had it shipped in. He promised to break me in on that

Johnny Clark, 1945. Courtesy of Bobby Miller.

bulldozer. But he also promised four others, so there were seventeen of us working there with a pick and shovel. Within thirty-three days, fifteen of the seventeen quit; they couldn't take it. All that was left was me, a kid, and old man Popovich. Pete put me on the bulldozer. I figured, "I'm going to for sure learn this great cause I'm sick of working with that pick and shovel!" In 1936, Miscovichs got a bigger Cat, a D-8. For many years, that was the biggest Cat available. For the next seven years I ran a bulldozer for different mining outfits. By 1938–39, I was bulldozing for a five-partner-owned mine, Alder Camp, headed by Jake Drablous and including Pete Miscovich and 'ol man [Martin] Sather Sr. on Fairbanks Creek. By that time, Wise Mike Stepovich was doing well on Fairbanks and Fish creeks. (His wife Vuka was the best woman who ever came across the Atlantic. Before, when the Stepovichs had been poor, Lavery and Bailey's grocery used to grubstake them.)

I've known those old Bohunks ever since I was a kid. The Bojanichs, who had the Model Café with Milo Hajdukovich, were all good guys. Nick Borovich was a mining partner with Spuroni, an Italian, who worked with some of the Bohunks. They and a third partner owned that rich hunk of property at Ester where the dredge sat. When I was small, Borovich and Spuroni came over and told my father how rich that ground was but that the problem was that the gold was too deep, down 135 feet. Back then, there weren't pumps to siphon all that water out. That land doesn't have much of a drainage, which is a big problem. Fairbanks Exploration Company bought the land; it was so rich that they couldn't even take a full bucketload before they had to stop for a clean up.

Back in 1939, Max built an apartment building on Illinois Street. I went into partnership with him. Most of the early Fairbanks truckers got their start by working for Max's General Transportation Company hauling from Valdez to Fairbanks. In 1938, Pete Daugherty gave Alfred Ghezzi a break and bought him a 1937 truck for $450. Max charged twelve dollars a ton to haul a load from Fairbanks to Livengood but Ghezzi cut prices by twenty-five percent and took my brother's business. Johnny Clark (whom I really liked) became Ghezzi's manager. He sorta became the trucking law. I wanted to work with him. Ghezzi offered me more than my brother had so I went to work for Ghezzi's Alaska Freight Lines! Ghezzi was the first in Alaska to get a diesel truck.

In 1940, I drove it all summer to Livengood. Since the road was full of potholes, and the trucks were under-powered then—even with the pedal to the metal—it was a rough fifteen-hour round trip. Ghezzi was a steamer all his life! One winter, Johnny Clark, Jess Bachner, Charlie Simmons, and I were each driving trucks to Livengood. But in those days before territorial or state road maintenance, we had to keep the road open ourselves.

After I returned from World War II, Max and I based out of his apartment building on Illinois and ran Interior Equipment. I bought and sold cars and trucks. Old man Stroecker

[Ed Stroecker Sr.] at the bank [First National Bank of Fairbanks] would always loan me money without security or a submitted payment plan. He knew I was good for it. He and— later his son, Bill—were an invaluable help to me.

In 1946, I got into aviation for two and a half years. Just after the war, the military began selling airplanes. Pollock and I got a fourteen-passenger DC-2, a forerunner of the DC-3, for fifty thousand dollars. When the military started selling, I bought. I got three DC-3s, the first big airplanes. Together, my brother and I had eight airplanes, beginning Northern Air Service. At that time, there were three major aviation companies servicing the Interior: Ray Petersen Flying Service in Bethel and Anchorage, [Frank] Pollock's Air Service, and our Northern Air Service. In 1946, we and five smaller companies, merged into Northern Consolidated Airlines. I ran it out of Fairbanks. We served Tanana, Kokrines, Ruby, Galena, Koyukuk, Nulato, and Kaltag and spider-webbed into the surrounding mining areas. Another run went to Bethel, McGrath, and Lake Minchumina. With good timing and simple maneuvers, we built up to thirty-three airplanes and serviced the entire Yukon and Kuskokwim drainages.

Wien Alaska Airways and Northern Consolidated already operated like siblings. Wien had all the government subsidies north of the Yukon River, and Northern Consolidated had everything south of the river. In 1947 to 1948 we merged with Wien and based out of Fairbanks. Together, we had all of Alaska. In 1948 when the Wien headquarters moved to Anchorage, I retired because I didn't want to live in Anchorage, but I stayed active on the board.

However, based on a claim of bankruptcy Wien sold out in the early 1980s to Household Finance. All of the forty-five hundred stockholders were forced to sell at a low price. At that time, Wien had ten Boeing 737 jets, an excellent airline. About nine months later, one of the Anchorage board officers who had handled the original sale to Household Finance bought Wien back, then shut down the airline and sold all the assets. I understand he made a lot of

Al Ghezzi, former owner of Alaska Freight Lines, 2003, Anchorage. Courtesy of Charlie Barr.

Bobby Miller driving Al Ghezzi's first diesel truck in Alaska, with a 3,000 gallon tank, Livengood, 1940. Courtesy of Bobby Miller.

Bobby Miller, Miller Bentley Equipment office, 1968. Courtesy of Bobby Miller.

money. I negotiated with Household Finance and told them I wasn't paid a fair price for my stock. Based on a related court judgment, Household Finance sent me a check for an additional $87,560.40. To my knowledge, no other stockholders were ever paid anything.

When I began buying airplanes from the military, I went to the first military surplus sale in Fairbanks where they had 109 pieces of equipment up for sale. Fairbanks was so small then. I thought, "Whoever gets that pile—that will be enough to last Fairbanks as long as I live. I wanted it all or nothing. I sat and thought and came up with the bid of $30,650. I thought, "If I get it, I'm going into the surplus business. If not, I won't because there would be no room in Fairbanks for two surplus yards. Wrong as hell." I won the bid by a mere $44 margin and moved the surplus out to the nine acres next to Noyes Slough where Fred Meyer East and Safeway are now, part of the old Bentley Brothers dairy. [Bentley Dairy operated under homestead grants in the 1920s through 1947.] In 1953 I went into business with George and Harry Bentley, who had run their dairy on their 849 acres north of Fairbanks. They had the money and the land. I gave my labor in exchange for not paying rent. I had the Miller and Bentley Equipment office there and could store surplus anywhere on their 849 acres. My Miller Salvage and car sales business headquarters was at Max's apartments on Illinois. Our salvage inventory included well over a thousand vehicles. I was the only one who knew the inventory and where everything was. I bought from all over the state: Anchorage, Big Delta, Fairbanks. A surplus expert once told me that I had the largest surplus yard in North America. In the 1960s, the Bentley brothers were getting old and asked me to help them set up a trust for their property.

I asked my nephew Cliff Burglin to handle it. He turned the 849 acres into the Bentley Family Charitable Trust in 1969 and sold a lot of my salvage to a Taiwan-based company. [Bentley Mall, Fred Meyer, Walmart, and the box stores on Merhar Avenue are on the Bentley Family Trust land. Merhar Avenue is named for Mary Burglin Foran and Bobby Miller's mother, Mary Merhar Miller. Miller Boulevard is for the Miller family.] By 1974, I moved the rest of the equipment out to the new Miller Salvage on Thirtieth Avenue. I sold the Illinois Street apartments and part of the Miller Salvage business to Alex Haman. I ran the remaining Miller Salvage at its new location on Thirtieth Avenue. I did a good business but lacking good help, I sold the business to Tom Carter about 1984.

When gold was high in the 1970s, I did dragline mining for a small company in Manley Hot Springs. To help the poor miners who were at the mercy of the local jewelers, I set up a fair gold buying business, Alaska Gold Sales, in the Northward building. I didn't take a dime and my assayer, Tiny Thomas, didn't either. We just bought and sold gold to help the miner.

In 1977, I conducted an Alaska gold nugget sale, the only gold auction in the world, held at Alaskaland. We hired First National Bank's security guard. The gold was laid out on tables. I had ten thousand ounces of gold, and I was very nervous. I told everyone I had insurance but in reality, they had cancelled at the last minute. I had volunteers that I didn't even know, but they were honest people.

In 1979, I owed Bill Stroecker, the president of Alaska First National Bank, $420,000 on an accumulation of notes. Well, I went to an auction that day and I spent $365,000 more on Alyeska Pipeline's big sale. I was there six days and got quite a few hundred tons of it.

I wrote them a check and went to the bank the next day and told Bill, "Well, you gotta loan me $365,000." I was in the bank then four times a month, borrowing and paying, paying and borrowing. I sold a lot of the surplus but a lot of it is still at the old Miller Salvage grounds.

In 1980, I bought Arctic Circle Hot Springs at Central on the Steese Highway. [In 1905, Cassius Monohan homesteaded 106 acres around the springs and then sold it in 1909 to Franklin Leach. In 1924, Leach built an early runway. By 1930, Leach had hauled materials for the four-story resort up the Yukon River and overland by wagon. His carpenter, John Ahoe, built the main buildings and cabins. The 139°F water from the springs was pumped at 103°F into the Olympic-sized pool.] On reconstruction, upkeep, and maintenance, I have poured millions into the resort. At the springs, I catered not to tourists but to the people of Alaska, the miners. I believe in meat and potatoes. Tourists weren't my class.

I have been in every business but never saloons 'cause I don't believe in that. In 1981, our two-story home built from the old Miner's Home saloon and located where the *News-Miner* parking lot is today was torn down.

Recently at a party, I asked Bill Stroecker, retired president of First National Bank of Fairbanks, "Hey, Bill—all those years, why did you loan me all that money?" He replied, "I thought you knew what you were doing." I did. Since I was five years old, I have worked hard. For me, it wasn't primarily about the money but for the people of Alaska, the miners. They came first. I worked hard and tried to treat people right.

Bobby Miller, Admiral (Hank) Miller, reporter Ip Lien, Mary Burglin Foran, and Albina Miller at Mary Miller's (mother) funeral, 1967. Courtesy of Bobby Miller.

Chapter 25

Jackovich: Owners of Samson's Hardware and the Big I, Digging Alaska's Future

Whenever I pump gas into my car and look down at the nozzle sleeve, "Jackovich Industrial & Supply, Inc." is a footprint of the Alaska-Yugoslavs. Like many of the Slavs, the Jackovich family began in the mines and bar trade. They benefited from the construction booms of Fairbanks: post World War II, the DEW Line, and the Trans-Alaska Pipeline.

Owners of Samson's Hardware, the Jackovich family closed the store on December 12, 2008, after 104 years of service. With plans underway for a new bridge connecting to Barnette Street, Samson's, the Carrington, Lounsbury, Cook, and Haman buildings are slated for removal, leaving only the Big I bar and the Fairbanks Daily News-Miner.

Joe and Melo Jackovich, Fairbanks, c. 1970s. Courtesy of Buz and Iris Jackovich.

Joe Jackovich, who with his nephew Buz Jackovich originated Jackovich Tractor, shared the family's story before his death in 2000.

ur family was from a relatively important market town Mrkopalj, Croatia, thirty-one miles east of the coastal town of Rijeka. Next to the neighboring town of Sunger in the mountains, origin of the Fairbanks Paskvans, Mrkopalj's main resources were sheep and timber. Under the Austrian Empire in 1785, Mrkopalj was declared a free, albeit Austrian royal town. During the end of the nineteenth to early twentieth century, the pan-Slavic movement became strong, resulting partly in World War I. To escape the foreign draft in 1912, my eighteen-year-old father, Ignac Jakovac, left Croatia, a part of the Austrian Empire. He got aboard an outbound ship to North America and arrived in Iowa, where he began calling himself Vance. After the end of World War I, my fifteen-year-old mother and her parents met my father in Iowa, where my parents were married. My father and his brothers began working in the coal mines. All the children except my older brother Vance, sister Mary, and I were born there. My

1920 · International Hotel built · 1930 · Great Depression · 1940 · WWII · 1950 · DEW Line · 1960 · Fairbanks flood · 1970 · Fairbanks Key Bank parking lot · 1980 · Trans-Alaska Pipeline · 1990 · 2000 · 2010 · New Cushman St. bridge

folks moved to Nebish, Minnesota, twenty-five miles north of Bemidji, where land was selling for fifty cents an acre. Along with thirteen other Croatian farmers, Dad got forty acres. Our family farmed with the Rilovich family.

As we kids began school, our name was changed to Jackovich. When I was eighteen, my uncles took me over to the mine and tried to talk me into working there. I said, "That's for mice, not for me!" When mine owners didn't have mules, they got Croatians. It was tough back then trying to raise kids and make it. I was the youngest but my older brothers were twenty-one and they had to go somewhere to find a job!

During the Depression, although it wasn't easy, my brothers got an eighteen-dollar train ticket to Seattle and a thirty-dollar steamship ticket, steerage class (down with the cattle), to Alaska. (If you knew someone on deck, you could go up from time to time.) In 1932, my oldest brother Frank went to the Independence gold mine in the Talkeetna Mountains where he got three to four dollars a day. He was lucky to get a job. Strandbergs' Tofty at Manley Hot Springs was paying three dollars a day. But Fairbanks Exploration Company paid four to six dollars: good pay! In a season, a man could make six hundred to twelve hundred dollars. For two years, Frank was intermittently in Alaska. In 1934, my second-oldest brother, Melo, came up to Palmer. In 1940, Frank was back in Minnesota where he got drafted. Melo went to diesel mechanic school in Chicago.

On December 7, 1941, Pearl Harbor hit; Melo, back in Anchorage, got drafted. After the war he met Marie, a girl from Broken Arrow, Oklahoma, and they married. He and Marie bought a home in Oregon so that Buz and his sister could go to "the better schools of the Lower Forty-eight." During the summers, Melo and Buzy would visit Fairbanks. Buzy remembered following his father through his bars, waiting on a stool and being treated to silver dollars from the old-timers.

In 1945, I was still in Minnesota where I married a nice Irish girl, Dolores. Oh, my father was upset. There was nothing but that I should marry a Croatian girl. My mother was

Jack Mistic, (Mary Jackovich's husband); Jackovich brothers and sister: Frank, Melo, Vance, Joe, Mary Mistic, c. 1970s. Courtesy of Buz and Iris Jackovich.

better about it. Hell, when you go to America, how many Croatian girls do you see? Yeah, Croats can be pretty bad about that. I wanted Vance, the brother closest to my age, to be my best man, but he was still in the service. Once married, Dolores and I came up to Alaska. Fairbanks had a short-lived formal Yugoslav society, headed up by Charlie Miller until he died in 1950. There were lots of Slavs here: Lupovich who had Fairbanks Liquor on College Road, Pete Voich, Jimmy Stupovich, Pete Mesich, Marco Vujovich (who helped my brother at the mine), and Sam Panovich, a miner who died in a strange fire.

In the 1940s, Melo owned two bars: the Riverside and the Savoy, both on First Avenue (later he bought Wise Mike's Stepovich Building and ran the Savoy there at Second and Lacey). I helped my brother Melo by running a bulldozer while my wife did the camp cooking at his mine, south of Rampart at Hunter Creek. I ran the dozer for four summers from 1946 to 1950. I worked for a percentage of yield, not for wages. (Nowadays, no one helps anyone. Now, everyone has to have money.) Two miles down, Little Minook was the only other mine in the area. They had four Cats and a dragline. We never had a dragline. We just had dozers and sluice boxes.

During the winters, I tended Melo's bars on First Avenue. My wife and I were raising kids at the same time. Funny thing if you're a Catholic, kids come with marriage, seven of them: Katie, Joey, Jeanne, John, Jennifer, Jaime, and Jeffrey. Also in the 1950s, the Sexton family arrived, including Bill, Gus, Jack, Mary Jo, and Mike. Bill began Bill's Drive-In. Jack bartended around town. He became friends with Bob Bigovich at the Nevada bar, and eventually he became like a son to "Bigo," a Montenegrin from Risan. Bigovich had a history with the Nevada and the International.

The original builder of the International Hotel, Emil Pozza, c. 1958, Courtesy of John Jackovich.

Pete Mesich, Croatian miner from Ophir, owner of Arctic and International Hotels, Fairbanks. C. 1938. Courtesy of Jack Sexton.

Blažo "Bob" Bigovich, c. 1989, Fairbanks. Courtesy of Jack Sexton.

Across the river near Samson's Hardware, the International Hotel was built in 1920 by Emil Pozza on property he didn't own. The railroad took the first building and deeded nearby land to Pozza to rebuild the hotel. In 1927 Chris Radovich bought the hotel from Pozza for thirteen thousand dollars, but business was poor. He tried to sell it back to Pozza, but Pozza hadn't a dime. In the late 1920s, Radovich went in with John Vukmir of the Nevada bar. After Radovich's death, in 1938 Vukmir sold to Thomas Paskvan Sr. who with miner Pete Mesich's help bought the hotel. Mesich and Tom Paskvan Sr. had worked a quasi-partnership of sorts. Paskvan Sr. traded labor for investment capitol with Mesich. In 1941, based on confirmed grievances, the International was deeded over to Mesich. In a subsequent lawsuit

Joe and Dolores Jackovich, Diamond Horseshoe bar, Fairbanks, c. 1955. Courtesy of Joe Jackovich.

in 1955, Thomas Paskvan (Sr.), appellant, v. Pete Mesich, an incompetent person, by his guardian, Blazo N. Bigovich, appellee, Paskvan lost any claim to the International Hotel. After paying off Mesich's heirs, the estate seems to have gone to Bob Bigovich.

By then, Curly Levi owned the Savoy at Second and Lacey and the Redwood next to Tommy's Elbow Room. Bigovich, Sexton and Lloyd "Curly" Levi shared the liquor license and various responsibilities within the Mesich estate which included the Nevada bar and the International Hotel. The Levi and Sexton arrangement ended in litigation. In 1962, Jack Sexton was the sole owner of the International Hotel. With Bigovich, he also continued running the Nevada bar across the river. Much later, my son John bought the old International Hotel, The Big I.

In the 1950s, I knew the DEW Line was coming and Fairbanks would be hopping. So I got in the nightclub business, running the Diamond Horseshoe bar out on South Cushman from 1952 to 1958. I sold the Diamond Horseshoe then and began working in a partnership with George Thompson, distributing vending machines. I used to drive routinely to Delta and Allen Army Airfield, later Fort Greely.

Melo's son Buz Jackovich arrived in Fairbanks to live in 1955. In 1959, Melo and I bought the Fairbanks Bar on Second Avenue across from today's Soapy Smith's restaurant. While Melo was out at his mine, I tended the bar. (He usually had people out there working with him as well.) The Fairbanks Bar building extended to First Avenue. We rented the half on First to a restaurant. One time I caught the manager, Sam Hudaka, trying to set the building on fire. He'd wired cans of fuel up to the ceiling and started a fire nearby, figuring that when someone opened the door, the rush of oxygen would cause a flash fire. But outside the firemen saw smoke, black soot on the inside of the windows, and knew the fire was oxygen deprived. They slowly eased the door barely open, slipped in, hit the fire with hoses, and saved the structure.

Mining was shut down during World War II but after the war, there was all that left-over junk that became surplus cached at Badger Road Six Mile Camp. Man, oh man: Caterpillars, Caterpillars, Cats! In 1945, mining started back up and that surplus became draglines and dozers for the miners, just what they needed! (Sure, it was great for the community but not competing against a business selling the same merchandise!) Melo got one cat for $1,800 and another for $3,200, both Le Tourneau! His partner bought a hydraulic dozer with forty feet of cable running off steam for $3,500. Here in Fairbanks for seven dollars an hour, I overhauled Roy Minook's complete dragline. For six years, my nephew Buzy worked for the Seattle-based Western Tractor.

In 1967, six of our Fairbanks Slavic families went to Yugoslavia: the Stepovichs, Franichs, Milos Boconovich, Sophie Krize, me, and Dolores, twenty-one of us. We and Sophie Krize rented a VW in Vienna. Communist survivors of the Austrian Empire, the Croatians didn't like our Austrian license tag. They wanted to know what we were doing. We about got run outta there with pitchforks. My Croatian was dated by sixty years. From the inbreeding of Romanian, Serbian, and Montenegrin, Croatian words had changed their meanings! At the outset of our trip, we had to submit our exact itinerary to the police. When we skipped a town, suddenly three cop cars pulled up on each side of us! Throughout our itinerary, they'd kept an eye on us, but there was no way when asked that I would give them my passport for whatever reason. But those were the days: Tito kept all the ethnicities together. Now, Yugoslavia's destroyed. Wish we had another Tito.

At Western Tractor, Buz had gotten to know all the contractors and the lines of heavy equipment. He knew the Alaska pipeline was coming. In late 1968, Buz called me to say the owners of Western Tractor in Seattle, the Fay family, had decided to sell their Fairbanks store. I told him to find out what they wanted. On January 2, 1969, we made an agreement: fifty percent down and the rest in payments. Melo sold the bar and we did the rest in payments. When he went to Eddie Stroecker Jr. at First National Bank for part of the down payment, he said, "Forget Western Tractor! Call it Jackovich Tractor!" He insisted the business needed personality and that familiarity would give us exposure. He was right! Buz enjoyed painting *Western* off the sign and inserting *Jackovich*. Melo was never in the business; I became fifty-one percent owner and Buz got forty-nine percent. Western Tractor had been only a tire warehouse before but we extended into cable rigging. The seller subtracted twenty-five hundred dollars so we could afford a wire rope cable press for making slings, used by miners for draglines. One of the older names, Le Tourneau, made trucks and scrapers that are pulled behind. They used cables for hydraulic lines. Caterpillars didn't have hydraulics yet; those didn't come out until the late 1950s to early 1960s. Then they got rid of the cable dozers and everything went hydraulic.

Buz Jackovich, 2004. Courtesy of Iris Jackovich.

To supply pipeline construction equipment, we built another Jackovich Tractor in Valdez in 1974. Two years later we added on to our Fairbanks store in the industrial sub-division. We were very busy throughout the construction of the pipeline, supplying the camps along the eight-hundred-mile road with ripper and digger (ground engagement teeth) buckets and cables and servicing what we sold. In 1976 we bought the Anchorage Western Tractor store and converted it to a third Jackovich Tractor outlet. In 1978 we closed our Valdez store. The same year, we built our larger Jackovich store in Anchorage, upgrading to a new building. In 1980, we did the same in Fairbanks, building across the street from the old store. That year, I bought Samson's Hardware, its warehouses, and the Johnny Albright apartment building behind Samson's. In 1985 we changed our name to Jackovich Industrial and Construction Supply Inc. In 1995 and 2000, we built the Parker Stores, specializing in hydraulic hoses and fittings in both Fairbanks and Anchorage.

Since we opened in 1969, all seven of our children have worked in the business. Joey ran the Valdez store. John was president of Jackovich in Fairbanks with Jennifer, Jaime, Katie, and Jeff working alongside. Jeanne had the Anchorage store.

An Ohio-based petroleum company offered loyal customers free gasoline pump sleeves imprinted with customized advertising. Shoot, it was free advertising so in 1995, we began sleeving all our gas pumps with the "Jackovich Industrial & Construction Supply" label. Every time someone pumped gas they thought of Jackovich.

The -viches began in mining and bars; what else was there then? Charlie Miller had the Dreamland bar; Danny Pekich used to work for Miller before he became the Odom distributor. The Klondike, Fairbanks Exploration Company, Cap Lathrop's coal mine: it was all about Slavs pushing carts; the Slavs did it all. Who else would? And stay in this country as well?

At the age of seventy-eight in 2000, Joe Jackovich passed away.

In 1971 when the Nevada Bar was torn down to enlarge the Key Bank parking lot, owner Jack Sexton moved his bar business into the existing bar at the International Hotel down from Samson's. The bar was nicknamed the Big I. After Sexton ran the bar for thirty-five years, and after John had shown Jack his interest and having started negotiations, Jack Sexton said that at that point there was only one person he'd sell the bar to: Johnny Jackovich. Six years after his father's death, Johnny began building up the old International, first built in 1920 by Emil Pozza. After the new Barnette bridge construction, the Big I is slated to be an island in the midst of a new traffic pattern by 2010. The family plans to relocate Samson's Hardware, which first opened in 1904.

Joe Jackovich with Jackovich Industrial and Construction Supply's ground engagement teeth and bucket, 1996, North Slope. Courtesy of Buz and Iris Jackovich.

Chapter 26

Who Was Big Ray?

very week we get asked at least once, 'So who was Big Ray?'" Monty Rostad, owner-partner of Fairbanks Big Ray's Classic Alaska clothing store, grinned. Like most of the Second Avenue business owners, Milan Raykovich, "Big Ray," was a Montenegrin! As we celebrate Alaska statehood anniversary in 2008–2009, the oil discovery that had a key impact on Alaska's case for statehood was linked to the Anchorage Army-Navy Surplus Store: the Kenai oil discovery of 1957.

In 1999, four months after the NATO bombing of the Federal

Alaska Agricultural College and School of Mines (University of Alaska Fairbanks) basketball team. Back, L: Al Malden, Stanley Hill, John O'Shea, Jack Wilbur, Milan Raykovich, Donald George, Harry Lundell, Roy Moyer. Front: Richard Mahan, Coach James Ryan, Manager Earl Beistline, Ted Kukkola. 1936–37. Courtesy of Monty Rostad.

Republic of Yugoslavia, I prepared to go to war-torn Yugoslavia and take aid with me. Fairbanks doctors donated medical supplies. Monty Rostad of Big Ray's also helped.

Petar and Zorka Raykovich (Rajkovic), Big Ray's parents, were from Kosijeri, Montenegro, a village nine miles from the birthplace of John Hajdukovich. Married when Petar was twenty five and she was fifteen, they immigrated to the mines of Washington state. In 1917, Milan "Big Ray" Raykovich was born on their family farm twenty miles outside of Ellensburg, Washington, in farming and coal country. Milan's father worked in the mines while his wife grew a garden, canned food, and raised their children, Milan, Phil, Ben, and Olga. Like many Montenegrins, the oldest son, Milan, was tall with a commanding appearance. Like other local Slavic families, they gathered for holidays at the Serbian fraternity hall in Seattle. Some of the Slavs had moved on to Alaska, making a network all the way to Fairbanks. Nick and Angie Borovich, John Vukmir, and Peter Miscovich in Fairbanks were friends of the Raykovich family.

Slavs love basketball, and at 6'7", on his Washington college campus Milan Raykovich turned heads on the basketball court. Family friend Nick Borovich mentioned to Raykovich that he might consider playing ball for the Alaska Agricultural College and School of Mines (later the University of Alaska Fairbanks). Raykovich transferred and between 1936 and 1937, he became the school's tallest player and a local star.

In 1940, Croatian-Americans from Minnesota's Iron Range, Tommy Paskvan Jr. and his friends Rudy and Louis Krize arrived in Fairbanks, looking for work. The Krize brothers got work bartending, soon bought their own bars, and managed somehow to buy the lower end of Second Avenue from Cap Lathrop. They began building on their new property on the rather vacant lower Second Avenue.

By then Raykovich and his brother were in Anchorage, running a pool hall and bar. As World War II threatened Alaska, vast amounts of money, construction and people poured in, more than all the gold rushes combined. Bar business skyrocketed.

Captain Glenn Miller of the U.S. Army Signal Corps and his sergeant John "Mac" McManamin liked to come in and play pool at Big Ray's bar. Graduates of the Great Depression, Miller and Mac saw Anchorage as a business bonanza waiting to happen. They figured that when the war was over, they would sell military surplus cold weather gear: boots, pants, parkas, jerry cans, and ahkio sleds. There was a market, and Miller and Mac could supply.

In 1947, Miller, Mac, and their friend Howard Cruver began selling surplus in their new Army-Navy Surplus Store on Fourth Avenue. It went so well that they decided to open a store in Fairbanks. A friend, "Honest John" Brennan, opened their Honest John's surplus store in Charlie Main's old five and dime between First and Second on Noble. However, Honest John died. One evening in Anchorage, Glenn Miller discussed with Big Ray their need for a partner in Fairbanks. Raykovich knew the town, knew how to run a business, and was good with the public. Miller offered Big Ray and his brother a partnership, saying the store would be called Big Ray's. The Raykovichs opened at Charlie Main's but then moved on to a Quonset hut on the river (near today's Morris Thompson building).

A year earlier, Rudy and Louis Krize had opened their restaurant, the Café Aurel, on lower Second Avenue. However, after many frustrations they threw in the towel. Knowing the Raykovichs were down at the river working out of a Quonset hut, they asked Big Ray if he'd like to buy the new Krize building on Second Avenue. In 1951, the Raykovichs opened Big Ray's Surplus Store on Second and ran it out of Krize's building for the next ten years.

Big Ray's Surplus Store, c. 1955, Fairbanks. Courtesy of Monty Rostad.

Big Ray bought the old Waechter's meat market complete with an elevator at 543 Second Avenue. He leased the building and the lessee operated the Crystal Room bar there.

Above Big Ray's Surplus Store, the Krize brothers, Ted, Louis, and Frank, opened the Flame Lounge; they also bought Top O' the World clothing at Third and Lacey from "Happy" Holter.

By the mid-1950s as northern oil exploration developed, major oil company geologists were arriving in Anchorage. Needing cold-weather clothing, they shopped at the Army-Navy Surplus Store. Miller's shoe clerk, Locke Jacobs, listened intently to the geologists and asked questions. With no money but through grueling research, Jacobs devoted himself to learn not only geology but the local land and oil possibilities. After recording reams of land office data and tracking on oil leases, he decided that the Swanson River Kenai Peninsula was the place to invest.

Glenn Miller's son, Mike Miller, recalled, "Jacobs approached Dad and the other employees repeatedly. Concerned that Jacobs' oil speculations might ruin his employees, Dad asked, 'How much would it take to

Milan Ray Raykovich, 1956.
Courtesy of Nick Stepovich.

shut you up?' '$1,000,' Locke replied. 'Fine,' Dad said, and wrote out the check." Eventually Miller along with thirteen other investors including Mac, the Raykovich brothers, Robert Atwood of the Anchorage Daily Times, banker Elmer Rasmuson, and Wilbur Wester of Westward Hotel invested, forming the Group of Fourteen. These key businessmen, particularly Wester, pressured Congress to drill in Alaska. In 1957 when Richfield Oil Company struck oil in Swanson River, the prospects of Alaska statehood improved, showing Alaska could support itself.

In 1961 when the checks from Richfield Oil (later, ARCO) began arriving, Big Ray and Glenn Miller were ready to sell Big Ray's. They ran into Louis Krize on the street. "Hey, we wanna sell!" they called out. Right there on Second Avenue, a deal was struck.

After Frank and Louis Krize took over Big Ray's Surplus Store, in 1967, the Fairbanks flood badly damaged the Top O' the World clothing store on Lacey Street. In 1968, the Krize Corporation managed by Dennis Krize expanded Big Ray's building and added an upstairs with offices and storage. He dropped the "Surplus Store" handle to "Big Ray's." He added Red Wing boots and clothes for the working man to his surplus inventory. He enlarged the Krize Building to also accommodate the Sportland Arcade and café and its newsstand as well as the new Top O' the World clothing. From 1961 to 1978, the Krize brothers owned Big Ray's with its entrance on Third and ran the Sportland café out of the Second Avenue entrance.

In the 1950s, Dick Cruver took over his brother Howard's partnership in the Anchorage store. Mike Miller and his friend Monty Rostad worked during the summers. In 1978,

Rostad graduated in business from college but intended to move to Texas. That same year Glenn Miller told Rostad the partners were buying Big Ray's back from the Krizes, and would Rostad consider running Big Ray's? Rostad agreed to for a year. For the next two years, Glen Miller continued to offer Rostad a check if he'd just stay one more year.

"In 1980," Rostad smiled, "I knocked out the separating wall and converted the café into Big Ray's boot department. We converted what had been the old Flame Lounge into warehouse space. We have continued to expand," he pointed out, "to over 23,000 square feet. In 2006, we purchased the building from Sophie and Shirley Krize."

Dick Cruver asked his son, Mark, to replace him while Glenn asked his son, Mike, to take his place. Rostad added, "I was very fortunate. Glenn and Dick offered me the same opportunity as they did their sons. In the 1980s, Mark, Mike, and I became equal partners in the two stores."

Mike Miller added, "In 1988 on a Seattle buying trip for the stores, we visited the Longacres Race Track. Big Ray had a horse competing. 'Well,'" Miller grinned, "'if it's Big Ray's, we figured it had to win!' We placed a bet and we won!" At the track, they learned that Big Ray had just retired from a career as a successful Budweiser distributor.

Angie Borovich Geraghty who'd known the Raykovichs for a lifetime, said, "Everything Ray touched seemed to turn to gold!" However, in 1989 at age 71, Big Ray was gone.

From 1979 to 2008, Mark Cruver, Mike Miller and Monty Rostad have been at the helm of the business, half of the stores' lifetime. "Between both outlets," Rostad said, "we have sold more Carharts per capita than anyone else in the world!

"Today," he continued, "we carry all the name brands. We listen to our customers and have customized a line of Alaska clothes based on their requests." He added, "In January, we also bought Mac's Sport Shop in Kodiak."

"There's no question," he added, "that we work harder today than we used to. A business has to evolve, be computerized, control its buying, have sharp advertising, pay good wages and benefits, and particularly, span the changes of ownership.

"Big Ray's," he added, "is a story of Alaska's development, of loyal customers, of Millers, Cruvers, McManamins, Raykovichs, Krizes and now, Rostad; each store is Alaska-owned and operated. We fill the niches the 'box stores' can not. We are so grateful to the people of Alaska for their support. The year 2007 was the sixtieth year for us; we are classic Alaska.

Monty Rostad, Big Ray's, Fairbanks, 2008. Photo by Judy Ferguson.

Note: Mike Miller remarked, "The Group of Fourteen were the only private oil leaseholders who have ever made money off of Alaska oil."

184

Chapter 27

Hello, Central? Get me Alaska: Fred Ferrell

*Territorial Alaska did not have telephone connections
with "America" until World War II. Limited capacity and multiparty lines remained the rule in much of
the state through the 1970s. As a soldier during World
War II, Fred Ferrell helped install the first telephone
lines from the Lower 48 to Alaska, following the Alaska
Highway. With only a sixth-grade education, for forty-
eight years he was associated with every new communications technology that came into Alaska, from 1942 to
1990. These days Fred and his Alaska Communications
System friends have breakfast together every morning at
Denny's in Anchorage. One morning when I was there,
Fred told his story.*

*Fred Ferrell Alaska Communications
System, c. 1943, Whitehorse, Yukon
Territory, Canada. Courtesy of Fred
Ferrell.*

wenty years after Lt. Billy Mitchell installed the telegraph wire for the Washington-
Alaska Military Cable and Telegraph System (WAMCATS, forerunner of Alaska
Communications System/ACS) in the Alaska interior, Fred was born in 1921 in Texas.
In those days, everyone was on the old analog, one-line party, ten-ring telephone
system operating on open wires, often disrupted by wind, frost, and ice. Many had
no telephones at all. Communication wasn't missed because we didn't know what it was. In
1926, my dad, a farmer, raised cattle, but to raise the falling price of beef, the government
bought and shot cattle in 1932 to 1933. Many were hungry, and the failure to help them was
a communications problem. The grocery stores had no refrigeration to preserve meat and no
telephone to communicate with the hungry families. The local butcher brought beef to the
store on Saturdays when people came to shop, but with daily communication, the grocer
could have dispersed beef more often to those in need.

When I was eleven in 1932, I had to quit school in sixth grade to help support my family.
By the time I was fifteen, I was working in the oil fields for Lone Star Gas. Just before I got
my draft notice, a new communications technology, the first twelve-channel cable, transcon-
tinental K system, was installed.
Working around the clock,
AT&T's Frank Borstedt had
completed installation of
the cable from Atlanta
to Los Angeles on Dec.
6, 1941, the day before
Pearl Harbor was hit.

After getting drafted in 1942,
I began basic electrical courses in Missouri,

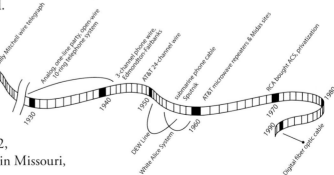

followed by six weeks at Michigan Bell telephone school. Then I was assigned to the Alaska Communications System in Seattle.

Following the attack on Pearl Harbor, the government feared the Japanese might block the shipping channel from the states to Alaska. The military began building the Alaska Highway in spring 1942 and completed it by fall.

(In those days, communication with Europe was limited to an infrequent radio channel, and we could not call Japan at all.)

Major Van Nort, a Bell Labs engineer, was working on a new technology for direct dialing when he received his military notice. Stationed in Edmonton, he became my superior for providing communication to the north.

By fall 1943, we had installed three channels on an open-wire system from Edmonton to Fairbanks. Alaska could talk to America for the first time. By April 1944, the first oil on the Canol pipeline reached Whitehorse.

During the war, the technology in Alaska was still the old one-line, ten-ring party system; each home had a designated number of identifiable rings. However, some of the analog switchboard circuits were noisy and the loss on them was great. Sometimes the switchboard operator had to repeat messages for people trying to communicate from Seattle to Fairbanks.

In the late 1940s, we overbuilt our original wartime wire cable communication line down the Alcan, bringing it up to twenty-four channels.

In 1946 when I was in Seattle, I considered returning to Lone Star Gas, my old employer, but I took one look around and decided, "No, I'll stay in communications." The next year, I was in Unalaska securing water-damaged transmitters.

As innovations in Alaska communications gathered speed, I was stationed with ACS at Lena Point in Juneau for the next twelve years. I was a master sergeant at the time.

Unlike the short-lived Canol pipeline, the new eight-inch Haines to Fairbanks pipeline transported fuel for the Korean conflict from Haines to Eielson Air Force Base for nineteen years. In 1955, I was again responsible for communication between pump stations, this time pumping sixteen thousand gallons of fuel an hour for planes bound for Korea. (The number of pump stations doubled during the Vietnam War.)

Sputnik and the Soviet Union Hammer and Sickle. Courtesy of http://www.uwsp.edu/.

In 1956, a new submarine cable carrying thirty-six channels of voice was put in from Eastern Canada to Scotland, significantly upgrading communication with Europe. From Port Angeles, Washington, another new submarine cable was installed to Ketchikan, with a leg over to Juneau and Skagway, and it seemed that Alaska was no longer such a remote colony.

At 3 a.m. on Oct. 4, 1957, I got a call from Seattle: "Get out to Lena Point and get a receiver tuned to the frequency and record when, how often, and the speed at which Sputnik comes over the horizon, orbiting the Earth. You'll hear a 'beep, beep, beep' until it disappears over the far horizon!"

After the installation of the cable in 1957, AT&T figured that upgrade would take care of Alaska's communications for the next twenty years. However, after Alaskans got dependable communication, civilian use, and the new Cold War technology and its communication flooded the system, necessitating an upgrade only three years later.

Beginning in 1952–57, newly developed UHF and VHF radar technology communicated by the Distant Early Warning system (DEW line) made a virtual electronic wall of defense across Alaska and Canada. The DEW line could transmit data by troposcatter a hundred to two hundred miles between repeaters back to the military's control center in Colorado Springs. However, that high-frequency radio technology could not carry as many channels as microwave, and it was also hampered by atmospheric conditions.

ACS and the Federal Aviation Administration combined to create the White Alice Communications System (WACS), installed by Western Electric. It provided circuits for remote military installations and to villages beyond ACS. In the late 1950s, featuring hundred-foot-high by three-hundred-foot-wide cupped troposcatter antennas, it provided upgraded communication for the DEW line as well.

As a further defensive innovation against incoming missiles, a satellite-based electronic warning system, the Missile Defense Alert System (MIDAS)

DEW Line Bell Systems pamphlet. Courtesy of Bell Systems.

sites, was built in 1961. Advanced MIDAS antennae collected satellite data to detect hostile missiles at launch, alerting Ladd Air Force Base and a base in California. We first tested the satellite-based technology by taking pictures of a parking lot in Greenbelt, Maryland. When we could make out the form of cars, gosh—that was exciting!

A further upgrade, AT&T's microwave technology, first developed in 1948, took time to get to Alaska. In 1960, eighty-four Western Electric installers arrived, putting microwave site equipment in the Tanana Valley. The guy in charge at Delta Junction began having problems with the contractors. One day Jack Bowman, vice president of defense communications at AT&T, was talking to Col. White in Seattle. Jack said, "Get someone like Fred Ferrell in Delta and we won't have a problem!" Col. White replied, "He'll be there in two weeks."

I arrived in Delta that fall, and we got the microwave repeaters up, enlarging the channel capacity to 480 as opposed to the original three channels we first installed in 1943.

RCA came as a contractor under our supervision a year later to maintain the enhanced White Alice system along the highway.

MIDAS, enhanced by the upgraded White Alice system, was the first time we could transmit 1,500-bit data over the telephone system. I worked every day with Bell Telephone to get that circuit connected with the satellite orbiting over Russia to send data back to

DEWLine "golf ball" antennas. Courtesy of www.greatarcticairadventure.com/.

Colorado Springs. The dishlike antenna, coined "Golf Ball," was cupped to the sky to track the satellite as it orbited. To prevent the dish from collecting ice, a spherical white cover was put over the six-story-high antenna, giving it a golf-ball-like appearance.

In 1969, Congress passed the Alaska Communications Disposal Act, enabling private bidders to purchase the Alaska Communications System. RCA won. In 1963 I switched from military to civil service, doing the same job, and in 1971 I began work for RCA.

In 1979, RCA Alascom was purchased by Pacific Power and Light Co. (now PacifiCorp) of Portland, Oregon.

Everything until the 1980s had been the analog system. In 1990, we laid a digital fiber-optic cable with ultimately several thousand channels from Portland to Japan, with a spur over to Seward.

Fiber optic transmits a light pulse; it can carry more bandwidth than microwave. The technology doesn't require much power; in fact, they can now go all the way across the ocean without a repeater. Most of the microwave sites are currently still in place, but some have been and more will be shut down in the north.

In 1960, when I first arrived in Delta, we were switching from the old operator-based, one-line-party, ten-ring to the dial system. The old-timers like Rika Wallen and Jack Warren were defiant, saying no, they weren't going to give up their old wall telephone. I spent days at Rika's Roadhouse talking to her and 'ol Jack. But when we changed the system, Jack was out of a telephone. We finally had to just cut off service to the old one and then put in the other phone. They liked talking to the operator, getting her to connect them to their party; they didn't want to have to remember the number!

In 1967, I was thinking about moving the old Billy Mitchell cabin from the WAMCATS Signal Corps military reservation near Rika's to Alaskaland in Fairbanks (now Pioneer Park). Engineers had told me it couldn't be done. A colonel at Elmendorf asked, "Do you really think you can do it?"

I told the colonel, "I need load booms, timbers, four railroad jacks, and a lowboy."

The colonel said, "Go to Fort Wainwright and get anything you want."

The Signal Corps had used old newspapers for insulation in between the cabin's two floors. We found an old July 4, 1904, newspaper, printed the same year Billy Mitchell and WAMCATS completed installation of the old single-wire telegraph system from Eagle to Fairbanks and Tanana to the coast. The year he finished, an engineer, Ken Cannon out of

Seattle, said in the article he was already installing a wireless radio station at Eagle. He expected that radio communication would replace all wire communication in Alaska within the year. We put that newspaper in the display case of the Billy Mitchell cabin and moved the cabin to Alaskaland on the Chena River in Fairbanks. However, two weeks later when the Chena flooded, the Billy Mitchell cabin was completely washed away.

Three years ago, Wayne Olsen, who used to work for me, came into a building where I was talking with others. He went out to the parking lot and returned, saying, "Hey, do you guys know who this man is?" He paused and continued, "He had more to do with Alaska communications than any two men." He went out and returned again, saying, "I take that back; he had more to do with Alaska communications than any ten men."

When I drove the highway in June 2005, crews were laying fiber-optic cable from Whitehorse, Yukon, to Edmonton, Alberta. At Muncho Lake, British Columbia, I saw the reels and I talked to the construction guys. In some places, fiber-optic will replace microwave—but not quite yet in others. Microwave will still be in use for a number of years.

These days I have breakfast at Denny's in Anchorage with my old ACS friends. To honor Veterans Day, I wore my old parka, issued to me in 1943. But at home on the Internet, I play the stock market.

Not learning new technology is for those who are old, and I'm not old yet.

Fred Ferrell, Denny's, Anchorage, 2005. Judy Ferguson photo

White Alice Tropo antenna. Courtesy of Fred Ferrell.

Chapter 28

Refugee to Magnate: Paul Gavora

For many years, Paul Gavora has enjoyed lamb roasts at Harding Lake with the Fairbanks "vich" families. Through his story, it's clear that the western system of business and government succeeds based on trust. Without it, an open society cannot endure. Paul remembered his long voyage from Eastern Europe to Fairbanks.

Paul Gavora, thirty-two, first American passport, 1963. Courtesy of Paul Gavora.

In 1970, I built the first shopping mall in Fairbanks, twenty-two years after I swam the Danube River to freedom in 1948 from my home country of Czechoslovakia.

I was born Vladimir ("Paul") Gavora in 1931 to Rudolph and Darina Gavora in Brezova (now in Slovakia). My father was a merchant who owned land, including a flour mill. In those days, there wasn't much cash exchange. People raised cows, hogs, grain, potatoes, and flax so as not to be dependent on the system.

In 1944, my father died while both my siblings were away at school. From the time I was thirteen until I left at seventeen, I was both a student and the surrogate head of the family.

Twelve hours after the Russians liberated us, the Soviet Army began building up our new armed forces, made up entirely of Slovaks.

The communists took over our stores, inventoried private property, and confiscated our flour mill, our land, and possessions. The public could say nothing negative and had to entirely subjugate themselves to the system. Later, my mother would go to jail for not declaring our entire domestic inventory.

I was pretty independent, the head of the family. I told my mom I was getting out. I changed some money into dollars through an illegal money changer. The Soviets didn't yet have lights or guards securing the river; with the clothes on my back and able to speak German, I swam across the Danube in November.

I headed for Vienna. Like Berlin, Vienna was an island in the midst of the Soviet liberation troops. I slipped past the Russian and British zones during the night, guided by locals. Outside of Stuttgart, I entered a refugee camp. I worked there for the United Nations and finished high school over the next sixteen months. After scoring high on an exam, I won a scholarship to Colorado State University. I began immediately to study English.

At the university, math and science were easy, because my study in Europe had been intensive. History and English, however, necessitated a

1960 — Fairbanks flood — Gavora Mall, Fairbanks first shopping mall — Nixon-Agnew re-election campaign — 1970 — 1980 — Market Basket in Fairbanks, North Pole, Anchorage, Ketchikan — 1990

dictionary; I could read English, but I couldn't speak it well. In Fort Collins, I met and married my wife, Donna. After two years in Colorado, I took the entrance exams for the University of Chicago, won a scholarship, and after two more years I graduated with a masters in economics. By that time, two of my nine children had been born.

After graduation, it was hard as a foreigner to find a job. There was a lot of bias. In 1958, I saw an advertisement for an assistant professorship in the Department of Economics at the University of Alaska in Fairbanks. The head of the department, Tom Jensen, invited me to come visit. However, when I arrived, the last territorial legislature had not funded the assistant professorship.

Having no other options, I found a job delivering milk for Creamer's Dairy and decided to wait for the next legislature to convene. While I was delivering milk to a local grocery store, the dairy manager asked if I would come to work for them. Needing the money, I began in groceries in 1958 and have never left since.

I became the manager for Foodland at Cushman and Gaffney. Later I went to work as manager for Joe Franich, who had two grocery stores, one of which was at Tice Center (which I later purchased and today is Shopper's Forum) and the other on South Cushman.

Using my house as collateral, I borrowed seven thousand dollars and, in 1964, I put a down payment on the old Piggly Wiggly, which was across the Chena River in Graehl.

In 1966, my mother visited us from Czechoslovakia. She couldn't understand why we lived in a frame rather than a stone house and why we did not have maids. She could not believe our store merchandise was out, entirely vulnerable to the public. "Back home, the people (who had nothing, no money and no variety of merchandise) would steal you blind, Vlad!" she scolded me.

"Our merchandising system here," I explained, "is built on trust." She couldn't believe it.

Merchandise floats out of Paul Gavora's original Market Basket store, during the 1967 Fairbanks flood. Center: Paul is peering into store. Gavora lost $750,000, the equivalent of four million dollars today. Courtesy of Paul Gavora.

However, nature was not so kind. In August 1967, the Chena River began to rise. The radio kept promising us it was about to crest, but suddenly, as if someone had opened the gate, water rolled toward my store. Pressing against the doors, the wall of water popped the doors open. I ran for my Wagoneer and jumped onto the hood to stay dry. When I knew the store was lost, I got on the radio and called people to come get the products before it all floated down the Chena.

I joined my friend who had a rowboat, and all night we ferried people from Hamilton Acres to Steese Market, a high point. The Salvation Army backed up an Army flatbed truck and rolled carts of groceries right up into the truck. About a month after the flood, I got a check from the Salvation Army for eighteen thousand dollars. (I had sent them no invoice, nothing.) Needless to say, I have supported the Salvation Army ever since. Many other people sent twenty-five or fifty dollars. I lost three-quarters of a million dollars, equivalent today to about four million dollars.

But in 1969, I reopened as Market Basket. I bought twenty-five adjoining postage-stamp-sized

Vice President Spiro Agnew, left, met with Paul Gavora, chairman of Alaska's Nixon-Agnew re-election committee, and other Alaska Republicans during a Fairbanks campaign stop in Fairbanks, 1972. Courtesy of Paul Gavora.

lots, called locally "the Native village." On that property, I built Gavora Mall, adjoining Market Basket, making the first shopping mall in Fairbanks. We opened in 1970, only a few years before the construction of the Trans-Alaska Pipeline.

At the same time, as a tenant of the Tice Center next to Le Monte's on Airport, I bought that property and built my second Market Basket, followed by the Northland Hub on South Cushman. In North Pole, I built the third Market Basket, followed by a fourth in Anchorage and finally a Market Basket as far south as Ketchikan. The headline of the *Alaska Business Monthly* in 1989 read, "From Milkman to Magnate: Fairbanks' Paul Gavora."

I owned three of the five major shopping malls in the Fairbanks area and three of the six major grocery stores. I moved the utility building of the former Tice Center to Cushman and Illinois, where it became my office as well as a small shopping complex.

I never became a professor, but over the years, besides heading up the Nixon-Agnew re-election campaign and participating in many community organizations, I did become the president of the University of Alaska Foundation.

Today, my business is a family-run operation, extending five hundred years of the Gavora family in Europe deep into the Alaska frontier.

Chapter 29

Montenegrin, Alaskan, and Russian Christmas: Pete Stepovich

The customs of a far culture's Christmas celebration add flavor and understanding, a window on where we have come from. Pete Stepovich, the fourth child of Alaska's last territorial governor Mike Stepovich, remembered his family's Roman Catholic Alaska celebration and that of his Orthodox family in Montenegro.

y parents represented two republics, two cultures of former Yugoslavia. My mother, a Croatian-American, was Catholic; my father's paternal side was Montenegrin, which traditionally is Serbian Orthodox. However, my father's mother was Croatian and Dad was raised Catholic.

To me growing up, it was all just Yugoslavia, not one particular republic or another. But from my uncle Nikola Radovich's 1993 memoir, *Reflections of the Past*, as well as from the former Russian Orthodox bishop of Alaska, I learned more of the Montenegrin and Russian traditions.

Back, L–R: Ted, Dominick, Pete, Mike, Chris, Maria; Middle, l: Toni, Nick, Jim, Matilda, Mike; Front: Laura, Melissa, Andrea, Nada Stepovich, c. 1968, Fairbanks. Courtesy of Bob Hajdukovich.

I was born in 1952 in Fairbanks at St. Joseph's Hospital. The nuns who ran St. Joseph's and Immaculate Conception grade school lived in the old Fairbanks Exploration Co. house on Illinois Street. We kids called it "the convent."

I attended Immaculate Conception grade school, and at Christmas, we kids participated in pageants at school. By the time I was fourteen, all thirteen of us Stepovich children had been born. There was never a quiet moment in our house on Charles Street.

In the weeks before Christmas, the Yugoslav ladies—Helen Vacura, Branka Pekich, and my mother—made *hrustala*, a fried sweet bread sprinkled with powdered sugar.

On Christmas Eve, we all opened one gift. Before bed, we left walnuts, oranges, and milk on the table for Sveti Nikola (Saint Nick) and said *Laku noc!* ("good night") to the adults. In the morning, we kids pummeled downstairs to our stockings and gifts.

Later that morning, we would attend Mass to celebrate the birth of Baby Jesus. In our earlier years, my brother Mike and I served as altar boys on Christmas Day. After church, we visited Mom and Dad's friends: the Bojaniches, the Vacuras, and Bob and Misha Bigovich. Bob would perform wonderful magic tricks for us kids. We also stopped at the nuns' convent to wish the Sisters of Providence "Merry Christmas." For Christmas dinner, Dad would invite the bishop and other clergy to dine with us.

Back, L–R: Mrs. Joyce Burglin, Vuka Stepovich (seated), Bev Sexton, Evelyn Franich, Dolores Dodson, Angie Geraghty, Helen Vacura; Front, L–R: Donna Gavora, Geri Fantazzi, Matilda Stepovich, Gertrude Linck, c. 1980. Courtesy of Angie Geraghty.

In his *Reflections of the Past*, Uncle Nikola described Montenegrin Christmas, a blend of Celtic and Orthodox customs, observed on Orthodox Christmas, January 7:

The little town of Risan on the Bay of Kotor was known for keeping Christmas. Even though the Turks occupied the area for three centuries, Christmas was a time for demonstrating Christian spirit. Before Badnjak (Christmas) we observed partial fasts, and kept the kitchen clean especially of oil. The house was decorated with vegetation from the Holy Land: laurel, rosemary, olive branches.

The main symbol in the celebration, Badnjak, was left over from pagan times, before the Slavs adopted Christianity from the Greeks. Badnjak is a log made from an oak or olive tree. The top is beveled to demonstrate the head or the upper end. For the young boys in the family, a sapling Badnjak was made for each of them. The fire place was a kind of holy place because the big Badnjak would be burned there before dinner.

On Jan. 6, before the sun rose, my father would select a young oak tree, called "Badnjak." He crossed himself (Orthodox style) to the right and left and kissed the tree three times, representing the Trinity. Striking the tree three times, he felled the tree to the east, toward Constantinople, the seat of Orthodoxy.

Seven small seedlings, called "Badnjaca," were also harvested. The trees were left upright outside near the front door leaning against the wall until the evening's festivities. During the day, the family ate special food: beans with onion, ornamented "Badnjus" bread, salted fish in oil, honey, nuts and wine but no meat.

That evening, the youngest son carried the small tree through the northern door and was greeted by two female cousins, holding two candles, who showered him with corn or rice.

The son greeted his father, "God's evening to you!" Everyone returned, "Congratulations, Badnjus' evening!" and set the tree in front of the chimney. The seven small seedlings were designed into two small crosses affixed to the chimney on either side of the oak. Wine and bread (the blood and body of Christ) were on a chimney ledge above the tree.

Straw, like Bethehem's stable, covered the floor. The girls tossed nuts into it, decorating Badnjak, singing, "Oh, Badnjace, jolly fellow, we give you bread and wine. In return, you give us happiness and peace."

Putting Badnjak, the Yule log, into the fireplace, the grandfather prayed, "As many as there are sparks, so will our blessings be from our children, livestock and dreams." Grandmothers lit candles by the Orthodox icons and prayed for their family. Outside pistols rang as Montenegrin men greeted Badnjus' evening. By the fireplace where Badnjak was burning, there was a pitcher, called *Bardak*, of wine. Everyone drank some and wished each other, "Happy Christmas Eve."

Before daylight on Christmas morning, a young cousin scurried to the house with brandy and money. Trying to get out of bed and beat that cousin to greet his house first, the man of the house ran to his house. Once received, each messenger was presented there with white wool socks and was expected to stay for dinner.

Christmas dinner was for family and for one guest only: a banquet of sheep steak, pork sausages, sauerkraut, fruit and holiday bread decorated with candles. For dessert, braided bread was served—like our Fairbanks celebration with fry bread. Each twist hid a gold or silver coin, one for each member of the family, as well as for the guest. The first to find a coin could expect riches in the coming year. (Note: Christmas

Dragan Petrović and nephew Miloš celebrating Badnjak night, Belgrade, 2001. Judy Ferguson photo.

trees were never used by the Serbian people but instead they used only "Badnjak." [A Serbian friend once called a western Christmas tree "Catholic Badnjak" as Badnjak was a more natural referent for her.] Christmas gifts were also not given as in today's western manner.

Pete Stepovich continued: When Mary Hajdukovich was growing up in the 1940s in Fairbanks, she remembered celebrating with a dinner of roasted pig's head stuffed with apples, surrounded by "uncles" singing the songs of Montenegro. In Juneau, the Serbian community wore traditional costume and hosted pageants.

The former American-Herzegovinan Russian Orthodox bishop of Alaska, Vladyka Nikolai, spent years ministering to the Yup'ik, Aleut, and Indian congregations throughout the state. In the Alaska Russian Orthodox culture, the Natives star or celebrate Selaviq, a Russian word for "glory." In the late nineteenth century, a Ukrainian priest introduced starring to Alaska Natives. It died out in Russia around the time of the Russian Revolution. Some experts feel that Alaska is the last place where starring congregants sing, pray, eat, and bless homes for several days after January 7. On Russian Orthodox Christmas, people carry large twirling brightly decorated stars from door to door, singing and eating until late into the night. The procession and the carols symbolize the journey of the three wise men who followed the star to Jesus' manager. The antique stars are typically three feet across, made of wood and glass with no nails holding them together (because Jesus was crucified on the cross). The star is decorated with pictures of native flowers and rotates in a flurry of tinsel and jingle bells. The men who carry the stars keep them spinning while the carolers sing in three languages: Yup'ik, Slavonic (the Russian Orthodox Church liturgical language), and English, all an Alaska twist to our Eastern European roots.

Bishop Nikolai also pointed out the uniquely Serbian Orthodox celebration of Slava: "The Serbs have a special individual feast day, Slava (a thanksgiving), celebrated on the family's patriarchal patron saint's feast day, even more important than the individual's birthday."

In Montenegro, the patron saint of our Stepovich family is St. Michael. Bishop Nikolai said, "Ever since Serbs became Christians, the patron saint's day has been celebrated by the family, unifying its members and giving glory to God."

Recently, cousin Vlado Stijepović in Risan explained that our Slava is celebrated with a round loaf of sweet bread, decorated on top with "CCCC: Only Unity Saves the Serbs," along with a bowl of sweetened, soaked wheat accompanied by some red wine, observing Christ's Last Supper. A candle burns near the Slava loaf, which is covered with white lace. The priest blesses each member of the family with incense and holy water. Father, mother, and children wave the incense toward their faces while crossing themselves.

The priest lifts the Slava loaf, supported by the family's hands, all rotating it together like the hub of a wheel. The priest carefully cuts the bread and then hands a portion to each member while each one hopes for the hidden coin in his slice.

Today, as a father, I share my Christmas stories and Yugoslavian heritage with my three grown children. On December 25, we Alaska Stepoviches will visit with some of our American-Slavic friends in Fairbanks, while in Risan, on Orthodox Christmas, January 7, the Montenegrin Stijepovićs will hurry to each others' homes to be the first to wish "Congratulations! It's Božić—Christmas Day!"

Bishop Nikolai, Russian Orthodox Christmas, Starring at Alaska Native Medical Center, c. 2005. Courtesy of Bishop Nikolai.

Chapter 30

The Alaska State Constitutional Convention:
Control of Natural Resources By and For the People

ifty years after the Alaska constitution was created, former state
legislator Ethan Berkowitz observed, "A constitution should describe
freedoms as well as outline the mechanisms
of government. The fathers of the Alaska
constitution put aside their differences and
made a document for the ages."

In 1912, the second Organic Act made
Alaska a territory and created a bicameral
legislature that met biennially. However,
even though it was one-fifth the size of the
entire continental United States, Alaska's
fifty-eight thousand people were only
represented in Congress by one voteless
federal delegate. Bureaucracies manipulated
by powerful mining and fishing lobbies
in distant Washington, D.C., controlled

*Governor B. Heintzleman signing bill authoriz-
ing a statehood convention to be held November
8, 1955 at the University of Alaska, College,
Alaska. Juneau, March 21, 1955. Courtesy of
John Almquist/Butrovich family.*

Alaska's destiny. Alaskans could not develop their own economy through local government
or control the harvest of their natural resources whose profits largely went Outside. In first
the district, and then the territory of Alaska, life amounted to (albeit, low) taxation without
representation.

With an economy based on fishing and mining, Alaska was not considered economically viable to support a state government. In 1916, statehood was first proposed by Alaska's
only federal delegate, James Wickersham, and then again in 1943 by Delegate Anthony
J. Dimond, but in both cases the bill was defeated in committee. With Alaska's natural
resources harvested by Outsiders and with a largely transient
Alaska population, statehood
seemed questionable. In 1950,
congressional delegate E. L.
"Bob" Bartlett got a statehood
bill through the House, but it was
derailed by pressing national matters.
The control of Alaska's natural resources wasn't considered "critical."

Salmon canneries in the Pacific
Northwest using large fish traps had caused

the near-destruction of Alaska's salmon runs. What amounted to the canneries' exclusive "right of fishery" with little taxation typified Alaska's colonial frustrations.

A fisherman and merchant, Frank Peratrovich, a six-foot two-inch Tlingit-Croat from Prince of Wales Island, knew firsthand the issues both of racial discrimination and the Outside canneries' monopoly. Peratrovich was the son of a Tlingit mother, Mary Skan, and a Croatian-born cannery manager, John Peratrovich. He was born in 1895 in Klawock, before Indians were even considered citizens. Peratrovich became a part of the Alaska Native Brotherhood (ANB), where he learned parliamentary procedure. He was educated at Chemawa Indian School in Oregon then Haskell Institute in Kansas. After serving as the grand president of ANB, he referred to a popular perception: "I wasn't singly responsible for the Natives' right to vote but I certainly supported it."

Frank Peratrovich, possibly in college, c. 1921. Courtesy of Frank and Nettie Peratrovich.

As a leader of the Southeast Seineboat Owners and Operators Association, Peratrovich fought against the monopoly of the Washington-Oregon canneries. In 1944, the seiners backed Peratrovich for election to the territorial House of Representatives.

When he wasn't fighting the monopolies, Peratrovich, his brother, Roy, and his sister-in-law, Elizabeth Peratrovich, worked to end discrimination in housing and public places. In 1945 they saw Governor Gruening sign into law their equal rights legislation, preceding the nation's by nineteen years.

By 1947 Peratrovich was a senator, and the following year he introduced the Fish Trap Referendum bill, calling for a popular vote. The ballot result was 19,712 against fish traps and only 2,624 in favor, sending a strong signal for self government and telling the national lobbies that their control was due for a change.

During the critical 1949 special session, Peratrovich was senate president when tax legislation was enacted on all businesses that derived their income from Alaska, including the transportation and fishing industries. This taxation helped support the territory and nationally demonstrated Alaska's ability to govern itself. In the following regular session, Peratrovich and Victor C. Rivers proposed a bill forming the Alaska Statehood Committee, consisting of eleven members including Peratrovich. Frustrated over inadequate roads, poor airfields, meager tuberculosis hospitals, undependable and expensive shipping, and lack of national defense and security, Alaskans pushed to have two senators and a representative each with a vote in Washington, D.C.

In that effort, Anchorage lawyer Wendell P. Kay in 1953 introduced a bill calling for a constitutional convention, which failed.

In his State of the Union address, President Eisenhower in 1954 favored statehood for (Republican) Hawaii but not for (Democratic) Alaska. When asked, Eisenhower denied that partisan politics might be the motive. With nothing to lose, Alaskans formed Operation

Statehood with Victor Fischer, Thomas B. Stewart, Niilo Koponen, and Territorial Senator John Butrovich to organize and begin research on constitution writing.

"Not many people in Alaska," Stewart said, "understood about how to write a constitution writing." On his own, Stewart left his job and traveled Outside to interview political scientists and experts in government regarding writing a constitution. Learning of the National Municipal League's Model Constitution, rooted in Eisenhower's State Constitutional Reform Movement, he became familiar with methods of routing power back to the state level. He established connections with the Public Administrative Service (PAS), which later provided the convention with constitutional studies and reference guides. In his research, Stewart was advised that Alaska should host its constitutional convention away from Juneau lobbyists and cloister in a university equipped with a library immersed in an academic atmosphere. He returned home, intimately informed on hosting a constitutional convention.

Wanting delegates representative of all Alaska, the legislature devised a special apportionment plan to elect delegates to ensure territory-wide representation.

November 8, 1955, fifty-five delegates gathered at the University of Alaska Fairbanks. Delayed three days by bad weather, traveling one thousand miles from Klawock to Fairbanks, Frank Peratrovich, the only Native delegate, arrived. Even while absent, Peratrovich was elected the convention's first vice president.

Convention president William Egan, a master politician and organizer, called upon former Territorial Gov. Ernest Gruening, who began, "Its greatest importance . . . [is] that [this] . . . is the first occasion which is wholly of, for, and most important, *by* the people of Alaska."

Congressional delegate Bartlett pointed out, "fifty years from now . . . people . . . may very well judge the product of this convention by the decision taken upon the vital issue of resources policy. . . . Only a minute fraction of the land area is owned by private persons or corporations. . . . Never before . . . has there been so great an opportunity to establish a resources policy geared to the growth of a magnificent economy and the welfare of a people."

For the next seventy-five days and through fifty-below temperatures, the gathering of merchants, lawyers, fishermen, housewives, homesteaders, and miners, representing two hundred thousand Alaskans, became statesmen, writing a document more appropriate to its time and place than any other state constitution.

Potential dilemmas facing the delegates were whether to have a unicameral versus bicameral legislature, the apportionment of the legislators from the Bush and urban areas, whether to have a strong executive, how

Jack Coghill and Frank Peratrovich studying considerations, Constitutional Convention, 1955–56, Fairbanks. Courtesy of Jack Coghill.

199

to select judges, voting age, the complexity of local government, voting qualification, and the relatively new topic of indigenous land claims and their selection.

In the debating about whether a voter should be required to be able to read, write, and speak English, Peratrovich, a member of the Suffrage, Elections, and Apportionment committee, wanted to limit suffrage requirements to "read or speak" only. He added that in his area some "can write their name...but...not letters." He reminded the committee, "These people are citizens entitled by the 1924 congressional act...and vote under that provision and should continue to do so."

Regarding indigenous land claims, Marvin R. "Muktuk" Marston, organizer and leader of the Eskimo Scouts, said, "Justice demands that something be done to help the Native people" (forty percent of the population) with their land rights. "The proposed Marston amendment," George McLaughlin responded, "would create a completely new set of property rights" that would cast a cloud over "every title in the Territory." After much discussion, the amendment was dropped. (This lack has been called the greatest failure of the constitution.) The legitimacy of land claims was, however, mentioned in the General Provisions article, deferring resolution of indigenous land claims to the federal government.

On the sixty-fifth day, Peratrovich pointed out that delegates with mining interests had protected Alaska's minerals from exploitation. After a debate on the correctness of including the question of fish traps in the constitution, Burke Riley, Eldor Lee, Seaborn Buckalew, W. O. "Bo" Smith, and Frank Peratrovich decided to include it rather in a separate ordinance on the statehood ballot. "It was a marvelous idea," chief clerk Katherine Alexander Hurley observed. Peratrovich summed up later, "It proved to be the linchpin in getting the Southeast vote out for statehood."

Although Hawaii had a constitution, it had not achieved statehood. Knowing more was needed, delegates listened to George Lehleitner, a New Orleans advocate for Hawaiian statehood, who advocated including the Tennessee Plan on Alaska's statehood ballot. Sidestepping an enabling act from Congress, the vote would elect provisional delegates to

Recess: L–R: John Hellenthal, George McLaughlin, (behind) Robert McNealy, Leslie Nerland, Steve McCutcheon, Wm Egan, Jack Coghill, Katherine (Alexander) Hurley, Dorothy (Awes) Haaland. Courtesy of Jack Coghill.

approach Congress, following the example of six previously successful states in their statehood bids, including Tennessee. On February 5, 1956, William Egan signed the Alaska constitution in the University of Alaska gymnasium.

For three years, disappointment dogged the delegates. With some concern about impending civil rights legislation, a national coalition of Republicans and "Dixiecrats" kept blocking the passage of an Alaska statehood bill. Delegate Bob Bartlett, the Tennessee Plan delegation, newly elected Senator William Egan, Senator Ernest Gruening, and Representative Ralph Rivers lobbied Congress vigorously. Finally, with the national coalition weakening, Congress passed the statehood bill on June 30, 1958. President Eisenhower signed the official proclamation making Alaska the forty-ninth state on January 3, 1959.

Fifty years later, former Republican delegate Jack B. Coghill reflected, "The form of government we set up in 1955 has worked well, serving both urban and rural Alaskans."

Jack Coghill, Fairbanks, 2007. Judy Ferguson photo.

University of Alaska professor of political science and author Dr. Gerald McBeath added, "Our founding framers constructed principles of effective government, observable by all. Patterning our constitution after the American constitution, they created a basic foundational document for state governance, guiding the state legislature's development. They did not lock up areas of concern in tight language for all time."

Judge Andrew Kleinfeld of the United States Court of Appeals for the Ninth Circuit (selected federally, not under the Alaska Constitution) observed, "Alaska's constitution and system of selecting judges works better than that of other states. Our system of using a judicial council, bar poll, and gubernatorial appointment of judges attracts a higher quality of judicial aspirants and shields our judges from excessive politicization. Also, the practice of law in our Department of Law is less political, compared to states where the attorney general's office may be a political stepping stone to other statewide elective office.

"Since the Alaska Constitution has worked (in these areas I know best)," the judge concluded, "it should probably be left alone."

Agreeing with Kleinfeld, Dr. McBeath observed, "Needs, passions, and events of the people change from day to day. Those majority issues should be brought before and sifted by the legislature rather than expressed in constitutional amendments. Indeed, the constitution should go beyond majority passions and not react to perceived 'emergency issues' of the day."

Jack Coghill concurred: "The document's strength was its simplicity and flexibility. Other state constitutions," he pointed out, "direct government. We, Alaskan citizens, gave power to the local government, to the people, rather than to a centralized government.

"Due to our lessons learned from the fish trap issue, no industry," he emphasized, "has ever been able to over-harvest us."

"However," current Governor Sarah Palin pointed out, "one of the biggest challenges of my administration is getting Alaska natural gas to market while at the same time ensuring Alaskans get their fair share of their natural resource's value.

"But," she smiled, "in working with legislators committed to open and transparent process, both the short, and long-term interests of Alaskans will, I am confidant, be served."

"Today on our fiftieth anniversary," Jack Coghill concluded, "only four of the convention delegates are living: Seaborn J. Buckalew, George W. Sundborg, Victor Fischer, and me." Adding, "In 1984, a day before Alaska's twenty-fifth statehood anniversary, Frank Peratrovich died on January 4."

Fifty years ago, Democrat and Republican, Peratrovich and Coghill, among the eight delegates born in Alaska, worked with the other fifty-three delegates for home rule, to prevent the exploitation of Alaska that she might forever retain her freedom and rugged beauty for the ages yet to come.

Above: constitutional committee, University of Alaska, Fairbanks, 1956. Below: signatures of the committee. Courtesy of Jack Coghill.

"Alaska State Constitutional Convention" was first published in the state's only official statehood anniversary publication, Alaska 50: Celebrating Alaska's 50th Anniversary of Statehood 1959–2009. *Special thanks to Katie Hurley, Vic Fischer, Jack Coghill, Nettie and Frank Peratrovich Jr., Judge Kleinfeld, Ethan Berkowitz, and Dr. McBeath.*

Chapter 31

Alaska, a Platform to the Ear of the Nation: Judge Andrew Kleinfeld

Judge Andrew J. Kleinfeld, U.S. Ninth Circuit Court of Appeals, 2008, Fairbanks. Judy Ferguson photo.

Jewish connections with Alaska from its beginning were critical. In 1964, my first connection with Yugoslavia was with a survivor of the Holocaust, a Serbian Jew, Misha David. Today Misha's brother, Filip David, is a spokesman for former Yugoslavia and for Eastern Europe as an advocate of equality for all.

In a series focusing on Alaska Jewish history, Robert Bloom and Meta Bloom Buttnick, Perry Green, Judge and Professor Kleinfeld, and Rabbi Greenberg of the Orthodox Chabad-Lubavitch Center/Alaska Jewish Museum in Anchorage present Alaska Jewish history, a bridge from the former Ottoman Empire that once included Serbia, a refuge then for Jews as Alaska is a refuge today.

Judge Andrew J. Kleinfeld, of the U.S. Ninth Circuit Court of Appeals, shared his family's origins in his Fairbanks home one evening. He began, "Jews like being in America. For over a thousand years, there has never been a country for Jews like America. From the country's inception, George Washington made it an American principle to be tolerant of all faiths, and this was something... *new*. There's never been anything like this before: America."

He continued, "We are Ashkenazi Jews from East Prussia. When Jews came to America, however, most didn't talk about the old country and they never went back."

As a child in 1895, Kleinfeld's grandfather, Jacob Wolfram Kleinfeld, arrived with his father in New York. "Historically," Kleinfeld said, "the careers no one else wanted were left to Jews: rag picking, peddling. Our grandparents were really poor. However, my mother's father, a fingerprint detective in New York, was considered the 'rich' relative. He got a salary, and salaried people's checks didn't bounce.

"When I was a little kid," Kleinfeld remembered, "we took drives. I'd get tired and want to stop at a motel. But my father would say, 'No, that motel is 'restricted,'" which meant that on check-in, there would suddenly be 'no more rooms available.'"

Kleinfeld's father, Irving Kleinfeld, was born in 1916 and graduated from Brooklyn Law School.

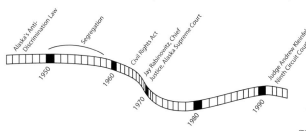

Alaska's Anti-Discrimination Law
Segregation
Civil Rights Act
Jay Rabinowitz Chief Justice, Alaska Supreme Court
Judge Andrew Kleinfeld, Ninth Circuit Court of Appeals

1950 1960 1970 1980 1990

In 1945, his son, Andrew Kleinfeld, was born in the Bronx. After the war, Kleinfeld Sr. became an adjudicator of veterans' claims. By 1951, however, the post-war demand had eased. To keep his job, Kleinfeld Sr. moved his family to Philadelphia.

Kleinfeld's first exposure to "colored segregation" was as a child on the train from New York City to Washington, D.C. "In Delaware, in what was perceived as the north," Kleinfeld said, "Blacks were suddenly separated behind a curtain from whites. Additionally, on Route Forty even black diplomats couldn't get a hamburger or go to the bathroom."

By 1959–60, when Kleinfeld was fourteen, he became interested in current events as well as in politics. He read newspapers closely, focusing on economics, trying to understand. "Discrimination didn't strike me as right," he said. In high school, Kleinfeld became a freedom rider on Maryland's segregated Route Forty.

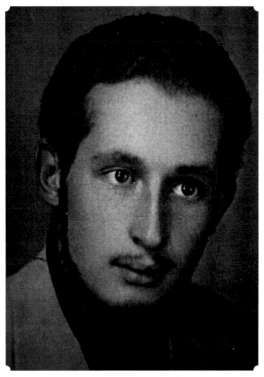

Mihajlo Mihajlov, Yugoslavian dissident, 1957. Courtesy of Mihajlo Mihajlov.

A move to the Washington, D.C., area where President Kennedy appointed Kleinfeld Sr. to the Board of Veterans' Appeals (now known as the U.S. Court of Veterans' Appeals), further opened Kleinfeld Jr.'s opportunities.

"In Alexandria, professors who were affiliated with think tanks, key governmental branches, and lobbies or unions invited bright teenagers to adult cocktail parties where opposing ideas were enthusiastically presented.

"I decided," he said, "to attend Wesleyan University in Connecticut where the faculty-student ratio was one to seven. Further, in the religious department, John Maguire was a personal friend of Martin Luther King, as well as a real leader in the civil rights movement. "Fraternities invited lecturers to discuss books; one fraternity brother was the son of the American ambassador to Yugoslavia. We discussed and concluded that when Tito died, Yugoslavia would be engulfed in a bloody civil war and would fall apart. We read about the Yugoslavian dissidents Milovan Djilas and Mihajlo Mihajlov. We debated the reality of so-called 'communism' in emerging African nations.

"When I met Judy," he added, "she wouldn't give me her phone number until I satisfied her standards regarding my position on civil rights.

"By 1968," he continued, "the world had turned upside down. I was the first Jew accepted as a summer law clerk at my law firm in Boston. My commitment has always been to liberty and unity; at that time, the Democratic Party best served those goals." Graduating with a degree in political science and pursuing a career in politics, Kleinfeld continued, "for several reasons, I began to consider Democratic-dominated Alaska." Kleinfeld figured an Alaskan candidate could run a low-budget campaign. Also, due to the election victories of Ernest Gruening who was half Jewish, Kleinfeld felt that ethnicity would not be an issue. And Alaska's population was only about a quarter of a million people. Kleinfeld figured if he worked hard that in ten to twenty years, he could connect across the state. Wealth and aristocracy weren't as big political factors as they were in Virginia.

"While a student at Harvard Law School," Kleinfeld continued, "I read a lot of the Alaska Supreme Court decisions. Jay Rabinowitz wrote the best. I applied for a clerkship with him; his cousin, who happened to be my criminal law professor, interviewed me, and I was accepted."

When Kleinfeld arrived in Alaska in 1969, he wanted to be a senator, to help shape law on the frontier, but he found that he didn't like politics; he greatly preferred the practice of law.

Under Republican Governor Jay Hammond in 1980 and two years later under Democratic Governor Bill Sheffield, Kleinfeld was nominated by the Alaska Judicial Council for the Alaska Supreme Court. "I was told," he remembered, "that if I wanted to be taken seriously, I had to be approved by Alex Miller, the powerful Democratic lobbyist. Miller gave me a green light even knowing my politics had evolved into the Republican Party camp." In 1986, President Reagan selected Kleinfeld for the United States District Court. Five years later, Kleinfeld, the former president of the state bar association, was appointed by President H. W. Bush to the U.S. Court of Appeals for the Ninth Circuit, whose decisions create law for one-fifth of the nation. Kleinfeld, a judge of plain-spoken opinions, said, "coming to Alaska led to an opportunity for the Ninth Circuit; my decisions are now clearly presented to other federal circuit courts as well as to the U.S. Supreme Court.

"Alaska," he concluded, "has been as good as I expected. We are an open, tolerant society, and offer people opportunities. We *appreciate* what people can *do*."

Judge Kleinfeld on Alaska History

"I wasn't here until 1969 but I think Fairbanks may not have changed much from its pre-statehood era to when we first arrived. In 1971, I opened my law office. In those early years, I worked frequently as co-counsel with (Gov.) Mike Stepovich. I learned from him some very important points in litigation, negotiation, and cross examination. Today, I still have occasion to quote him often.

"In that pre-pipeline era, times could be hard for lawyers. We used to say there was just five thousand dollars in town. When it got to you, you paid your bills. Fairbanks bar owners were

Mike Stepovich, Fairbanks, c. 1959. Courtesy of Stepovich family.

among the most substantial business people in town. They had a real business, a steady flow of revenue. Some pretty impressive people too—from the leading families, like the Paskvans. Naturally the older, better-connected families gravitated where there was money: bars, government contracts, government positions, places where people actually got paid. At that time a bar owner in Fairbanks was different than today; gambling was also not what it is considered now. Both were a more respectable thing.

"Most of Fairbanks' economy was based on construction, but by October that money dried up. With Christmas, everyone had spent their last nickel. Then there was just plain no money in town. No one could pay their lawyer bills, or any other bills. In the bar trade when a customer got a beer, the owner got two dollars. In March I'd provide legal services and by June, I'd hope to get paid. But serve a beer, and the owner got paid right then.

"Each of the bars had its own clientele. The Big I was an artsy bar, catering to local actors, musicians. The clientele at Tommy's Elbow Room were journalists, politicians, lawyers, professors, Natives, and working people.

"A good bar will not let dysfunctional alcoholics in but bad bars make money off chronic inebriates.

"The pipeline changed things, and wounded downtown. It brought in hoodlums and prostitutes. With the extra revenue in town, malls were built, and people didn't have to go downtown anymore. It hurt the Co-op Drugstore, which carried a huge inventory to supply the Bush; business was drained away."

Memories During the Pipeline Era

"The project manager of Alyeska was in charge of pipeline construction and hired the subcontractors. The critical factor was time. It was a twenty-four/seven project; no delay could be risked. Of course, it was union work. If an outsider could incite a strike, the company would pay to avoid it. Alyeska couldn't afford a walk-out or to have the police breaking up a strike. The work had to get done, and contracts were judged on that basis. Any company that didn't deliver was history. So whatever a company had to pay, it paid.

"There was a lot of money around, and everything was cost plus.

"There were so many things happening in so many places so fast. No one knew everything, only their little part.

"The phones in town (and a lot of the infrastructure) didn't work. In a short time, Fairbanks had gone from a small town to handling a large population. There weren't enough phone lines, or enough switches. Much of the time, the phones had no dial tone. Those businesses that had to talk every ten minutes, the first thing in the morning, they'd pick up the phone and keep that line open all day. It was like a war."

Judge Kleinfeld (selected federally, not under the Alaska Constitution) on Alaska's Legal System and State Constitution

"James Wickersham was our great judge, a pioneer who created our effective judicial system.

"Before statehood with its quite different legal system, Fairbanks was probably a much rougher place. With only the U.S. attorneys, assistant U.S. attorneys and the FBI, it would have been impossible to have the effective law enforcement system afforded today with state troopers, city police, state-appointed judges, and state-appointed prosecutors. Our Department of Law is less political as contrasted with states in which the attorney general's office is potentially a political stepping stone to other statewide elective offices. Because our judges are appointed by the governor and our district attorneys are selected by the attorney general (also appointed, not elected), this tends to produce an effective, clean law enforcement system.

"Regarding Alaska's constitution, Alaska's constitution and system of selecting judges work better than in other states. It's obvious because lawyers in Alaska don't try to move their cases over to the federal judiciary as they do in other states. This is partly because the Alaska constitution set it up well, and partly because we've developed traditions that fill in around that constitution and make the constitution work well.

"We depend on the knowledge of lawyers regarding which of their colleagues would be good judges. The Judicial Council and the bar poll filter out possible bad judges and encourage the application of potentially good judges.

"Nothing is perfect, but when something has worked as well as the Alaska constitution (in these areas I know best) it should probably be left alone."

Regarding America's History of Tolerance

"In 1790, a year before the Bill of Rights was ratified, George Washington wrote a famous letter to the oldest synagogue in continuous operation in the United States, the Touro synagogue in Newport, Rhode Island. He stated the American principle of tolerance, saying it would be applied to the Jews. '...*the Government of the United States...gives to bigotry no sanction, to persecution no assistance.... May the children of the Stock of Abraham, who dwell in this land, continue to merit and enjoy the good will of the other Inhabitants.*'

"Under General George Washington, Jews fought for America's freedom. George Washington had a lot of beliefs that were considered novel in Europe. For instance, after winning the Revolutionary War he returned to his farm rather than become a king as the Europeans expected. This American tolerance for Jews is really extraordinary."

Touro Synagogue, America's oldest synagogue building, dedicated 1763, Newport, R.I. (http://www.thirteen.org/edonline/studentstake/jewsinamerica)

Chapter 32

Working Across the Aisle to Deliver: Nick Begich Sr. and Tom Begich

On November 4, 2008, Anchorage Mayor Mark Begich, son of former U.S. Congressman Nick Begich, won the U.S. Senate seat held for forty years by incumbent Senator Ted Stevens. In what was the largest voter turnout in the state's history, the outcome of the election was in doubt until the final counting of ballots on November 18. As he accepted the position, Begich said, "I am humbled and honored to serve Alaska in the U.S. Senate. I will work in a bipartisan manner in Washington, D.C."

Mark Begich, Nov. 19, 2008. Courtesy of Tom Begich.

I n 2007, Mark's older brother Tom Begich told me the story of the Begich children growing up without their father and the story of their father, U.S. Congressman Nick Begich.

Until I was nearly twelve, I grew up with a man who was a legend, the son of Croatian immigrants, but who disappeared on Oct. 16, 1972, into the clouds. No trace of him was ever found. My father, U.S. congressman Nick Begich, was critical in the 1971 passage of Alaska Native Claims Settlement Act.

In 1960, I was born in the old Anchorage hospital, the third child of Nick and Pegge Begich.

My dad grew up in the Mesabi Iron Range in Eveleth, Minnesota, where his father, John Begich, spent his life working in the iron ore mines.

My grandfather, John Begich, was born in 1893 in Podlapaca, Croatia, a country without a history of strong democratic institutions, in an area that later experienced the twentieth century's worst genocide.

After growing up in an impoverished nineteenth-century village whose survival depended on backbreaking farming, and armed with an eighth-grade education, my grandfather left Croatia in 1911 to join his brother in Minnesota. He found work and his wife in the Iron Range, and they raised three sons and a daughter. The youngest, my father, Nick, was born in 1932. His older brothers worked in the mines, but Nick was destined for the books.

Eleven years after Dad was born, the mine, mill, and smelter workers were finally allowed to organize openly, and Dad was introduced to the world of politics and debate.

During World War II, my grandfather lost most of his relatives back home to Tito's partisans, causing him to hate communists and always support an independent Croatia. He was very active in the CFR, the Croatian Fraternal Union, as was his friend John Blatnick, an American-Croatian

Republican Gov. Hickel
Hickel fills U.S. Senator Bob Bartlett's vacated seat with Ted Stevens
Alaska Native Claims Settlement Act
Nick Begich's plane missing
U.S. Senator-elect Mark Begich

1970
1980
1990
2000
2010

Nick and daughter Stephanie Begich, Anchorage, 1972.

politician. Blatnick greatly influenced my father when he was only eight years old. Blatnick encouraged my dad to go to college and to consider politics.

In high school, my father excelled in everything from sports to academics. He accumulated a year of college credit and enrolled at the local teachers college in St. Cloud. He pushed so hard that he got his bachelor's degree in three years and graduated with a cum laude degree in history and political science. While teaching high school, he got his master's degree two years later, and he was working on his doctorate when he died. A member of the Farmer Labor Young Democrats, he supported Hubert Humphrey for his second term in the U.S. Senate.

As a teacher, Dad's plans for a Minnesota political life changed when he fell in love with a former student, Pegge Jendro. In 1956, Dad's mentor Hubert Humphrey got Dad a job in Anchorage, where he could jump-start his political career. He moved, and that winter he returned to Minnesota to marry the student, my mom.

In 1957 Dad and Mom drove up the highway to Anchorage, where my father pursued his career as a teacher and politician. He always believed that an educated population was critical to Alaska's success.

In 1960, as principal of the elementary school at Fort Richardson, Dad was elected president of the Alaska Principals Association. As he fought for teachers for the next two years, he was still naive about public service. He believed people naturally served altruistically. He was aggressive about politics and didn't understand compromise.

That same year I was born, Dad decided to run for the Alaska Senate. He went to union leaders for backing, but they used him to pressure other Democrats who were in office. Taking advantage of his ambition, they convinced him to run against an incumbent. Although he lost the primary, the incumbent was weakened and he lost the seat in the general election. Determined to be his own man, Dad realized he must create his own base, and he turned to the Alaska Education Association, for which he lobbied.

A key to Dad's lifelong success was the three-by-five-inch cards on which he recorded the names of everyone he met, their personal information, and their issues. He opted for public exposure and became a more professional, streamlined Nick Begich. In 1963, Dad became the superintendent of the Fort Richardson schools and the youngest-ever elected state senator, with a district of 1,200 square miles that included one-fourth of the state's population. By long distance during legislative sessions, he supervised the Fort Richardson schools and taught classes at the University of Alaska.

Already a father of three—Nichelle, Nick, and me—he announced his second candidacy for the Senate the year his fourth child, Mark, was born in 1962.

Part of growing up in a political family with a man who was a workaholic was that I didn't know my father. In those days, the legislative session was unlimited, and although the Democrats dominated, they were often not aligned, and sessions could stretch into mid-June. My dad would drive to Juneau in January and not return for almost six months.

Before reapportionment made the previous geographic-based Senate districts invalid, Dad's district was enormous, stretching from Spenard to Adak. During the summer he campaigned, and Mom and we six kids drove, visiting relatives in the Lower Forty-eight. Sometimes Dad joined us.

At home, Dad had an inner sanctum that was off limits to us kids. Today it seems kind of funny: old photos show only a rundown teacher's office with jury-rigged shelves lined with books, most of which I now own. One of my first memories was when he invited me in and showed me the headlines of John Kennedy's assassination.

Throughout his years in the state Senate, Dad won twenty-three of twenty-four listed goals for teachers. By the time his Senate career finished, Alaska's teachers drew the nation's top salaries and benefits.

Alaska traditionally voted Democratic, but in 1966 we elected a Republican governor, Walter Hickel, and a Republican-dominated legislature. U.S. Senator Ernest Gruening, a Democrat, was seventy-nine years old. In 1968, Hickel appointed Republican Ted Stevens to replace Senator Bob Bartlett, a Democrat, who had just died.

In 1968, Nixon ran against Dad's mentor, Hubert Humphrey, and Dad ran for the Democratic nomination for the U.S. House against John Rader. Dad's teacher-based Democrats beat Rader.

Early on, Dad hadn't realized others played hardball, but he learned and built his own organization. He forged together the teachers and the Native Democrats and defeated Egan's establishment Democrats. In the general election, however, the nation went for Nixon and Dad lost to the Republican Party's Howard Pollock.

Throughout 1960, '62, '66, and '68 (and later, 1970), Dad campaigned. When he ran for Congress, he campaigned statewide, not just in his Senate district. My Dad's obsession with work finally triggered my mother to file for divorce in 1969. Devastated, Dad offered to leave politics. Mom left us kids with him, spent the summer in Minnesota, and returned in the fall supporting a Nick Begich who had discovered there was more to life than political pursuits.

In 1970, Bill Egan was in the race of his life. Frankly, all the Democratic Party's resources were focused on Egan and his running mate, Wendell Kay. My dad was

Nick Begich campaigning for state senate, 1960. Courtesy of Tom Begich.

running against Frank Murkowski for the U.S. Congress, and many thought Murkowski would win, but Dad beat him soundly.

With the expected oil pipeline blocked by pending Alaska Native land claims, Dad had one goal: get a land claims bill passed. The previous Congress had gotten a bill through the Senate, but if a bill didn't make it through the House, the legislation could die. Dad asked Guy Martin, a lawyer who knew land claims well, to be his legislative aide.

The chairman of the Senate's Interior and Insular Affairs Committee, Henry "Scoop" Jackson, had a bill and was pushing hard for settlement. The chair for the House's Interior and Insular Affairs Committee was a crusty ol' guy from Colorado, Wayne Aspinall. In those days, a chair held that post for life and ruled with an iron hand. It was known that Aspinall didn't support Indians or favor settlement, and he didn't like being pushed around at all. He was a conservative Democrat, hard to handle, but he would favor a member who attended all his committee meetings.

Our family had moved by then to Washington, D.C. On the weekends, Dad would touch base back in Alaska, then return to D.C. twelve hours and five time zones later (this was be-

Nick Begich and Alaska Federation of Natives staff, c.1970. Courtesy of Tom Begich.

fore they changed the time zones in Alaska in 1983) and drive madly to the committee hearing room just as Aspinall convened the Monday-morning meeting.

From the day Dad first arrived in Washington in December 1970, he made sure he knew every person, Republican and Democrat, in the House of Representatives. He saw each one as a potential vote for the settlement act. Every morning he left his office for the House floor with a three-by-five-inch card with the names of ten congressmen, saying, "I am going to get to know these guys and find out the three most important issues to them."

When he met with the Alaska Federation of Natives, he said, "Tell me what you want." They said, "Half a billion dollars, ten million acres, and the corporate structure." He responded, "We can do better." So Dad carried the bill forward with forty million acres and a billion dollars.

He spent a huge amount of time on the bill, discussing with oil companies and talking with his aide, Guy. He supported issues relevant to the colleagues he lobbied. He spent the entire first year positioning himself to get claims passed.

He didn't make the rousing speeches typical of his past but patiently worked his strategy, becoming a true statesman. When opposing members baited him, he nodded, made factual corrections, and didn't argue. He wanted a bill Natives could live with and one that worked.

Aspinall wanted to dictate the solution for the Natives. Dad and a supportive legislator from Washington, Lloyd Meeds, worked out a dynamic. Acting as a "no prisoners, no compromise" spokesman for the Natives, Meeds took the confrontational heat with the opposition, freeing Dad to be the connective tissue between Native and non-Native Alaskans and the politicians.

When Aspinall still wasn't delivering on Native terms, Dad called Aspinall's bluff, threatening to drop the bill. Aspinall replied, "Convince Bud Saylor of Pennsylvania, and we'll have a deal."

Before the final vote, Speaker of the House Carl Albert spoke: "I know of no one who has done more for his state in his first term of his first session than the hardworking, conscientious, never-say-die Nick Begich." On his chairman's advice, then, to combat possible amendments, Dad finally gave one of his fiery speeches, replying to all attacks with facts, dates, and numbers. In 1971 a billion dollars was a lot, and Congress was not so inclined, but the bill passed without amendment.

Later, I was told that if all the United States' indigenous land settlements were combined, they would not equal ANCSA's (Alaska Native Claims Settlement Act). While handling three committees, Dad, a first-session freshman, got a landmark bill that set the model for all subsequent Alaska land development. To this day, Dad is revered in rural Alaska.

From the outset, this quick-passage legislation was intended to be tweaked continually to meet the needs of the evolving Native community: addressing the rights of those born after passage, the descent of stocks, and the accountability issue of the new corporations. The great tragedy of ANCSA is that has not been done effectively. ANCSA is one of the most-amended acts ever, but only ten to twenty percent of those amendments have been to perfect the act. Rather, they have been to improve ANCSA's playing field, to get additional bites of the apple.

The morning of Oct. 16, 1972, Dad, Louisiana congressman and majority leader of the House Hale Boggs, Dad's aide Russ Brown, and pilot Don Jonz climbed into Jonz's Cessna 310 in Anchorage, bound for Juneau. The next morning, after the plane had not been heard from in twenty-four hours, our mother broke the news to us before we went to school.

House Majority Whip Democrat Tip O'Neil and Senator Nick Begich, Washington, D.C., c. 1971. Courtesy of Tom Begich.

As my brother Nick and I walked to classes, I looked up and saw a cloud formation. "See that cloud?" I said, "There's a plane and a mountain. You see, Dad must have made it through all right!"

When the votes were cast three weeks later, Dad won his congressional seat with 56.2 percent, even though he was suspected dead. Later, at the March special nominating convention, Mom, though a candidate herself, threw her support to Emil Notti and put him over the top as Alaska's first Alaska Native candidate for Congress. That was an election Don Young won by about one percentage point.

At age thirty-four, Mom was a widow with six children.

When I was twenty-one, in an attempt to "find" the father I lost when I was eleven, I interviewed over eighty people and drafted a book about his life.

Unlike my grandfather's native Yugoslavia, our multiethnic issues in Alaska are addressed within the confines of the state and federal constitutions. One-fifth of the legislature in Alaska is Native, mirroring the population, which is unusual in a state with a "minority" population.

Before the pipeline, times weren't easy in Alaska. Sure, Republicans and Democrats fought—but when we were finished, we talked with respect. That legacy and the gift of our father's instinct for public service have helped keep five of his six children here in Alaska.

Last December, Mom and I retraced my parents' first trip up the Alaska Highway in 1956. Fifty years after her marriage to Nick Begich, we drove and savored the journey.

Journey Back Home to Croatia

In the twenty-first century, after the 1990s wars that imploded former Yugoslavia, in October 2006 I returned to my grandfather's village Podlapača near Bihać, which borders the ancient military border, the front lines in the War of Croatian Independence. The military border (locally, Krajina [kri eena]) was one of two Serb historical areas inside Croatia.

Most Croatian Alaskans are from Croatia's coast. Our family originated from over the mountains that separate the Romanized and Venetianized coast from the interior.

The Begich family, Mark, Nick, Nichelle, Tom, Stephanie, Paul on Pegge's lap, Nick Begich, Anchorage, 1970. Courtesy of Tom Begich.

I'd heard my grandfather often describe his village, but I'd never seen a photo of Podlapača. In the fall, I drove along the Adriatic coast, where Rome had had its ancient network of roads. I enjoyed the Mediterranean ambience, the fruits, the modern expressway, the special flavor. But once I crossed over the boundary of the mountains, I was in central Europe, in the Balkans, and the feeling was completely different. Not only did I go from an arid climate to forested mountains, but in Gospić, desolation filled the air. Eleven years after the war, the buildings were still pock-marked and bullet-ridden. Not wanting to embarrass people, I didn't take photographs.

Tom Begich, Anchorage, 2006. Judy Ferguson photo.

On my way to Podlapača, road maps became suddenly irrelevant. West of Gospić, I tried to follow tarmacked roads but to my consternation, they dead-ended repeatedly at berms. I circled around and took a back road that finally went all the way into Podlapača. In my grandparents' village, there was not a building that wasn't scarred. Electric wires hung like stripped veins, dangling from eaves. If there was any electricity, it must have been underground. I wouldn't have believed anyone lived there except that I saw an occasional disinterested person. There were a post office, a health clinic, and two houses.

All over Croatia, I had seen granite memorials to the dead but in this small town, there was a much larger monument, out of proportion to the size of the town. When he was living, my grandfather said there were other families in the village with our same last name but that they were unrelated. So I looked on the granite not just for Begich but also for my grandmother's maiden name Martinić as well as Paun, and the name of my grandfather's boarder, Sertić. Those names were there but there were no dates alongside.

As I walked I thought I might've discovered the rock wall and big tree that my grandfather had said bordered his farm. At the church there was still a safe haven U.N. sign posted in front.

On the way back to Gospić, I followed a road sign but it soon became a dirt track no bigger than the width of my vehicle. Obviously the road hadn't been used in years. I began noticing rocks painted with slathers of red paint on my right and left. (I remembered then I'd been told on the coast that the area around Podlapača was still actively mined.) I thought I better turn around. At the entrance to a farm, I saw a cap that appeared to be a land mine. I realized that if I turned around where the red paint was splashed on the rocks behind me . . . I was terrified. It was getting toward dusk. I figured I'd better stay on the road because since someone had driven it to paint the rocks, the road must be okay. But there was no habitation. Nothing. It was like being in the middle of nowhere. For twenty miles, there was no sign of anything alive. Then I came up to one of those berms. I realized suddenly why the roads going into Podlapača dead-ended in berms. Only I was on the wrong side of it! I gunned my engine and drove right over the berm. On the other side of the mound there was a sign, *Ne Prilažite*, with a red skull and crossbones and the word, "Mines." Posted next to

214

Partial map of Croatia showing the two historical and previously Serb population areas in darker grey: upper right: portion of eastern Slavonia; lower is Krajina. Courtesy of Tom Begich.

it there was a map of the large mined areas, where I had just been!

That night, I drove to the Plivice National Park and intending to stay two nights, I checked into a hotel. Someone told me that the first guy killed in the war had been shot at this hotel. Early on, the hotel had been converted into a Serbian barracks, a notorious staging ground against my grandfather's region. The next day, I checked out early.

Just west of the old Krajina military border—now the boundary between Croatia and Bosnia—the Serbs had earlier occupied and held the Krajina. Podlapača was on the western border of that region and was held by the Serbs during the war. Hence the area heading toward Croat-held Gospić and to the east of Podlapača had been mined and its roads bermed.

The war in the Krajina took a brutal toll on Podlapača and the surrounding villages. Initially occupied by the Republic of Serbian Krajina, it was later recaptured by Croatian forces. Both these occupations displaced people, and in some cases, the original Croat and Serb inhabitants were killed.

In August 2008 when I returned, the town was still in disrepair. However, on the red-marked, once-abandoned road, I was surprised to see farms restarted, logging again occur-ring (cordwood was stacked for miles), and the berms that once blocked the roads were removed.

Nationalists killed Yugoslavia. But not communicating under Communism for fifty years to resolve the great wrongs done in World War II created flint and tender, ready for ignition by the mutual nationalist propaganda.

Talking across borders is critical. Here in the New World, the ancient hatreds in the Old World are not the same, but we have our own issues. Democracy works if people get past the boundaries of the aisle and travel roads together past their ideological berms.

Approaching Podlapača, Croatia. Tom Begich photo.

Chapter 33

A Foundation Stone: Judith Kleinfeld

 n 1969, before the Trans-Alaska Pipeline was built, Professor Judith Smilg Kleinfeld arrived in Alaska and became among the first to meet Alaska Native bias issues headlong. Knowing discrimination personally, Professor Kleinfeld described her own family history: "As a new pogrom in the early 1900s began killing most of the Jews in my grandfather's Lithuanian village, he got out and immigrated to New York. In those days, immigrants, particularly Jews, didn't talk much about their roots; they kept their Jewish culture but they also wanted to assimilate into America, our country.

"My father, Benjamin Smilg," she continued, "became an aeronautical engineer at Wright-Patterson Air Force Base in Dayton, Ohio, where he met my mother."

Judge Andrew Kleinfeld interjected, "Benjamin Smilg was a real engineering genius. During World War II, the vibrations in airplanes were shaking them apart. He solved the problem so that airplanes could travel at much higher speeds. He made supersonic flight possible!"

Professor Kleinfeld continued, "I was born in Dayton, Ohio in 1944. As a junior in high school in 1961, I saw a photo in the Dayton *Daily News* showing beefy policemen with cattle prods herding Blacks

Professor Judith Kleinfeld, c. 2006, Fairbanks, Courtesy of Judy Kleinfeld.

into buses when they protested against discrimination. I was shocked. I began developing College Prep, a forerunner of Upward Bound, a college preparatory program for black kids.

"In the 1960s, there were 10 percent quotas on Jewish admittance to major universities," she remembered. "When I went to Wellesley and later to Harvard, there was discrimination against Jews. In those days, W.A.S.P. [White Anglo-Saxon Protestant] country clubs were exclusive, and top law firms were mostly open only to non-Jewish lawyers."

At Wellesley, Professor Kleinfeld majored in psychology with the goal

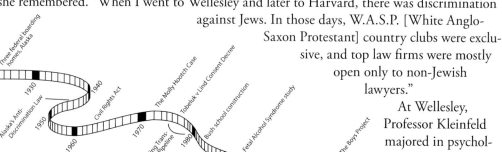

of helping educate African-American children. Later while earning her doctoral degree at Harvard, she worked with Pathways to Identity, a college prep for African-American adolescents.

"When I first met Andy at a Harvard mixer," she grinned, "I gave him my usual civil rights quiz. When he passed it, I let him have my phone number.

"As we courted," she added, "he suggested Alaska would be a great place to live."

Judge Kleinfeld added, "I knew what I'd do in Alaska—law and politics—but what would Judy's niche be? However, when I read in *Esquire* about the Institute for Social, Economic, and Government Research at the University of Alaska, we thought, 'Right topic, right place.'"

In 1969, Alaska had enormous opportunity because there were few skilled researchers studying the educational problems of Alaska Native children.

Professor Kleinfeld began collaborating with many Alaska Native groups studying boarding schools and boarding programs to see what effect they were having on Alaska Native adolescents. She studied the unusually high spatial intelligence skills of Eskimo children as well. She suggested teachers be educated in the local cultures. Kleinfeld also studied children with fetal alcohol syndrome and found what parents and teachers could do to help alcohol-affected children succeed. She gave hope that such children everywhere could lead fulfilling lives.

In pre-pipeline Alaska, there were no high schools in Alaska villages. The children were shipped to high schools away from home and even outside the state. Boarding school programs were an effort to bring the children back home to the state. However, the program often meant Native children lived with non-Native parents while attending local schools or that Native students were sent away from home to boarding schools.

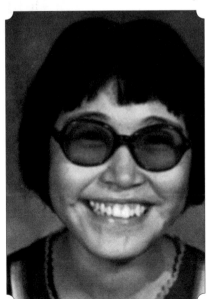

Anna Tobeluk, Nunapitchuk, c. 1978. (http://www.lksd.org/nunapitchuk/ Anna2.JPG)

"My research plan," Professor Kleinfeld explained, "was to study 160 young people who'd never been away to school, and track their progress in boarding schools, religious schools, and in the boarding home program to see what happened to them. To my surprise, the boarding programs were not working for most Native students. Their parents missed them; the children worried about their parents and relatives, and the villages lost the energy of their youth. I recommended establishing high schools in their villages so they could maintain their cultural heritage."

At that time, Alaska Legal Services was suing the state in the "Molly Hootch" case, claiming "denial of education" because the state had built high schools in communities of the same size as Native villages but not in Native villages.

Judge Kleinfeld pointed out, "In the Supreme Court decision, Judy's research was quoted extensively."

He continued, "Molly Hootch lost her case; however, an incomplete part of the conclusion was sent back to the Superior Court. At the same time, oil revenues had begun to come in; the state could afford to build high schools in the villages. The Alaska Department of Education entered into a consent decree enabling villages to establish local high schools."

Judge Kleinfeld continued, "Judy was the first to come to Alaska with a doctorate from Harvard, with knowledge of research methods. She became one of Alaska's first serious research educators focusing on Native education. Her boarding schools project completely changed the system of the education of Native children in Alaska. Something was wrong; she helped change it."

> Nettie Peratrovich, Haida-Scot, District Director of Indian Education Act Programs Title IV Party, State Operated School System. "The Molly Hootch consent decree in the late 1970s was a godsend; the state committed to provide local high schools for Native communities as it had in predominantly white communities. Using oil tax dollars, rural schools began to be built."

Recently, Professor Kleinfeld has created the Boys' Project, an international program to help boys who are dropping out of high school to help them make use of their talents.

"America," Professor Kleinfeld pointed out, "is a very fragile experiment. Cynicism can breed a lack of faith that will collapse the country from within.

"To me, the United States with its generosity, prosperity, and power is a real achievement of human civilization. It's not perfect," she said, "but we need to appreciate what we have. My purpose in my recent book *Go For It!* is to encourage people that the American dream can be lived on the Alaska frontier as well as on the frontiers people create for themselves. Through America's open society, people are able to find their own frontiers *wherever* they live.

"Alaska is open to talent," she emphasized. "It is particularly tolerant of Jews, even finding them *interesting*. But one big stain on Alaska's record has been its treatment of Alaska Natives."

> ### Speech to University of Alaska Symposium, February 27, 2004
> Excerpt by Stephen E. Cotton, Attorney, Andover, Massachusetts (http://www.ankn.uaf.edu/SOP/SOPv9i4.html#hootch)
>
> "I didn't document the disaster—Judith Kleinfeld did. Her 1973 study, A Long Way From Home, should be an inspiration to any of the students, educators, or researchers in this room who want to know whether the research you do can affect public policy. Because Judy's work did.
>
> She looked at the dropout rates—42 percent in a single year in the Bethel dorm, 65 percent over two years in the Anchorage Boarding Home program. She looked at the dismal academic performance these schools inspired. And, with a consulting psychiatrist, Dr. Joseph Bloom, she examined the social and emotional problems the students experienced. Some of Kleinfeld's findings are quoted word for word in the settlement of this case. In the end, the State had no choice but to agree that she was right."

Chapter 34

An Insecure Bridge: the 1984 Sarajevo XIV Olympic Winter Games, Mary Pat Maloney-Henderson

From 1998 to 2003 when a visa was required to enter the Federal Republic of Yugoslavia (FRY), I had to send my passport first to the FRY embassy in Washington, D.C. but after the 1999 NATO air strikes on FRY to Ottawa, Ontario, Canada. At Fairbanks' FedEx office, I relied on Mary Pat Maloney, a very dependable agent. As we filled out paperwork, she told me she'd gone to Yugoslavia as a liaison for the 1984 Sarajevo XIV Olympic Winter Games. Sarajevo, in Bosnia and Herzegovina, Socialist Federal Republic of Yugoslavia, was the first social-ist country to host the Winter Games, the second to host the Olympics, and the only time it was held in a predominately Muslim city. Chosen as a member of a travel agency consortium, Mary Pat left for Sarajevo in late 1983 to negotiate lodging for the American winter sports teams. Recently she shared a vi-gnette, a taste of that time that was a promise of Sarajevo's glory, in a Yugoslavia never to be revisited.

Mary Pat Maloney-Henderson, c. 2004.

ur American athletes were still qualifying to go to the Sarajevo Winter Olympics in late 1983. We were down to the wire to secure lodging for them. I flew first to New York City and met George, the head of Yugoslav Internal Affairs with the Department of Tourism for the winter Olympics, a big blonde guy. I flew on to Belgrade where I met the president of the Sarajevo Olympics. With sixteen hundred dollars to secure hotel space for the athletes, I was driven to Sarajevo to the Holiday Inn. On the way through Bosnia, I noticed that there were still bridges down from World War II. In Sarajevo, I met with the Olympic *predsednik* and a woman representative. With them, I inspected hotels and dormitory space. They demanded a deposit of sixty percent on rooms at the Holiday Inn and forty percent at the student apartment building: more than was normal. Their terms were "pay now and we'll deliver later." When I was hesitant, without warning they erupted into excited aggression, determined to intimidate me. I didn't understand their process for making a deal, nor their language, and their manner was confusing. For a half an hour, we were watched as our conversation was taped. They walked away from me to confer. I felt very uneasy but I was out of options. Some kids had already passed qualifications to come to Sarajevo. I'd come a long way, and we had to secure space. Apprehensive of losing the money, I didn't give them the percentage they demanded but only the sixteen hundred I had brought, and we never really reached a decision. I had to go on to Dubrovnik, and the *predsednik* was to drive me there. On the way, he didn't have money but he used chits for benzene (gas). I was getting a fever and I wasn't feeling up to par. In the dark on narrow

Sarajevo market, Olympics sign, 1983, Sarajevo. Courtesy of Mary Pat Maloney-Henderson.

curvy mountain roads he drove very fast. He kept reaching over and touching me suggestively. I was so scared that I started crying. He taunted me. Finally I could hear the ocean; I couldn't wait to get to Dubrovnik. Once I was safe in my room in the Old City overlooking the sea, I decided I'd fly to Ljubljana on my way home, not as planned to drive with him to Slovenia. I wasn't going to deal with that guy again. I let him keep the money, and I went on to Slovenia. While I waited for my plane, I realized I needed to buy something at the store. Police with rifles blocked my path and asked me where I was going. I wasn't used to a Communist state. When I had toured the marketplace in Sarajevo with Bosnians, my escorts were great people. But the Yugoslav big brother police state was intimidating. The system perpetuated fear in everyone. When I returned to the States, I got a job with FedEx and began working in Fairbanks. I don't know how things turned out with the travel agency getting the needed rooms for Sarajevo. I was just glad to be home.

Sarajevo, Bosnia and Herzegovina, Socialist Federal Republic of Yugoslavia, first socialist country to host the Winter Games; President Tito on building, 1983, Sarajevo. Courtesy of Mary Pat Maloney-Henderson.

Chapter 35

The Snows of Croatia, Fairbanks Gospel Outreach

I first met Brad Snow on New Year's in 1984 when he and the Gospel Outreach Fairbanks' ministry team visited Delta Christian Center.

Seven years later when I was going to church at Whitestone Farms, it was announced that Whitestone had purchased Brad Snow's ServiceMaster janitorial service for a church business. On the buffet, there was a photo of the Snow family missionaries going to war-torn Croatia.

In 1998 while research-

Dubrovnik, 2007. Judy Ferguson photo.

ing the builder of Rika's Roadhouse, John Hajdukovich, cousins Branko and Dr. Dragan Hajdukovich asked me to visit Hajdukovich's country, Montenegro, despite the possibility of imminent war. Although we were yet strangers, I called the Gospel Outreach pastor, Brad Snow, and told him of the invitation. He responded, "We have been praying for Montenegro." Continuing, "When we were there, 1992–95, the border was, of course, closed."

Two years later and after two trips to the Federal Republic of Yugoslavia, I stopped by Pastor Brad Snow's Gospel Outreach/Open Door church office. Overhearing the ensuing conversation, staff member Susan Brown commented, "Hmm, Montenegro. I was praying in October-November 1998 for Montenegro." I told her that even though it was under threat of bombing, I had been in Montenegro and Serbia October-November 1998.

In 2002, I asked Susan to accompany me to Belgrade to publish my first book, *Parallel Destinies*, the Hajdukovich story.

Throughout the early twenty-first century, we have enjoyed the Snows' link with Croatia and mine with Serbia/Montenegro, an unusual bond in the Alaska Interior. Over the years as I researched the Alaska-Yugoslav immigrants, I asked Brad and Andrea Snow if they might also tell their story, beginning with the Snows' first encounter with their Serbo-Croatian tutor in Fairbanks, Kate Miscovich, daughter-in-law of Flat/Iditarod/Fairbanks pioneer miner Pete Miscovich.

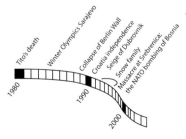

A voice from the implosion of former Yugoslavia, Fairbanksans Brad Snow and his wife, Andrea, lived the death of a nation in the 1990s while protected in the midst of a war zone.

In 1978 during a short stint in the Fairbanks Correctional Center, Brad Snow, a descendant of Alaska pioneers, committed his life to Christ. The day of his release, Brad met Pastor Tom Flint of Gospel Outreach church, who invited him to live with his family. As Brad began running the church's janitorial service, ServiceMaster, he met Andrea Stein, a lifelong Fairbanksan whose father mined Discovery Two, one claim up from Felix Pedro's original 1902 Discovery claim.

One night in 1982 while cleaning Nerland's Home Furnishing, Brad paused before a poster of Dubrovnik, Yugoslavia, that promoted a trip to the historic city as a reward in a sales contest. Snow recalled, "There was a glory, a light around that map of Dubrovnik. I felt the Lord say, 'Someday you'll be going to Dubrovnik.'

"During the following months," he said, "as I courted Andrea Stein, I told her one evening, 'I'm called to go to Yugoslavia.'"

"After we married," Brad continued, "I mined with the Steins, just one claim down from Andy Miscovich's mine. Somebody said we might be able to study Serbo-Croatian with Andy's sister–in–law, Kate Miscovich, a Fairbanks-Croatian, over at the library."

As the Snows began to study with Miscovich, she mentioned she had a niece, Ružica Miscović, a Dubrovnik attorney whose family was quite influential in Croatia. Kate went on to tell the Snows the unique history of the port city on the Adriatic Sea. Dubrovnik, called Ragusa or "Little Rome," had never been conquered by force. To maintain its independence during the Ottoman Empire, Dubrovnik annually paid the Turks a gold tribute. The first port on the Adriatic, Dubrovnik stole a lot of trade from Venice, which tried to conquer them but never could. "Napoleon," Kate said, "outwitted Dubrovnik, saying, 'If you let us in, we won't take you over. He came in and immediately took over, but due to events in France, he had to leave abruptly."

Joseph, Bill, Elsie, Ben, Sarah Snow; (back) Brad, Andrea Snow, Leaving for Croatia, c. 1991. Courtesy of Brad and Andrea Snow.

Dubrovnik was related to another walled city, Kotor, "Key," further down the coast on the Bay of Kotor, "Boka," a protected Montenegrin bay. (The Bay of Kotor, a multiethnic area more often ruled by the Venetians and then by the Austro-Hungarians, was the ancestral home of several notable Alaskan-Montenegrins: Marco [Mike] and Vuka Stepovich as well as Mary Pusich Miller and Mike Pusich of Juneau.)

As the Snows prepared to go as missionaries to Yugoslavia, they sold their janitorial business to a Christian community, Whitestone, in Big Delta. Snow's parents, Bill and Elsie Snow, also wanted to go with their son, Andrea, and their three children to Croatia. When the payments from Whitestone began arriving, the family decided to test living abroad and made a month-long trip to Germany in September 1991. Brad, not knowing that Croatia had declared independence and that Vukovar had been overrun in August, was eager to visit Dubrovnik. By early September, access by sea into Dubrovnik was beginning to close. Many of the non-Serbs in the JNA (Yugoslav People's Army) refused to fight their Yugoslav brothers. To replace them, Serb (nationalist and criminal) volunteer militias began raids into Croatia. When the militias invaded the District of Dubrovnik, fifteen thousand refugees ran to Dubrovnik's New

Dubrovnik tourist sign. Judy Ferguson photo.

Town hotels. Based out of Herceg Novi, Montenegro, and Trebinje, Bosnia, the JNA positioned themselves on top of the hills above Dubrovnik and began lobbing white phosphorous bombs into the city, burning everything in their wake. From land and sea, the city that Mussolini's force had avoided in World War II was shelled.

Nonetheless, Brad and his mother decided to scout out Dubrovnik. They drove from Germany to Italy, took a boat to Korčula, overnighted, and continued the next day to Split, Croatia. Ferry service to many Dalmatian islands had stopped; there was only limited service to Dubrovnik. "As we drove past burning buses into the Old City, we could hear machine-gun fire and bombing," Brad remembered. "We contacted Kate Miscovich's niece, Ružica Miscović. The Croats were nervous of course, not knowing if the Serbs were about to invade.

"Mom and I decided to fast and pray. Out in the harbor," he remembered, "there was a British boat going out daily to a battleship where peace talks were underway.

"As we prayed," Brad said, "the Lord gave me a scripture. It was the story in II Kings 19:32-34 when Hezekiah, king of Israel, fearing that Sennacherib, the king of Assyria, might invade Jerusalem. Hezekiah prayed. The Lord promised him that Sennacherib would not enter the city." Wanting further confirmation, Brad asked for another scripture. He turned then to II Chronicles 32:7-8 where again the same story was recorded. "I had a promise and peace then," Brad said. "For some reason, the JNA air support turned in midflight and returned to Belgrade. Without their air support, the Serbs never invaded.

"Later," Brad said rather incredulously, "we found out that the Serbs were less than a mile away, waiting for that air support."

A soldier friend had been poised with an anti-tank weapon, waiting just past a tight corner in the Old

Pedestrian walking in Dubrovnik's Old City, 2007. Judy Ferguson photo.

223

City. He later confided to Brad, "I was waiting for the tanks but they never arrived. Good thing—later when I tested my weapon, it didn't work!"

On October 1, the Snows were back in Fairbanks, but by then in Dubrovnik only one well remained working. To get water, townspeople risked sniper fire running to the well or boating out to ships. Dubrovnik was blockaded, hemmed in at the border with Croatia and Bosnia-Herzegovina and by the Navy from the sea. After heavy shelling December 6, the JNA forces quieted down for several months.

"By January 1992, we were finally on our way back to live in Croatia. We sold everything and hand-carried all our worldly possessions, including the Croatian version of the 'Jesus film' in our seventeen checked bags," Brad explained. "The airline staff looked, scratched their heads, and passed us on through. With perfect peace, we flew from Seattle to Rome. The Dubrovnik airport was closed so we flew to Split where we rented a van and hired a driver. We arrived in Dubrovnik, a city of seventy thousand with only two stores and one restaurant open. We had no connections to anyone there," he said, "besides Ružica Miscović, Kate Miscovich's niece. For eight months then we rented a two-bedroom apartment with my parents from a friend of Ružica's, Franica Čagal, who'd been in the police department for twenty-three years, a good contact for us. Even during war, Franica had no problem getting us visas, the only Americans in war-torn Dubrovnik! Her husband was also an influential hotel owner and became our good friend."

The Snows had two goals: to start a church and to give humanitarian aid to the seven thousand refugees who remained. "To the Croatians' credit," Brad pointed out, "they took in and fed the rural Croatian and Bosniak refugees.

"Except for one commuting Red Cross worker," he continued, "for three years, we were the only Americans in Dubrovnik."

Andrea remembered, "There was an oppressive feeling in the air: you couldn't talk openly, express what you were thinking or feeling."

Franica's apartment was small and expensive so the elder Snows moved into a new apartment, renting from a Serbian lawyer. Brad and Andrea Snow rented from a lady on King's Way street who turned out "to have issues," Brad smiled. In the city, electricity was rationed: six to eight hours per twenty-four hours. "Even though my parents' Serbian landlady had been born and raised in Croatia," Brad pointed out, "she lost her lawyer position. Croats also killed her father and her grandfather. In her own hometown, she was completely ostracized.

"Croatia's tie to Germany," Brad said "was very evident: the look of their new money was very similar to the German mark, and certainly during World War II, they cooperated with the Nazis.

"An attraction to the Serbs would've been Croatia's beautiful coastline," Brad said, "some oil, and it was also more progressive. Of course," he clarified, "what the Croats did to the Serbs during World War II was terrible, far worse than what the Serbs did to the Croats in the 1990s."

The moment to save Yugoslavia was past. "At some point," Brad said, "records were reputedly found stored in Croatia that detailed a conspiratorial one-hundred-year-old plan for a Greater Serbia." Rather than accept Lord Carrington's proposal of recognizing independent ethnic regions, President Slobodan Milosevic preferred to fight, citing the need to protect the Croatian Serbs, fearing another genocide as had been during World War II. "Milosevic," Brad continued, "fought for a Greater Serbia, to take Bosnia and fill that Yugoslav state with the Serbs of both Croatia and Bosnia." When Carrington's compromise was rejected, the blood bath went on.

In 1989, nine years after the death of President Josip Broz Tito, JNA senior officials (suspiciously) demilitarized the District of Dubrovnik. Throughout the siege of Dubrovnik, the JNA tried to take the strategically located Napoleonic Imperial Fort on Mount Srdj, through which they could have controlled the city, but they could not. They bombarded villages, including Gorniji Brgat, five kilometers behind Dubrovnik. "In a village near Brgat," Brad recalled, "I became friends with Elar, who was in charge of all humanitarian aid in Dubrovnik, caring for those seven thousand Bosniaks.

"It's important to understand," he emphasized, "the war was always going on around us in other parts of Croatia and in Bosnia. We were only four miles from the Bosnian border.

"Elar warned me," he said, "'Don't go off the beaten path. Not all this area has been swept for mines.'" However, while looking for wild asparagus and without thinking, Elar's daughters later stepped on a mine. One was killed and the other lost her leg.

"We had a Yugo car," Brad explained. A New York lawyer from Helsinki Watch needed a driver to go and interview a former Croat prisoner who'd been imprisoned in Montenegro. "At that time, the world didn't know about the detention camps across the border in Montenegro, one at Morinj," Brad said. "At the interview, former prisoner 'Mihalj' remembered that in 1992, he and other Croatian prisoners were taken across the border in cattle cars to Montenegro." As the prisoners were unloaded, Serbs dressed in Nazi S.S. uniforms hit them with their guns, shouting, "This is what you did to us in World War II!" Along with 250 other people, the prisoners were then shoved into a thirty-foot-by-thirty-foot metal shed with only a small breathing hole. The only liquid the prisoners had was their own sweat. Mihajl was beaten

Bill, Andrea, Sarah Snow, the adopted family in Brgat holding Joseph and Ben Snow. Young man is holding a Russian made Serbian launched shell, Brgat near Dubrovnik, 1992. Courtesy of Brad and Andrea Snow.

and for three days, left for dead. "Many times as he spoke," Brad said, "the man broke down, weeping. I told him, 'The Lord saved you for a reason.' 'I know,' he agreed."

In Dubrovnik, a small Protestant church contacted the Snows. For forty years with twelve core members, they had endured Communism. Brad said, "Connected with the faith movement and holding services in a blown-up hotel by the sea, the church eventually grew to sixty people." The pastor, Vladimir ("Vlado") Krajičić, worked as a government tax collector as well; like other professionals, he earned about two hundred dollars a month. Since churches in Yugoslavia were required to register with the government, "Vlado could easily cover that," Brad said. "His wife," Brad pointed out, "said that during the blockade of Dubrovnik when she was praying against the JNA invasion, the Lord had given her the same scripture that I had gotten, the story of King Hezekiah and the possible invasion of Sennacherib, the king of Assyria. She got the same promise of safety." He smiled, "That was pretty cool!"

"The Protestant churches in Croatia," he continued, "all network together. With Vlado, I attended a Protestant conference in Osijek near Slovenia, where I met a lot of people, including our friend Mihelj Janke. Mihelj ministered via radio and distributed Derek Prince material. Also, Vlado had first received the Lord," he said, "through the well-known local ministry of Peter Kuzmić, cofounder and director of the Biblical Theological Institute of Croatia."

Vlado frequently visited the state-run local orphanage, Dječji Dom Maslina. Even during the Communist period, the Protestant church had a strong influence on the orphanage. "However, the older boys," Andrea said, "remembered sometimes having to meet clandestinely. Sometimes the police followed them."

Ivica, of the Dječji Dom Maslina orphanage, Dubrovnik, 1992. Courtesy of Brad and Andrea Snow.

"We have this photo of one young man, Ivica," she smiled, "holding up his Bible trium-phantly, framed by the Old City with the sea behind him. I called him 'My little sunshine.'"

Through their pastor, the Snows met Vinco, a Croatian Serb married to a Croatian girl, Romana. "Vinco also served in the Croatian Army!" Brad said incredulously. "He told us stories from the front of the Catholic priest blessing them to kill the Serbs. The ethnic cleansing included pushing the Serbs out of Croatia, pressuring mixed families and eliminat-ing any Serbian word usage in their common Serbo-Croatian language while retaining only Croatian word usage."

In asserting their new post-Communist identities, formerly atheistic Croats and Serbs sud-denly embraced their historic, traditional churches. Serbs began wearing Orthodox bracelets, more families celebrating family Slavas, hanging church icons from their car mirrors, and genuflecting east (toward Constantinople) to west. Croats wore crucifixes and crossed themselves west (Rome) to east. "The Catholic priests had a lot of control," Brad said. "With such religious identification in the new nation," he pointed out, "Croats could better advance in their jobs and be accepted.

Pero with his Bible, of the Dječji Dom Maslina orphan-age, the Adriatic Sea, Dubrovnik, 1992. Courtesy of Brad and Andrea Snow.

"The issue that destroyed Yugoslavia," he continued, "was power and control." An ancient network of tribalism based on ethnicity defined through religion and culture was the means by which power-brokers and global criminals profited from a national meltdown. (By anal-ogy it has been said that if the United States' media and organs of power were controlled by the Ku Klux Klan, as ultra nationalists controlled both Serbian and Croatian seats of power, that there would also be violent ethnic outbreaks in America.)

"As Protestants (less than one percent) in a society that was ninety-five percent Catholic, our family—despite our mission—was considered a religious 'sect, cult,' suspect," Brad explained. "For a Croat to become a Protestant is equivalent to betrayal of family, society." While exemplary in hospitality, all former republics of Yugoslavia tend to xenophobia. While church and state now tend to function essentially as one, a visitor should never confuse hospitality with Christian charity and ethics. "Along with the Croatian Muslim minority, we Protestants," he explained, "were also 'persecuted.'"

During Ramadan, the Snows' Muslim neighbor invited them to his mosque, where the men were separated from the women. Andrea recalled, "When the Croatian Muslims spoke, there was a social feeling, but when the visiting Saudi spoke, there was a terrorist-feel about him." Brad added, "My neighbor leaned over and confided in me that he was the number

The Snow family, children from the Dječji Dom Maslina orphanage, and church staff. Dubrovnik, 1993.

two political leader for all Islamic Croats!

"He was praying for my conversion," Brad grinned, "and I for him.

"Every holiday," he warmed with the memory, "his wife would bring us a handmade, seventeen-layer baklava: filo dough, sugar, oil, and nuts! I was deeply touched."

A year and a half after the Snows' arrival, a team of Gospel Outreach Fairbanks intercessors arrived in 1993. "We felt," Brad said, "that the Lord was calling the people out, to walk 'the length and breadth of the land' as Abraham had also done" (Genesis 12). "We decided to begin our 'prayer walk,'" he continued, "beginning at the oldest Sephardic synagogue in the world [built in 1652], and walk on top of the Old City's twenty-foot-thick walls. At the end," he said, "we'd show the 'Jesus film' [Paul Eshleman] in Croatian at the Marin Držić theatre, built in 1865 when the common people couldn't afford to enter." The Snows met with the director of ministries to get access to the synagogue and the theatre. The director said that during World War II, the Nazi Croat/Utashe had sectioned off the Jewish neighborhood, including the synagogue, making a ghetto. The Jews had hidden their most precious items: the Ark of the Law and the Torah scrolls first brought in 1492 by the Sephardic Jews leaving Spain due to the Edict of Expulsion. All these precious items survived the World War II Holocaust.

"At church before the prayer walk," Brad explained, "we announced the showing of the Jesus film. To my amazement," he said, "the man who had originally translated the film into Croatian was there from Zagreb! When I asked him for permission to show the film, he answered, 'Yes; before the war, we had elaborate plans for it. But after the war began, our plans went out the window.' Amazing, that he was there!" Brad said.

The team made advertising posters and rented a projector and large screen. The theatre for the showing was across the street from the main Catholic church. Priests warned Croats not to attend the Jesus film. "I put the Jesus poster on my car," Brad said, "and someone sliced my tires. We just didn't know," he paused, "how this event was going to go."

The prayer team began their walk from the ancient synagogue, following the Old City walls and back to the Marin Držić theatre, off the main square. "A half an hour early," Brad smiled, "waiting to get in, there were already two hundred people lined up! The film," he added, "was a great success!"

Later, Brad felt led by the Lord with his parents to visit the Catholic bishop of Dubrovnik, a "surprisingly delightful meeting," Brad recalled. "The bishop encouraged 'New Evangelism,' an opportunity for even priests to evaluate if they indeed had a personal relationship with Jesus. The bishop publicly apologized for the 1545–1563 Council of Trent and

Marin Držić theatre where film was shown, built in 1865, Dubrovnik. Courtesy of Brad and Andrea Snow.

its judgment on Protestantism. The Dubrovnik Catholics were hosting crusades in a stadium filled with thousands of people! It was very refreshing to hear," he nodded.

With their first three children, the Snows always had home births. By 1993, Andrea was expecting the couple's fourth child. Through a nurse acquaintance, Dragica, Brad had contracted with a midwife, but he was obliged to have a doctor also as a backup. To complicate matters further, housing was again an issue. "In Croatia," Brad explained, "renting always means that you are an extension of a local family; you live with a Croatian family or are close to that family. They have a lot of control in your life." He emphasized, "In Croatia, there are no renter rights. If a landlord decides to arbitrarily evict you, you have to go. Three days before Andrea had Miho, our landlady decided she suddenly wanted her home back. Trying to ignore that, Andrea gave birth to Miho with the midwife in attendance. However it was soon obvious that the midwife had left too soon. Andrea began having complications. Even though we had no place to go the landlady kept trying to evict us. She called the police. I met them at the door and asked in Croatian, 'It's not yet the end of the month. Why are you here?' They turned, looked at each other, and asked, 'Why are we?' then the cops got mad at the landlady for bothering them."

Earlier in the open market, the Snows had met and helped a merchant family. Whenever the Snows had extra funds, they helped that family upgrade their home. During the war, houses that were vacant in Dubrovnik were immediately filled with refugees without the owner's permission. The family's brother had a beautiful vacant apartment in the most affluent part of Dubrovnik. Deciding it was best to have the flat occupied, the brother rented the apartment to the Snows. "I just lay there, unable to help, while Brad and the kids packed our stuff to move," Andrea remembered. "After we moved into our new place, I began bleeding profusely and passing out." Brad needed an ambulance quickly but didn't know his new phone number or address. He reached Dragica, who through the doctor got an ambulance. "Suddenly my wife was in the bullet-ridden, bombed hospital complete with cockroaches," he said. "The Serbs had bombed everything, including the hospitals." The midwife had apparently done a bad job; some of the placenta remained inside. The only way to locate it was through an ultrasound test. We hoped she wouldn't need a transfusion.

Not only was Andrea in a hospital for the first time, and in crisis, had just been evicted, but she was also in a foreign country, surrounded by a difficult language. Befuddled, she listened to the hospital staff chatting in the background about the prime time TV show "Santa Barbara" while they discussed "this terrible American who'd done the awful thing of having a home birth." "Croatia was ten years behind the United States," Brad added. Andrea smiled, "The best was that I didn't need a transfusion and our youngest son, Michael (Miho), was okay and had been born at home on King's Way."

As the Snows struggled in ministry for three years, experiencing both rejection and the Balkan double standard of adultery even among some in the congregation, they looked with yearning at the very successful Christian crusades in the former Soviet Union. "Our pastor told us," Brad explained, "that the war had softened the Croats, making them more receptive. But even in war, they were still a very hard, loveable, but very stubborn people."

In late 1994, the Snows prepared for their three-month-long missionary furlough back to Alaska. On both their 1991 and 1992 entrances, they had never registered with the American Embassy in Zagreb. But needing a passport for their new two-year-old son, Michael, to return home, they registered at the embassy.

While in Alaska, pastor's wife Nancy Campbell awakened during the night. Nancy said she felt the Lord say, "Tell Brad and Andrea, 'If the war kicks up, they must make plans to leave and…LEAVE! They will not want to but they must leave.'" "I had sold out my life, sold everything," Brad protested. "I figured if I rode out a war with the people, I'd win their hearts." Brad didn't think there was much chance of the war kicking back up, but within a few months after their return, the familiar signs began to happen. In April, "the Serbian troops returned and began blocking the main, coastal highway between Dubrovnik and Split, which," Brad pointed out, "would isolate us, our chief concern. NATO began threatening to bomb.

"The American Embassy in Zagreb," Brad said, "kept calling us to get out." Andrea inserted, "The most significant thing to me was that I lost my peace; I was fearful." The people felt as long as the Americans were there, there must be *some* hope. In early May with only a three to four day advance notice, Brad hurried to get airplane tickets for his family and paid nine thousand dollars. "As I was getting my tickets," he remembered, "the agent was so nervous she could barely write." To protect the airport (with Bosnia only a few miles away), the Croats had their big guns trained on the Serbian guns up in the hills. "Not knowing if we'd be shot down, our plane took off, banked steeply hard right, and flew directly to Rome. Just after we left," he pointed out, "the Croats pushed the Serbs out of the military frontier/Krajina. By July, General Mladić had murdered eight thousand Bosniaks in the U.N.-declared safe haven of Srebrenica. By August, NATO was bombing Bosnia. We were very thankful to be back in America.

(Left) Brad Snow, (right) Andrea Snow, Fairbanks, 2008. Judy Ferguson photos.

"Back home, living near Fort Wainwright, I'd hear a helicopter," Brad remembered, "and I'd think, 'Is it theirs? Are they coming yet?' I had to remind myself I was no longer living under threat of war."

Not long after the Snows' return, Brad became Gospel Outreach's associate pastor. The next year, he began the first of ten years as senior pastor until he retired in 2006.

"Since leaving, we have returned twice to Dubrovnik," Brad said. "When I visited our little church there by the sea once I happened to see Lydia, a member of the congregation, who told us Vinco and Romana and some of the young men from the orphanage were still there: a remnant."

In 2008 Brad said, "The only possibility for reconciliation between Serbia and Croatia is through Christ. I'd love to be a part of that, to attend Christian reconciliation conferences there." He said quietly, "What I feel for that country is very real."

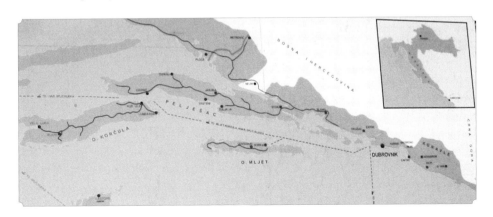

Pronounciation key: Dragica=Drahgeetza, Ruzica=Ruzheetzuh, Franica=Frahneetza; Ivica=Eéveetza; Kuzmic=Koozmeech; Osijek-Oóseeyek; Mihalj=Meéhiil; Čagal=Chagal, vić=vich. Note: Bosniaks refers to Bosnian Muslims.

Chapter 36

Born to Fly: Christopher A. Stepovich

SOME REAL INTER
IN HIS WORK.

Chris Stepovich is one of several MarkAir pilots from
Fairbanks who have graduated to flying our Boeing
737s. Born and raised in Fairbanks, Chris comes from
a long line of Stepoviches who call the Interior home.

And like the 1,300 other MarkAir employees who live and
work throughout Alaska, Chris wants to continue to provide Alaskans
with low-cost airfares. And if the state approves MarkAir's request
for a loan guarantee, he'll be one of the thousands of employers
who will ultimately own a majority interest in the airline.

So if you'd like Chris Stepovich and MarkAir to keep
flying and serving Fairbanks, write or call the governor's office, and your legislators, and let them know
you support the loan guarantee. Because in the
long run, the state's guarantee to MarkAir is about
turning local experience into local ownership.

MARKAIR

*In 1998 in Fairbanks when I used to visit Vuka
Stepovich, she told me her step-grandson Chris
Stepovich was a saint, someone very special. I never
met Chris until he telephoned me in September
2001, a year after Vuka's death. Since then, Chris
and I have worked together.*

*Here Chris tells the story of his life-changing
day, February 1999, and his subsequent eleven
years filled with pain and joy.*

"As I sat for six hours in that destroyed
airplane, I did the necessary. Far away, my family and friends did also. It took a lot of moving parts to accomplish one goal: search and
rescue."—Christopher A. Stepovich, pilot.

"The only thing on my mind that night was
the person inside that plane, the survival of
that human being."—Junior Riley, Hageland
Aviation Services, St. Marys Station Manager

*Christopher Stepovich, MarkAir pilot,
c. 1994. Courtesy of Christopher Stepovich.*

was born in 1953 in Fairbanks when Alaska was a territory, the fifth of Mike and
Matilda Stepovich's thirteen children. As the last territorial governor, Dad flew often to
Washington, D.C., lobbying for statehood. When I was five, I flew with my family on a
Pan Am DC-6. Because I was the governor's son, the captain put me on his lap and let
me hold the yoke of the plane. He showed me the instruments and described invisible
airways. On another flight with Dad, two Alaska Air National Guard Scorpion jets flying off
each wing escorted the governor back into Alaska. Looking out the windows, I knew I
wanted to be a pilot.

As I grew up, I collected airplane models and aviation books. On my bike, I imagined I
was flying on the wind.

When pipeline construction began in the 1970s, I worked on the North Slope and saved
my money for an airplane. I flew for three years using floats, skis, and tundra tires. Flying
my Piper PA12, a very forgiving airplane, I flew all over Alaska.

With money from the slope, I took a year off for more pilot training. In nine months,
I got my student, private, commercial, instrument, and multiengine ratings. Like a surfer
catching a wave, I loved flying and decided to make it my career.

I returned north and flew co-pilot on DC-3s for Frontier Flying Service. For the next
twenty-five years, I flew 737s, DC-4s, KC-97s, and many small craft. I flew with MarkAir
for five years to both coasts, followed by six months of 747 training in Japan. Since 1975, I
have accumulated fourteen thousand hours of flying time. Many pilots in the military retire
after only thirty-five hundred hours of flying.

Antonia, Maria, (standing) Dominic, and Matilda (pregnant with Nicholas); (front) Michael, Peter, Christopher, (in the governor's arms) Theodore, 1958, governor's mansion, Juneau. Courtesy of Nick Stepovich.

I have experienced engine failures, fires, and icing. In a dead-stick landing, a pilot knows by the gauges and the feel of the plane how to get the wind under the wing for a controlled landing.

In 1999, I was based in Fairbanks, working the night shift for an Anchorage aviation company. I'd gone to bed one morning in February when I got a call that they needed pilots to fly out of Anchorage to St. Marys that night. Bad weather was backing up their Bush freight.

"By the time you get here and get out, you'll be starting a new duty day. I'll owe you one," the dispatcher promised. Reluctantly I agreed, so they flew me to Anchorage to pilot the Beech 1900C, a large plane capable of carrying nineteen passengers. However, these contracts were cargo only.

When I got to work, the blizzard was still in the St. Marys area, but the minimums for landing were legal: two-hundred-foot ceiling and 1.5-mile visibility. It was a single-pilot operation with forty-nine hundred pounds of soda pop on board. The soda pop was braced so it could not slide from back to front, but nothing held it firmly to the floor. Also, only recently had the weight capacity for the Beech 1900C been increased by a thousand pounds.

As I neared St. Marys, which is on a bluff, after being cleared for approach two miles out at two hundred feet AGL (above ground level), I set my flaps at the first notch and let my landing gear down. Instead of getting the expected headwind, a thirty-knot crosswind from the right suddenly lifted the wing and threw the cargo to the side, upsetting the plane's balance. I corrected, but without enough wind at that level, the plane dropped but avoided cartwheeling.

When I awoke in the darkness, my Mini Mag flashlight was shining in my eyes. I thought it was a snowmachine; it seemed like a spotlight in that immense darkness. A thousand feet away, the plane's tail was on the hill; the fuselage had opened from the cockpit and was in a ravine. I had been thrown eighty feet, just missing the spinning plane. I didn't know at the time, but I had dislocated both knees and fractured the left one.

Wearing a vest, insulated pants, and left with only one boot, I jumped to get up but screamed when my left leg collapsed. It was –5° F with winds gusting up to thirty-eight mph blowing snow. With bare hands, I crawled to the fuselage and opened the side door. The snow sifted in everywhere. I stacked pop cases as far as possible against the open fuselage and wrapped the wall of case lots with a space blanket. I urinated in emptied Pine-Sol bottles and used them for hand warmers. I traded socks to cover my exposed left foot and wrapped a plastic space blanket around me and one over my head.

Junior Riley with Chris' Beech 1900C near St. Marys, 1999. Courtesy of Jr. Riley.

For the next six hours, the wind blew on the ripped metal, sounding like an approaching snowmachine.

When the plane was reported overdue, the Alaska Army National Guard at Bethel, eighty miles from St. Marys, could not fly their helicopter because they had no available certified night-vision pilot. The local Alaska State Troopers were ordered not to go out in the storm. The troopers told the local Hageland Aviation people that they would look for the body in the morning. Hearing that, St. Marys Hageland Aviation station manager Junior Riley, who was at home off duty, got dressed and rounded up his crew. Unpaid, they headed out. They were familiar with the terrain, armed with no coordinates but only a handheld aircraft radio, hoping to pick up the emergency landing transmitter signal. On snowmachines, they searched blindly for two hours. When they couldn't see, they waited for the wind to settle.

At home, my company notified my wife, Joan, who called the family in Fairbanks. My brother, Mike, called Senator Ted Stevens, hoping the senator could get someone certified to Bethel to fly the helicopter. At home Joan, who was sympathetically feeling my cold, turned up the stove and made a fire in the fireplace. She called our church and Gospel Outreach/ Open Door church next door to pray. Intercessors prayed all through the night.

After five and a half hours in the plane wreckage and snow, I began to think I'd better write notes in case I didn't make it. Just then I suddenly heard snowmachines. "Hey, it's down there!" someone yelled.

My ELT beacon had guided the Hageland crew from a mile and a half away. "Otherwise," Junior Riley said, "we would never have found you. The white plane was drifted over with snow, buried in a ravine." Looking at the wreckage, Junior later said, there was one in a million chance the pilot could be alive.

Inside, I could hear them, but my voice wouldn't work and I couldn't whistle. Finally, as they descended, I yelled, "Hey, I'm in here!" and someone hollered, "He's alive!"

Fighting my destroyed knees, frozen hands, bloody head, snowdrifts, and with no snow toboggan for a litter, the crew put a jacket on me and put me on the back of Junior's snowmachine. Hanging on, we rode two miles to where EMTs met me at the terminal. My adrenaline had subsided and pain hit me like a tsunami. For the next twelve hours, I endured until I was finally rolled into surgery in Anchorage.

Since February 12, 1999, I have had seventeen surgeries. However, I came home to my wife and four boys. We knew that God had been my co-pilot.

My aviation partner once asked me what I liked about flying our Piper Cub. I told him it was catching a tailwind. "The tail goes up and I ride the crest. With the wind at my back, I'm one with the plane."

Chapter 37

Learning to Fly in Every Weather: Ivan and Chris

In September 2001, I knew I was entering another long round of pending surgeries. As I sat in my car before going into the doctor's office, I pondered what my brother Nick had told me the night before about a young Serb, Ivan Mišković, who wanted to come to Alaska to play basketball. I thought back to that long night, February 12, 1999, buried in the snow-covered ravine outside of St. Marys. I thought, "Maybe I lived to help this young man, maybe this would save his life." Before going into the clinic, I called Judy Ferguson and told her to send Ivan to us.—Christopher Stepovich

Chris Stepovich and Ivan Mišković, flexing his knees, first night, Nov. 2001. Judy Ferguson photo.

ost of us are full of good ideas for others, but few will pay the price. Quietly the Stepovich family steps up to the plate and does what needs to be done.

In 1998 to 1999 when I used to visit Vuka Stepovich, she talked about her nephew Simo Radovic of Risan, Montenegro, whom she'd put through college in California. When I was traveling in Seward, the Banic family with great respect told me how their brother Sammy had stayed with the Stepovich family in Fairbanks while attending University of Alaska Fairbanks (UAF).

In 2000 as I finished up my research on John Hajdukovich of Rika's Roadhouse, I began to consider printing my book in Belgrade for the Alaska market. I went to my friend Miša David's brother Filip David, a well-known author in former Yugoslavia. He referred me to a tall man in Belgrade experienced in book layout, Dragan Mišković. After meeting me, Dragan agreed to design the Hajdukovich/Rika's Roadhouse book *Parallel Destinies.* Also, Dragan wanted help for his son Ivan.

In 1989 as Yugoslavia began to unravel, President Slobodan Milošević fed the fire by pumping nationalist incendiary propaganda through the state-owned TV station RTS. An RTS employee, Filip David, and others including Dragan walked out. They couldn't afford the loss of salary but they wouldn't be a part of destroying Yugoslavia.

At home in 2000, Dragan's six-foot-eight-inch tall sixteen-year-old son Ivan loved basketball. His father was concerned about Ivan's future. As a result of wars, criminals, and international sanctions, out of the once-prosperous Yugoslavia there remained only Serbia and Montenegro, living behind a wall, isolated, poor,

Plane accident & NATO bombing of FRY (Yu.)
Vuka Stepovich died
Bombing of World Trade Center Twin Towers
UAF Nanooks, Div. II team, won BP Top of the World Classic
Nanooks, NCAA Div II Sweet Sixteen

2000
2010

and driven by crime—every day uncertain. Unemployment, murder, and drug abuse soared. With little hope or vision, children roamed the streets most of the night and slept during the day. To get a job, it was said a person had to be connected. Certain that there was no future for Ivan in Belgrade, Dragan sent a basketball video of Ivan's skills with a promotional of him speaking to prospective coaches to me. I copied the video and at his direction, I sent it out to high schools and colleges, wrote letters, made calls, and contacted immigration. Dragan suggested firmly that I talk to Fairbanks' Slavic-Alaska families regarding Ivan's future.

For four years, throughout the NATO bombing, I'd tried to help my friends behind their wall. My efforts had fallen mostly on deaf ears. I had experienced disappointment with some I'd tried to help and with Americans who weren't interested. I'd lost my oldest Serbian Jewish friend to brain cancer. I had little optimism and not much remaining energy. On a shopping trip to Fairbanks in early September 2001, I went to see my friend retired Key Bank president Bill Stroecker. I began, "Bill, I have another cause." When I explained, he said, "Go see Nick Stepovich." In my research on John Hajdukovich, Nick and I had conferred, but I didn't know him well. In 2000, Vuka had passed away. Very tired, recovering from a broken leg and getting a cold, I wanted to just drive the one hundred miles back home. But at 9 p.m. on Stroecker's faith, I hobbled into Fred Meyer's noisy vestibule to the pay phone. I braced myself for rejection as I dialed Nick's home number, and began, "Nick, this is crazy but..." He listened quietly and said, "Well, sure. Our family has always done that kind of thing. But...will he mind?"

One morning a week later, a stranger's voice woke me at 7 a.m.: "Judy, my name is Christopher Stepovich. We want Ivan. We will send him to Monroe Catholic High School. We wanted him a week ago. Send us the information and we'll take care of the documents. Maybe we could arrange a trans-Atlantic phone call with him and his parents. You bring

him; we'll take care of him." I was transfixed and transformed. When I had done nothing, a response beyond my wildest hopes had presented itself. When I e-mailed Dragan, he was blinded with his tears. The next week on an international phone call, Dragan and Ivan talked with Matilda and Chris Stepovich. Matilda and Dragan spoke in Serbo-Croatian; they discovered their families were from the same Dalmatian island, Hvar, Croatia.

A few days later Christopher had an accident with his Skil saw, requiring surgery to his hand. Then the Twin Towers were hit. We didn't know how September 11, 2001 would affect Ivan getting a visa. However, Chris worked with Senator Ted Stevens and Congressman Don Young, and two months later, he was able to secure Ivan's visa.

On November 17, 2001, I joined Chris and Joan Stepovich and their four sons to pick up the new "big

Ivan Mišković meeting Judy Ferguson, Fairbanks International Airport, 2001. Judy Ferguson photo.

brother" at Fairbanks International Airport. After nearly a year of effort for me and Dragan, Ivan looked down at us, the grinning Americans below him, waiting at baggage claim. It was the beginning of a long journey. Ivan was seventeen, and he still needed his own home. His childhood had been ten years of bombing, sanctions, confusion, and implosion.

From the beginning the Stepoviches adopted Ivan and he them. Chris was a true father; his twelve siblings became Ivan's *tetkas* (aunts) and uncles. Craig Compeau, the Gavoras, and the Monroe community got behind supporting Ivan. However, there were many adjustments and disappointments waiting for him. He spoke English but everything around him, including the money, was strange. A Serb from war-torn Orthodox Serbia, to Ivan Catholics represented Croatia, with whom his republic had just fought a bitter war. However, he was required to attend but not partake of Catholic mass at Monroe Catholic High School. Because he had not come through an official foreign exchange student agency, during his remaining senior year he was not allowed to play competitive basketball. He could practice but he could not compete. It seemed this was all he'd ever have in America. As a true team player, Ivan rooted with all his heart, supporting kids he'd only just met. While many of the Fairbanks high schools were interested in the towering Serb, Chris and I waited to see if any opportunities might really open up for Ivan. Honoring the students' parents one evening, Monroe recognized Ivan's "parents" by presenting flowers to me and to Christopher. May 2003, at Ivan's Monroe graduation, each student was given a rose to give to his mother. With purpose in his eyes, Ivan strode down the aisle and over to the section where I stood. He embraced me and handed me the rose.

An adopted child is something very special. Ivan was supposed to go home that spring, and it seemed that would be the end of his American experience.

However, that spring, Chris and I met with Coach Al Sokaitis at UAF regarding Ivan's possible future with the UAF Nanooks basketball team. The university extended a partial

freshman scholarship to this out-of-country student. Chris made sure Ivan could be in the dorm. That winter was Ivan's first opportunity to play competitive American-style basketball. In Belgrade, the schools did not have sports teams, only extracurricular athletic clubs that played a European-style

Chris Stepovich, Ivan Mišković, Joe Stepovich, Randy Lam, Joan Stepovich; Front: David in front of Marko, Lawrence, Christopher Stepovich, 2001. Judy Ferguson photo.

Ivan Mišković and his painting of a Serbian Orthodox church and cemetery. Fairbanks, 2003. Judy Ferguson photo.

basketball. Ivan's future depended on his performance at UAF. He also had to do well in school, perform in an American venue, and write with academically correct English. The pressure and the stress of being away from home on him was enormous. Sometimes he felt he might break.

Since 2000, UAF had hosted BP's Top of the World Classic, in which seventeen national Division One teams contested every November at the Carlson Center. During Ivan's first winter at UAF in 2002 the UAF Nanooks took the BP Top of the World Classic, the first time in NCAA history that a Division Two team had won a Division One tournament. Everyone and particularly the kids were ecstatic. The next day, they rode down First Avenue in a parade celebrating the unprecedented victory.

Throughout the winter, Chris never missed a game. When I was in Fairbanks (even though I had no interest in basketball and knew nothing about it) but especially during Top of the World, I frequently caught a game. In 2003, the Nanooks made the NCAA Division II Sweet Sixteen.

The winters got long for Ivan. Pushing hard at practice every day, learning American-style basketball, enduring the clash of culture, language, personality, away from all that was familiar, and spending more time on the sidelines than seemed fair, Ivan had an uphill battle. Anyplace else sounded good to him, particularly the beaches of South America.

Every August for at least two weeks, Ivan returned home to Belgrade. Every fall, Chris and I had a meeting with the coach to see what finances might be available for him and what else had to be done. With no green card, immigration's permission to work, he could only work small jobs on campus. From fall 2001 to spring 2004, we fought and hung on, but in Ivan's junior and senior years, he received a full scholarship. For the 2005-2006 season, the Nanooks posted a seventeen to ten record including wins over Division I teams Montana State and Kennesaw State for a fourth-place finish in the BP Top of The World Classic.

The summer before he graduated in business, he went to Boston for an internship with T. Rowe Price investors. When he returned in the fall, he was really happy. He'd met people he liked back East and enjoyed the challenge of the investment world.

However, once during the following winter, he said with a half smile, "I've stayed here too long. I don't fit in in Serbia anymore. Fairbanks has become home." Even with her four growing boys and working a full-time job, from the beginning, Joan Stepovich's home was Ivan's home.

In December 2006, Ivan graduated in business. Very happy, Chris said, "It was never about basketball. It was about equipping Ivan for life after basketball is over. Basketball was just icing on the cake." Through Coach Frank Ostanik, a basketball agent contacted Ivan. The Danish professional basketball team Horsens IC invited him to come to Denmark for a tryout. The Danish coach was so impressed that he asked Ivan to begin immediately. Ivan played for Horsens IC throughout spring 2007. He returned to Fairbanks to help with the UAF basketball camp in May and June 2007. When I was selling books on June 21 at the Fairbanks Midnight Sun Festival, Ivan stopped to say goodbye.

Ivan no longer sits on the sidelines. In fall 2007, he quickly moved up to a European Division One team, Denmark's Bakken Bears. In 2008, Ivan became their top scorer. He is now almost twenty-five years old. It has been eight years since the Stepoviches and I first greeted Ivan at Fairbanks International Airport. From time to time, he e-mails Chris' boys and calls his Alaska Yugoslav uncles. As Joan says, "Ivan knows he always has a home here."

What Vuka first extended to her nephew Simo and what Governor and First Lady Stepovich gave to Sam Banic of Seward, a young UAF student in the 1960s, the Stepoviches continued in Chris, teaching by example, living what he believes. Chris has found there is more than one way now to ride the wind; he has learned to fly in every kind of weather.

Ivan Mišković (center, top) at BP Top of the World Classic, Fairbanks, 2005. Courtesy of Christopher Stepovich.

Chapter 38

His Grace the Right Reverend Nikolai, the Retired Orthodox Bishop of Alaska

I first met Nikolai Soraich, called "Vladyka," the bishop of the Orthodox Church in America, Russian Orthodox Diocese of Alaska (RODA), in 2003 in Anchorage. I was delighted to meet a Herzegovinian-American bishop in Alaska. From the beginning, the Vladyka impressed me with his genuineness and kindness. In October 2007 at the Alaska Federation of Natives conference in Fairbanks, the Vladyka (Serbian for bishop) described his history and that of Alaska.

However, in spring 2008 tragic events within the church resulted in the bishop being asked to leave. Not knowing where God might take him, in June at the invitation of Serbian Orthodox Bishop Irinej, Vladyka moved to Australia. Now he resides in a Serbian Orthodox monastery near Melbourne, and ministers to Serbs throughout the New Zealand and Australian diocese. Through Vladyka, the story of Orthodoxy in Alaska and in North America is told and is better understood.

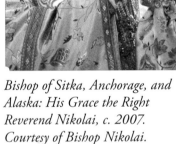

y father, Nikola Soraich, followed his brother to the United States from Ljubinje near Trebinje, Herzegovina, Austro-Hungarian Empire in 1909. His oldest brother, Sava, paid his way to join him. Like many American Slavs, my sixteen-year-old father came to

Bishop of Sitka, Anchorage, and Alaska: His Grace the Right Reverend Nikolai, c. 2007. Courtesy of Bishop Nikolai.

make money in the copper mine in Butte and the coal mine in Red Lodge, Montana, where there were a lot of Serbs. In the early 1900s when Dad was working at Red Lodge, there were five hundred men working in that mine.

The first church in Butte was consecrated in 1905 by St. Tikhon, who at that time was the only Orthodox bishop in North America. (His official title was bishop of the Aleutian Islands and Alaska. See the Orthodox church in Alaska timeline at the end of this chapter.)

My father intended to make money and return home to seminary. However, World War I broke out. With that delay, he married but unfortunately, that union ended in divorce. During World War II, Nazi sympathizers, Utaše, killed my father's sister and brother in Yugoslavia. After the war, my father married my mother Vera Grace Obilović, born in Butte. Her family was from the Bay of Kotor ("Boka'), Montenegro, which borders Herzegovina, a republic of Yugoslavia.

As I was growing up, we were very poor. When my father was retired on a pension but could finally afford to return home (By then Yugoslavia was Communist), he asked, "Why

241

would I? It's better to remember the people as they were." As I grew up, our parents regularly took us to church and lived their faith at home. My father was the secretary, a more permanent position than that of priest. In those days in Butte, the position of priest changed frequently. The secretary was the connective tissue between the bishop and the rotating priests. My mother was the president of the Young Mother's Club whose focus was the youth and who helped raise funds.

I always wanted to be a priest. For vestments when I was small, I wore a dish towel on my back. My Baba, my grandmother, gave me a plastic cross, which I offered to all to kiss. Like the priest, I gave bread to each relative.

After high school graduation, I enrolled in Christ the Saviour Seminary, Johnstown, Pennsylvania. My mother was a tremendous support to me in this big decision. At the end of my third year in seminary, I was dating a very nice young lady. We both attended church where it seemed the local parish priest's wife was pretty nearly perfect. As my girlfriend and I discussed marriage, she concluded finally that she could never be a priest's wife.

At the same time, my mother, fifty-two, was dying of cancer. The summer of 1970, I went

home. I petitioned the bishop, whom I had always known, to be ordained. He honored my request. On August 8, 1970, I took monastic vows and was given the name Nikolai. My baptismal name was the same as my father's, Nikolai. Three months later while I was at her bedside, my mother died on November 8, the day of St. Dimitrije, Mitrovdan.

In 1972, I was ordained as a priest at St. Stevan Serbian Orthodox Cathedral, Alhambra, California. I first served in Billings, reorganizing the St. Elijah parish. To allow my parishes to grow, I supported myself. Working as a juvenile parole officer for the state, followed by two years as assistant principal of Billings Central High School, I continued supporting myself. During this time, the Montana Pekich family, now of Anchorage, invited me to officiate at their daughter's wedding in February. The Vuka and Mike Stepovich family brought me back to Alaska during the summer. In 1978 to 1979 during the Tito-Communist era, I did my post-graduate studies at the Belgrade Serbian Orthodox Church in Yugoslavia.

Vladyka at the Alaska Federation of Natives Convention, Fairbanks, 2007. Judy Ferguson photo.

A difficult period followed in the 1980s as I worked to organize the St. Simeon church in Las Vegas. I wondered, "Do I want to be a social manager or a priest?" I decided that social issues would remain secondary. In 1988, I received a canonical release from the Serbian Orthodox church. I was received into the Orthodox Church in America (OCA), the successor to the Russian Orthodox Church.

On March 21, 2001, the church's twelve bishops elected me the bishop of Baltimore, the auxiliary of the metropolitan to Alaska.

I was elected by the Holy Synod as the ruling bishop on November 14, 2001.

The next year, I was installed as the ruling bishop of the Diocese of Sitka and Alaska, the birthplace of Orthodoxy in North America, and was presented the Staff of St. Innocent.

To honor the early Russian heritage, the OCA here is called the Russian Orthodox Diocese of Alaska (RODA).

Slavs were the first outsiders to shape Alaska and to bring Christianity as well. In the 1700s, the Orthodox missionaries defended the Alaska Natives from the Russian fur traders.

Orthodoxy began in Sitka, went south to Kodiak, spread through the Aleutians, over to Prince William Sound, through the Kenai Peninsula, to Lake Iliamna, the Nushagak River, around the coast to the Kuskokwim and Yukon rivers, and over to Fairbanks. In 1840, St. Innocent became the first ruling bishop of Alaska. He returned to Russia and became the metropolitan (same as patriarch, the head) of the Russian Orthodox Church in Moscow. In 1898, St. Tikhon, who was the only Orthodox bishop in North America, became the bishop of the Aleutian Islands and Alaska. He later returned in 1907 to Russia (just before the Russian revolution) where he later became the patriarch of the Russian Orthodox Church, the first in two hundred years, but not for long due to the Bolshevik Revolution.

To Alaska, Russia had not just sent Slavs; they sent the best they had. Today there are fifteen self-governing Orthodox churches in the world. It's broken down ethnically: Russians, Greeks, Serbians, Antiochians, Romanians, Bulgarians. Historically in Eastern Europe, the czars built the churches. The people reaped the benefits. (Yes, they were poor serfs so indeed, it is a two-sided story.) As a result, the people have never felt any obligation (as in western democratic societies) to support their church. The people tend to identify culturally with the church rather than to apply Christ's axioms to their personal lives; there is a lack of personal responsibility. The same entitlement rather than accountability plagues the endowed people of Alaska. In the church, we have to teach responsibility.

During my tenure in Alaska, there were many improvements, including the complete renovation of several churches, including at Koliganek on the Nushagak River.

The Russian Orthodox Diocese of Alaska has a hundred churches and with my tenure, forty-three priests and nine deacons. Even though the number has more than doubled since I first arrived, priests still have to do double and triple duty to cover the diocese.

At St. Herman's thirty-year-old, four-year program seminary in Kodiak, there are eleven transindigenous [indigenous persons whose purview transcends their original culture] students who will graduate also as substance abuse counselors. They will be able to minister to anyone in the village.

Cultural diversity is very important here. Our congregation is principally Aleut, Yupik, and Tlingit. We are partnering in the Family Wellness Warrior Initiative with the Southcentral Foundation, working with the drug, alcohol, and sexual abuse programs.

Vladyka at a (pure beeswax) candle workshop in Moe near Melbourne, Australia, December 2008. Courtesy of Bishop Nikolai.

Without much church presence here from 1898 to 1967, our people in Alaska are not used to having priests in the villages. Faith has devolved sometimes to tradition, a part of the culture. It's a similar situation as in Eastern Europe. Faith in Christ has to be first; everything else, including culture, flows from that. We're in a critical time now. The villages that have priests are far healthier than those who don't. We're rebuilding the churches so people feel, "It's our church and like anything else, we have to support it."

We're addressing bringing Orthodoxy back to our villages, meaning the faith, and traditions only as they are tied to the faith. We're going to start by following the scriptural precepts and by example: by mandate if we have to, to draw people back to what they need to do.

In 2006 in Belgrade, I attended the consecration of Bishop Irinej, also a Serbian-American like myself. Today he is the bishop of both Australia and New Zealand. He has a bigger territory than I do, forty parishes.

We just built a new church in south Anchorage, off of Rabbit Creek. The consecration will be on Thomas Sunday, a week after our Pascha, after Easter, 2008.

In May 2008, Bishop Nicholai left Alaska and the Orthodox Church in America. He traveled throughout the Lower Forty-eight, visiting old friends and family. At the invitation of Serbian Orthodox Bishop Irinej in June, Bishop Nicholai, Vladyka, moved to Australia where he began a ministry to his people: the Serbian diaspora. Australia and New Zealand have large Serbian communities, many of whom are refugees or displaced persons due to war and economics. Vladyka stays in touch with his friends and shares this new frontier by e-mail with them, sharing a world where Serbs are making a new life in the Land Down Under.

BOSNIA AND HERZEGOVINA

244

Timeline

1741   Divine Liturgy celebrated on a Russian ship off the coast of Alaska.

1794   Missionaries, including St. Herman of Alaska, arrive at Kodiak Island, bringing Orthodoxy to Russian Alaska.

1824   Fr. John Veniaminov comes to Unalaska, Alaska.

1825   First Native priest, Jacob Netsvetov.

1834   Fr. John Veniaminov moves to Sitka, Alaska; liturgy and catechism translated into Aleut.

1836   Imperial *ukaz* regarding Alaska education issued from Czar Nicholas I that students were to become faithful members of the Orthodox Church, loyal subjects of the Czar, and loyal citizens; Fr. John Veniaminov returns to Russia.

1840   Russian Orthodox Diocese formed; consecration of Fr. John Veniaminov as bishop with the name Innocent. Bishop given permission to use Native languages in the liturgy.

1841   Return of St. Innocent of Alaska to Sitka; sale of Fort Ross property to an American citizen; pastoral school established in Sitka.

1843   First mission school for the Eskimos was established at Nushagak by Russian-Greek Orthodox Church

1844   Formation of seminary in Sitka.

1848   Consecration of St. Michael Cathedral in Sitka.

1867   Alaska purchased by the United States from Russia.

1888   Bp. Vladimir (Sokolovsky) becomes bishop of the Aleutians and Alaska; ordination of first American-born Orthodox priest, Fr. Sebastian Dabovich.

1891   Nicholas (Ziorov) becomes ruling bishop of the Alaska diocese.

1898   Tikhon (Belavin) becomes bishop of the Aleutians and Alaska.

1918   The Bolshevik Revolution pitches the Church of Russia into chaos, in essence leaving the fledgling Russian mission in America alone.

1943   Founding of Federated Orthodox Greek Catholic Primary Jurisdictions in America.

1967   Consecration of Theodosius (Lazor) of Sitka.

1970   Russian Metropolitan reconciles with the Church of Russia and is granted autocephaly, changing its name to the Orthodox Church in America (OCA); glorification of St. Herman of Alaska in separate services by the OCA.

1971   OCA receives rebel ROCOR parish in Australia.

Chapter 39

Rabbi Yosef and Esther Greenberg:
Rebuilding Jewish Infrastructure from the Ashes of the Holocaust

Nineteen years after World War II, when I was eighteen in France, I first met Misha David, a Serbian Jewish survivor of the Yugoslav holocaust. In 1941, Nazi General Milan Nedic proclaimed Belgrade the first Judenfrei (Jew-free) city in Europe. During the war to survive, the David family traveled with Tito's Partisans. In 1942, Misha David was born under a tree in Serbia's Vojvodina. Before World War II, there were 86,000 Jews in Yugoslavia. After the war, ninety percent of Yugoslavia's Jews were dead.

In response to the Holocaust, young Jewish couples around the world left home to relocate where they can strengthen Jewish infrastructure. Alaska has never had a permanent traditional Jewish rabbi. Today, Rabbi Yosef Greenberg and his wife, Esther (Estie), of the Anchorage Lubavitch Jewish center have pledged themselves to Alaska's people and to memorializing Alaska Jewish history by preserving it in a museum. Rabbi Greenberg shared the story of his roots and an overview of Jewish history and its relevance to the Last Frontier.

"My family comes from a lineage of distinguished rabbis," Rabbi Greenberg began, "the ninth generation of the second leader of the Hasidic movement, Rabbi Dov Ber of Mezritch."

In the late 1600s in Russia, Poland, and Ukraine, Hasidism began as a spiritual response to Judaism's perceived overemphasis on the intellectual. Some would say Hasidism saved Judaism. At that time, the average, poor, uneducated, hard-working Jew had no time to study the Talmud. Consequently, the vast majority of Jews felt alienated from Judaism. Rabbi Israel ben Eliezer (1698–1760), the Ba'al Shem Tov, "the Besht," taught that every human was of great value. This Hasidism was based on the Kaballah, esoteric Judaism, and involved special meditations. "That Hasidism also implies something more practical," Rabbi Greenberg explained, "as to why I am in Alaska."

He began, "During World War II, my maternal grandfather Rabbi Aaron Hazan fled Ukraine under fire to Tashkent

Misha and Filip David, Young Partisans, 1945, Novi Sad, Vojvodina, Serbia. Courtesy of Misha and Majda David.

Hitler invaded Poland
Belgrade proclaimed Judenfrei
the Rebbe
1940
1950
1960

246

in Uzbekistan. In just Babiyar, Ukraine, the Nazis shot 100,000 to 120,000 Jews. My paternal grandparents fled Bucharest, Rumania to Tashkent as well. Life there was also very hard," he pointed out, "but it wasn't a concentration camp as in the Nazi-occupied countries. Because the war destroyed all the crops," he said, "my paternal grandparents starved to death there, but still my grandfather was smart to flee. As a result, all his children," he explained, "including my father, Moshe Greenberg, survived."

Before the war, Rabbi Greenberg's grandfather studied Hitler's writings. "Any Jew who was a reader knew what was coming with Hitler's rise to power. But no one," he emphasized, "expected World War II to be as bad as it was. The Holocaust, however, clearly demonstrated to all how far racism, anti Semitism, could go."

After the war, Rabbi Greenberg's family tried to reach Israel. However, due to Stalin's persecution of Polish Jews and the subsequent deluge of people trying to get out, the exit was slammed shut. With no other choice and hoping to evade persecution, Greenberg's family went to Moscow, trying to blend into anonymity. For the next twenty-five years Moshe Greenberg supported his wife Devorah and their children as a diamond cutter. A year after Rabbi Greenberg was born, his grandparents left Russia for B'Nai Brach, a small religious town near Tel Aviv. Two years later, Greenberg's family joined their grandfather in Israel, where Moshe Greenberg then managed a diamond-cutting factory. To help Russian Jewish immigrants in another town, Moshe Greenberg asked the factory owner to open another factory there and teach them the art of cutting diamonds in the Russian language, helping forty to fifty families.

After the Holocaust, a debate had arisen among Jewish sages. Some Hasidics wanted to just build a wall around what remained of Judaism, to make sure those souls didn't fall away.

Misha David's Maternal Judich Family, Kragujevac, Serbia, 1918. (Most in the Judich family died in World War II.) Courtesy of Misha and Majda David.

"Not only were many Jews killed or wounded," the Rabbi pointed out, but those who survived were uprooted from their communities, their rabbis; they were torn in two. They went into new societies, new countries where there was no Jewish infrastructure. As a result, millions of Jews left Judaism. That vast defection was primarily because the Jewish infrastructure had been destroyed."

Rabbi Greenberg and photo of Rebbe Menachem Mendel Schneerson, Anchorage, 2007. Photo by Judy Ferguson.

However, the man who became the post-Holocaust leader of world Jewry, Menachem Mendel Schneerson, or "Rebbe," had a different message than isolation. Teaching from Brooklyn, New York, Lubavitcher Rebbe Rabbi Schneerson believed survivors had been spared for a reason: to rebuild Jewish infrastructure from the ashes of the Holocaust. Rather than making a new kind of ghetto, he encouraged young couples to go wherever Judaism needed strengthening, creating bridges to the local community.

"When I was only seventeen," Rabbi Greenberg continued, "I came to the United States to study for ten years, sitting weekly under this great sage, the Rebbe. During the Sabbath and holidays," he remembered, "ten thousand would come to hear the Rebbe speak for six to eight hours; I was very humbled to hear him."

Schneerson's Chabad Lubavitch Hasidic vision for Jewish revitalization meant "for us, young couples," Rabbi Greenberg explained, "leaving our family, community, and comfort zone; this would be the answer to the Holocaust." He continued, "A rabbi chooses a town; the town chooses him. It's a marriage, for life. There are about four thousand couples like me and Estie," he said, "who are called shluchim representatives who shoulder the mission to rebuild Jewish infrastructure in the world. Every major town in America and in the world has a couple like us. Some have three."

"A classmate of mine, Rabbi Lazal, went to Marina district in Moscow two years before I came to Alaska. According to his estimate, there are about two million Jews in Russia today.

"Where my sister and her husband went, Odessa alone has about forty-five thousand Jews. The first seven years there were very hard. But global Jewry," he said, "was fascinated by the rebirth of Judaism in Russia and poured in millions of dollars. The local population began to emerge, including some wealthy Jews," he added. "Now from the local Jewish population, there is a fairly good commitment, including a synagogue and two Jewish day schools, with four hundred students each.

"My classmate in Moscow has three hundred rabbis under him and an operating budget of seventy million dollars a year!

"Russia," he smiled, "is the third largest Jewish population in the world after Israel and America. After the Holocaust and seventy-five years of communism, to rebuild Judaism in Russia is the greatest miracle!"

During 1983–84, Greenberg studied at a small rabbinical Seattle college headed by Rabbi Levitin, who had long-time contacts with the Alaska Jewish community. In 1990, the Anchorage Jewish community asked Rabbi Levitin for a local, permanent traditional rabbi. He asked the students who might be ready to go. "The summer of 1990, my wife, Estie," Rabbi Greenberg said, "and I came to Anchorage to visit and fell in love with the mountains, the people, the hiking, and said, 'This is the place where we would strengthen Judaism.'"

Rabbi Greenberg estimated there are about six thousand Jews in Alaska, located mostly in Anchorage, Fairbanks, and Juneau, adding, "From the beginning, Jews were extremely significant in early Alaska."

In 1866, two San Francisco Jewish fur traders, Lewis Gerstle and Louis Sloss, asked the Russian-American Trading Company for exclusive license to do business in Alaska, only to discover that Russia wanted to sell Alaska. "Gerstle and Sloss ran to Senator Cole in California," Rabbi Greenberg explained, "and basically said, 'These Russians are nuts to sell Alaska. Bring them to their knees and buy it for peanuts, seven million!'" As a former classmate of Secretary of State William Seward, Senator Cole contacted Seward. After the sale, Gerstle and Sloss got exclusive right for twenty years to do business in Alaska if they would establish the infrastructure: trading posts. "De facto," Rabbi Greenberg pointed out, "Gerstle and Sloss were the first governors of this territory although they never set foot here."

There are many Jewish Alaskan stories that could be included in Rabbi Greenberg's Alaskan Jewish Historical Museum and Community Center, including that of Dan Cuddy, president of Alaska National Bank, who was born and raised in Alaska. As a World War II veteran, he was among those who first liberated Germany and visited Buchenwald. "He saw the concentration camps first hand!" Rabbi Greenberg emphasized.

"There is a lot of Alaska Jewish history but no one knows it because there has been no museum to bring it to light. The museum will further promote the spirit of pluralism here. As contrasted with the lessons of historic Russian oppression, Alaska's open society welcomes ethnic diversity, critical to a frontier of diverse cultures."

Alaskan-Jewish Chronicle, *Elmendorf Air Force Base, c. 1940s. Courtesy of Rabbi Greenberg.*

Chapter 40

Hajduks' Frontier Airlines: A Full Circle Alaska Bush Economy

The Hajdukovich and Stepovich families are the oldest Alaska-Yugoslav families in the Alaska interior.

Milo Hajdukovich, grandfather of Frontier Alaska President and CEO Bob Hajdukovich, was born in Kolašin, Montenegro, in 1883. John Hajdukovich of Rika's Roadhouse was from the arid rocky mountains near the border with Albania and Kosovo. For centuries against relentless enemies and poverty, Montenegrin tribesmen lived exclusively for independence and freedom. Tribal laws often overrode both biblical and later, sometimes civil precepts; the tribal ethic was life's interface. The revered bishop-prince Vladika Peter II Njegoš' (1813 to 1851) epic poem Mountain Wreath *dictated Montenegrins' moral code; it was quoted chapter and verse. Two maxims ruled behavior: heroism and survival. "Hajduk" was the title for the tribal mountain warriors, those fighters of the Turks (which included Slavic Muslims) who kept Montenegro secure.*

Through their tribal holdings to the north, Milo, Filip, and their four brothers held large amounts of fertile land, while John Hajdukovich's family in the karst limestone hills to the south scratched out a meager living.

In 1903, John got on a ship for America. Two months later, Milo followed his cousin John. The Hajdukovichs followed the gold strikes to Dawson, Fairbanks, Richardson-Tenderfoot, and then up the Goodpaster River in 1906.

Milo's children, Mary and John, were born in 1936 and 1938, just before Yugoslavia melted into the chaos of World War II. As the Serbs and Montenegrins fought the fascists, Ellen Hajdukovich served in Fairbanks as head of the Yugoslav Relief Agency. She, Vuka Stepovich, and Mary Bojanich all served as volunteers in the Fairbanks Red Cross.

Marko Hajduković, Bob's great grandfather, Milo and Filip Hajdukovich's father. In the 1880s, Montenegro held its own Olympic games. Marko took the gold in all the events. C. 1875, Kolašin, Montenegro. Courtesy of Branko Hajduković.

In 1944 and 1945, Ellen and then Milo died. Their children were entrusted to their guardians, Charlie and Maritza (Milajic) Miller.

Mary and John's Uncle Filip, Milo's brother in Montenegro, was murdered along with his two brothers and a nephew by Tito's Partisans. Filip left behind his three-year-old daughter,

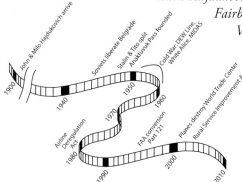

250

Danica, and a new son, Branko. In a society in which the pride of a family was its warriors, the Hajdukovich clan had suffered a great loss. On both sides of the Atlantic, the first cousins grew up without their fathers. In 1944, Soviet troops helped liberate Yugoslavia. Until 1948, Prime Minister Josip Broz Tito and Joseph Stalin were allies. However, Tito's Yugoslavia broke with Stalin because the Yugoslavs were dedicated to independence. Fear and poverty gripped the new Communist state of Yugoslavia. Loyal Yugoslav Stalinists were sent to Tito's gulag; no one could be trusted, not even within families.

In the West during the 1950s, Yugoslavia was behind the Iron Curtain. With minimal trans-Atlantic telephone cables and worse telephone systems in Yugoslavia, international communication depended on the slow mail system.

In 1998, I was invited by the Branko and Dr. Dragan Hajduković families to Montenegro. My presence became a sort of connection between Alaska and Montenegro. Proud and overjoyed to have contact with his first cousin John, Branko sent suitcases of gifts, family photographs, and valuable information to his cousins Mary and John Hajdukovich in Fairbanks. One evening in 1998, we gathered for a gift-giving, a kind of reunion, six years before Mary died in 2004.

In 2008, President and CEO of Frontier Alaska Bob Hajdukovich, the third child of John and Marcia Hajdukovich, shared his family's story: his grandfather's fur trade that grew into Frontier Flying Service as well as meeting today's challenges of an economy in recession with fluctuating oil prices.

John Hajdukovich wearing Montenegrin traditional cap, gift from first cousin Branko Hajduković, Fairbanks, 1998. Judy Ferguson photo.

Mary Hajdukovich Hollander looking at a photo of her mother Ellen Hajdukovich. Fairbanks, 1998. Judy Ferguson photo.

My granddad Milo Hajdukovich was old country and a pretty straight guy. In 1922, he bought Uncle John's run-down trading post at Nabesna, fixed it up really nicely, then sold it back to Uncle John. He came to Fairbanks and invested in real estate. He owned several commercial properties, including the Model Café. One day on their way home from school, Dad and Aunt Mary stopped in at George Bojanich's to see their dad. They tried to wake him up but could not. He was gone. Since the death of their mother Ellen in 1944, the children were already living with Charlie and Maritza Miller but with the death of their father in 1945, the Millers became their legal guardians. (Dad remembered that Charlie had the only Lincoln in town, a purple one!) With the Millers and then the Vacuras, Dad and Aunt Mary grew up in the Fairbanks Yugoslavian community. When Uncle John (of Rika's Roadhouse) came to town, he stayed at the Nordale Hotel or my Dad would run into him at the Model Café. (The Model Café was the nicest restaurant in town, extending from First Avenue to

Marcia, Bob in arms, John, Lynn, Johnny Hajdukovich, c. 1967, Florida. Courtesy of Bob Hajdukovich.

Second, across the street from the Mecca bar. In those days if you wanted to see anyone, you went to the Model Café.)

In high school, Dad would go down to Big Delta and visit Uncle John in his cabin behind Rika's Roadhouse. Uncle John had stacks of photos and letters documenting his life in Big Delta from 1906. Dad loved to pore over the history.

After Dad graduated from college in business, he and Mom got married in 1959. With his estate partners and with Al Vacura Sr., Dad started Florcraft in the Hajdukovich Building at Fourth and Cushman. Seven months before I was born, Uncle John died. Dad asked Rika for Uncle John's historical material to archive at the University of Alaska Fairbanks, but she refused and put it all in the pink roadhouse. The winter of 1965, the roadhouse burned, injuring Rika and destroying all of Uncle John's records. Not long before I was born in 1966, Rika came to our house to heal from her frostbite and burns. Mom remembered that Rika was deathly afraid Mom would have me while she was there.

When Uncle John's letters to his daughter Andje in Montenegro were later found, there was a letter written a year before he died mentioning that my father had a son and a daughter. I understand that in Montenegro, family is dedicated to having sons. My father had four, and he was very proud how he managed to alternate having boy-girl with every birth: Johnny, Lynn, me, Tracie, Mike, Kathy, and Jimmy.

While Dad was still at Florcraft, one weekend he took his new high-powered riverboat out hunting in Minto Flats, but his engine blew up. Seeing Don Wallace, a Pan American captain, he hitched a ride back to Fairbanks in Don's Super Cub. Impressed with the fifteen-minute return to Fairbanks, rather than eight and half hours by boat, Dad immediately turned in his boat for an airplane!

Normally most people take ground school, then the pilot's test, followed by a solo, later with passengers. Not Dad. About 1970, while he was in Florida at the Piper dealership buying his first plane, Dad figured his first solo would be returning from Florida to Fairbanks. However, the weather and sheer distance made it a harrowing trip.

John Hajdukovich, father of Bob Hajdukovich, c. 1977, flying to Brooks Range. Courtesy of Bob Hajdukovich.

When he finally safely arrived, Dad sold the Hajdukovich Building and became a Cessna dealer. He began buying and selling planes and training pilots, beginning Alaska Airco, which he started from scratch. I remember growing up and just hanging out there. I wasn't old enough to help fuel airplanes but Johnny was. It was a pretty cool place.

For over twenty years, big game guide Dick McIntyre operated Frontier Flying, ferrying his clients to his hunting camps. In 1974, Dad bought Frontier Flying from McIntyre and located on the airport's east ramp with a hangar and pilot shack and ten to twelve employees, a pretty small family business. We moved a couple of trailers, hooked them up, and over the years put a roof over the trailers. Frontier flew three to four single engine planes to the Brooks Range, contracting from Wien, a scheduled airliner.

It was the heyday of big air carriers. The Civil Aeronautics Board (CAB) selected who flew which routes, giving an airline like Wien in Alaska a monopoly. Wien made a lot of the air strips up north. During the 1950s and 1960s, a lot of development was going on in the Bush: the DEW Line, White Alice, and the Midas sites, along with surveying and mining. Typically villages didn't have good strips. But in my experience, I've always had pretty decent runways. Nothing like the strips that pilots had to use in the 1930s to the 1950s. For instance, when Noel Wien made the first flight from Fairbanks to Nome, there were no airports in between. The sand bar where he was supposed to land at Ruby was under water. So he flew to the top of Ruby's hill, landed on a potato field, and flipped the airplane on its back. In 1930, Ruby residents had never even seen a plane. The women of the village repaired the tail by sewing the fabric back up. He had a spare prop and slapped it on. Somehow he got the plane airborne again. This was nothing like my flying experiences.

After the 1978 Airline Deregulation Act, Frontier got their Department of Transportation 401 certificate, which allowed them to offer scheduled flights to the public. The next year we got our first Navajo, a twin engine plane. For the next twenty years, we served north of Fairbanks.

I graduated in 1984 from Monroe High School. At that point, I was just doing ramp rat work for the company. I was the operations person. It was a great

Marcia, Bob, Lynn, Johnny, Tracie, John, Kathy, Jimmy, Mike, Fairbanks, c.1985. Courtesy of Bob Hajdukovich.

family atmosphere. Johnny, Lynn, and I worked there. Mom would bring lunch every day and serve it on the same conference table we use today. There was no stress. But I am sure I was protected from a lot of it. From the beginning, Dad was pouring his life into aviation, mortgaging his house ten times over.

From 1984 to 1988, I was in college. During the summers, I worked part time at Frontier. By 1988, I had graduated from the University of San Diego with a major in business and a minor in computers. When I returned, Dad made me the office manager. For the next five years, I sat across from him at his desk, learning every facet of the business: talking to the banks, the IRS, the airports, and the governor. Over the next three years, there were a couple of bank failings, one in which we had an account. The FDIC wanted to repossess our planes. I was only twenty-two; it was very stressful.

When I first came on board, we had Victor 9000 computers with the big five-and-a-quarter-inch floppy drives. The accounts payable were on one 512 kilobyte disk and the accounts receivable on the other. Today we have eight terrabytes of data in our current server.

In college, using the Apple 2E, I'd developed databases. My first year at Frontier, I got a first-generation MacIntosh with the embedded screen and the handle in the back. I considered that a portable computer. I started developing programs for everything, from accounting to flight management: dispatching and manifesting. Since then, with that original database language, we have built Frontier's website, reservations, flight tracking, and other systems. Dad just kinda let me grow it. Anytime I saw anything redundant, I'd program it out. Not to throw the person out but to make the system work better. Computers can handle repetitive functions while leaving employees free to make decisions. Today it's called "risk assessment": get the chaff out of the way for the priorities, taking care of those who entrust their lives to us. I have fostered efficiency and safety. For over twenty years, we have had no fatal accidents.

During our tenure in the Brooks Range from 1980 to 2000, business grew. On a daily basis, we had probably 95% of the traffic. After thirty years of serving that community, that was a tough place to leave.

In 1996, the Federal Aviation Administration mandated that smaller air carriers like Frontier had to convert their operations over to the more stringent safety standards of Code of Federal Regulations Title 14 Part 121 regulations. One of my hardest decisions ever was deciding whether to convert our operation to the more challenging Part 121 or remain forever small as a Part 135. I went Part 121. In thirteen months, we changed maintenance, dispatch, and flying, training people and everything, costing us a million dollars that we didn't have but giving us the potential to grow.

By 1997 to help offset those conversion expenses, Frontier began looking at a slightly larger, nineteen-seater airplane, the Beech 1900 Airliner. Four years later, Frontier was leasing six 1900s from Raytheon Company. But after the tragedy of September 11, 2001, it became untenable to buy the insurance required by Raytheon. When other efforts failed, I turned to First National Bank of Alaska which financed the aircraft, allowing Frontier to continue.

The mail subsidy for Alaska has always been very important to our operation. Before 2003 if an aircraft serviced a village, it was entitled to one share of the mail. As a result, there were up to fourteen air carriers claiming service in communities that had as few as a hundred residents. In reality, only one to two carriers bore the main air service while the others transported some mail. In 2002 Senator Ted Stevens wrote RSIA, the Rural Service Improvement Act. If a carrier were hauling 20% of the passenger traffic or 25% of the freight, it was entitled to a bigger share of the mail, but otherwise it got nothing. After RSIA from 2003 to 2005, air carriers fell from fourteen to an average of four. Frontier wound up buying the assets of one of the more tenacious competitors, Cape Smythe, which gave us twelve more aircraft.

By 2006, Hageland Aviation Services, a large competitor based in southwest Alaska that also served Aniak, St Mary's, Nome, Kotzebue, Bethel, Unalakleet and Barrow, remained. We were looking to replace our PA-31 fleet with a newer but expensive aircraft like the Cessna Caravan. Hageland had fourteen. Conversely, they liked our operating system. To make an enduring airline, we combined forces. Together now, Frontier Alaska has twelve Beech 1900s, eleven Navajos, nineteen 207s, four 406s, Hageland's original fourteen Caravans, and close to five hundred employees! Hageland's side continues to operate the forty-plus smaller, Part 135, airplanes, while Frontier's 121 fleet can continue to grow.

I am the CEO and president of the new Frontier Alaska, responsible for the operations of both airlines, as well as the CEO of Frontier Flying Service and its director of operations. It depends on what day you catch me as to what role I am playing. Today I was in a board meeting with the other two owners from 8 a.m. to 6:30 p.m. I missed forty-four e-mails and fourteen messages that I have to return before bed. Tomorrow, I go in and start all over again. But it's coming together; the Frontier-Hageland combination will make this airline one that can last.

This year the amount of fuel we burned last year will cost ten to twelve million dollars more for the two combined companies. There is also the further issue of the challenged village economies.

In 1996 as I sat at Raytheon's table to buy one of our first aircraft from them, I began signing documents. It asked for a personal guarantee. I said, "I don't own anything. I don't own the company. I'm just Dad's son, the general manager. I have two kids and a tiny house on Dunbar." The banker said, "Bob, we're not selling this to your dad but to you. It's your story; you are the one running the company. We're believing in you and we want you to believe in us." That sounded good. I signed my first personal guarantee and haven't looked back since. It's a big responsibility. The first big guarantee I did was in 2002 for 3.7 million bucks, more than my house was worth. I said, "I can't even count this high." They said, "It's more of a personal commitment that you are making than a guarantee. We're not going to come and take your house." I realized then I was doing more than selling a yarn. I was representing what I was committed to. I've tried to run the company not to succeed for us but for those to whom I have made commitments. If we're late on payments, we try to communicate with people, to work with them. My approach has always been to tell it like it is so that my banker, and everyone else, knows what to expect.

Bob Hajdukovich, c. 2007, Fairbanks. Courtesy of Bob Hajdukovich.

Aviation is really tough to be involved in. As the two companies consolidate, we are targeting markets, cutting back stations and personnel, phasing out aircraft, and looking at new aircraft. We've got a really busy time ahead of us. But like my mom, I try not to get worked up over anything. I'm pretty much of an optimist. But there's only one way to pick up a 2,000 pound boulder: break it into pieces and pick up two-pound chunks, one at a time. I try to back away from a problem and look at it in pieces. I always say, "It's tough but I prefer struggling with success than dealing with failure."

Aviation has clear benefits to the Bush as well as bringing in the urban mindset and its problems. Back in the late 1940s, pilot Sigurd Wien asked Simon Paneak, a leader of the inland nomadic Nunamiut Inupiaq at Chandler Lake, to relocate to the Anaktuvuk valley. If he would stop following the caribou, Wien could trade goods with him. By 1949, five families from Chandler Lake, followed by eight families from the Killik River, moved to a plateau at the headwaters of the John River and founded the village of Anaktuvuk Pass, at the continental divide of the Brooks Range. Before long the community had its own school, airstrip, and church.

I have seen a lot of changes in the Bush and the struggle of the kids. In getting educated, they lose time in subsistence experiences while they are also losing their elders, their heritage.

It especially hits home for me because I never knew my paternal culture, my heritage. In Grandad's and Uncle John's day, they had invaluable relationships like Uncle John had with the Kirsteatters at Healy Lake. Those are special, but I have grown up in a different era. My identity is my family and the communities Frontier Alaska serves.

Frontier is not an airline just flying businessmen from point A to point B. It's flying people's kids, providing necessities and medical transport. We serve over ninety communities, including all Alaska's cultures. We provide service to the people of Alaska with whom my grandfather, Milo Hajdukovich, and "Uncle" John Hajdukovich, first traded. It is very satisfying to know that we're a continuing part of that lifeline: a full circle Bush economy.

Back: Jim and Michelle Hajdukovich, (fifth) Bob Hajdukovich; (seventh) Jake and Kathy (Hajdukovich) Carlisle; Sheli and John Hajdukovich; Michelle and Mike Hajdukovich. Middle: Rick and Tracie (Hajdukovich) Wilhelm, (Bob's wife) Leslie Wien-Hajdukovich. Front: Lynn (Hajdukovich) Cornberg, John and Marcia Hajdukovich, (Marcia's mother) Grandma Rose Hanson, c. 2006, Harding Lake, Alaska. Courtesy of Bob Hajdukovich.

MONTENEGRO

Chapter 41

The Multicolored Threads of My Five Yugoslav Friends

In 2007, Zorica Petrović, Majda David, and I attended an art exhibit at the Belgrade Ethnographic Museum in Serbia where Zorica first took me forty-four years ago. The exhibit was VRATA: Doors. An introduction to the exhibit stated, "Doors can be simple, ornate, wooden, ancient, or new but all doors can be opened or they may be closed." The same may be said of bridges: they can be spanned or they can be bombed. Similarly, open windows can allow fresh air, or during air strikes they can be closed and to prevent breakage, taped. There is a choice.

I begin my story with my first friends, my doors, my teachers, my bridge to the Balkans. Nineteen years after World War II and during the Cold War era, the story began, followed by the years of wars and the end of Yugoslavia. Just as Kosovo was about to erupt in 1998, my windows to Yugoslavia reopened, just before NATO's 1999 strikes necessitating taping of windows in case of a blast.

Zorica Petrović and Majda David, Belgrade Ethnographic Museum, Belgrade, Serbia, 2007. Judy Ferguson photo.

grew up in the tornado-ridden Bible-belt Midwest during the Cold War era. In case of impending nuclear disaster, every Wednesday we practiced air raid drills at school. Since we lived across the street from the school, the siren blasted in my ears as I practiced my piano weekly. If I wasn't worrying about being ready for my piano teacher, I was concerned about the prevailing polio epidemic, or worse, the Red threat. In 1957, the Soviets shocked the United States when they launched Sputnik. The surprise success of the Russians sent the United States into a space race and underscored the Cold War, adding greatly to American fear of the Soviets. In tenth grade Ancient and Medieval History class, Miss Kelly said that Yugoslavia was the gate between East and West. In my urban 1950s world of couples, best friends, hamburgers, the telephone, and rock n' roll, Yugoslavia meant nothing to me, but I did remember. There were synagogues in Oklahoma. Many of my friends were Jewish but theirs was a world shared, in Tulsa's rather WASP-like world, only up to a point.

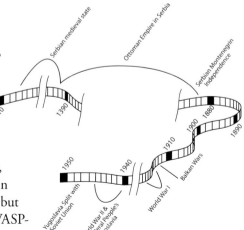

Across the sea, an equally young man was growing up in old Belgrade, in a country I could not have pointed to on the map. Only twelve years past Yugoslavia's concentration camps, Miša David had narrowly escaped Hitler's camps and extermination. To protect themselves, his parents Fred and Roza (Ruška) David had joined the Partisan resistance. Born under a tree, Miša had not been among the 110 of his family who'd been killed in the Balkan Holocaust.

Miša David [Misha]

Miša taught me that there'd been two major worldwide Jewish migrations: the Sephardim and the Ashkenazi. In 1492, the Jews, the Sephardim, were expelled from Spain. In contrast to western Europe, the Ottoman Empire not only tolerated but valued Jews. The first significant wave of Jews into former Yugoslavia were the Sephardim in the 1500s. They were often given responsibility, privileges and lived

Janina and Friedrich David, Vienna, Austro-Hungarian Empire, c. 1897. Courtesy of Miša and Majda David.

in the urban centers. They spoke an old form of Judeo-Spanish, Ladino. Miša's mother was Sephardic; her Judić family had lived for generations in Kragujevac, central Serbia. In Bosnia, the Jewish men could wear a sword while the Serbian peasants in the villages could not. The Jews frequently were businessmen while the Serbian peasants scratched for a living in the rocky rural areas.

From 1717 to 1739 when the Austrians held Belgrade, the second wave of Jews, the Ashkenazi, came from central and northern Europe. Miša's Ashkenazi grandmother, Janina David, was a cousin to Sigmund Freud. She came from Vienna, the dual capitol of the Austro-Hungarian Empire. Her husband, Hermann David, was from Lvov, Poland, an ancient cultural center. As a lawyer for the Austro-Hungarian monarchy, Hermann and Janina were assigned to Sarajevo in 1896. They returned to Lvov for the birth of their first son, Friedrich "Fred," but three years later Janina had her youngest son, Arthur, in Sarajevo. Like all Jewish (and Muslim) boys, Fredrih and Arthur dressed in traditional Bosnian clothing. From 1896 to 1914, the Davids made a lot

The Miša and Flora Judić family: back, (2nd from left, the eldest) Uziel (Bata, Buki) Judić, baby, Mihailo "Mika" Judić. Seated on floor: Ruška (Miša David's mother). All but four: the baby, Mika Judić, the oldest, Uziel Bata Judić, a brother, Avram Judić and daughter, Ruška, were killed by the Nazis. Photo c. 1926, Kragujevac, Serbia, Kingdom of Serbs, Croats and Slovenes. Courtesy of Miša and Majda David.

of friends in Sarajevo. When World War I began, the Davids identified less with Austria and more with the local Bosnians and Serbs.

According to protocol, when Fred was of age his mother asked a matchmaker to go to the Serbian Jewish community and find Fred a possible bride but to report back before she sealed the deal. The matchmaker wanted to keep things simple. She went to Kragujevac where she met Miša Judić a tailor of Manchester-style men's suits, and his family. Moše Eli, an excellent surgeon and humanitarian, was a cousin to the Judić family in Kragujevac.

The matchmaker talked with Miša and Flora Judić; their youngest daughter, Ruška, agreed to marry Fred. The matchmaker didn't want to bother with reporting back to the Davids and just sealed the deal. When the matchmaker returned to Sarajevo, Janina was horrified that the matchmaker had given the honorable David family name to a Sephardic inner Serbian family. Provincial-Serbia and Sephardics didn't have the reputation for education and culture that the metropolitan Ashkenazi had. Nonetheless, the arrangement was already made. Fred met and liked Ruška and the wedding took place. Under the new Kingdom of Serbs, Croats, and Slovenes, Fred became a judge in Sremska Mitrovica, Vojvodina, northern Serbia.

However, in 1938, on Kristellnacht in Germany, the Third Reich began their pogroms, killing ninety-one Jews and sending thirty thousand to concentration camps. They destroyed two hundred synagogues and thousands of Jewish businesses. According to *Jews in Belgrade* by Djurić-Zamolo, Almuli, Demajo, and Levi, as a result under the growing influence of fascism, as early as 1938, Yugoslavia's eighty-six thousand Jews (of Yugoslavia's total population of 15,400,000) began to be affected. University enroll-

Friedrich and Arthur David, Sarajevo, Bosnia Herzegovina, c. 1890. Courtesy of Miša and Majda David.

ment for Jews began to be limited. Jews began to even be denied the right to trade for food. In 1939, Hitler invaded Poland. Miša's older brother, Filip David, was born the following year in Kragujevac, central Serbia. In 1941 when the Kingdom of Yugoslavia was invaded by Hitler, seventeen-year-old King Petar II went into exile. The country was partitioned, and Serbia was occupied by Hitler's Wehrmacht troops, backed by the local collaborationist Serbian Quisling government, traitors to their own people. Initially the communist Partisans and the royalist Chetniks tried to collaborate in their resistance, but according to Danilo Udovički, it soon became clear that the Chetniks were not willing to fight but wanted to wait for the Allies to liberate the country. As the Partisan movement grew and liberated large swaths of the country, the Chetnicks realized they would be overwhelmed. They started collaborating on occasion with the Wehrmacht, and there were times when together they even attacked the Partisans. Until 1942, the Allies attributed the Partisan victories to the Chetniks, but by 1943 the Allies had dropped their connection to the Chetniks.

The fascists introduced a swift genocide against the Jews. Jewish men were loaded into a special gas chamber on wheels from Germany and taken to the Belgrade prewar fairgrounds where their bodies were dumped. Their wives and children were kept in the "holding facility" at the fairground.

When some German soldiers were killed in Kragujevac where Miša's Judić's family lived, following the hundred-for-one Nazi policy, the Wehrmacht rounded up thousands of Roma, Serbs, and Jews. Unlike in other Nazi-occupied countries, to satisfy their quota, the Germans pulled entire classes from the secondary school and killed five hundred students and their teachers. Included in the massacre were the Judić family and the famous doctor Moše Eli and his brother; nearly five thousand were killed. German soldiers and officers who refused to shoot the school children were also killed. In 1942, the Serbian Quisling Milan Nedić, who worked with some of the Chetnicks, wired Hitler that Serbia was the first Judenfrei (Jew-free) country.

The Independent State of Croatia, an Axis puppet state that controlled Croatia, Bosnia, Herzegovina, and parts of Serbia, was led by the Croatian ultranationalist fascist Ustaše. This puppet regime promised to cleanse the state of Serbs, Jews, and Roma. Miša's grandmother, the former Austro-Hungarian representative in Sarajevo Janina David, was taken to the Stara Gradiška concentration camp near the larger Jasenovac camp in Croatia. Without blankets or bathroom, Janina died of dysentery on a concrete floor. Several hundred thousand people, mostly Serbs but including Jews and Roma, died in Jasenovac.

In 1942 Fred, Ruška, and Filip David were escaping with the Partisans near Fruška Gora in Vojvodina, northwest of Belgrade. One night on the ridgetops, they were surrounded by a Nazi contingent. Two-year-old Filip began to whimper. A Partisan hissed at Ruška, "Kill him or I will." The Davids let their protectors go and they melted into the night. When light came, the David family found that all the Partisans were dead while they had been overlooked; they'd been cloaked by the night.

On foot and within eyesight of her husband, pregnant Ruška David and two-year- old Filip David used Serbian aliases and kept on the move from village to village while Fred continued with a new group of Partisans. Some Serb villagers knew Ruška and Filip were Jews but politely believed their (fictitious) Slavic names. When Ruška was near term, a kind German Serbian, Dr Lederer, allowed her to use his vineyard. When her labor began, she laid under a tree. Filip wasn't far away, playing in the orchard.

Ruška, Filip, Fred, and Miša David, Belgrade, c. 1949. Courtesy of Miša and Majda David.

On June 7, 1942, Miša David was born. The family lived in the village of Mandjelos under false Serbian names while Fred was in the Partisans until 1944 when the Soviets helped liberate Belgrade. A colonel and a judge in the army of the Federal People's Republic of Yugoslavia, Fred began working in Novi Sad where he moved his family into a flat. When Ruška David found out that almost all of her family had been killed, she quit speaking for a time. After the war, the Partisans wished to separate themselves from their "free love" reputation and quickly within their ranks they expedited a number of weddings. In a photo of one of the weddings, five-year-old Filip David was holding a Partisan's pistol.

Miša, Ruška, Fred, Filip David, Novi Sad, Serbia, Federal People's Yugoslavia, c. 1946. Courtesy of Miša and Majda David.

When the family went into a flat previously occupied by Germans, Filip deliberately shot the crystal chandelier. For years although he was fluent in German, Fred David refused to speak the language.

In 1948, Josip Broz Tito "wanted to be somewhat independent of Stalin's Russia," Miša said. Knowing Stalin's nature, Tito sent Milovan Đilas alone to Moscow to meet Stalin in 1948 to try to bridge the gap between Moscow and Belgrade. Because Tito refused to be a satellite of Moscow, the Cominform (a Soviet-dominated Communist organization) decided to excommunicate the Yugoslav Party and called on party members and leaders to overthrow Tito.

However, the USSR did not invade Yugoslavia because in 1945 at Yalta, Stalin made an agreement with Roosevelt and Churchill regarding the partition of Europe. Yugoslavia was agreed upon as fifty/fifty: east and west. Therefore an invasion of Yugoslavia would have been perceived as an attack on the west as well.

After excommunication from the Cominform, Tito ushered in the Informbiro period, a Tito-dominated Yugoslav Communist organization active from 1948 to 1955.

From 1948 to 1953, party members who were suspected of loyalty to Stalin were sent to Goli Otok, a horrible concentration camp on an island off the Croatian coast.

In the early 1950s, the David family was given an apartment in Belgrade's center near the embassies on Kneza Miloša street.

In a famous Nazi war criminal trial in Belgrade, Fred David was the presiding military judge. His photo was published in a prominent European newspaper about 1958. Janina David's brother in Vienna noticed the photo of a Judge David. He immediately left for

Belgrade to look for the trail of his dead sister. After much frustration in Belgrade, he secured Fred David's home address, went to his home, and introduced himself to his sister's son and family. Fred was determined to go to his sister's grave. They traveled together to Stara Gradiška, Croatia, where the local Catholic church had labeled the graves of the exterminated Jews with crosses. In a book, the church had recorded the particulars of each victim's death. After that, every year Fred and his family visited his mother's grave in Croatia.

As Miša grew up, ethnicities were not noted. The 1950s and 1960s were the pure Yugoslav period. Every July or August, the family vacationed at the seaside.

Miša grew to five-foot-nine and had sandy-colored hair; his brown eyes alternated from deeply reflective to dryly mischievous. He often had a wry self-pronounced "very clever joke." His feet, in thongs, turned outward while he walked. He was always meditatively thinking. His eyes were cloaked behind tinted glasses and his heavy eyebrows furrowed with thought. His shoulders stooped a little with life's cares, reflecting his own humble opinion of himself. Very controlled, polite, and inward focused, Miša chose carefully what he said, keeping much to himself. In the 1960s, Miša stayed close to his father as for ten years he watched him decline with multiple sclerosis. Danilo said, "It was a very hard period."

Danilo Udovički-Selb [Duh´ nee loh You´ doh vich kee]

A friend of Miša's, Danilo Udovički, was black-haired, alert, smart, warm, and friendly with a boyish charm that drew friends to him. Danilo grew up partly in Belgrade as well as in France and South America. Danilo had an exotic background. In 1918, his grandfather, Milenko Udovički, was part of the failed Soviet Hungarian movement led by Bela Kun.

After World War II, Yugoslavia's King Alexander gave plots of land to Yugoslavs returning home. Udovički was given land in Mol, Serbia. The Communist party was illegal in Hungary and in Yugoslavia (but not in Czechoslovakia). A poor cobbler, Milenko kept his passion hidden from everyone. His son, Lazar, grew up and left to study in Prague, Czechoslovakia (at the time, the most democratic country in Europe). There Lazar also became interested in Communism. When he prepared to return to Serbia, he hid Communist propaganda under a false bottom in his suitcase. When he arrived home, his father helped him unpack, but the false bottom fell out of the suitcase and the propaganda with it. Lazar thought he was in trouble, but to his surprise his father showed him the correct way to smuggle such things.

Danilo and his father Lazar Udovički at the Mostar bridge by Ottoman Turk architect Mimar Hayruddin, Neretva River, Bosnia-Herzegovina. Built 1566, destroyed 1993, rebuilt 2004. Photo c. 1966. Courtesy Danilo Udovički-Selb.

Lazar and twenty-five fellow Yugoslav students from Prague were traveling through France when the Spanish Civil War (1936 to 1939) broke out. International freedom fighters from many countries, including the Abraham Lincoln Brigade from the United States and the Yugoslav Brigade, arrived in Spain to defend the republic from Franco's fascist invasion. Lazar and his friends headed to Spain where they joined the twelve-hundred-strong Yugoslav Brigade.

A beautiful French girl, Camille "Mimi" Selb, had been raised in France in a school run by nuns. She was disgusted by the Catholic church. She and her friend Nadine Rouge

Yugoslav students from Prague. Back, third from left is Lazar Udovički. Courtesy of Danilo Udovički-Selb.

began looking for the political group closest to their humanistic ideas; they chose the French Communist party and joined in Paris.

In 1939 when the Spanish Republic fell, thousands of people began crossing the Pyrenees into France. Hundreds of thousands of people, including Lazar, were held in a concentration camp at the border in a partly German-occupied France. The only way the refugees could enter France was if they had a sponsor. Mimi was working with an organization that was helping the prisoners get a sponsor and out of the camp. She helped Lazar and began corresponding with him. In the process, they fell in love. The twenty-five students, including Lazar, joined the Yugoslav Partisans.

In Paris, Mimi's friend Nadine began giving piano lessons to the daughter of the

Mimi and Danilo Udovički, Milan, Italy, 1949. Courtesy of Danilo Udovički-Selb.

American consul. However, as the Germans began occupying half of France, the American consul left for Switzerland. To prevent the Germans from requisitioning the house, the consul gave Nadine and Mimi permission to let the twenty-five students live in the house. Little by little through the French underground, Lazar and Mimi began to get the Yugoslav Partisans back to Yugoslavia. Just before Lazar's turn, the underground channel was cut, causing him to stay in France where he continued working in the resistance. Mimi worked for the underground in Paris while Lazar organized a network in the northern city of Lille. His group planted booby traps in places frequented by German soldiers.

Once when the Gestapo went to arrest Mimi, she locked herself in a bathroom and got from the second floor outside to the ground. Then she rode her bicycle twelve kilometers to Paris to warn a German resistance fighter hiding on the eighth floor of a Paris residence. Just as the Gestapo was pulling up, the German and Mimi left the building. They walked slowly like a couple until they reached the corner. The concierge saw them leaving but told the police that yes, they were upstairs.

Danilo Udovički-Selb, 1943, France. Courtesy of Danilo Udovički-Selb.

Mimi became pregnant. Lazar and Mimi's daughter was born in winter in an unheated German-occupied hospital in Paris. The child was not blanketed nor given to her mother and she froze to death. In 1942, Mimi became pregnant again. On the Fourth of July 1943, she gave birth to Danilo in a German-occupied hospital. Before the Gestapo came to arrest her the next day, she escaped. Her mother, Elvina Cas, was from Burgundy; she gave her daughter addresses where she could hide and keep moving. By the time Danilo was two, he and his mother had moved eleven times.

In Lille, Lazar and a married female Partisan were based in an apartment. Lazar was arrested in a cafe. There was an agreement among the Partisans that if someone were arrested, he would give no information for the first twenty-four hours, allowing his comrades a chance to escape. Lazar was beaten for those twenty-four hours and kept saying that he couldn't give his location to protect the married woman's reputation. After twenty-four hours of beatings, he figured that such feigned loyalty was no longer credible and he gave the Gestapo the information they wanted. However, the woman had not done as agreed and was still at the apartment, where she was arrested. From 1943 to 1945, Lazar spent the rest of the war in a German prison.

After he returned to Yugoslavia, he was made president of the Republic of Serbia but was not given a position in the federal government of Yugoslavia. If the incident in Lille had not happened, Lazar would have had a much higher position in the government. In the early 1950s, Lazar became a Yugoslav ambassador. Danilo grew up traveling the world with his parents, learning languages and living in embassies.

In 1959 while stationed in Caracas, Danilo's mother became sick and died of cancer. For a while, Danilo and his father lived alone. He remembered helping his father issue visas and stamping passports. When he was sixteen, his father remarried. It seemed best to send Danilo back to France to his adopted Aunt Nadine, who was by then living in the village of Le Chambon-sur-Lignon, France. In 1961, Lazar felt that Danilo should return to Belgrade to finish his last year of high school. A man should have a country, Lazar reasoned, and when possible, a true Yugoslav should live in Yugoslavia. Danilo moved from his beloved aunt's to his father's Belgrade apartment where he knew no one and lived alone.

Danilo's first love was theatre, but discouraged by his father, he enrolled instead in the school of architecture at the University of Belgrade where he met Verica Šostarić, Spasoje "Paja" Krunić, Zorica Jovičić, and Miša David. Verica remembered that Danilo used

Lazar and Mimi Udovički, 1941. Courtesy of Danilo Udovički-Selb.

to swallow his "r's" like a Frenchman and didn't roll them like a Yugoslav. The two loved to be silly together and make jokes. Danilo was vivacious, talented, and had a heart like an open window. His apartment was an open house, an oasis for anyone in need. From his life abroad, Danilo was familiar with a pluralistic dialogue and a healthy civic society. Danilo often visited the Miša David home on Višegradska, near the government ministry buildings at the center of old Belgrade. The boys grew up speaking of the intellectual ideas of the day: Ghandi's nonviolence and French existentialism. Miša joined the Communist party at the university. He, Danilo, and Paja tried to direct their country, encouraging a multiparty system. Danilo began reading a publication, Praxis, published in Zagreb by the philosophy faculty from 1964 to 1974. Under the relatively more liberal conditions of Josip Broz Tito's Communism, the Praxis Group in Yugoslavia was the first public oppositional group to emerge in Eastern Europe. Marxist philosophers and sociologists with a humanist orientation, they presented a Marxist alternative to "state socialism," Stalinist dogma, and orthodoxy. The members of the editorial board included the American Herbert Marcuse, the Frenchman Lucien Goldman, the Hungarian Agnes Heller, and Danilo's friend Nebojsa Popov. From 1964 to 1974 the Praxis Group hosted the Korčula Summer School, attended by well-known Western Marxist theoreticians. These inquiring intellectuals discussed and published articles that vigilantly critiqued the performance and health of Communism. Danilo attended the summer school. Ultimately in the spring of 1975, the printing and distribution of the journal itself became impossible.

During the summers when he could, Danilo returned home to Le Chambon.

Praxis Group summer school (left, second: Danilo; lower right: Nebojša Popov) at Korčula, Yugoslavia, c. 1966. Courtesy of Danilo Udovički-Selb.

Spasoje Krunić [Spasoyeh Krunich] "Paja"

"Paja" came from Herzegovina, a part of old Serbia. A young man with soft brown eyes, a straight back, a love of poetry, and the majesty of a Serbian prince, Paja was born in the cradle of the Serbian language, Herzegovina. Spasoje meant "to save." When Paja was later the city official, a mayor of Belgrade, speaking only in Serbian, in 1998, he told the following story while Miša acted as his interpreter.

The family name of Krunić was originally something else. After the battle of Kosovo Polje in 1389, because so many of the Krunić men had fought for the Serbian crown, a bishop changed the family name to Krunić, crown. Everyone called Spasoje "Paja" [Pi yuh].

Spasoje "Paja" Krunić, Le Chambon, France, 1964. Courtesy of the Camp du Travail.

The grandson of a proud patriarch, Paja's grandfather Spasoje had sixteen children. Many times at the dinner table there were more than sixteen. When the grandfather pointed to one and asked the child's identity, the grandmother would just say, "Oh, that's your other child." Paja remembered two traits of his grandfather; he never asked anything of anyone; he told them. He never apologized and he never said thank you. He ordered everyone. In 1912 he led strong Herzegovinan warriors to the Balkan Wars. The men proved decisive against the Ottoman Turks in the victory of the Battle of Kumanovo in Macedonia. In thanks, grandfather was given a gold medal and several other medals as well as an envelope with title to a piece of land. When the envelope was given to him, grandfather banged his fist on the table and exclaimed, "I didn't go to fight for medals and land but to serve my king." The medals were on display in front of him. To be sure his men were of equal nobility, to test their appetites, and to reassert who was boss, he dared his warriors to try and come forward to take any of those medals. None did.

When the 1912 Balkan Wars began, Paja's father, Vojislav, was in America. He organized shiploads of Serbs to return home to fight.

After the 1917 Russian revolution, Paja's grandfather decided to see what Marxism was for himself. When he returned to his wife, he said quietly, "Jelo, it is a great evil. A great evil."

In October 1939 when Paja's father was fifty-four, Paja was born. When grandfather heard the crying of a baby, although he was gravely ill, he asked what it was. When one of his daughters told him a boy had been born, grandfather for the first time in his life asked, "Please name him after me" [Spasoje.] Paja's aunt was shocked and announced to the family that the patriarch for the first (and last) time had said "Please." When she returned, he was dead.

Paja's father was poor, always moving from job to job. During World War II when Paja was six in 1945, his two uncles were shot by Utaše in Herzegovina and thrown into a pit. Three years after the war, Paja's father died of a heart attack. Not long after, the village decided to move all the graves to a new cemetery site. Noticing the activity, nine-year-old Paja hid behind some trees and watched some men enter with a shovel. He watched the men dig up his father's grave. They pulled the corpse out of the casket, with strips of colored cloth intertwined with crawling maggots through his father's rib cage. Paja never told his mother.

In 1998 as we sat in the mayor's office with Belgrade under threat of bombing, Paja turned to recent events. He said that under Tito, if the Serbs and Croats had been permitted to address the great grief done during World War II rather than to feign "Brotherhood and Equality," possibly the wounds might have been healed in a healthy civic manner rather than exploding in the 1990s wars.

Paja became a successful architect, a university professor, the mayor of Belgrade, and a spokesman for the (neoroyalist) Serbian Renewal Party and its leader Vuk Drašković.

Spasoje "Paja" Krunić, President (a mayor) of Belgrade City Assembly, Belgrade, Federal Republic of Yugoslavia, 1998. Judy Ferguson photo.

Zorica Jovičić

My dearest friend, a sprite-like pretty young woman, Zorica is smart, wise, loyal, and very warm. Zorica's background was also difficult, but not until over forty years later when I asked did she bother me with the story. Emotive, responsible, strong-willed, and subtle, Zorica is a true nurturer.

Before Zorica was born, her beautiful mother from Valjevo married a wealthy young man who lived in the family's upper middle class home on a main boulevard in Belgrade. The matriarch disdained her son's choice for a wife and made life in the family home difficult, which finally resulted in a divorce. Very close to her mother but with a strong sense that her father needed her care, Zorica chose to stay in her grandmother's home and take care of her father. When I met Zorica, she was midway through the faculty of architecture at the University of Belgrade; her grandmother had just died. Zorica and her husband lived briefly in Paris. Moving back to Belgrade in 1969, she eventually became a professor of architecture for sport facilities at the University of Belgrade.

Verica Šostarić

Verica's father was half Croat and half Serb while her mother was a Serb. Verica lost both her uncles during World War II but toward the end of the war, her father was killed in the battle at Sremski Front. Verica grew up with her mother in Belgrade. She learned to play the violin; she drew beautiful illustrations on greeting cards depicting Yugoslavia's multiethnic traditional costumes. For my birthday in 1967 in France, she made a three-foot-wide baklava.

Because she was among the best students in high school, without telling her, Verica's high school teacher registered her in the party. Not knowing what it might mean, she allowed herself to become involved because to succeed in her field, it was helpful. However two years later, when she realized the implications of the party's agenda, she abandoned the party. In 1968 she met and married Slobodan Raspopović, who became one of Belgrade's leading architects. Throughout the years at holidays, Verica always kept in contact with me.

Miša, Danilo, Paja, Zorica, and Verica were five friends, five threads in the fabric of Yugoslavia's multicolored, complicated, and ancient fabric. They were my windows into another land, into a history of global empires.

Later I met Mihajlo Mihajlov.

In the mid-1960s, Nikita Khrushchev, the head of the Soviet Union's Communist party, began de-Stalinization and introduced sweeping liberal reforms in the USSR.

During the summer of 1964, when Khrushchev was in power, the son of a Russian émigré, Mihajlo Mihajlov, a

Mihajlo Mihajlov, Moscow, 1964. Courtesy of Mihajlo Mihajlov.

professor in Zagreb, went to Moscow to pursue his study of Russian literature. While he was there, he was deeply impressed with Khrushchev's reform measures. When Mihajlov returned to Zagreb, he published his experience in Moscow Summer. That fall what Mihajlov didn't expect was that Khrushchev was removed from power and replaced by hardliner Leonid Brezhev. As Russia tightened up, the Russian ambassador to Yugoslavia publicly accused Mihajlov to Tito: "Must Russia always bring it to your attention when you have someone like this?" With a public issue stated, Tito himself then denounced young Mihajlov and sentenced him to prison. Throughout his life, Mihajlov fought for freedom of speech and press. As a result, Mihajlov spent a total of seven years in prison. He became very active in Amnesty International and Radio Free Europe.

The summer that Mihajlov went to Moscow, Danilo Udovički returned to his second home in France, Le Chambon-sur-Lignon. He brought his friends: Paja, twenty-five; Miša, twenty-two; Verica, twenty-one; Zorica, twenty-four; and Mirjana, twenty-two. It was only nineteen years after World War II had destroyed Yugoslavia, but citizens had passports for travel and they were allowed to leave their country with twenty dollars. Brave with hope, they were proud of the country their generation was building.

Chapter 42

Le Chambon and a Young Yugoslavia: 1964

n the fall of 1963, I entered the University of Oklahoma. On November 22, as I was in elementary French class, an announcement on the public address system interrupted: "The President of the United States, John Fitzgerald Kennedy, has just been shot in Dallas." The university dismissed all classes. As we exited a classmate sobbed, "Nothing will ever be the same, again."

While Miša, Danilo, Paja, Zorica, and Verica, still strangers to me, studied at the Faculty of Architecture in Belgrade, I sat in the language lab at the University of Oklahoma listening to the story of *The Little Prince* in French. As I began to understand the prince's words, the wonder of language broke over me; "Draw me a sheep," the little prince said. As I left the lab, I decided, "I am going to learn French, and I am going to go to France."

For years I had participated in my church's youth programs. "But," I told my youth pastor Jim MacDonald, "This summer, I can't do anything. I am going to get a job so I can go to

Work camp at College Cevenol, Le Chambon-sur-Lignon, Haute Loire, France, 1964: International student/workers L to R: in window: Danilo Udovicki-Selb (Yu-French). On top of truck cab: Aline Phluger (Swiss), Zorica Jovičić (Yu), Katerine Belle (French); In truck bed: Constance Hoguet (American), Alan Richtor (American), Mirjana Marković (Yu); René Westphal (French); Seated and hidden: Georginette Hanes (Dutch), Katerine "Sophia" Christian (French), Judy Eskridge (later, Ferguson) (American), Sharland Trotter (American), Donna Eastman (American); Foreground: Miša David (Yugoslav), Olivier Vernier (French), Spasoje "Paja" Krunić (Yugoslav). Courtesy of Zorica Jovičić Petrović and Danilo Udovicki-Selb.

Europe." He said, "We have a program with the American Friends of the College Cevenol in southern France." He read the story of Le Chambon sur Lignon:

> During World War II in Le Chambon-sur-Lignon, Haute Loire, France, pastors Edouard Theis and André Trocmé inspired the Huguenots in the twelve surrounding villages to save about five thousand refugees, including over three thousand Jews, during the Holocaust.
>
> Pastor Andre Trocmé, a moral compass for the village, came from a long line of Huguenots and Germans; he was born in 1901. A teenager during World War I, he met a German soldier who held to his convictions as a conscientious objector, which deeply impressed the boy. Trocmé came to Le Chambon, seeking a remote parish where his pacifism would not be conspicuous.
>
> One cold, dark evening during the winter of 1940-41, Trocmé, the Protestant pastor of Le Chambon-sur-Lignon, answered a knock at his door. A cold, hungry woman, a Jewish refugee fleeing the Nazis, asked if she could come in. Trocmé's simple act of kindness in letting her in led to hundreds of people fleeing the Nazis and the Vichy government to safety in Switzerland or Spain via the well-organized underground network that saved some five thousand refugees over four years.

"Love One Another," sign on church at Le Chambon-sur-Lignon, France. Judy Ferguson photo.

The ordinary Les Chambonais, often poverty-stricken themselves, protected the Jews at great risk, taking in more than their entire population. Under the noses of the Gestapo, they fed, schooled, and protected them, not for days, but for years. No one ever turned away, denounced, or betrayed one Jewish refugee. One of the villagers later recalled: "As soon as the soldiers left, we would go into the forest and sing a song. When they heard that song, the Jews knew it was safe to return."

Meanwhile French collaborators delivered eighty –three thousand Jews, including ten thousand children, to the Nazi death camps; only three thousand ever returned.

In 1938, Pastors Trocmé and Theis founded the Collège Cévenol International a French middle and high school, an international pacifist school, with a wooded thirty-acre campus near the Lignon River in a mountainous village in the Cevennes Mountains, five hours south of Paris.

In 1939–40, when a national leader of the Reformed Church called on Trocmé to ask him to stop aiding Jews because it could damage French Protestantism, Trocmé refused.

The Vichy authorities knew what was taking place, since it was impossible to hide such wide-scale rescue activities over time. They demanded that the pastor stop. He said, "These people came here for help. A shepherd does not forsake his flock. I do not know what a Jew is. I know only human beings."

In the summer of 1942, two Vichy French police busses arrived at the village. The police captain went to Andre Trocmé and demanded a list of the Jews. The pastor refused. The next day, the busses left without prisoners.

Eventually, Trocme was arrested along with a number of his friends, but after a few weeks he was released without having signed a commitment to

"The Memory of the Just Shall Live Forever. Homage to the Protestant community of this Cevenol land and to all those trained by their example, believers of all confessions and nonbelievers who during the war 1939–1945 blocked Nazi crimes at the peril of their lives. While under occupation, they hid and saved thousands of the persecuted. [From] the Jewish refugees at Chambon and in the neighboring communities." Judy Ferguson photo.

obey. The Nazis arrested his cousin, Daniel Trocmé, and sent him to the death camp Majdanek, where he was killed. Andre Trocmé went into hiding. His wife continued his legacy, and many Jews continued to live in relative calm.

After the war, the French Pacifists and Huguenots wanted to educate children from different countries so that never again could a holocaust happen, to prevent the misunderstanding that leads nations to kill one another. During the winter, students from all over the world came to study but in summer, international students came to build the school's facilities. Together they dug foundations, mixed cement, trenched septic tunnels, and erected frame houses.

In 1990, Le Chambon-sur-Lignon became the first community to be honored as Righteous Gentiles by the Yad Vashem, the Holocaust Martyrs' and Heroes' Remembrance Authority in Jerusalem. There are two trees dedicated to them at Yad Vashem. Mordecai Paldiel of Yad Vashem said, "the village was unique in that almost all the people of the plateau were involved in saving these Jews, and no one said a word."

Jim added, "We have some scholarship money left in the fund. We'll send you."

Three weeks later when I was eighteen years old, I left with my mother for Pottstown, Pennsylvania, to meet the American Friends in charge of the trip. I waved goodbye to Mother and took a train with them to New York City, where we boarded a student ship, the SS *Aurelia*, for Le Havre. In early July 1964 from the Le Havre harbor, I took a train to Le Chambon where I was met and brought to the chateau, a large old French farmhouse overlooking its fields and hills. In wonderment I stood on a hill overlooking Chambon and

Back, L–R: Mirjana Marković (Yu), Pierre Vernier (French), René Westphal (French), Zorica Jovičić (Yu); Front, L–R: Miša David (Yu), Spasoje "Paja" Krunić (Yu), Danilo Udovički-Selb, Le Chambon, France, 1964. Courtesy of Zorica Petrović.

the Lignon River. I watched six laughing young people below, kicking a soccer ball with the abandon of a child. My eyes locked on the happy scene. They were healthy, uninhibited, unpretentious, and complete. They were different than anyone I'd ever seen. I was told they were Yugoslavs. But they spoke in a language that locked me out; it was very foreign. Georginette, a happy, blonde Dutch girl, was sweeping out the upstairs porch. Students from Holland, France, Germany, Switzerland, and America were arriving. In the kitchen dining room by the big wood cooking range, René, a small wiry smiling man, explained in French-accented English that the work camp usually was hosted in the school's dormitory, but this summer it was under repairs. For only this summer, we'd have the work camp at the chateau farmhouse. In the kitchen we girls opened a door that led up steep wooden stairs to a row of four sinks (where we took spit baths but we bathed in the river) and two toilets. We went into a larger room with ten cots lined around the walls. I chose the bunk under the windows overlooking the yard. The Yugoslav girls called Zorica and Mira took the cots to my left against the wall. Sometimes their friend Verica visited, but she was studying violin, visiting Danilo's grandfather and adopted Aunt Nadine and she lived at the college itself. Americans who were older and more sophisticated than I took the bunks to my right. Three French girls and Georginette filled the rest of the room.

In the morning we woke at six. Zorica and Mira were the first up. A mountain chill filled the room. While I was crawling deeper in my bed, the girl Zorica, with proletarian steel, put on her short shorts and her Mao-type olive drab green jacket and slipped on her shoes. I put on jeans but quickly learned that by 10:30 a.m., shorts were needed.

A Norwegian woman and her daughter ran the kitchen downstairs. The wood cook range was crackling with heat. Kettles of hot coffee, cocoa, and hot water for tea were ready. I watched the Europeans fill their bowls half full with the coffee, add whole milk to the top, with sugar to sweeten. French bread, real butter, and fruit jam lay on platters. We ate and listened as René Westphal, a teacher from the high school, and Pierre Vernier, the school's physical education coach and a French farmer, explained the work camp projects for the day. We began digging a drainage trench by the roadside to the chateau. At 10 a.m., we came in for a brunch of bread, butter, and jam. Then we worked until noon. After lunch, we bathed in the Lignon River. We could go to town, but we had to be back at 2 p.m. for afternoon discussion in the field.

As we lined the gravel road with our picks and shovels, foreign languages swirled around me. I felt lost. With my smooth hands, I picked up a pick, guessing how it might be used. I began working away from everyone else. The diminutive, exotic girl in pig-tails dressed in her Chairman Mao form-fitting jacket hailed me. "Why are you working alone?" Zorica inquired in French. In my best University of Oklahoma French 101, I responded, "To be alone with my thoughts." Laughing like a thousand bells twinkling across the galaxy, she called to me, "Come!" She herded me over to her friends, the bare-chested Yugoslav boys I'd seen playing in the pasture the night before. A different air came from them. They represented a society entirely unknown to me. They laughed and talked with their young women. Gradually, I became accustomed to Serbo-Croatian flow-

Zorica Jovičić Petrović, 1979, Belgrade, Yugoslavia. Courtesy of Zorica Petrović.

ing over and around me like water. I liked it. A few days later, working in the sand pit we'd dug, they drew a map of Yugoslavia for me in the dirt, teaching me its location. They taught me their songs: "*Tamo Daleko*" was sung during the Balkan Wars by the Serbian calvary in Albania and during World War I. We sang "*U mog dike oci povelike*," a comical song about "my guy," a captain and his rooster. All morning in the hot sun, Miša and I dug sand and mixed it with cement and water, making concrete for our newly dug foundation. Pierre's son, Olivier, carried buckets of water while his little brother Etienne scurried after the smaller ones. For my nineteenth birthday, Zorica and the others gave me a Tito-style work camp uniform like theirs. That afternoon, I sat on the farmhouse's stone windowsill and sang for them, in my new work camp uniform, "Oklahoma, where the wind comes sweeping down the plain..."

In afternoon study sessions, the French work camp's "father," Pierre Vernier, presented his deep convictions against national chauvinism, patriotism, "the breeding ground for war." He refused to sing "the Marseilleise," the French national anthem. Nationalism separates people, gives rise to "otherness," and leaves a breeding ground for hate and wars.

Pierre was a simple farmer who'd endured two great wars. He spoke only French and gestured with large hands, rough from a lifetime of work and raising children. His thought-ful blue eyes had a perceptive light. They twinkled as he gave his time and his energies to teaching. He chewed blades of grass while Danilo, fluent in French and English (as well as seven other languages) translated Pierre's thoughts to our intimate circle. Danilo translated

Les Chatoux, the French farmhouse. Going to lunch. Far left: Miša David, Judy Eskridge (Ferguson), Sharland Trotter; middle: girl in darker dress: Zorica. Le Chambon, France, 1964. Courtesy of Zorica Petrović.

into Serbian for Paja lounging on the grass. Miša buried himself within, as in a cocoon, or rocked forward with his tinted glasses shielding his warm, brown eyes and considered all that was said to him. Zorica and Verica understood Pierre's French, but I was just learning. Danilo was our United Nations communications center.

Every afternoon, each of the kids presented his own country, explaining his own culture. One afternoon, Danilo and Zorica presented Yugoslavia to us. They explained the uniquely Yugoslavian factory self-management system. Blue-collar factory workers directed the factory's management themselves. In turn, the board represented the workers' needs to the state. It seemed a true workers' utopia, with the people exercising dialogue between labor and management. The kids had great hope for the future.

During the afternoons, Miša and I walked to town together. "Plavi," he would carefully teach me. "Blue," I repeated. "Nebo," he continued. "Sky," I smiled. Miša shared his life; in English, it was hard for him but he worked at it. He said he'd joined the university's Communist party. He'd tried to help liberalize the party, make it multiparty. But pluralism was forbidden, and they told him to leave. He told me his beliefs were probably best understood through the writings of Jean-Paul Sartre, the existentialist.

At the end of the work camp, we gathered one last time in the kitchen. I drew pictures of each one and made a memory card for all of us. My friends invited me and another

275

American, Donna Eastman, to join them in Belgrade. Pierre said, "Our friends, the Yugoslavs, are only allowed to leave their country with twenty dollars. They'd like to see Paris." We passed the hat. While Donna and I toured Italy, the Yugoslavs took the train to Paris. As architecture students, they were eager to see the City of Light. When we arrived in Belgrade, Miša, Danilo, Paja, Zorica and Mira met us. Danilo greeted me with, "Did you bring your scissors? To cut the Iron Curtain?"

Zorica and Mira locked elbows with me and we clicked down the sidewalk together in our European sling high heels. All street and store signs were in two alphabets: Cyrillic, which was unrecognizible to me, and the familiar Latin alphabet. Exotic Turkish Serbian shoes with upturned toes enticed me in the market. I bought a pair, a Serbian doll, and a man's green leather-covered canteen. In the afternoon, we toured the Ethnographic Museum. Display cases illustrated Serbian life under the Turks. "FIVE HUNDRED YEARS," Miša and Zorica impressed upon me; "five hundred years, we were ruled by the Turks," more than twice as old as the United States. My mind tried to comprehend what Ottoman domination meant: dark, exotic, foreign.

On a perfect night, we dined on top of the ancient Roman fortress Kalemegdan, overlooking the confluence of the Danube and Sava rivers, the division of the Western and Eastern Roman Empires. We had a delicacy: a tender steak of ground veal and pork, topped with a cheese-butter dollup, called *kajmak*. I remembered that meal for the next thirty-one years.

We returned to Zorica's classical Belgrade home where the six of us waited. Miša stood looking out Zorica's dark picture window. We took the bus to the train station. I climbed the train's dark metal steps with a sense of the distance from Byzantium to the American West, like the moon was distant from the earth. In the dark, Miša ran alongside my train car's platform, holding on, his young face shining up at mine. He looked down, ran a little, and then he was forced to let go.

I stood in the night, looking out from the train at the Serbian fields. Under the full moon, a man was still out working with a horse-drawn plow.

I returned to the university, where youth pastors sadly mentioned how changed I'd become. I kicked along through Oklahoma's autumn leaves that covered the cracked sidewalks of sorority row and sang sad songs of separation.

I wrote to Miša and Zorica and looked for their letters from JNA and Višegradska streets in Belgrade. I bought Yugoslav folk songs on a 33 ⅓ record. On the record jacket, director Emil Cossetto wrote,

In the Balkans, where two ancient cultures meet and where East and West for cen-

Danilo Udovički-Selb, Miša David, and Verica Šostarić, Le Chambon, 1964. Courtesy of Danilo Udovički-Selb.

turies fought a bloody battle for power, a powerful creative vitality produced something new, something Slavic: music from Serbia, Croatia, Macedonia, Montenegro, Slovenia, Slavonia, Istria: Yugoslavian harmony.

In one language, I could hear polkas, kolas, Montenegrin heroic wailing, and Serbia's searching minor key. In 1964, theirs was a multilandscape, multiethnic rhapsody flowing around me on a black plastic record.

I studied Yugoslavia and represented them in my university's model United Nations. Inside me, a small nation was living: Zorica, Miša, Danilo, Paja, Verica, and Mira. I was nineteen; I would return.

What I'd encountered was a small nation in its development. The post-war developer of Yugoslavia's nuclear lab at Vinča, Dr. Srboljub Hajduković, later recalled to me how it was to build Yugoslavia. "The closest similarity to building the country was being in love. Scientists were up half the night, bending over their microscopes. We were making a new country."

Back: Alan Richtor, German work camp leader (a sub-work-camp unit), Sharland Trotter, Three Germans; Front: Miša David, Donna Eastman, Martha Lanning, Georginette Hanes, Spasoje "Paja" Krunić, Katerine "Sophia" Christian, Oliver Vernier, Judy Eskridge (Ferguson), July 21, 1964, my nineteenth birthday, Le Chambon. Courtesy of Le Camp du Travail.

People spent their summer holiday in work camps rebuilding the roads, bridges, and railroads the Nazis, Allies, Chetniks, Utaše, even Partisans had destroyed. The most famous work camps were those in 1947 to 1950, which were responsible for the railroad from Sarajevo to Šamac, Bosnia-Hercegovina, as well as the cross-country highway, the so-called Brotherhood and Unity highway from Ljubljana-Zagreb-Belgrade-Nis-Skopje. After the war, people could not afford a vacation; they labored together in the day, sang and danced around the campfires in the evening, and slept in tents at night.

Later when we were adults, Miša more clearly explained Tito's Yugoslavia:

In 1948, Yugoslavia separated from the Soviet Bloc, wanting to be independent of Stalin. Not too much, but enough to be able to make its own decisions about development. The Soviets didn't want to, because they'd have to free others, too. Yugoslavs wanted to develop certain industries. Soviets thought that was stupid because they had the same industries. Otherwise, they thought very similarly.

But Yugoslavs didn't like too much to listen to other people. It started some fight between Soviets and Yugoslavs. Soviets thought they could easily move Tito because Yugoslavs professed loyalty to Stalin, to international communism.

But Tito was a wise person, without too much scruple. He liked, like Milošević, to be in power. He decided to ask the people, "Who is for Tito and who is for Stalin?" During the Communist meetings then, they had to decide. For most people, it was a total shock. Most of the people answered, "I am for both Tito and Stalin." (Stalin was at the top of the international communists.)

Tito sent a million people to prison for declaring fidelity to both leaders. Those prisoners spent three to five terrible years, from 1948 to 1953. More than a million persons were on Naked Island, a horrible story. These were political prisoners devoted to international Communism; their prison guards were devoted to Tito. It was a horrible conflict. It was very dangerous then if anyone whispered to the secret police, "I think that person likes Stalin."

Yugoslav Communists had been bonded with the Russians, who'd helped liberate them from the Nazis, and some of whom had died with the Partisans, fighting the fascists. Yugoslavs couldn't forget, and they couldn't say that Stalin's troops were now criminals. And they could not also lie, saying that the Soviets didn't help during the war.

Tito wanted to change history. It was propaganda. It was dangerous if anyone was accused; no proof was needed. This happened to my uncle who was in the diplomatic corps.

The Secret Police liked to test suspects' loyalty by asking them to kill someone. My uncle was told to kill a certain person in the Yugoslav

Zorica Jovičić in Yugoslav work camp, c. 1966. Courtesy of Zorica Petrović.

Embassy, but that person was my uncle's friend. My uncle had no idea what his friend's Communist loyalties were, and he didn't think it was important. He and his wife escaped to the USA. For the rest of his life, he was insecure because the Yugoslav police were very dangerous. My uncle got money from his brother, Avram, and went to South America. He was too afraid after 1948 to visit our family in Belgrade. The Secret Police were very dangerous. He was very careful.

Danilo's wife Jasminka Udovički later wrote in her book, *Burn This House*:

Tito was a leading figure in the Movement of Nonaligned Countries which was launched in 1954-55, and he remained a prominent figure in it until his death. For the better part of two decades, the 1960s and 1970s, Yugoslavia was in the forefront of nonalignment and contributed effectively to the movement's leadership.

Chapter 43

1967: From the Adriatic to Alaska

n 1967 when Danilo and Miša registered for the military draft in Belgrade, they were asked for the first time what their ethnicity was. To satisfy the system, Miša, a Jew, simply wrote: "Ancient Greek." Danilo wrote "French" and later, simply "Yugoslav." Much later, Danilo's wife, Jasminka Udovički, wrote of this period in her book *Burn This House*:

Miša David, hiking with work camp, Le Chambon, France, 1967. Courtesy of Camp du Travail.

In early post-war Yugoslavia, the criteria for public responsibility had been meritorious war service, belief in the party's goals, and readiness to work hard....Gradually, however, personal loyalty became the decisive element. In the 1970s, an unconditional pledge to one's republic and ethnic leaders was required for advancement.

As values began to shift in Yugoslavia, unaware, I prepared to return there. From January through early June 1967, I worked and saved, traveling to a new location every two months. I stayed with friends and family, waitressing first in Berkeley, California, then Yellow Springs, Ohio, and finally in New York City. I always had my Serbo-Croatian primer with me, trying to learn the language. In June 1967, my cousin put me on an airplane. I kicked my father's World War II footlocker onto the baggage scale and flew to Paris, where Zorica was living and where Miša and I had agreed to meet and then go on to the work camp at Le Chambon.

After the work camp of 1964, and after graduation from college in 1965, Zorica had been unable to find work in Belgrade. January 1966 she moved to Paris where after a hard month of searching, she got a job in graphics in an architectural firm. That fall she met Dragan Petrović, an architect from Belgrade and in November, they were married.

In June 1967, Miša hitchhiked from Belgrade to meet me at Zorica's flat in Paris. Reunited finally, we looked at each other outside Zorica's door, incredulous and happy to be together again. That night, we drank plum brandy and talked until late into the night but in the confusion of language and youth, we misunderstood one another. Many years later, Miša and I briefly discussed this turning point in Paris. Apparently it had been a case of feeling mutually rejected while not realizing it.

In 1967, the following day as we left Paris and began hitchhiking to Le Chambon together, I said to Miša, "We love each other but let's agree to be friends. If we ever need to talk to each other, let's always feel free, and let's

Soviet Union and Yugoslavia split

Yugoslavia's most purely Yugoslav period

Ethnic documentation required

1940 1950 1960 1970

Zorica and Dragan Petrović, Paris,
c. 1966–67. Courtesy of Zorica
Petrović.

not ever play games." We sang, "We shall overcome," slipped our arms around each other and walked down the highway together, feeling a fraternal peace. But in the following weeks at Le Chambon, we didn't talk to each other and we did play games. Once I tried to approach Miša to talk but feeling an opaque wall, I stopped.

In Le Chambon, the work camp had returned to the school's dormitories, which were sterile and lacked the ambience of the farmhouse-chateau of 1964. Verica and I shared a room. Danilo stayed at his Aunt Nadine's, but he was busy preparing for his graduation exams. Paja was not there. Mira had married and was in Germany. At the camp, I was surrounded by young kids, including Gordana (who later became Miša's first wife). Except for Verica, I felt quite alone. One weekend we hiked all day and camped that night in a barn. The hay in the loft gave me asthma so I slept outside in the chill and near dried cow dung but I could breathe.

At the camp's end, René, a young American girl named "Max," and Miša drove me and my friend Judy Tucker to the road outside of Chambon to begin hitchhiking to Yugoslavia's Dalmatian coastline where we would join Verica. Max wept and slipped a friendship ring on my left hand. Sweaty and dirty from working in the hot woods, Miša scantily kissed my cheeks, then looked down. There seemed no words for a bridge. Judy and I hitchhiked to Zagreb, where we stayed with Verica and her Catholic Croatian paternal grandmother Draga Šostarić in her two-room flat. From Zagreb, Verica, Judy, and I took the bus to Murter near Šibenik to where the family of Verica's close friend Zdravka Jovanović lived in a two-story house with a sun roof near the beach. Every morning at ten and every afternoon at three, her *tetka* (*aunt*, a term of respect for someone older) left a tray of shot glasses filled with *eau de vie* (*rakija*, brandy) on the landing of the stairs. By day, we lay on the beach and ate figs from the trees when we returned to the house. In the middle of the day we ate young cheese with fresh garlic, and in the evening, we had fresh boiled octopus. We went to the open market where the vendor wrung the chicken's neck and handed it to Verica. One balmy evening at an outdoor restaurant, we had grilled fish over a small fire. As the season began to turn, Verica sighed, "Oh, my poor country. When I return I will start work for the rest of my life and from then on, I'll have only two weeks of vacation per year---the rest of my life." My plans included the possibility of my waiting in Paris until fall for a friend from the University of Oklahoma. She and I had talked about me meeting her there and then our spending the winter together in France. I had to decide whether to go on to Paris and wait for her or return home to school. (In fall 1965 to fall 1966, I'd studied at the University of California in Los Angeles which I didn't like. Returning home would mean to the University of Oklahoma, which wasn't appealing but it was familiar.) I said goodbye to Verica and began hitchhiking, first to Zagreb. I had written my parents that I would probably go to their friend Howard Harris in Munich. Standing on the mountainous road overlooking the Adriatic Sea, I prayed about my decision about my future. I got quiet to see what I wanted: the answer was a horse, a cabin open to the sky, and a good man. With that settled, I hitchhiked to Verica's grandmother's in Zagreb to see if I had any mail. A trembling ghost who'd lost her three sons in the war and her husband just before the war, Draga Šostarić barely opened the door, thrust my mail at me while the wind blew, and slammed the door shut. Verica told me that when the wind blew her grandmother would get nervous and start to shake.

As I hitched from Zagreb to Austria, a driver made passes at me and scared me badly. As soon as we were across the Austrian border, even though we were in a small German-speaking town with night coming on, I demanded that the young man let me out. Annoyed, he roared off in his fast car. Down the street of the village, I saw a sign with *Zimmer* [room] above the door. Thinking it might be a hotel, I went into the downstairs beer hall and asked for a room. The owner explained in German that it wasn't the place for me. Back on the street, shaken and alone, I walked toward a group of middle-aged men and women talking under a streetlight. In pigeon German and sign language, I explained I'd come from Yugoslavia, was an American, and needed a place to stay. A kind woman took me home and made a bed for me at the top of her stairs, where I slept like a secure child.

Miša David, Judy Eskridge (Ferguson), French girl, and Verica Šostarić waiting lunch, Le Chambon, France, 1967. Courtesy Le Camp du Travail.

In the morning the woman made me a beautiful breakfast, told me that she'd been a cook for American soldiers during the war, and that she respected and loved the Americans. Like a mother, she gave me an Austrian skirt and tall socks, packed me a lunch, and walked me across the street where she insisted on buying me chocolate and a bag. When I arrived in Germany to a youth hostel, I was relieved to be nearer Munich and the home of Howard and Gwen Harris. I waited outside the Harris' apartment building until they returned home from work. Gwen had just made me a drink to share with her and Howard when the phone rang. A voice at the other end asked, "Howard, do you have any idea where my daughter is?" "She's right here with me and Gwen having a drink," Howard chuckled. Daddy simply said, "Good God almighty!" That night I talked to Howard and Gwen like they were my parents regarding my choice to stay in Paris or return to Oklahoma. They didn't press but they gently guided me. That night, I lay awake a long time, praying and agonizing about whether I should stay or return. I had dreamed so long of Europe; my fantasized dream was just within my reach. However, in the end I felt that I should return home and finish my education. The Harris family drove me to Belgium, where I caught an Icelandic Airlines flight home to New York City. Soon I was back in Oklahoma for my last year of college. In February the friend I had been supposed to meet in Paris arrived at my house at the University of Oklahoma. To my surprise, she had become a heroine addict. It became necessary to sit with her while she went through withdrawal. Afraid for her in the last stage, I carried her into the hospital. My decision to not remain in Europe had been a divine choice. In June 1968, after finals, I got a ride with a friend in his World War II jeep to Alaska. In Anchorage, he joined AmeriCorps VISTA. After we met Verna Canter in the Yukon Territory, Verna and I continued to Big Delta. There, I met a man who had the horse and a cabin in the woods. Later that year, Reb and I married and began our family of three children. I closed the door on Yugoslavia and Europe. We lived remote up the Tanana River, upstream from John Hajdukovich's Rika's Roadhouse. Hajdukovich was an exotic Alaska name; I, like many Alaskans, thought the *vich* names were Russian. For a lifetime, I didn't know Hajdukovich was Yugoslavian.

Over the next thirty-one years, Verica Šostarić wrote to me. She shared when she met Slobodan "Boba" Raspopović and when they married. Every holiday, we exchanged annual news, but she never told me of Danilo, Miša, or Zorica. Over thirty-one years, I watched Verica's four children grow as she told me about their *slavas*, Christmas, New Years, and work. I never heard about the big events. We were both raising kids. For a lifetime, Danilo, Miša, Zorica, and Paja seemed to no longer exist. I mushed my dog team to church once a week, home schooled my children, and lived a wilderness lifestyle.

Verica Šostarić digging a septic pipe drainage ditch, Le College Cevenol, Le Chambon, France, 1967. Courtesy of Le Camp du Travail.

Verica and Slobodan Raspopović, wedding, c. 1969, Belgrade, Yugoslavia. Courtesy of Verica Raspopović.

Chapter 44

1968: "This Generation Was the Most Fully Yugoslav of Any Generation" —Danilo Udovički-Selb

When Miša was twenty-six and Danilo twenty-five, Tito invited new ideas. He asked the young people to engage in dialogue with him. Miša, Danilo, and those at the Philosophy Department at Belgrade University proposed an anthropological, humanist Marxism formed by flexing more to the people's needs.

Danilo, Miša, and their colleagues wanted open dialogue, accompanied by ruthless criticism, between workers and management. New blood might save the Marxist utopia and its bosses from ossification. The system should evolve toward its ideal. The Department of Humanistic Sciences would be the base of operations. A society could be built, demands articulated, programs designed to implement a truly classless populace, the communist ideal: a pure dialectic. Danilo's generation, educated in post-war Yugoslavia, had come of age. They had assimilated the system's fundamental values. They were not against Communism but they wanted to see it flourish. Danilo said, "We were outraged at the hypocrisy of our government, sending its proud Yugoslav workers out to Germany. People were emigrating at something like a rate of about ten to fifteen per minute. Obviously our system was in conflict with itself; it should be creating jobs at home. But instead the system was depending on capitalistic countries and was selling out its working class, making them

Danilo Udovički, Mirjana Marković, Spasoje "Paja" Krunić, Miša David, and Zorica Jovičić in afternoon work camp discussions, presenting our countries, Le Chambon, France, 1964. Judy Ferguson photo.

vulnerable to exploitation." He added, "There was a tendency also to create private industries; as purists, we protested against that." He observed that Yugoslav citizens were encouraged not to think about state affairs, the future of their country, or the political health of society. The government gave the people money to afford a good life and encouraged them to travel. He said, "Those who were lower class went to Trieste to shop; the rich went to London." But whenever plurality of party was suggested, the possibility was crushed. He continued, "Many, not all, of us also wanted to see true equality implemented." The students were pushing for more intellectual freedom: to be free to publicly express themselves without threat of imprisonment. They wanted to see full implementation of the constitution as well as the party's program, not strident police presence. They wanted to be able to help shape their country.

On June 3, 1968, when Tito rejected the students' ideas, there was an explosion of discontent. The philosophy department called for a strike but in twelve hours, it had ignited across the campus. The faculty joined the students; they were also unhappy with the inequalities with the government authorities. Danilo said, "We hoped the workers would join us, which would've affected public transport and touched off a country-wide strike." For a week, the students and protesting faculty controlled the campus.

However, Tito trumped the strike. He made a pernicious speech, saying, "I'm with you. Not all of you are bad. Only ten percent are weeds. Come out, let's talk and we'll make some changes." Danilo concluded sadly, "That ten percent was us, those who wanted a rational civic society." The others, the younger students who had only known Tito as the great father who held Yugoslavia together, relented.

The Tito who had once faced off the Nazis and Stalin himself had become too geriatric to challenge his socialist bureaucracy's ossification. In 1974, Tito made a new constitution, installed himself for life, gave more autonomy to the individual republics, and effectively made the provinces as powerful as the republics. Rather than try to save Yugoslavia, he set up a fragmentation process. For five years after the 1968 strike, Danilo kept sharing his political sympathies with friends. An architect, he worked with Miša at the Yugoslav Institute for Town Planning. Miša had formed a focused team of urban architect engineers with a good working relationship. A brilliant thinker with responsible shoulders and a full work ethic, Miša maintained a complete staff, including Jasminka Gojković,

Danilo Udovički, Mia, Gordana (Miša's first wife), Lea, and Miša David, after Danilo's release from prison, Danilo visiting David family, 1976, Belgrade. Courtesy of Majda David.

a sociologist. These were Miša's happiest years. A multidiscipline team working in a good environment, they became well known, building two thirds of Serbia and Montenegro's communities and contracting in Eastern Europe and Africa.

One morning in 1972 before he left for work, the police knocked on Danilo's door. Apparently Danilo had written some incriminating letters to a friend in prison. One day the letters were discovered in the man's bunk. Following the lead, the police arrived and began ransacking Danilo's apartment. By 11 a.m., when Danilo hadn't come to work, Miša became worried and hurried to his apartment. As he knocked on Danilo's door, he walked into a possible trap. The following day, Danilo was officially charged. He was defended by two lawyers during a long trial. They might have prolonged it, but Danilo's father could not stand it anymore. He was sentenced and led downstairs to a maze of cells. The son of a Yugoslav ambassador and a French citizen, Danilo, at age twenty-nine, was locked up for two years. As the door clicked behind him, the head guard yelled, "Political criminal!" (The term was a two-edged sword. Yugoslavia claimed to have no "political prisoners" only "political criminals," which meant they could not have special treatment.) But the term "political" inferred to the jailers not to beat Danilo, that he was different from the usual criminal. While investigation for an appeal was underway, Danilo spent three months in solitary confinement. During the rest of his two years of imprisonment, Miša visited Danilo every week. Danilo's friend Nataša Kandić, a human rights activist, also came with Miša. On Danilo's birthday, Miša published a newspaper greeting signed by everyone in the government-owned firm. However, under Tito's regime, this was almost too confrontational. While he was in jail, Danilo and his colleague Jasminka Gojković decided to marry. When Danilo was freed, his release made newspaper headlines. Danilo said, "Not one of my friends, except Miša, called me. Not one." He returned to work at Miša's firm, but things didn't go well. Some of Miša's colleagues didn't want to be affiliated with Danilo's prison stigma. They felt it was a handicap in a Titoist world (although it had become only a Tito world). It was thought that Danilo's signature compromised the federally owned town planning firm and that contracts were being lost. Danilo suggested he and Jasminka might move to the United States. Miša agreed, "That would be an option." In 1979, thirty-six-year-old Danilo, who'd had a country for only twenty years, two of them in prison, was left no option but to adopt yet another country. Danilo and his wife were in Boston by the time Tito died in May 1980. A country that had no substantial democratic or capitalist past, no connection to populism, Yugoslavia became further manipulated and destroyed by nationalism based on irrational myths.

Chapter 45

Yugoslavia's Slide Into Civil War

In my life in Alaska, raising children and homeschooling, one night in the 1980s I thought of Miša and almost wrote to him but I wouldn't have known where to write. Jasminka Udovički wrote of this transitional period in Yugoslavia in her book *Burn This House*:

Verica, Nikola, Simona Raspopović, Dalmatian coast, 1976. Courtesy of Verica Raspopović.

> Still perceived as a country that had rebuffed the Soviet Union, Yugoslavia in the 1970s obtained cheap loans from many foreign sources. The federal government borrowed and spent more recklessly. Meanwhile [Tito's] 1974 constitution encouraged the republics to believe that mutual responsibilities would disappear in the near future. Concerning themselves with only their own affairs in the 1970s and 1980s, the republics imposed on the federation an enormous foreign debt. Regional spending was not determined by economic criteria but orchestrated by local bureaucracies increasingly governed by nationalist selfishness. The façade of prosperity was maintained but the economic underpinnings of Yugoslavia were crumbling. The overriding concern was to keep up the appearance of progress, measured by the fictitious standards of "self-management." In reality, Yugoslavs were squandering their future.... This building up of foreign debt boomeranged by the beginning of the 1980s, the time of a worldwide recession. The debt would not have been nearly as grave had the borrowed funds not been managed poorly by "political factories," giant operations built to satisfy political and not economic objectives. The malfunctioning of those industries, equipped with state-of-the-art technology, and their failure to yield expected results produced an economic calamity of staggering proportions. Foreign debt increased four hundred percent by 1980. Interest on the foreign debt alone brought about three-digit inflation. Prices for food, clothing, electricity and other daily necessities rose to sixty percent about every six months.

Rather than implement restrictions, the government just printed more money. Jasminka continued, "Still many from the burgeoning middle class found it possible to maintain their lifestyle, eat at good restaurants, and furnish their homes with good sofas and tiles, even if they were no longer able to afford winter vacations in Austria or France." In December 1982, Verica wrote me in Alaska:

Cheap loans to Yu

New Constitution

Global recession & Yu. foreign debt

Milošević's Kosovo speech

Croatia & Slovenia secede

Serb attacks on Vukovar & Dubrovnik, Croatia

1970

1980

1990

There are many restrictions on my country's investments that greatly affect us. There is no work for the builders, the architects. The other professions are in the same crisis. There are all sorts of such restrictions: a huge sharing of electricity. There is no gas: no naptha or coal or oil. A driver can only get 40 liters [10.5 gallons] of gas for the car per day. There are none of the food essentials: oil, butter, meat, coffee, chocolate. The smallest car costs twelve annual salaries.

That year, they went to the Greek seaside for vacation rather than the Dalmatian because that was more expensive. She said for winter vacation they had considered going to Austria for skiing, but with the current economics they couldn't afford that.

Bad Hofgastein, Austria: (Right, seventh and eighth): Simona and Nikola Raspopović, 1980. Courtesy of Verica Raspopović.

For me, living in my cabin up the Tanana River and commuting by dog sled weekly, it was a world about which I knew nothing. I didn't watch the news; I never thought beyond my family, church, dogs, garden, and horses. I prayed for the persecuted Christians in the Soviet Union. I raised our three children as they grew up on our hill overlooking the river. I never thought the door to Europe and certainly not to Yugoslavia would ever open again.

In the late 1980s, Pam Selvaggio arrived in my children's Christian school community. Pam had minored in Russian and she began giving language classes. Remembering my long-ago desire to learn Serbo-Croatian, I reasoned that Russian was the next best thing. In 1987 and 1988, I began walking across the frozen Delta River to her home to study Russian. Then in the early 1990s, as former Soviet Union Christians began arriving in my town of Delta, I began studying with a Ukranian woman, Vera Berezyuk. Once while I was visiting some friends who were doing missionary work in Russia, they invited me to consider the same. I surprised myself and said, "If I went anywhere, it would be to Yugoslavia."

As the Soviet Union began to weaken, Communist Slobodan Milošević saw the end of the party coming. With Tito gone, he reasoned that someone could still be the next Tito. In Kosovo on the six hundredth anniversary of the battle of Kosovo Polje in 1989, Milošević stumbled on the means. For decades in the autonomous province of Kosovo, the roles of abuser and victim had alternated between Serbs and Kosovars (ethnic Albanian), depending on the balance of power. In 1989, the Kosovars were the vast majority and had almost as much power as a republic. Pledging to protect the oppressed Serbs, Milošević discovered that nationalism was a natural and convenient means to glory. Milošević promised the Serbs of Kosovo and Metohija, "No one should dare to ever beat you again," which incited the Serbs and sent fear into the Muslim majority. In 1989 to 1990 to strengthen Serbia, Milošević stripped Kosovo and Vojvodina (the northern substantial Hungarian minority province) of much of their autonomy.

Long-time Croatian ultranationalist Franjo Tudjman formed the Croatian Democratic Union, the HDZ. Slovenia could not live in a Serb-dominated Yugoslavia and sought independence. Bosnia-Herzegovina was a microcosm of Yugoslavia with its Muslim (ancient Slavs converted to Islam), Croatian, and Serbian populations. Sandwiched between Croatia and Serbia, Bosnia had the most to lose; they tried to avoid war and keep Yugoslavia going. However, both Milošević and Tudjman were set on gathering their ethnic populations to themselves and gaining Bosnia as enlarged territory.

Slovenia was the first, followed soon by Croatia, to pull the string on the wavering and fragile pile of blocks that was Yugoslavia. The weak confederacy that Tito had set up in 1974 could not hold Yugoslavia together, leading to the Pandora's box of the 1990s. With the secession of Slovenia and Croatia, the Yugoslav Army began to fragment. Paramilitaries and criminals augmented what remained of the once multiethnic army.

Veran Matic of B92 opposition radio once explained: "Yugoslavia's vulnerability to a demogogue was intensified because seventy percent of its adults are high school drop-outs. A mere three to five percent deal with social events with any sophistication. Consequently, the population clings to a paternalistic autocrat the same as they do to their Orthodox priest."

After the secession of Slovenia and Croatia, and following the Serb attacks on Vukovar and Dubrovnik in Croatia, Verica wrote me from Belgrade in May 1992:

> The political situation here is very bad. I think of you and all the other places in the earth where life is normal. Yugoslavia no longer exists. We find ourselves in a brutal war. It's a great attack on our soul. We are unhappy, sinister, destroyed. It is a great disaster. The Serbs aren't guilty in this war. The roots go back fifty years. The guilty are the Communists; they are the ones who had the power. All our life, we were against the official political policy. We were always against but this was a totalitarian regime as it is now. The people themselves had not enough power to change anything. All the politicians, all the generals were under Tito and the Communist Party. Here it is terrible: the sadness, the dead young people, the invalids. There are a lot of refugees. A huge inflation. Prices go up every day. Food is very expensive. Banks have confiscated our savings and our money is all lost. We are completely against this war. To

Ana, Verica, (front) Jelena, Boba Raspopović, Spain, 1993. Courtesy of Verica Raspopović.

get our son Nikola away from the draft, at the last moment in November, I got him out to Czechoslovakia. Two days later, the border closed for boys and young men. In February I was able to get a visa for him to Belgium. He is there now with friends of ours, a family, in Belgium. He is going to an international high school there. I would've sent him to Le Chambon but the French wouldn't give a visa. I am giving this letter to an American going to Virginia because I have a great fear of writing these things.

That year, Verica and her youngest daughter Jelena got out of Yugoslavia, followed soon after by Nikola and their middle daughter Ana; together, they began the long road of beginning a new life in Portugal. During the summer, her oldest daughter Simona had to leave her studies in Boston and live in Portugal. At the end of 1993, Verica's husband Boba gathered up the remaining family furniture, caught a boat, and narrowly got out of the country. In December 1993 when Boba was still in Belgrade, Verica wrote:

> The situation in our country is well known. I can't bring myself to talk of the political situation but the war and the sanctions against Serbia are catastrophic. There is no medicine, the basic foodstuffs [milk, oil, little meat]. There is no transportation, no gas, electricity, et cetera. The inflation is terrible. [With unrestrained inflation, fifty million and then fifty billion dinara bills were printed in 1993.] What is worse is that the country is completely dead. It is the cultural death because ties with all the world are completely cut for a long time.

In 1995, Verica wrote:

> Here in Portugal, I spent the whole last year in such worry that it almost became chronic depression. We go often to the seashore to enjoy the waves, sun and clouds. With every wave we feel strength from that big ocean; the great sky above allows us to feel like we are at home. The ocean views erase all differences among people and gives us the satisfaction that we belong somewhere.

I was isolated, uninformed, and poor. I wanted to help Verica but my efforts didn't get far. I called immigration, who told me that the only way to get a professional into the United States was for him or her to have a job offer from an American employer and to show evidence that only this person from another country was qualified to fill the job rather than an American. I was told that to sponsor a foreigner, an American had to share his financial information with immigration and become financially responsible for that person. Feeling frustrated, I put it on the shelf.

Verica and Boba Raspopović, Portugal, 2005. Courtesy of Verica Raspopović.

Chapter 46

Reunion on the Eve of Bombing: 1998

Writing was always natural to me: an outlet, a means of expression, a documentation of life. As a child, I illustrated, wrote, and bound my own little books.

In the late 1990s as my children grew up, I longed to create those little book packages to tell the unusual life I'd had. In 1995, after returning from a particularly dramatic caribou hunt, I told the story to a newspaper editor, my friend Diana Harper. She urged, "Why don't you write it?" Diana offered to edit my work. In 1996, the *Fairbanks Daily News-Miner* hired a new editor, Patricia Watts. She advertised the *News-Miner's* annual Christmas story-writing contest. I submitted a trapline Christmas story for the newspaper's *Heartland* magazine; Patricia asked me to begin writing a monthly column for the Sunday edition.

Democratic movement Studio B, located at top of the large Beogradjanka building. After three months of riots, fired Democratic journalists briefly regained the studio. February 26, 1997, Belgrade, Yugoslavia. Courtesy of Dr. Miroslav Konstantinović.

The Christian community of Whitestone, in which Diana Harper lived, was the concessionaire for Rika's Roadhouse, built by John Hajdukovich in 1914. The following fall Diana asked me to consider writing a book on Rika Wallen and John Hajdukovich. She suggested that I research and write in increments, publishing biweekly in my newspaper column. I

290

knew nothing about research and I was just learning to use the computer and the internet. I got quiet and prayed about it. To my surprise, I felt a solid promise and I took the leap.

Through a good Swedish website, I successfully researched Rika Wallen. I wanted to search out John Hajdukovich through a Yugoslavian website, but due to the wars, I wasn't optimistic. I looked at some websites in Yugoslavia. One, *Radio Mileva*, sounded intellectual and appealing so I tried e-mailing them. Immediately I got an answer from Dr. Miroslav "Miro" Konstantinović, a geneticist at the Institute of Molecular Genetics and Genetic Engineering in Belgrade. Miro was a writer as well, exactly my age, and was quite interested in my research. He told me about Blažo Sredanović, president of the Montenegrin Association of America, and Dr. Dragan Hajduković, a physicist in Geneva, Switzerland, who had also run for president of Montenegro.

I told Miro about my long-ago connection with his country and about my original friends Miša, Paja, and Zorica. He did a little homework and three days later he said, "I know how to find Miša. I grew up a block and a half from him. He's on the street every night with the rest of us marching in the protests against Milošević." Stunned, I felt a door on the vault of time begin to open.

A month later, Miša's son Eli David typed an e-mail to me from his father. It was short and friendly and he mentioned being worried about Kosovo. I had no idea what Kosovo was.

Jane and Dušan Pavlović's wedding, c. 1917, Belgrade. Courtesy of Dr. Miroslav Konstantinović.

291

As Miro and I corresponded, he told me some
of his life. His great-great-grandfather Pavlović was
a merchant from Knjaževac in eastern Serbia. He
caravanned wheat on the old trade routes east to the
Ottoman Empire around the 1850s. On one of his
first trips, he met a beautiful Turkish girl, Fatima,
from the Sultan's court. He married her and brought
her home, much to his mother's and family's displea-
sure. But soon, Fatima was renamed, baptized Serbian
Orthodox, and life proceeded normally. Around 1890,
when their son Ljubomir was thirty-two and was
starting his own family, Pavlović and Fatima bought
a small house in Belgrade. In 1904 Pavlović built a
beautiful block-long home with marble steps leading
to an enclosed garden on Rešavka Street, in the outskirts at that time (now, in the center) of Belgrade. The
house had an apartment for each of his children and
their families. Ljubomir's son, Dušan, born in 1888,
became a lawyer. Dušan met a French Swiss girl,
Jane, who had gotten a job as a nanny for a family in
Belgrade. Dušan and Jane fell in love, but because she
was a foreigner, Ljubomir did not approve. However,
the couple had their way and soon they married and
had two daughters, Borislava and Zorka. Zorka was
Miro's mother. They had one of the first automobiles in Belgrade, and when Zorka was a
young woman, the family used to take drives to Austria and Switzerland. Zora had a classical education and was fluent in French, English, and of course Serbian. She married Milutin
"Cico," a skier and the president of the Yugoslav Ski Association, who served on the Olympic
committee. She and Cico were members of the Communist party but even so, she said, "We
were called *bourgeois*."

*Zora and Miro Konstantinovic
mountain climbing in Yugoslavia's
golden years, Slovenia, c. 1957.
Courtesy of Miroslav Konstantinovic.*

One day toward the end of World War II, Zora was in the market when she heard an
ungodly sound. The Allies had begun carpet bombing Belgrade, running the occupiers out.
As the bombs began to fall, Zora felt something in her heart die. When she returned home
to the house on Rešavka Street, to her horror, a bomb had struck her home. The house was
destroyed; her beautiful mother, Jane, and Cico's mother were both killed. After the war,
Dušan rebuilt half the home where Miro was born and lived until the 1970s.

As a young man, Miro spent several months living abroad in the 1970s. It was easy living
in Holland. Finally after several months, Miro's good friend Marjolein challenged, "You can
either choose the easy way and remain here but always be a foreigner, or you can go home
and help your own country." Miro decided to go home, but when he arrived, his family
home had been taken by the government. The beautiful marble home was swapped out for a
much lesser home in a distant and less attractive part of Belgrade.

Miro had finished his studies, and started to work. Later he did post graduate work, and
without ever being a member of the Communist party, he became a doctor of genetics. In

1983 as a part of the Galenika group, he, his wife Dr. Vesna Maksimović, and two other colleagues cloned human beta-interferon gene in bacteria. It was the first time in the former Yugoslavia that someone cloned a human gene in a bacterial cell.

In the early 1990s as the wars in Yugoslavia began, Miro and his family almost left Yugoslavia, but disease in his extended family prevented their leaving. Feeling his call was then to write a weekly internet publication of life in Belgrade, he began journaling *Radio Mileva*, sending updates from home to the Yugoslavian diaspora abroad. Describing life in Belgrade in the turbulent 1990s, Miro summarized for me:

> In the center of Belgrade, the local Belgrade radio and TV station, Studio B, was located in the top of the Beogradjanka building. Studio B represented a movement for democratic processes. However, in the beginning of the 1990s, everything changed. The best journalists from Studio B got fired.
>
> Between 1991 and 2000, there were several street riots against the Serbian Radio Television Serbia (RTS, so-called TV Bastille) [Milošević's propaganda mouthpiece]. In 1991 we had the first big street riot against Milošević. He used armed military force (tanks) against us, the citizens of my birthplace, Belgrade. I will never forgive Milošević for such an act.
>
> After city officials in Milošević's party lost the city elections in September 1996, Milošević manipulated the results. The citizenry were enraged. For the next three months, November 1996 through January 1997, forty percent of the people demonstrated with street riots against the Milošević regime. In Niš and several other cities across Serbia, they marched.

Demonstrator from the Zajedno (students and citizens) movement, 1996, Belgrade. Photo by Miroslav Petrovic of DT Foto, Vreme *magazine. Courtesy of Miroslav Konstantinović.*

Many like Miša and Miro knew Milošević for what he was, while others were just angry that Milošević had not won in Croatia and Bosnia. For three months, cold, wet, and exposed, the students took to the streets. Armed only with whistles, they tried to drown out the nightly news hour when Milošević propagandized. Up to five hundred thousand residents of Belgrade banged on trash can lids to drown out the evening news on TV Bastille. Several students drummed for many hours on the frozen street until the blood flowed from their hands. Students were supported by their parents who marched after their work day. Hot soup and coffee were trucked to the protestors. Miro continued:

> After three winter months of street riots a group of Studio B journalists returned to their former positions at Studio B in the top of the Beogradjanka building on February 26, 1997. The energy was fantastic as every light in every apartment was on in Belgrade. I took this photo of the Beogdradjanka building. The visible aurora above

the building must have been the energy released during those three months of street riots; that aurora was only there because the elite of the STB (Studio B) journalists had returned.

In the end, a public vote was taken but the results were manipulated. A deal was reputedly struck between some of the opposition leaders and Milošević, Slobodan's dance of one step forward and three steps back. The movement's efforts retreated into a game of smoke and mirrors and dissipated into shadow boxing. People felt trapped: their bank accounts had been taken; their meager salaries amounted to "a hot lunch ticket." "It will never change," Miro once reflected of the Balkans. "I am worried about my children's future."

In October 1997, my father unexpectedly called me. "Judy," he began, "how'd you like to go to Europe with your daughter, mother, and sister this spring?" I hadn't been to Europe in a lifetime.

In May, my daughter Sarah and I flew to meet my mother and sister in Paris. After a couple of weeks of traveling, we approached the Swiss border where we had bed and breakfast reservations. However, the place was closed. I made a couple of calls in French and found us a place. The next morning, feeling like the trail was warm in my search for Dr. Dragan Hajduković, I prayed. That evening as I told the story of my search for Dragan Hajduković to the daughter of the owner of the B&B, she said, "Oh, he probably works at CERN laboratory with my father." She flipped open the phone book and in a second she'd found Dr. Hajduković's number. I called but there was no answer.

A week later I left my family at an English-speaking B&B in southern France while I took a three-day bus trip to Portugal to be rejoined after thirty-one years with Verica. On the Portuguese bus, I managed to trade for a Portuguese coin. On the street in Porto, Portugal, I found and figured out how to use the Portuguese pay phone. I told Verica I was there and then got a cab. As we drove, the driver and I reminisced about 1968, "the year," he said, "the

Judy Ferguson and Verica Raspopović, Portugal, 1998. Judy Ferguson photo.

294

world was turned upside down." Waiting on her street corner, Verica was waving. She looked the same. With moistened eyes, she stroked my cheek and whispered, "La meme, la meme" (the same, the same). When we walked into her apartment door, she announced, "Boba, my Judy is here!" He said, "What do you mean? You mean OUR Judy is here!"

Verica and I had twelve hours before I had to return on the bus. As we sat and talked at their kitchen table, they spoke of their long deep struggle to adjust to having lost so much. In 1991–1992 as the wars raged, Boba, one of Belgrade's most successful architects, had decided it was time to get out, that all of Yugoslavia might go. Boba helped catch me up to the present situation in former Yugoslavia. He summarized Tito's history:

Marshall Tito, leader (in 1944) of Yugoslav partisan forces, stands near his pet dog "Tiger" near his cabin in the Yugoslav mountains, from which he later escaped when it was under attack by German paratroopers and glider troops. From John Hajdukovich's original June 28, 1944 (anniversary of Kosovo Polje), Fairbanks Daily News-Miner *issue. Newspaper courtesy of Judy Ferguson.*

Tito was half Croat and half Slovene. As a soldier in the Austro-Hungarian military during World War I, he was captured on the Russian front. When the Russian Revolution began, Russia stepped out of the war; Josip Broz Tito joined the Red Force and entered the Communist Party. As a communist apparatchik [an agent of the Communist bureaucratic apparatus], he made a career in the international Communist movement (the Comintern). He traveled around Europe and the U.S. for the Comintern doing some espionage and even terrorism. At the beginning of World War II, Tito's superiors made him the head of the small Yugoslav Communist party (about nine hundred members). He was fifty-five then when he became the chief of the Communist Partisan movement. From the beginning, Tito was only interested in the transformation of society through revolution and in gaining power. His movement had nothing to lose and everything to gain. He was an international hustler without the slightest idea of what patriotism was. From the outset, Tito said he was the first enemy of the royal Serbian forces who had fought the Germans. Through the strong support of British and American friends and Stalin's acquiescence (who knew quite well what Tito was and never fully trusted him but preferred Tito to the restoration of the monarchy), Tito

came into power in 1945. During World War II, he used the propaganda of brotherhood and unity to build his Partisan force. The Partisans were predominantly
Serbs from Bosnia, Serbia, and Croatia. One tragic result of the party was that Serbs
were divided into two opposite groups: the royalist Chetniks and the Communist
Partisans. For the most part, Croats fought in the Ustaše, which was both anti-Ser-
bian and anti-Semitic while others served in the less extreme Domobran. In Tito's
forces, there were Croats, but on a smaller scale.

Although the majority of the population in post-World War II was anti-
Communist, Tito came to power as a revolutionary leader supported by the Allies.

As head of the new Yugoslavia in 1945, Tito's first political step was to divide
Serbia into three parts, making the provinces of Vojvodina and Kosovo autonomous regions and reducing Serbia's power. Before this, because Serbia had the
nonautonomous, nonvoting provinces of Vojvodina and Kosovo, Serbia had the entire voting power of all three parts. After Tito made the provinces autonomous, they
still were an integral part of Serbia, but they had the power to vote against Serbia.
Tito completely forgave the Ustaše's actions, proclaiming brotherhood among all,
even though the Ustaše had just killed several hundred thousand Serbs, including
children and women. Tito's policy just tamped the Balkan powder keg to ignite once
he was gone.

In the early 1990s when Croatia gained independence, the Croats sang "Danke
Deutschland," ("Thank you, Germany") because of the speed with which Germany, Austria,
and the Vatican recognized the new state of Croatia.

Verica told me that Serbs had always had a strong, one-man, patriarchal leader regardless
whether it was tribal, later clerical, monarchal, or Communist. It seemed to require an oppressive father figure to gather the Slavic persona. Boba added:

> Before World War II in Belgrade, there wasn't a trace of anti-Semitism; the
> Jewish community was well established and perfectly respected. During the war,
> many Serbs helped the Jews escape from the German zone. Young lawyers and
> intellectuals managed false papers for entire Jewish families and got them out of
> Belgrade through friends. The Chetnik movement got them to the Adriatic coast to
> reach Italy. Recently in Politika, Yad Vashem representatives and the Israeli ambas-
> sador in Belgrade decorated two Serbian families for hiding two Jewish families
> throughout the entire occupation.

When asked, Boba said:

> My paternal grandfather was a lawyer and a republican, not a monarchist. He
> belonged to a small political party but with an advanced program. After the war
> the Communists sentenced him to five years in prison because he gave advice to the
> Chetnik leaders to attack Germans with more force, in spite of the German retali-
> ation policy of one hundred Serbs for every dead German soldier. He was never in-
> volved with any pro-German organization. In addition to prison, he lost his rights as
> a citizen, was prohibited from practicing law, and was denied an appeal. My father

who also became a lawyer in 1936 never joined either the Chetniks or the Partisans, but because of his father, he was also put in prison. Obviously our whole family was profoundly anticommunist.

Verica said that unfortunately she had found out the hard way that the Portuguese ethos was "May the buyer beware." The Portuguese took pride in getting the best of any deal no matter the deception. When Verica first arrived alone in Portugal, she had not read the fine print in a contract for a flat that she signed. The landlord robbed her with a pen, setting the family back considerably. As former Yugoslavs, in 1998 Verica and her family still did not have the documents needed to travel freely. For the first time, Verica told me that Danilo lived in Boston, that Miša was divorced, and that she'd lost contact with Zorica. With sunrise, Verica packed me a beautiful homemade lunch along with a small bottle of homemade cherry liqueur. We didn't know if we'd ever see each other again. It was very hard to say goodbye so soon. Back in France, I met my family and to honor Daddy, we traveled north to Normandy to see where the Allies had landed on D-Day, June 6, 1944.

When I returned home to Alaska, I wrote to Dr. Hajduković. After our family's annual caribou hunt in September, the telephone rang. A man began, "This is Dr. Dragan Hajduković. The Hajduković family, which is a small one, strongly supports what you are doing. However you cannot write about John Hajdukovich (of Rika Roadhouse) without writing about Montenegro. You can't write about Montenegro without coming here. We want you to be our guest. If you can get to Zurich, we will pay all your expenses to and throughout Montenegro. We will drive you to meet all the Hajduković family and to see the beauties of Montenegro. You will be surprised." For someone who'd lived up the Tanana River and had been to Anchorage twice in thirty-one years, this seemed like Dorothy going to the moon. When I told my husband, he said quietly, "Well, this is where I met you."

I went for a run and then sat, thought, and prayed. Motionless, I pulled scraps of memory from a vault; a scene came to me that I'd almost forgotten: Zorica's Belgrade home in 1964.

Dr. Dragan Hajdukovic as we boarded to fly into Montenegro, October 1998. Judy Ferguson photo.

I handled each memory, slowly entering back into the moment. I wondered how I'd put it away, left it complete and as unprocessed as the moment it was lived.

I wondered that the roadhouse next to where I'd lived for thirty-one years was built not by an Alaskan but by a Yugoslav. I pondered that I'd been asked to write the book. I, the only person probably in a hundred miles who had ever been to Yugoslavia, had been asked to write the book about this roadhouse. Without ever thinking of it, my life had come full circle.

Not long after that, my father called. He was alone at home. He told me about a trip that he and Mother were taking to Israel. I paused and said quietly, "I'm taking a trip also." "Oh, really?" he said. I told him the whole story carefully and thoroughly. I waited for the reaction. He said, "What an opportunity! What a great opportunity. You must do it. If I were twenty...no, forty years younger, I'd go with you. You must go; the worst that can happen is that you'd die but you'd die happy. I wish I could go." I was overwhelmed. It was perfect. My pastor's wife, Bette Grier, said something similar, "You must go. You have to go where the story is."

A couple of days later, my husband, Reb, was looking at the newspaper. "You know, Judy, it sounds like we are about to bomb Yugoslavia." Not wanting him to focus on the possibility, I just said, "Oh, you can't believe everything you hear. The media always blows everything up." Aware of Yugoslavia's current dark and questionable reputation, I set my face to go while my nerves were in a rumble. I wouldn't think about it. The morning I was to leave home, I got an e-mail from Miša, who never e-mailed at all. He wrote to Reb reassuring him that I would be okay and not to worry. He and Miro had talked; they had arranged for me to stay with Miša's grown daughters Mia and Lea at their penthouse apartment but warned me that there were seven flights of stairs with no elevator (always the dry wit). Miša said I could stay as long as I wanted.

On September 30, 1998, as I prepared to get on the plane, the *Fairbanks Daily News-Miner* headlined the assault by Serbian troops on ethnic Albanians in Kosovo, a province of the Federal Republic of Yugoslavia. I flew to Switzerland to meet Dragan, who strikingly resembled John Hajdukovich of Frontier Flying Service. (So much so that John had once commented, "I hope the FBI's not looking for him 'cause they'll come looking for me.") Dragan and I had dinner in Zurich and prepared to leave the West and fly into internationally sanctioned Montenegro. As we got on Montenegrin Airlines, which had given me a free ticket through Branko Hajduković, I felt like we were vaulting over a wall. I held my breath as I looked out the plane window and for the first time since 1967, I saw Yugoslavia, something unbelievable. We landed on the Tarmac at Podgorica, the capitol, and crossed damaged pavement into a small building with some standing water. I stood in a line with others waiting to have our passports and visas checked. Yugoslav customs required that I register my computer; they noted its serial number in my passport both on entrance and exit from the country. Standing on the other side of a rope, there was a beaming and proud man dressed in a suit and tie: my host, Branko Hajduković. He waved to us. I was soon introduced to him and the lovely woman next to him, his sister, Danica Hajduković, "Dana." Dana was an elegant earthy woman whom I later called "my Yugoslav Sophia Loren." Branko also introduced Aleksandra, "Saša," his teenage daughter, who would help translate. Branko congratulated me on my courage. In the car, he clapped his hand over mine and welcomed me as "Dzudi Hajduković." They were warm, wonderful, and only spoke Serbian. My Delta Junction Russian didn't work either. Branko would laugh at my efforts and say, "Polyglot Dzudi!" Always stable, warm, and in the background, Branko had initiated, arranged for, and paid for everything. For several days, they showed me Montenegro, followed by meeting the family and then going to John Hajdukovich's original home in Podgor Utrg. We toured the old capitol of Cetinje with its former embassies built after 1878, King Nikola's palace (1863 to 1867), a small museum, and Cipur where the relics of the royal family are today. We drove the circuitous mountain road down into the breathtaking Bay of Kotor where we took the ferry over to Risan. Branko ran up and down Risan's cobblestone streets, looking for relatives of the Fairbanks Stepovich family. He returned to us with Dr. Vladimir Stijepović and Vuka Stepovich's nephew Savo Radović, who spoke only Serbian. I got Vlado and Savo's contact information and took photos.

We drove south down the Montenegrin coast where we saw the man-made "island" of Sveti Stefan, a fishermen's village converted on the inside into a luxury hotel. Dragan frequently gestured at the empty resorts and hotels, saying, "Because of the war, these can be bought for little today!"

One night we stayed in a very nice hotel but due to sanctions and poverty, it was a miserably cold night. Saša let me shove the sofa together and pile cushions on top of us to stay warm. The next morning, we had the empty elaborate restaurant to ourselves. Nonetheless, the waiter was dressed elegantly and had formal manners. I begged for hot coffee to warm my hands and hopefully in a cup large enough to accommodate an American. Branko ordered traditional Montenegrin foods and pointed to each one, teaching me the name: *prsuta*, a smoked meat, various sausages, cheeses.

Down the coast at Sutomore and in Podgor Utrg, we met many Hajdukovićs. In Podgorica, we visited the maternal Hajdukovich family, the Lesperovićs. In Kolašin to the north, we visited the Hajduković patriarch Marko Hajduković's grave, paying homage to a monument paid for by Branko, who'd lost his father in the war. Branko explained that in the 1880s, Montenegro had held its own Olympic games. Marko, Milo, and Filip Hajdukovich's father had taken gold in all the events.

Dragan, Saša, Branko, Danica Hajduković, Podgorica, Montenegro, Judy Ferguson photo.

John Hajdukovich's village, Podgor Utrg, was the highlight and the reason for the trip. Ilinka Hajduković and her husband Jovan had taken care of John Hajdukovich's daughter, Andje, in her latter years. When I walked into their driveway, Ilinka met me with some of her roses, hugged me tightly, and said, "Finally someone has come!"

At the home of John's wife, Milica, and Andje in Utrg, we searched for any research gems. The house was rotting from the 1979 earthquake and subsequent exposure. A blue-eyed neighbor girl, Jelena Mijač, (who at that time spoke only Serbian) helped us look for any gems. The upper floor of the bedroom was rotten. We skirted the outside edges of the floor, searching for clues, but there seemed to be nothing. Suddenly with determina-

Jelena Mijač, Dragan, Danica and Branko Hajduković exploring yard and house of John, Milica, Andje Hajduković, Podgor-Utrg, Montenegro. Judy Ferguson photo.

tion Jelena leaped across the bad floor to the table near the beds, pulled open a drawer on the far side, and bingo! Inside were layers of letters from John in Big Delta to Andje, from John Butrovich in Fairbanks, and from Rika Wallen to Andje! Out in the dry outside air, we gingerly spread the onion-thin moist stationery across surfaces to dry. Later Dragan carefully translated John's letters in Serbian to his daughter. To my great joy, it opened the hidden dimension of the father-daughter relationship. As we sat at the Mijačs' table, Branko suddenly had an epiphany moment. He proposed that we get title to John's house and convert it into a roadhouse, a museum saluting the Montenegrin Diaspora, a parallel to Rika's Roadhouse. I agreed but had no idea what that might entail. After a very wonderful week, I was ready to go to Belgrade to see Miša, to meet Miro, and maybe find Zorica.

One morning at Dana's flat in Podgorica, Dragan fingered a newspaper on the breakfast table. He translated the headlines of the newspaper, "Embassy staffs evacuate Belgrade." Nervously, I noticed the photo showing lines of foreigners lining up on the Tarmac to fly out. I suddenly felt like hidden goods. We realized it wasn't wise for me to go by bus or train to Belgrade when NATO was threatening to bomb. I needed to be with a Yugoslav; traveling alone wasn't a good idea. Branko didn't want to make the seven-hour drive, and he really wanted me to stay. One morning, as we looked at each other, I said, "If you had a chance to finally see your family in Fairbanks, wouldn't you go? I have not seen my Yugoslav friends in Belgrade for thirty-one years. I will go." He nodded in complete understanding. Because of the long-awaited reunion with her Alaska family, Dana suddenly burst into tears as I left, probably partly caused by ten years of tension. Not long after we'd started driving north, Branko's cell phone rang. Dana was calling her greetings and to check our progress. Branko smiled and said, "*Pada kiša*" as his windshield wipers comfortingly and rhythmically swished back and forth. "*Pada kiša*"; it is raining.

As we neared Belgrade, it felt like we were approaching Mordor, a descent into the eye of the dark. Before leaving Alaska I had asked for prayer. At that moment, I had seen a very distant, deep dark space, but in the dark, there were candles, lots of them, like on a cake, burning on a slightly tilted planet in the dark, but very far away from Alaska, in another realm. (I hadn't known that Serbs light tall candles and stick them in sand at church, symbols of prayers.)

As we approached Belgrade's outskirts, it was dark. Branko had talked several times on his cell phone but I had no idea what he was saying. Suddenly with no warning, Branko pulled the car over onto a traffic island in the highway. A strange form in the dark opened the door; Branko quickly moved into the back seat and a stranger slid into the driver's seat next to me. I wasn't scared but it was pretty strange. Later I realized Branko wasn't comfortable driving in Belgrade. He'd had a Montenegrin doctor who lived in Belgrade meet us to drive us. Everything was very dark. After searching, always using cell phones, we pulled up on a sidewalk on a dark street. A strange man opened my door. I got out. Just a couple of noses away from me, he stood waiting, an open face with an inquiring look. A man my size but with a very Turkish face, he was a stranger who'd just appeared out of the dark. I began, "Excuse me, do I know you...?" Then like a thunderbolt it hit me, it was Miro! We burst into laughter, grabbed each other, and laughed and laughed.

I was embarrassed at how much scavenging of artifacts I'd done at John Hajdukovich's house. None of it was packed. This train made up of three men and I each carried an armload of my archeological finds up seven flights of stairs. Above me, I could hear a soft familiar comforting melodic voice. I knew the voice, and when I saw him, I knew the warm twinkling eyes but I'd never seen the middle-aged, sandy-brown haired man with a slight paunch who wore glasses. The voice was Miša's; we took each others' hands. Upstairs, in a long and intimate charming room, Miša had chairs arranged in a circle, with a beautiful spread of food on a tray in front of him for his guests. We were all there: Montenegrins, journalists, doctor, scientist, Miša the town planner, and his wife Majda, and children Mia, Lea, and his son Eli. I brought out gifts; everyone talked and we began getting acquainted. I was amazed but Miša told me Zorica was living in Belgrade and I would see her! Further, Paja was "lord mayor." Miša smiled; he was the head of the Belgrade City Assembly with an office in the downtown city assembly building.

That night, Lea and I sat up till 2 a.m., looking at photos of the family and trying to catch up on thirty-one years. Miša had left a note on the coffee table with Zorica's phone number.

Miša David, reunion, Vlajkovica Street, Belgrade, 1998. Judy Ferguson photo.

I had hoped Branko would overnight with a friend but I was afraid he might drive the seven hours back home.

Before bed, I walked outside onto the balcony with its view of the city, including the dominating Beogradjanka building with its Studio B at the top. I said, "Hello, Belgrade, it's been a long time." I was really there. Under Milošević, both Studio B and the RTS building were Milošević's mouthpiece, destroying what was left of Yugoslavia. However, the night blanketed the city's urban restlessness.

The next morning, Miro picked me up and brought me to his house to meet his wife, Vesna; his children Nenad, Ivan, Duda, and Neda; his dear mother, Zora; and Vesna's parents, Raša and Milena. It was intimate, warm, and wonderful. Zora and I were instant friends.

Sunday morning, Miša arrived from the open market with fresh vegetables and fruits. In the background the radio was on nonstop as Serbian newscasters monitored the ongoing high-tension talks between U.S. Special Envoy Richard Holbrooke and President Slobodan Milošević. Because of the ongoing battles between Milošević's army in Kosovo and the Kosovo Liberation Army, bombs could fly at any moment. After the wars in Croatia and Bosnia, NATO wasn't going to wait long.

Miša and I walked out on the balcony. We sipped coffee and ate rolls sitting on the girls' garden seat surrounded by their flowers. It was wonderful to see the subdued twinkling eyes, to hear the voice and dry wit I hadn't heard in many years. As he assessed the current events, his profoundly sane intellect was dear and familiar. Our reacquaintance was abruptly interrupted when Lea entered and announced, "NATO is definitely going to bomb." My throat tightened; after three decades, we had so little time. I pictured burning buildings, cut water lines, food shortages, and people running in all directions. "Time to make a plan," I suggested. "Oh, we made a list once, Judy," Miša smiled. "We have a few bottles of mineral

water for our storage." Miša asked, "Judy, what to do? The state has taken our bank accounts. Our salaries barely exist. If we tried to start life over, we are middle aged and cannot stay with relatives for a year, two years. No, I am too lazy and too old." He was dry even in a crisis. "I do remember," he added, "that my Jewish uncle in Lvov, Poland, thought everything would be okay. He just kept waiting for life to again become normal. He died in the gas chambers. I hope we don't wait too long. But you must remember, Judy, we have lived with this tension, the uncertainty and crime around us for ten years. (And fifty years of Communism before that.) The stress is new to you; you're not used to it."

Milena, daughter, and Zorica Petrović, Belgrade. Judy Ferguson photo.

302

Miša went on with our plans for the day, postponing the storm clouds for our sunny day in Belgrade. Later, Lea discovered she had heard the radio wrong. The "bombardevanje" was still in the discussion although critical stage.

The next evening, Miša gave me Danilo's contact information. I had not known Danilo lived in the States and that he had for twenty years! I was flabbergasted that no one had told me. Nor had anyone told me he had spent two years in a Yugoslav prison in the 1970s. When I returned, I would contact Danilo.

Miša had arranged for us to see Zorica, whom I'd not seen since 1967. As we drove, I could hardly believe she was within reach. We pulled up in front of her house on Boulevard JNA, where a dear person I would not have known waited for us at the gate. Her eyes like Miša's twinkled at me; inside, we were the same but it took time to become acquainted with the new outer person. I embraced her, thrilled to find her. In the living room where we seven had waited in 1964 for me and Donna to catch the train, I was again with Zorica, Miša, and now with Majda. On the coffee table in front of me, Zorica had laid the 1964 photos of Chambon and the little memory book I had made, carefully stored for thirty-four years and in mint condition. I'd never seen the photos. Running my eyes over the jewels in my hand, I slowly relived the memories.

Majda and Miša went on home. Zorica began to briefly explain the current situation of her beloved country: "Serbia was under the Ottoman Empire for five hundred years and was almost destroyed through two world wars. Struggling to live, the country has grown like a gnarled Slavic tree. Milošević came to power as a communist. When the party began to crumble, he played powerful nationalist strategies to gain more and more power and got public support behind him. Now all of our youth are leaving. They have no future here. We hate it but they must go abroad to have a life."

I listened to Zorica's brave attitude as we discussed the possibility of NATO bombing 160 sites just in Belgrade alone. "So they are going to bomb. So bomb. We are so tired of the tension. Just do it."

Miša David, Judy Ferguson, Spasoje Paja Krunić, 1998, Belgrade. Judy Ferguson photo.

Miša said he'd told Paja, now the president of the city assembly, a mayor of Belgrade, that I was coming. Back at Mia and Lea's apartment, Miša had left me his phone number and said to call Paja. He wasn't sure with the threat of bombing if Paja would have time to see me. I phoned and asked, "Is Paja there?" An affronted woman demanded, "*Who is this?*" Then I remembered protocol and introduced myself and used his formal name and was given an appointment.

From evening news on TV, Miro's mother, Zora Konstantinović, greatly admired Paja, the mayor, and wanted very much to meet him. The next day Miša, Zora, and I waited in an elegant meeting room with red velvet drapes, crystal chandeliers, paintings on every wall, and a grand piano. When our name was called, we followed the receptionist up the carpeted wide steps, past the oak furnishings, across the marble, and into the reception room. We waited for "Lord Mayor," as Miša affectionately liked to say. After a half an hour, Paja majestically opened the double doors greeting me with his old work camp name for me, "Judy! *Dobra Budi!*" [Judy dohbruh boodee] "Judy, be good!" We kissed three times (the Orthodox salutation, kissing each cheek, three as in the trinity). We were overjoyed. Paja presented me with a replica of an artifact dating back to 4500 to 3500 B.C. from the Neolithic settlement of Vinča. The packaging explained that Belgrade's Roman predecessor was Singidunum. I had large sheets of photo collages of my visit in May to Le Chambon with me, along with collages of Verica, Boba, and their family in Portugal. Savoring each photo, Paja exclaimed, "Fantastično!" over and over and crossed himself saying, "*Slava Bogu!*" [Praise God!] Sitting

under crystal chandeliers and surrounded by oak doors, we were served drinks on a silver tray by a man in a suit. My head swam with the wonder of it. Since Paja spoke neither English nor French, Miša translated everything. I wanted to interview Paja, to hear him tell his life. As I tried to organize how to do it, Paja stopped me and said, "I will tell you how we'll do it, not you." He began telling of his grandfather the patriarch, his medals, of his parents, and of the situation which Yugoslavia now faced. He said, "Under Tito, if there had been civil exchange, open dialogue between Croats and Serbs, to work through the wounds of World War II, maybe things would've been different. But we were supposed to act like all those things during the war never happened. We had become the new Yugoslav comrades of brotherhood and unity."

Over the next couple of days, October 11 and 12, Lea and Mia kept turning on

Mia, Lea, Miša, Eli David, Belgrade, 1998. Judy Ferguson photo.

304

the state-controlled radio. Rivers of Serbian in a flat sort of machine-gun tone pummeled my ears, punctuated with "Holbrooke" and "Milošević." Each news release on the possibility of air raid strikes tied us together with stress. "What?" I'd ask Lea, anxious for a translation. She responded, "Nothing new. They're still talking." "We could take you hostage," suggested twenty-two-year-old Mia, her view slightly jaded by her uncertain surroundings. "Sure, whatever I can do to help," I returned. "It'll be a new experience; I've never been bombed before," Lea commented with black humor. When she wasn't exorcising Belgrade's deep futility, she relaxed and said honestly, "It isn't the bombing that scares me. It's what comes after: the looting, the chaos.... But I'm not going anywhere. All the people who were going to leave have done it already."

That evening my family e-mailed Miša, warning me to get out of Belgrade while there was still a city from which to leave. Miša said, "It's possible we don't even know here what is really going on since all the media here is state controlled," tightening the cord of paranoia around my decision-making. At that point against my desire, Miša insisted that we go to the American Embassy and at least register my presence. We sat in some tense silence there for the remaining staff to take my information. I was afraid they'd force me to return, but my registration was just a formality.

One night as I worked until 3 a.m. on my research, I thought I heard a prolonged whistling sound outside our penthouse flat. I hurried to the dark balcony to see if I would be the only one awake to hear the missiles coming. We had heard that when it came it would be with no warning. Studying the city from the balcony, I felt like I was in a pot on a burner, set on simmer. Day and night, car alarms shrieked from burglars and rampaging youth.

Gordana, the girls' mother and Miša's first wife, entered her girls' apartment the next morning. We hadn't seen each other since the 1967 work camp in Le Chambon. She grinned dryly and said in French, "What are you waiting for? For the missiles to carry you out?"

The tension was reaching maximum on Monday October 12. In the workplace, Belgrade was calling itself "Bombay," with dark humor to relieve the stress.

That evening as we were driving, Miša, concerned about paying me enough attention, asked, "Are you happy?" "Ecstatic, thrilled," I assured him. "Good," he beamed, "I am happy when you are happy." He continued, "I am sorry you aren't here in normal time. It's very nice city in a time, not like last ten years." To understand the years we'd missed, Miša went over his life. The year I'd seen him last in 1967, he'd graduated from Belgrade University Architectural Faculty. (I still had the postcard photo of his architectural graduation project.) For two years, he'd freelanced as an architect. For five years (during the time Danilo was arrested), he was a researcher at the Yugoslav Institute for Town Planning. For fifteen years until just after the fall of the Berlin Wall, he was the general manager at the Center for Developing Urban Planning. (During the formative years of that department, from 1978 to 1982, Miša's wife left him with their two daughters to raise until he met Majda.) During those fifteen years, Miša became well known throughout Yugoslavia and worked abroad in Africa. (When I later met a Muslim architect in Montenegro, I mentioned I was a friend of Miša's. The man responded warmly, "Miša is not only a great architect but he is an outstanding human being." When I told Miša, he said, "You see? I pay them to talk so.")

In 1990 when it became legal in Yugoslavia to privatize, Miša went from office to office, searching for the right firm: one with a plan, with an appealing position, but most of all a good working atmosphere. Against the advice of his more conservative colleagues, Miša went into business for himself, beginning Koni Consulting. He believed that private enterprise would develop a middle class, making an informed, healthy citizenry. (But in an aside he added that it was like trying to push a fat man uphill.) Miša was the president of Belgrade's Zemun Rotary club. After dinner,

Brothers Filip and Misa David, 1999, Belgrade. Judy Ferguson photo.

he peered at me with a wry expression over the top of his glasses and said, "I believe as Willy Brandt. If a man, when he is young, does not feel the world's pain sufficiently to follow communism . . . nor, when he is old, he does not sufficiently feel that pain to become a capitalist . . . he is not a worthy man."

One day Miša took me to Koni Consulting, where he introduced me to his business partners. As he showed me some of their projects, he explained the intense pressure of running a firm under international sanctions. Koni had to present a sense of security to entice investing in Serbia. Liquidity was important. Sometimes the firm had to make a down payment to hold a lot before the foreign investor could begin development on it. However, under sanctions, banks had no money to loan. Only criminals, the "grey Mafia," or the mafia itself had money to loan. As he drove us home one evening, Miša said that once when they were speculating on buying a lot downtown for MacDonald's that a man, *"real Mafia,"* with a pistol appeared in Miša's office. He began, "If you get that lot, we know you have a wife and a son." With a similar problem that night, Miša's knuckles tightened on the steering wheel as he tried to find a solution to the day's dilemma: how to keep the client interested but how to get the needed money to begin transactions. As he searched for the answer, his cell phone rang repeatedly. He and members of the Jewish community were organizing a bus caravan in case of bombing to evacuate their children from Belgrade to Budapest.

That night as we walked through Belgrade's downtown shopping district, Knez Mihailova Street, Miša and Majda ran into a friend. After polite exchanges, the friend looked me directly in the eyes and warned ominously in Serbian, "Caution is the mother of wisdom." Miša shrugged it off. He put his arm around me and I him. I'd forgotten but Miša had not. He began singing softly, "We shall overcome." I joined him, "I know that deep in my heart, I do believe that we shall overcome some day." I wondered if the English would get unfavorable attention but we kept strolling as if gliding, singing, "We shall overcome some day."

Miša David, Miro and Duda Konstantinović and Majda David, Belgrade, 1998, Judy Ferguson photo.

Majda, Miša, and I walked together in the dark twinkling night. They took me to an old artists' quarter where we stopped and had *kafa* (coffee).

Later one day after work, Miša sank into his TV chair, depressed. That day, he said, a journalist had been car-bombed and had lost both his legs. He thought about his brother Filip, an author, filmmaker, professor, and a spokesman for Yugoslavia as well as for Eastern Europe. Throughout all of Milošević's ominous veiled threats, Filip and other pro-Democratic dissidents, including Nebojša Popov, remained in their country, working to inform society. They met daily at the Medija Centar, hosting discussion at their respective tables. As Miša reflected in his chair at home, he said, "Milošević needs to be punished. What has been done to innocent people is terrible, terrible. But I am afraid that with bombing more innocent people will die."

Earlier in Montenegro, Dragan had said, "Much as I hate Milošević, I have to agree with Milošević that bombing is an infringement of a sovereign nation; it's interfering in the internal affairs of another country. I am afraid bombing would swing the undecided people into Milošević's camp to 'save country and sovereignty.' Also dropping bombs in an underpopulated country may allow for a wide margin of error but not here. The populace is too close together. The historic sites and beauty of the Montenegrin coastline would also be at risk."

A couple of days before I was due to leave Yugoslavia, the telephone rang. A friend called to say that the bombing had been delayed. Stress flowed off me like rivers; what a reprieve!

Miša debated whether the Jewish children already in Budapest should be brought back or not. Miša knew Milošević's cat-and-mouse game of one step forward and three steps back, a deadly waltz of populace control.

The day before I flew out, Milošević closed three independent newspapers and a student-run radio station, *Radio Index.* "That's terrorism," Miro snapped. Miša, Majda, and Miro took me to the airport. As I presented my ticket at Surčin, a police matron ordered me to empty all my pockets. She went through all my carry-ons and escorted me behind a curtain and gave me an external personal exam. Concerned, Miša came over to me and asked what they were looking for. "Money," she said. I had a silver coin that Branko had given me to give John Hajdukovich. But thank God, I had insisted that Branko give me a signed letter of permission for the silver piece. With that letter, I was able to

Downtown Belgrade, streets filled with up to 200,000 protesting the Milošević regime, 1996. Courtesy of Miroslav Konstantinović. Photo by Draško Gagović, Vreme *magazine.*

keep the coin. The matron and her colleagues disappeared. Suddenly frightened about leaving Miša in this oppressive Bombay, I began to pull out some money to give him. He hissed in my ear, "Put it away! I don't need it! They have cameras! Put it away." Once I was cleared, I went back and hugged each one but I felt so helpless, leaving them behind in that country, standing behind the railing with warm smiles. With my backpack on, I waved and turned the corner.

Miro e-mailed later that a demonstration was scheduled that day but only a few hundred people had showed up. Over the next weeks, he introduced me to the new independent internet news website in Belgrade: B-92. I watched B-92 grow from a few students with laptops keeping a low profile in a storefront space to a major TV network later in the twenty-first century.

At home, I called Danilo in Texas. I was overjoyed to find him. I would be going to see my family in Tulsa in January. Danilo and I planned for me to swing over to Austin and visit him for a couple of nights.

In Austin, we went out for dinner. We talked for hours, reviewing the years and sharing things only close friends can. Danilo's wife, Jasminka, and their daughter Kini lived in Boston where Jasminka was a professor. Jasminka had just released a new book on Yugoslavia, *Burn This House.* I was eager to read it. Danilo had obtained a tenured professorship at the University of Texas. It was during this visit that Danilo explained to me his years of incarceration and the reason for his leaving Yugoslavia.

Chapter 47

1999: NATO Air Strikes and Meeting the People of Yugoslavia

After my visit with Danilo at the University of Texas, I continued to monitor events as they unfolded in Kosovo. Throughout the winter of 1998–1999, the Kosovo Liberation Army (KLA) attacked and the Serbs responded. In July 1998, two thousand Albanians were displaced from the village of Račak, central Kosovo. The Organization for Security and Cooperation in Europe (OSCE) encouraged the Albanians to return, and in early January, about 350 people went back home. However, on January 16, 1999, OSCE monitors found the bodies of forty-five people in and around the village. A six-nation Contact Group, made up of delegates from the United States, Britain, France, Germany, Italy, and Russia, began meeting to resolve the conflict. They issued an ultimatum to the Yugoslavian government and the Kosovar Albanians to attend peace talks

Temporary pontoon bridge in background; front, NATO bombed bridge at Novi Sad, Vojvodina, Yugoslavia. 1999. Judy Ferguson photo.

in Rambouillet, France, from February 6 to 23. Negotiations went awry, however, when both the Serbs and the KLA rejected the terms of the agreement. The U.S. had been counting on the KLA signing and the Serbs walking away, which would then have paved the way for NATO air strikes against Serbia. But the KLA refused to sign unless the agreement promised them future independence, not simply self-rule, which was not on the NATO negotiators' agenda. The KLA's all-or-nothing position in effect meant that they preferred to continue their ground war against the Serbs—one in which they were vastly disadvantaged—and stick to their demand for independence, rather than agree to curtail their plans for the immediate future but thereby gain the military backing of NATO: NATO essentially operating as the KLA's air force.

A proposed peace agreement was drawn up; it was signed by the KLA but it was rejected by Yugoslavia. On March 18, 1999, the Albanian, American, and British delegations signed the Rambouillet Accords while the Serbian and Russian delegations refused. The accords called for NATO administration of Kosovo as an autonomous province within Yugoslavia; a force of thirty thousand NATO troops to maintain order in Kosovo; an unhindered right of passage for NATO troops on Yugoslav territory, including Kosovo; and immunity for NATO and its agents to Yugoslav law. This too was rejected despite Russian help at compromise. The notorious paramilitary terrorist Arkan appeared at the Belgrade Hyatt hotel and ordered the Western journalists to leave. In Kosovo, the international monitors withdrew, and NATO initiated air strikes March 24. Without the consent of the UN security council or of the approval of the U.S. Congress, the Kosovo War was initiated against a sovereign country who had not attacked outside its borders. This happened even though General Klaus Naumann (chairman of NATO Military Committee) cited that Ambassador Walker had said in the North Atlantic Council that the majority of ceasefire violations were caused by the KLA. The NATO air strikes were the first in its fifty-year history when without invitation, NATO aggressively entered a country based on its internal affairs. However, with the history of the Bosnia and Croatia wars, NATO decided not to wait this time.

Three days before the bombing began, on March 21, 1999, the *Fairbanks Daily News-Miner Heartland* magazine published my feature article "The Montenegrin Connection," the story of Alaska's Yugoslav pioneers, a result of my 1998 research on John Hajdukovich.

When NATO made the announcement, Miro e-mailed me from Belgrade in the middle of his night: "I lay down to take a sleep. When I woke I thought it was normal time. I looked out the window and saw a cherry tree in bloom. But—remembered we are war with the whole world. Nobody asked me."

When the missiles came, it was without warning. Incredulous that my country would bomb the country of my friends, I was devastated. With no experience with modern warfare, I imagined that my internet contact with my friends would be cut, that they could disappear in the black chaos of war. My husband said, "You might try fasting." For forty-two of the seventy-eight days of bombing, I began a juice fast. In the evenings, I went for a walk in the star-studded spring night and prayed. As I stood in the crusted snow looking toward the warrior constellation Orion, I felt a personal promise that God would protect each one of my friends. Incredible as it seemed to me, I embraced the promise with a daring faith.

I e-mailed with Danilo in Texas, Miša and Miro in Belgrade, Branko

Right: Vlada Stojanović, between south Serbia and Kosovo, 1999. Courtesy of Vlada Stojanović.

in Montenegro, and Dragan Hajduković in Switzerland. In Fairbanks, I visited often with Vuka Stepovich and Angie Geraghty, my Montenegrin Alaskan friends. I monitored five websites and kept a map of Serbia-Montenegro on my wall to check what had been hit.

NATO flew over thirty-eight thousand missions involving one thousand aircraft. Tomahawk cruise missiles were used extensively, fired from aircraft, ships, and submarines. But NATO seriously underestimated Milošević's will to resist.

On the ground with Yugoslavia's army and paramilitaries in Kosovo, 850,000 Kosovo Albanians fled. Targets used by civilian and military began to be bombed, including the Radio Television Serbia building, downtown buildings in Belgrade, bridges on the Danube, oil refineries and fertilizer plants along with the erroneous target of a train, a Saturday marketplace, and the Chinese embassy (reputedly being used as a relay station for Yugoslav army radio signals). Some of the many mistakes were termed "collateral damage."

A Protestant believer in Niš, Vlado later told me his story of being a soldier in Kosovo:

We had plenty of time to empty buildings, to dig in before the war. Two months in advance, I was in place. [January 1999.] In the beginning we really enjoyed protesting on the bridges. [Citizens danced and sang on the bridges of Belgrade, believing their presence would protect the bridges.] NATO dropped pamphlets and the Serbs thought they were poisonous to touch.

We had Stealth technology. When we destroyed NATO's NightHawk, we wrote on a big banner, "Sorry, we didn't know it was invisible." We did not use our best weapons because they were not a match against the USA.

The sky was the crossroads for different flight paths. Sometimes they flew so low we could see the plane's outline, but no one attacked us. One morning, a missile came so close that we didn't know why it didn't hit us. We searched until we found it. There was a Bible verse on the missile, Revelation 6:8, "—behold, an ashen horse; and he who sat on it had the name of Death; and

Far right: Vlada Stojanović, NATO rocket, Kosovo, 1999. Courtesy of Vlado Stojanović.

Hades was following him . . ." Scrawled next to it was, "Now you shall be free from Slobodan. This shall bring you peace," illustrated with a peace symbol. I really wanted to find that guy. I have a few words for those nice guys. There were lots of messages, "If you're a Serb, run faster."

There were five hundred soldiers in my barracks. I think there were fourteen radar, including mine, on the border with Kosovo. The battles were very near us but we did not feel them. The roads were closed and our job was to check cars coming and going.

Anti aircraft lights sweeping the sky for NATO aircraft, Belgrade, 1999. Courtesy of Miroslav Konstantinović.

While we were in the field, NATO destroyed my barracks and switchboard. Our job in Kosovo was to be a target. So with radar that didn't work, we'd play, switch on our nonfunctioning radar and act out "running with the missiles." We were under command from Belgrade. For a week, we had no communication. Maybe they tried to make contact but God really cared for us since Belgrade could not reach us. Just to have something to do, we switched the radar on and off. Not only was I in the war with a broken radar but we soldiers had borrowed 150 bullets for our machine gun. When we were finished, we were supposed to return them. We were fighting with sticks and rocks, weapons from the 1970s. We beat them because we lasted so long with just sticks. If you saw how many of our weapons were destroyed and how many kilos of bombs they dropped. They tried all their new weapons on us. We should not even exist. (Since our beginning, we Serbs have been in a war.) I kept trying to turn on the radiation in my radar but it was too weak. As planes roared overhead, we roasted meat and played football. But it was a miserable situation. We knew our hands were tied. We had no weapons and no airplanes. What tortured us was thinking of the ones left at home. We could see the fire of Leskovac when the missiles hit. Every morning, we wanted to call home but we could not use the line often or long.

We were a major attraction. People brought us rakija and meat every day. It was hard to go to Leskovac and see the guys who'd been where the real fighting was, those who really did something and had real wounds. What they did was for Milošević. I could see hell in my friends' eyes; some looked crazy. It was hard when they bombed Niš. I couldn't believe they would bomb the center of town. On Lenina Boulevard, just a street with families living on it, they hit forty-four people

312

in the flea market. After we shot planes down, they started dropping cluster bombs and depleted uranium bombs. People were really scared.

Between being both a Christian and a Serb, I really struggled. I didn't want to die for that kind of idol: nationalism. Sometimes I wanted to take on NATO and the Albanians but I didn't want to die for that. I could only trust God; no one else. I really prayed about this country, the wounded, the presence of foreigners. God really gave me peace. All this stupid war. God has both Clinton and Milošević in His hand.

We're not good guys; they're not good guys. I can live with that. The problem is, "Who gave the West the right to get involved?" That is very painful. Many years will go by before the truth is known about this war. Governments lie: NATO planes did go down.

I had my own battles with myself. The most difficult battle is fighting Serbian pride. For instance after Belgrade gets their milk, we in south Serbia have to wait in line with those on a pension to get our milk.

Everyone has his own reasons. In the Balkans, it's a spiritual war. During the time of Serbia's medieval kingdom in 1389 at Kosovo Polje, Knez [chieftain] Lazar said of Serbs, "Whoever is a Serb and of Serb birth; And of Serb blood and heritage; and comes not to fight at Kosovo; May he never have the progeny his heart desires! Neither son nor daughter. May nothing grow that his hand sows! Neither dark wine nor white wheat."

Serbian villages are really closed. Who knows what you can find there? I have heard that whole villages were swallowed up in the earth because they were so evil. But I got used to the lies and demons. I can recognize them and fight against them. I couldn't live anywhere else. But as a Christian, I must be ready to die for any other

Ušće Business Center, bombed twice by NATO, April 21 and 27, 1999. Photo by Velimir Savatić, Studio Strugar.

nation: Croat, Muslim, Serb. Still I don't know how I would be with an Albanian or an obtuse Westerner.

Throughout the bombing, I wrote e-mails to a protestant evangelical body, LeChurch in Leskovac, which was how I later met Vlado. During the bombing, normal schedules stopped; families were at home; many monitored the internet like unofficial war monitors. From his infrequent e-mails, I pictured Miša at home.

A man stood with his hands jammed in his pockets staring out the window onto the street where he'd spent his life, Višegradska, in downtown Belgrade. His back and shoulders were built for carrying and so they were always slightly rounded. His sandy hair wisped over his forehead. His brown eyes darted slightly as he sought to find the solution he knew must exist.

His wife Majda was cleaning up from *ručak*, the main meal of the day. Inured but depressed after ten years of Balkan insanity, Majda sat on the insulated stove trying to get warm. She simply shook her head. Miša swayed back and forth. Before he was evacuated to Budapest, their son, Eli, spent his time on his computer, listening to music in his bedroom, but tonight he was in Budapest. As night began to descend, the piercing wail of the air raid sirens began their scream. Dread slid into Belgrade as the nightly run of NATO's planes began to fill the skies, as they had for the last sixty nights. The Yugoslav antiaircraft lights swept the sky, comforting the suppressed terror of the populace. Coming in low and dependably, the robotic planes laden with "smart bombs" usually glided to their precise targets.

Miša David, Belgrade, 1998. Judy Ferguson photo.

Just inside the lighted windows of Belgrade homes, teenagers who'd dubbed themselves "Captain Commandos" were ready at their PCs. Their fingers poised on a mouse, they seemed to nod at one another, "Gentlemen, start your engines…" They filled cyber space with their quick-draw pistols, reporting, anticipating, e-mailing what the next target might be, what collateral damage NATO might incur tonight. They were ready to defend the family who might lose a child, the train or market that might be impacted.

In the surreal world of this twentieth century war, they e-mailed new pen pals around the world. The Serbs implicated President Clinton in his recent affair with Monica Lewinsky, asking, "Has anyone seen *Wag the Dog*?!" They cursed the bombs imploding their factories, their bridges, their homeland, their future. They monitored their wall maps and telephoned their friends as explosions rocked the dark night. Their electronic running commentary on beograd.com was translated into multiple languages as the Serbs fought to control their helpless situation.

Belgrade grafitti: "There's no use for barricades anymore; we're coming! SDS [a political party in the Serb Republic connected to Milošević's party], Serbia-Montenegro." The "CCCC" emblem, "Samo Sloga Srbina Spasava;" "Only unity saves the Serbs," Belgrade, 1999. Judy Ferguson photo.

Milošević's army was on the hunt to fulfill the military draft; any man up to sixty years old was liable. Many hid to avoid being sent to Kosovo. Citizens went to work erratically; life rotated around air raid sirens. Miša stepped over to his son Eli's computer. He began to write me.

April 9, 1999: I don't understand this computer. From the time NATO attack started, I sent you two messages but I got your e-mail from April 4 in which you didn't mention my e-mails so I don't think you got them. Do you know that Majda and me evacuated Eli and Lea to Budapest? So I am now the new commander of the computer and probably I can't use it the right way. The night alarm has just begun again. Lots of bombs and the barrage of antiairplane firing makes for a very unpleasant noise. It's time for sleep. Good night. Miša David.

May 12, 1999: Danilo wrote from Texas: Judy, I just received a note from Miša. You'll probably get it too. The wooden shutters and the plastic covering over his windows have been blown off their house from a nearby explosion. Miša expects the U.S. is about to cut off Yugoslavia from the internet. Milošević couldn't dream up anything more effective to win people to him. D.

May 12, 1999: Beograd.com wrote: We have reliable information that the U.S. government ordered shutdown of the satellite [Orion] feeds for internet customers in Yugoslavia. This action may happen as soon as later tonight or tomorrow, May 12 or 13.

I was devastated and intensified my prayer. Apparently President Clinton relented and allowed the satellite connection to remain. By June 2, twenty thousand bombs and missiles had been used. Depleted uranium ammunition and cluster bombs were poisoning the land, air, and water along with the implosion of the refineries and fertilizer factories. Night after night on Kneza Miloša Street, Belgrade's main artery, NATO continued surgically imploding one government building after another. Citizens prayed for cloudy nights to pause the nightly bombing. The RTS (Radio Television Serbia) building was hit and sixteen young people were buried under tons of cement. On global television, President Bill Clinton and the UK's prime minister, Tony Blair, agreed that the bombing of Yugoslavia was not so much about Kosovo but about the survival of NATO in the twenty-first century. On Public Television's McLaughlin Report, McLaughlin posed the question of the profile of a global dictator. California senator Tom Campbell waited for the full legal sixty days to elapse in which the president's emergency military action was no longer permitted without the consent of Congress.

Working with Miro, on April 10, 1999, I wrote an article for the *Anchorage Daily News Metro* section:

ILLEGAL NATO ACTIONS SHOCK PRO-DEMOCRATIC SERBS

Kosovo caught the American public unawares. Considered the Jerusalem of the Serbs' Orthodox faith, it is to Serbs the heartland of the Federal Republic of Yugoslavia.

Early ethnic tensions were described in a *New York Times* headline of Nov. 1, 1987: "In Yugoslavia, Rising Ethnic Strife Brings Fears of Worse Civil Conflict." Initially, the Serbs were the victims, until skirmishing became more or less mutual with the establishment of the Kosovo Liberation Army.

In a *Newsweek* interview (April 5, 1999), Henry Kissinger said the Rambouillet peace initiative, the only document offered to Milošević, may have pushed "Milošević into accelerating the repression against the KLA before the bombs fell." Exacerbated then by the North Atlantic Treaty Organization's bombing beginning March 24, the violence is now completely out of control.

Though "we cannot ignore Slobodan Milošević's brutality," Kissinger continued, "...we must remember that Yugoslavs fought at our side in two world wars and stood up to Stalin at the height of his powers."

With the media focused on Kosovo's desperate refugees, the world is unaware of the prodemocratic Serbs, repressed for 10 years by President Slobodan Milošević. Today the West is bombing their country.

One of those Belgrade Serbs, ethnically mixed as are many, Dr. Miroslav Konstantinović, a veteran of the prodemocratic demonstrations of 1996–1997, described this week, by e-mail, his democratic colleagues: "They sit silent in the bomb shelters of Belgrade, shocked by the illegal actions of NATO." The international 1992 sanctions against the former Yugoslavia hobbled the country's middle class, the carriers of democracy. Barely able to survive in dysfunctional Belgrade, they had their bank accounts frozen by Milošević. In this limited state, independent radio stations sprang up, but since the bombing, the regime has silenced them.

Dr. Miroslav Konstantinović, Belgrade, 1999. Judy Ferguson photo.

An early demonstrator for democracy, Dr. Danilo Udovički-Selb, now resettled in Texas, fought for democracy in Belgrade in 1968. Five years later, Tito put him in a Belgrade prison. Explaining today's bombardment, Danilo said, "Certainly international law does not permit the bombing of a sovereign country. NATO, an organization of 19 nations, knew there would be a veto by the 185-member United Nations and its security council. Skipping the step of the UN's approval, NATO illegally began bombing the sovereign state of Yugoslavia on March 24."

Three years ago, when Milošević's municipal officials were dismissed through Belgrade's free elections, the president illegally overturned the results. Demonstrating for three months in the rain and snow, Miro and 500,000 other residents protested daily.

"We were trying to solve … by peaceful, legal process," he said.

After 10 years of isolation and struggle, today's

Zora Konstantinović, Belgrade, 1999. Judy Ferguson photo.

bombing has crushed the hopes of Miro and the potential democratic fifth column in Belgrade. Instead of fighting Milošević, they are, Miro described, "clustered citizens, independent of political orientation, trying to defend their homes."

Fulfilling Milošević 's prophecies of Western persecution, the West has played into the regime's hands.

Before the bombardment, Gary Demsey of the CATO Institute warned the United States that bombing might trigger martial law and "we would not see a democratic, post-Milošević era for many years."

Exhausted and depressed after two weeks of bombing, geneticist Konstantinović wrote: "I am analyzing NATO's strategy. When I do my experiments, I fix all factors which could impact the result. Then, in a separate example, I change one factor at a time, searching for the difference it may bring."

There are many variables the West has missed in the Yugoslav experiment.

According to Laura Silber, author of *The Death of a Nation,* we have played catch-up. With the Rambouillet document, we insisted that NATO occupy Kosovo, the heartland, or else it would suffer bombing. We did not foresee the multitude of refugees soon to pour into neighboring Macedonia, Albania and tiny Montenegro, a trigger for internal chaos there.

"Stop the bombing and get FRY to withdraw its troops from Kosovo," Misha Glenny, author of *The Fall of Yugoslavia,* said March 31 on the Charlie Rose show. "Have a peacekeeping force of Russians, Greeks and two western nations. This is a tragedy," he said flatly.

Kissinger concluded, "World War I started in the Balkans, not from ethnic conflicts but because outside powers intervened in a local conflict."

Struggling to understand, Miro puzzled, "When someone says he brings peace but he systematically ruins my country, that is 'homelandacide.'"

Kissinger's interview concluded: "Let us handle" any other Balkan state of emergency "with greater foresight than the prelude to the current crisis."

Staring out at his beloved Belgrade, Miro, watching it burn, said, "I am bleeding."

Later my Belgrade book layout artist, dissident Dragan Mišković, said, "You were taught that the people who suffered were the Serbs; that they were the victims. They spent their efforts yelling at the rotten West instead of driving out their own leaders."

In early April, NATO countries began to think seriously about a ground operation, an invasion of Kosovo. Finally through Finnish and Russian negotiators, Milošević realized NATO would not relent and that Russia would not intervene militarily. Milošević agreed to terms and he allowed the UN-directed NATO military presence in Kosovo.

When the bombing finally ended on June 10, 1999, it was a new day. I planned on returning to see my friends at the first opportunity in the winter. I'd stay longer this time and interview people throughout Serbia and Montenegro. It was not a light decision. I asked for prayer and got some clear answers. Miro wasn't comfortable with my coming nor was Miša. Miro said, "If anything happened, I couldn't help you. I don't know if you'll be safe." Knowing this was something he had to say, I said, "It's okay. I know." But when I called Washington, D.C., to get a visa to enter Yugoslavia, the Yugoslav embassy was closed. I called the Chinese, Egyptian, and Croatian embassies trying to get a lead where I could

Benzin dealer putting benzin in Dragana Ranković's car, as was the only and normal way in 1999. Belgrade. Judy Ferguson photo.

get a visa to enter Yugoslavia. Nothing. The other embassies acted as if Yugoslavia never existed. I felt like a blind woman searching an unexpected wall for a crack to find entrance. (When I told Miša about this later, he said, "Most people would've given up.") Finally I called a Montenegrin public relations office in Washington, D.C. Almost as if it were a secret, the representative told me to call Ottawa, Canada. I did, but I needed a letter of invitation from a Yugoslavian citizen. Miro e-mailed his official invitation, which I sent with my passport by FedEx to Ottawa. Miša asked Zorica if I could stay with her. However, heating was very hard in those years. Zorica's family kept their house unheated except for their small upstairs living facilities. In winter, there was no way to heat the downstairs. Zorica got me a rented room through a colleague at the university, Ratka Marić and Lazar. Miro warned me that according to a new law, I would also have to go with Ratka to the police department and register my presence as soon as I arrived. Medical supplies were scarce in

Serbia. I visited doctors and Fairbanks Memorial Hospital and asked for donations for supplies and even winter clothing from Big Ray's. I called Northwest Airlines to get permission for extra baggage intended for charitable donations. Because Yugoslavia was under sanctions preventing international air traffic and because the area surrounding Surčin airport (including the military airport Batajnica) had been repeatedly bombed, I asked Miro how I could get there. He arranged for me to catch a minivan that ran from Budapest to Belgrade.

My twenty-two-year-old daughter Sarah, who was living in Oklahoma, gently asked me, "Mom, do you really want to go? You may be very disappointed." I knew I could be facing something difficult. But I told her that I'd backed off in 1967 when I didn't understand the culture, and if I was ever going to understand, it was now.

But at home, it was hard to watch my fifteen-year-old son walk down our snowy drive to school knowing that I'd be gone for the next two months. In early October 1999, four months after the bombing, I flew to Amsterdam where I caught another flight to Budapest. Feeling like an awkward American with two very large boxes along with my big bags, I met the minivan driver. I knew the Yugoslav border could be a problem. All the passengers sat in stoic silence while the driver talked to the border guards. I explained carefully several times to the guard that I was taking medical supplies in. I also told him I had a computer. The young man thought about not allowing my boxes through. He thought about how to follow the right procedures, then finally decided better of it and passed me on through. Seven hours later, I was delivered with all my freight in front of Miša's flat

Cigarette smuggler and dealer, Podgorica, Montenegro, 1999. Judy Ferguson photo.

where he, Majda, and Miro met me. A few minutes later, Zorica joined us at Miša's table. They were very concerned about my presence in a city NATO had just bombed. Suspected spies had been arrested in several cases. Zorica and Miša leaned forward and gave me two rules to follow religiously: No cameras in public, and don't speak English in public.

Majda brought us coffee and cakes. We were very happy to be reunited. Together we drove over to Zorica's colleague Ratka Marić. Miro took my medical boxes to his house because he would help me distribute the supplies. All of us gathered in Ratka's small living room and got acquainted. Ratka's daughter had moved out temporarily so I could have her room. The next day, Ratka and I went to the police station to register me. The men gave her a hard time because she had not registered me the very day I came in as the law required. Also, they demanded to see her title to her apartment. One policeman was disturbed and challenged, "Why should we let her stay here!? She bombed us!!" Trying to get his attention, I said, "Sir, I am very sorry. I am very sorry." A man standing next to me smiled at me and shrugged, saying, "Don't pay attention." Back at the flat, Ratka, Lazar, and I chatted and talked about sharing the kitchen. They gave me a key, and I began unpacking. I went

Police in Terazije Square, Belgrade, 1999. Judy Ferguson photo.

up to the top of the tall apartment building and from there, I could see a sweeping view of Belgrade: the river, its bridges, and the dominating Sv. Sava church. The building's watchman, a refugee Serb from Krajina, told me that when they were run out of Croatia, Milošević would not allow the refugees entry into Belgrade and told them to find another town. Most of them had nothing but what they could carry. The next day, Miša and Majda came by for me. As we drove, we never stopped but they showed me the collapsed buildings from the bombing.

I quickly learned to adjust to a flat without heat and with routine four to six-hour electrical outages. Electricity was being shared. I learned to back up my computer and be ready at any moment to be reduced to candlelight. Neighborhoods varied as to their heating supply but at Ratka's, the city didn't turn on the winter heating until the latter part of October. I went to bed dressed for the Alaska trapline: wearing my down jacket, pants, trappers hat, and mittens. Ten days later the central heating came on and the temperature was okay. The daytime was Indian summer weather. Miša encouraged me to go for walks because the rainy cooler weather was coming. Miro's mother, Zora, and I walked around the grounds of the ancient Kalemegdan fortress at the confluence of the Danube and Sava rivers where Miša, Danilo, Mira, Zorica, Donna, and I had dined a lifetime ago in 1964.

For the first two weeks, I interviewed in the Belgrade area and spent my weekends with either Miša's or Miro's families.

In 1998 after Miro and I first began researching John Hajdukovich, Miro prepared to take his family on their annual summer vacation to Montenegro. His wife, children, and her parents went by train to the family home in Nikšić while Miro followed by car. On his way, he had decided to look for the Hajduković village of Podgor Utrg. Trying to read a map, he tried an asphalted mountain road. Feeling like a fool, he followed a goat trail that seemed to go on and on. But when he stopped at a house to ask directions, who should he meet but eighty-year-old Anica Hajduković and her brothers. They invited Miro over for watermelon and lemonade. Anica pulled out the family photo album and showed Miro the photo of John's cousin, Archbishop Rade Hajduković. Miro took a photo of John Hajdukovich's fantastic view of Lake Skadar and of a photo of the archbishop. In the fall when he returned to Belgrade, Miro sent me his news and photos: a fantastic cornucopia of discoveries. In October when I visited Belgrade, Miro and I spent the evening with Anica where I met her daughter, Gordana, and granddaughter, Dragana Ranković, an engineer who was very proficient in English.

Pancevo refinery bombed by NATO, 1999. Courtesy of Nada and Ivan Stojkovic.

In 1999, Dragana took me to Novi Sad to see the bombed bridges and to interview some of the local people. As we looked from the banks of the Danube, trucks and cars were driving over a temporary pontoon bridge. Downstream, the inverted V of the bridge was protruding from the water, a quiet testimony to a decade of violence. As we walked, I saw taxi drivers pushing their dilapidated cars down the street to wait in line for benzin (gas).

Whenever Miro needed gas, he watched for a jug along the roadside with a sign, Benzin, on it. He'd look around and pull over. Day or night, shadowy figures emerged from the bushes, carrying a three-gallon fuel container and a funnel. First looking around, they poured the benzin into Miro's tank while his wife, Vesna, shuddered over who they might be dealing with.

Under international sanctions, most of the essentials of life were blockaded but were being smuggled in. The criminals who worked for Milošević lined his pockets with the illegal retail while he publicly penalized the illicit trade, a smoke-and-mirrors game. The same was true of changing money. The banks had little money. It was illegal to change money with the money changers on the street or in a retail store, but everyone had to. Any Hollywood movie, name brand music CD, software or Play Station games were available at the illegal street vendors' kiosks that operated openly and prolifically. Most retailers seemed to be lucky to have adding machines and didn't have cash registers. Sales were not recorded for the government nor taxes paid. Cigarette smugglers peddled their goods on every corner in Montenegro. All across Serbia and Montenegro, the public system was broken but an unofficial efficient system greased along in the shadows. A Serb once told me that Yugoslavia was far more free than in the United States because a person could easily get lost and leave no trail in the Balkans.

Sometimes Vesna Maksimović made a mental note of the taxi she put me in just in case something happened. But taxi drivers were some of my favorite storytellers. Of course, in those days, they had no seatbelts and smoking was prolific everywhere. Oxygen was at a premium. It was daring for me to roll down the car window.

Part of the family of Ellen Hajdukovich, Ivan and Nada Stojković, brought me to their home Pančevo for a sumptuous feast. After dinner, we drove along the Tamiš River to see the bombed refinery. It was never a good idea to pause when looking at the damage throughout Serbia; we always kept moving. In Pančevo's museum, there were large photos on display of fire pouring out from the refinery.

One night, wearing a small backpack, I crossed a Belgrade street in the dark. I didn't see a huge pothole and stumbled, hitting the asphalt. A woman ran over to me asking in English if I were all right, saying she was a doctor. I was very touched. Another night, I rode in a taxicab with a Serbian lady driver, Spomenka (which means "Forget Me Not"). Serbian names are very warm and imaginative, varying from Snow White to Strawberry. Spomenka told me she had two jobs to support her family. In her lapel, she wore a cross stick pin. She was worried about her son. She said it was very hard to see physicians and other professionals selling pencils on the street. As I prepared to say goodnight, she smiled and patted the cross on her lapel, and with a winsome smile, said full of faith, "But I believe."

I decided to ride the train to Montenegro that Vuka had told me about, the one that slid along the mountaintops and rattled through long tunnels. While waiting once during the night at the train station in Bar, I asked Dr. Srboljub Hajduković in Bar how he knew the train schedule. With his pipe in his mouth, and looking like a tall Sherlock Holmes, he smiled dryly and said, "It's the people's train." Apparently Eli David wasn't of that generation. In Belgrade, he dropped me off at the main train station and said, "I don't know

Vasko's Cerovo valley, near Bijelo Polje, Montenegro, 1999. Judy Ferguson photo.

anything about the train and I don't want to know!" I got on, wedged myself into a train car, and was pressed body–to–body in the corridor with no way to sit down. Filled with cigarette smoke, choked with peasants and bags, we stood. When I had to use the john, I hopped over bags, pushed open the broken handled door, kept one foot on the door to keep it shut while the goods fell through an open toilet onto the railroad tracks. Once while looking out the window, a large man tried to grab me and hustle me into a private area. I leapt over bags in the corridor back to the safety of my cigarette smoke-filled train car.

Implanted within a destroyed infrastructure, there was an unwritten system based on trust that worked well. Once while traveling in a taxi with Zora, at her urging, I handed the driver fifty dollars to change for me into dinar. He got out, kept the taxi running, ran through traffic, and soon returned with the correct change in dinar. One evening when I was walking with Zora, her gentleman neighbor said, "Take care of Baba [grandmother]. Without her, you have nothing."

From late October 1999 to mid-January 2000, I interviewed people from all walks of life in the Balkans: a former Yugoslav army captain who observed, "Every fifty years, the Turk must come"; journalists; filmmakers; scientist Dr. Srboljub Hajduković, who had invented Yugoslavia's atomic laboratory from nothing at Vinča after World War II; Orthodox priests; and prodemocracy, solitary, hated public figures. Four months after NATO had destroyed bridges, buildings, businesses, and marketplaces, I traveled alone and no one ever bothered me based on political bias. On the contrary, they helped me. Often a taxi driver would say to me, "Oh, it's okay. It's politics," and they'd help me learn to speak Serbian.

While I was visiting Branko Hajduković in Bijelo Polje, Montenegro, in the old Sandzak Ottoman administrative district, I met a ten-year-old-Hajduković, Vasko. A warm, impulsive, spontaneous child who embraced life, Vasko and I hit it off. He loved to talk about his lovely mountain home. One day we decided to hike up there. Knowing where I was going, Branko bought me some sturdy high-topped tennis shoes. All the way up the mountains, Vasko cavorted. We played and were silly. Once he stopped, pointed out a military fuel cache, showed me a distant military sentinel outpost that appeared quite vacant, and urged me to film it. Like an idiot, I did. As we neared his home, he began perfectly imitating the various Serbian and Montenegrin politicians. He bounced easily and seamlessly from one man's voice and mannerisms to the other. He began singing, "Crna Gora, how I love you," dramatically rolling on the ground with an imaginary *gusle* and wailing his passion for his country in dramatic fashion. But when he came to imitating Milošević, he began to explode, saying with all his vigor, "MILOŠEVIĆ!! I HATE HIM!! HE DESTROYED YUGOSLAVIA!!" The soul of the land was implicit in this very earnest, passionate boy. Before he jumped a creek, he paused in an eloquent stance, gestured, and said, "THIS is

Vasko Hajduković, Cerovo, Montenegro, 1999. Judy Ferguson photo.

MINE!" He crossed the creek in a small leap, and proclaimed, "And, THIS is MINE! Look, Judy, isn't it wonderful?!" he cried. And it was. In his village highland valley home, he showed me his room with its alpine view of the valley. Apples were strewn drying on his parents' bedroom floor.

We tramped down the valley in the falling snow, singing and then trying to stay warm in the heavy wet snow. We stopped at his cousin Dragan Hajduković's, where we would spend the night with Dragan's family: Nina, their son, and his parents. That night, Nina gave me a bed in the room with her small family. The alpine chill filled the Heidi-like house as I slept under my eider-down, secure and happy as if I was family.

In Bijelo Polje when I first met Nenad Božanović, a Serbian physicist, it was mentioned that he was a refugee from Priština, Kosovo. My eyes widened and he said in understatement, "Oh, is that important?" Over the next days, Nenad spent hours

Nenad Božanović, Bijelo Polje, Montenegro, 1999. Judy Ferguson photo.

teaching me. Puzzled over the endless Montenegrin cacophony that surrounded me, I found it hard to get a moment of quiet. He explained to me that it was a deep and profoundly black heritage: too dark to deal with. Pain, killing, and death that Serbs had known for centuries. "It is so deep and so black, Judy, that intimacy and quiet is not something they generally welcome. Music, *rakija*, and song help to alleviate memories of such long suffering." He added, "No, of course, you cannot understand it. Yes, Serbs hoped Milošević would win." Once he brought me a tape of Orthodox monks singing in their timeless monasteries cloistered high in the rocks. He asked me to let myself experience the timeless ancient history of Byzantine Orthodox culture as they chanted. He told me there were important gates in the spirit in the Balkans and he felt there were also in Alaska.

[I met a woman, Verica, whose story was riveting. However, because she died soon after and therefore I could not make corrections to her story, the family has preferred I use a pseudonym. In deference to their feelings, the names have been changed.]

One evening, Verica, her daughter Ratka, and I gathered by ourselves in their living room where Verica began telling her story:

> I was born Verica Šilović in Okučane, Slavonia, Croatia, in 1922. My mother Danica was Montenegrin from Podgorica. My mother lost her own mother at birth and she was raised by a cruel stepmother. During World War I, my mother met

Verica and her brother and sister, Croatia, c. 1931. Courtesy of the family who wishes to remain anonymous.

my father in Podgorica. He was a Serb from Slavonia in Croatia serving in the occupiers' army, the Austro-Hungarians. Montenegrins had suffered at the hands of the Austrians, and my mother's family in Montenegro would not accept my father. My step-grandmother accepted the marriage but only to get rid of my mother, Danica. The rest of the family excluded my mother from the family. My parents went to Slavonia but with the war going on, they sought refuge with fellow Serbs in western Slavonia in Krajina, at Okučane. [In 1995, Serbs were run out of Krajina during the war in Croatia.] When I was four, my mother decided she wanted to return to Podgorica. My father was an electrician and could get a job easily. My two sisters and brother were born there, and eight years later, my third sister was born. We were a middle-class family and I was raised Orthodox Christian. My father never liked Montenegro but Mother really wanted to be there. He was the head of the family; we kids followed in importance, and my soft gentle mother came last. My father was a hard pressuring person. From the western culture of Croatia, his experience was more of a democratic nature, and he felt like a stranger in Montenegro.

I had finished a school of economics and wanted to study law, but my father thought I'd had enough education. Toward the end of my high school, I met Peko Janković, a good-looking, charismatic young man. He was a communist from Cetinje but because of his politics, he had gotten kicked out of school and had to finish in Podgorica. I went to Belgrade, lived with my married sister, and began studying medicine. Peko and I met there again in the post office. We were both nineteen, fiery, ideological; from him, I learned Communism. The love between us became a very big love. March 27, 1941, Belgrade held a huge demonstration refusing to be a part of the monarchy's official agreement with the Nazis. We said it was better to go to war than to be in a pact with the Germans. April 6, 1941, we Yugoslavs got our thank you. With no warning, on Easter 1941, the Germans began carpet bombing us. My father decided to take my mother, brother, and two sisters back to Okučane, Slavonia, Croatia. But because of the Ustaše there, it was a very dangerous thing to do. Serbs and Jews were targets in Croatia. Before the big round-up of Serbs in Croatia, their Croatian neighbors got my brother and sisters out of Slavonia to Belgrade to my sister's.

During the bombing of Belgrade, Peko went to Podgorica to organize the Partisans. I stayed in Belgrade but we were determined to not let the war destroy our connection. We arranged to marry. I put my suitcase on my shoulders and walked for a week from Belgrade to Podgorica [seven hours just by car]. I slept wherever night found me. My suitcase made my shoulders bleed. But that is love. Our daughter Ljuba was born later, and she has always had the nature of a lover. Her name means "love."

My parents in Slavonia were taken to Auschwitz and moved from there to the concentration camp at Jasenovac. There my father was knifed to death and my mother was gassed in the shower room. I didn't know until the war was over. In Serbia, the partisans were being put in prison while noncommunist Serbs continued to live somewhat normal lives. My brother and sisters were very lucky they were in Belgrade, not in Slavonia.

(In the 1990s, Serbs saw the same signs in Croatia as happened in the late 1930s and 1940s. Serbs were very afraid that a Ustaše roundup and killing of Serbs could happen again.) [These feelings were largely a result of Milošević's intense, end-less manipulation of the media.] But because of my communist training, I didn't hate Croatians. I knew that behavior isn't dictated by nationality but by political convictions.

When I arrived with my suitcase in Podgorica, Peko and I married. Because I was pregnant, I stayed with Peko's mother and his five sisters. Because his father had been dead from Peko's youth, and Peko was the only son, he was very busy with family business. I never saw him. At the end of my pregnancy, the Italians made a big push in Montenegro. Montenegrin partisans, including Peko along with partisans from all over Yugoslavia, gathered in Bosnia. I went to Cetinje where our daughter Ljuba was born in 1942. When she was only seven days old, we—Peko's mother, his sisters, I, and Ljuba—were all arrested. We spent a few months in the prison in Cetinje and then were taken to Perugia prison in central Italy. (The female prisoners from Montenegro, Slovenia, and Croatia were transported to Perugia.) Ljuba was one of several babies in prison there.

Border crossing Serbia Montenegro, 1999. Judy Ferguson photo.

In Bosnia, there were big Partisan battles in the forested mountains. A chief commissariat, Peko was there with them until the end of 1942. Suddenly, however, Peko reversed his convictions. He left with the Germans, switched sides and became a Chetnik, led by Popojuić, in a certain kind of Chetnik group. He wrote articles against Tito.

When Italy capitulated in 1943, we prisoners were released at Susa, Italy, to Istria, which was then part of Austria. On our return to Montenegro, I met people fleeing Cetinje. They told me that my husband had changed sides. I couldn't believe it, but I saw articles written by him in the newspaper. I thought I would die. Ljuba was two years old. I was only twenty-one. Filled with pain and passion, I had to decide if I was truly committed to Communism. I decided Ljuba would be safer with Peko's mother in Sušak, Slavonia, where the Communist party would support them. I left a way of connection and as a trained nurse, I went to fight with the partisans in Bosnia. I got a pistol and a grenade off of dead Germans.

At the end of the war, I returned to Belgrade where there were a lot of young Serbs from across all of Yugoslavia. I think they may've been rounded up by the Croatians and dumped at the border. Since it was the end of the war, there was no point in killing them. My brother had fought with the Partisans. A lot of Serbs including my brother died at the end of the war at the battle of Sremski Front.

Verica and her daughter Ljuba, c. 1946. Courtesy of the family who wishes to remain anonymous.

I went to Zagreb and contacted a special soldier collaborator from the Domabran militia who wanted to work with Partisans. We found Peko's mother and Ljuba. Peko's mother had had a hard time of it, and my daughter Ljuba didn't know me. She clung to her grandmother, insisting that she was her mother. I took them to Belgrade and then to Cetinje where I left them with her family. I returned to Belgrade to get a job. I was eager to get an education and Ljuba preferred her grandmother. I got a military fellowship and after only two and a half years, I graduated in 1949 from the university's faculty of economics. After the war, Peko and I only spoke once by phone.

I found out later that Peko had run away with the Germans to Zagreb where without a divorce from me, he married a woman in Zagreb, the second of his six marriages. For awhile he'd worked for Italian intelligence. Hoping to save his skin, he took a lot of their files, returned waving a white flag to Yugoslavia, cried repentance, and fell on the mercy of the country. At his court trial, he gave such a moving speech of guilt, saying he was completely wrong and all he wanted now was to see his baby. Women cried and the trial was a sensation. As good looking as a movie star and oozing feeling, he managed to get his possible life sentence reduced to seven years.

In 1951, I got a job in Čačak as a bookkeeper at a military factory where I dragged Ljuba with me. I met Milutin Ranković at the factory. There was a lot of tension between Peko's family and me. Ljuba preferred to be with her grandmother in Cetinje, who had a good job as did her daughters. I sent Ljuba back to them. Ultimately they moved to Belgrade where as good communists they got secure jobs. In 1955, Milutin and I married and we moved to the capitol, to Belgrade. Milutin was soft toward Ljuba and she liked him. Finally before Ljuba's graduation from high school, she began to accept me. When my son Nikola was born and then my daughter Ratka, I retired and stayed home and raised them. I remained politically active, always reading books and newspapers.

I never admitted it before but now that I am old, I think Ljuba was right; I should have put my child before my convictions. But I think such confessions should be made only before dying. I will tell her then.

I am very disappointed with the results of communism. It makes me sick how that beautiful dream turned out.

With that gift of deep confidence, Verica, Ratka, and I returned to join the rest of the family.

Life was independent and comfortable at Branko and Keka Hajduković's house. They always gave me a big bedroom to myself. Everyone ate when he was hungry, used the pantry and refrigerator as needed. But one evening it was time for me to catch the train back to Belgrade. Branko dragged his feet getting me to the train. At the last second, we threw everything into his car and roared off to the train station, catching it barely in time. He thrust my dufflebag and suitcase through the train's open window into the arms of the Yugoslavian soldiers. In the same tight corridor, the Montenegrin police kept passing through. There was tension between the two units. It was too late for me to be anonymous. With my luggage outside my compartment and me sandwiched in the car between Yugoslavian special forces, I tried to keep quiet. My feet in their "Baba" (grandmother homemade) wool socks and Montenegrin tennis shoes stuck out. I was warm in my Yugoslavian hand-knit sweater vest, a gift from Miro and Vesna. A soldier itching for a fight as well as satisfaction began to interrogate me. Looking out the window, he said, "Belgrade! It's like a house on fire, surrounded by walls, and they are going to burn, baby, burn!" Turning his attention to me, he quizzed, "What do your Delta Special Forces think of us, Yugoslavian special forces?" I said, "They don't even know you exist." He muttered to his window, "Probably so, probably so." He and his fellow soldier demanded to look through my wallet, my purse, check my belongings. They found Paja's business card, a member of SPO, a royalist, "opposition" group. When I said he was my friend, they clucked their tongue. They and the Montenegrin police began viewing my movie film on my video camera. At peace, I prayed silently. I knew there were two controversial filmings on there. By a millimeter on both ends of the film they viewed, they just missed viewing the filmed military fuel cache and on the other end, Vasko Hajduković screaming, "Milošević, I HATE HIM!" I settled into my train car in some measure of peace. I was beginning to get to know what I called Byzantium. Like soft clay, I was being written on, embossed with experiences foreign to me.

Painting of the critical Orion satellite, the internet link for Yugoslavia in 1999. When I prayed in 1999 looking at the constellation Orion, I did not know this star cluster was the name of Yugoslavia's key satellite. Painting by Christian believer, Dragan Mladenovic, Nis, Serbia. Judy Ferguson photo.

Over the years, whenever I visited Branko and Danica Hajduković he always put me on TV and had me interviewed by magazines and newspapers. I never discussed politics but only my Hajdukovich research. In 1999, he had a full press conference, but I was astounded at the behavior of all but two of the reporters. The majority almost got into a free-for-all as to how I could've spent a month prepping a book in Belgrade. They were not interested in my subject matter but in a tug of war as to where I'd spent my time. The one European experienced journalist apologized and said that most of them were not serious journalists but puppets employed by special concerns.

In 1998, Branko seemed to have never-ending lists of Hajdukovićs for me to meet. One night when Danica told me there was one more, I rolled my eyes in mock agony, protesting, "No, no more Hajdukovićs!" But this Hajduković in his eighties was a jewel. I took the train to Bar on the coast where I met Dr. Srboljub Hajduković. A tall, elegant man who smoked a pipe and wore a beautiful overcoat and scarf, he peered at me from under thick black eyebrows and asked in aristocratic English, "What can I tell you? I am single and like my name, Srboljub, I love Serbs." He had lost his wife the previous year and he had a marvelous wit. Trained as a medical doctor, Hajduković was asked after World War II if he would start the atomic laboratory at Vinča, not far from Belgrade. When he mentioned his other specialized training, he was told that he was the best they had. When he arrived at Vinča, he said, "Well, show me what you have." His colleague answered, "Can a man saw off the top of a head and pour in a brain?"

All the scientific journals were in English and none of the Serbian newly appointed scientists spoke more than a couple of hundred words of English. Dr. Hajduković began living at the library. He set about learning sixty English words a day, took private lessons, and finished up with a trip to London. He loved his first years at Vinča, because they built something of nothing, using only the proverbial "stick and a rope." But during the 1970s and 1980s, the young zealots who had built

Dr. Srboljub Hajduković, an originator of the Vinča Institute of Nuclear Sciences; Bar, Montenegro, 1999. Judy Ferguson photo.

the new Yugoslavia were replaced by petty bureaucrats who cared more about opportunism than about learning and earning their monthly wage. Dr. Hajduković tired of such mindless chaff taking up offices and he retired. Something in Hajduković's English reminded me of Zora Konstantinović's English, Miro's eighty-year-old mother. I told him he so reminded me of someone. The next time he was in Belgrade, would he meet me and I'd introduce him to Zora. When this happened in 1999, I was waiting with Zora at her flat when Dr. Hajduković rang the door buzzer. On entry, he exclaimed, "ZORA!" "Srdja!" she answered. Zora was the English teacher who had prepared Dr. Hajduković to be able to read the scientific journals that ultimately developed atomic science for Yugoslavia at Vinča. Zora and Srdja were matching and rare souls.

In Belgrade during New Year's, the memorable Y-2K, the rolling from the twentieth into the twenty-first century, arrived. I celebrated with Miša, Majda, and Eli in Trg Republike Square, and Plato Terazije. Trg Republika, Terazije. We sat in a restaurant with his family speaking in Serbian. We went out in the plaza and I thought, "How unbelievable this is that I am welcoming the new millennium in Belgrade." Of course, Miro the scientist was quick to tell me that in calculating the calendar correctly, New Year's 2001 was really the beginning of the new millennium. I asked if that were a special Serbian calendar. He laughed.

In the evenings in his home, Miša attempted to teach me, "Truth," he said, "is not in black and white as you perceive it but in the grey. You pick out the truth and you learn; it's in the whole mix." He added in defense of my rosy view of Serbs, "I don't know much about Christianity. But I know we are supposed to forgive our enemies. My people did not." A man who'd lost 110 relatives in the Holocaust, Miša was qualified to speak of forgiveness.

It takes some getting used to for a westerner in Orthodox Serbia and Montenegro that New Year's precedes Orthodox Christmas, which is called *Badnjak*, January 7. For Badnjak, I celebrated with the Konstantinović and Maksimović families. After a beautiful dinner surrounded by Vesna's parents, Milena and Raša; the children; and Miro and Vesna, we retired to the living room to the sparse evergreen tree with its single strand of lights that Miro had cut from the family tree lot outside of town. We sang Serbian songs and watched a home movie I'd made.

One day at the university, I visited with Zorica at her job and met her colleague whose family had been among the Serbs living in Krajina, a centuries-old settlement of Serbs at the old Austro-Hungarian military border. He described briefly how Croatian soldiers in Operation Storm in Knin in northern Dalmatia in 1995 had awakened his grandmother and family in the middle of the night. They had no time to get anything but the bare essentials. They left by whatever means, taking only what they could carry, traveling hundreds of miles to Serbia, all the time under threat, pushed by soldiers. It was too deep for him to speak at any length.

My landlady, a professor, taught me from time to time. Once she said, speaking of the depth of pain in the Balkans, "If you stay here long enough, you'll feel the hurt. You will get hurt as we have been."

Miša exhorted me that the next time I returned that I should bring my family with me. I told him I had no money to pay for such a trip and my family had no interest in visiting the Balkans. However, it was Miša's directive that caused me to later get a job when I returned home, the beginning of a completely different way of life.

In early January, Miša began complaining of his vision. It was blurred, sometimes double, and he couldn't rub it clear. Having experienced this before with a friend, I suspected what it could be, but hoping I was wrong, I said nothing. I asked him if he'd go to a doctor, and if he did, would he later tell me the results. "My secret," he answered, smiling wryly, yes, of course, he would. As he helped me on with my coat, I looked him in

Miša David, Belgrade, 1999. Judy Ferguson photo.

Miša and Majda David, looking down at me from their upstairs window, Belgrade, 1999. Judy Ferguson photo.

the eye and said, "I'm going to miss this."

Distraught to leave my friends once again in a mafioso police state that could explode again at any time, I left envelopes, gifts of money to tuck them in, to leave some protection. I sat on a bed, melting in tears as I prepared to leave Zorica. "Judy," she said, "I don't need it, really. If I needed a glass of water, I would know to come to you. But really, I don't need this." For my peace of heart, she did allow me to leave the envelope but she kept it safe. Zorica always wore mid-high heels, a skirt, and always accompanied me home on foot to my flat even though it meant that she had to walk several blocks to catch a late city bus back home across town. (During those years when Benzin was scarce, she rode the bus which was far slower than a car.) I watched her retreating and ever-brave back. In her wisdom, she knew this era would pass. "Every ten years," as the army captain in Niš had said, "the Turk must come," meaning the ever-recurrent dictators and wars in the Balkans, that cauldron nestled into the center of the world's cultures.

In mid-January 2000, Miša embraced me goodbye. It was so hurried. Too casual, I thought, as I stood at the door of Miro's house. But we thought there'd be many more times, and the Konstantinovićs were inside, waiting with a dinner party. We spoke many times, but I never saw Miša again.

After the party, I stuffed a gorgeous wooden hand-carved *gusle* from Branko to Jim and Michelle Hajdukovich of Fairbanks in my bag along with many other of his gifts. Miro and I carried the luggage out to the street where I boarded the minibus with no heat to Budapest. The Konstantinovićs stood in the snow, waving good bye to me with all their might. I boarded and sat with the other huddled, silent dark figures on a seven-hour car trip through border checks to Budapest. At one brief stop, I got out, dug in the dark in my bag for my Baba wool socks to use as gloves, and found a hat and another down jacket. When we pulled up at the Hungarian airport, heat from the well-lit interior smacked deep into my chilled bones. A ceiling-high lit Christmas tree (Catholic tradition, not Orthodox) filled the foyer. This was the West, the land that didn't buck the world. I'd crossed through a divide, east-west, from Byzantium into the ancient western Roman Empire, the continental divide. I put my dinar back in my pocket, my Serbian into the back of my mind, thrust a dollar into a cafeteria hand, and spoke English. It was the long road back home to the West.

Chapter 48

2000: Millennial Changes

After I got home in mid January, I got a job working for the U.S. Census. I wanted to have an income so I might be able to help my friends. In the spring, I began teaching English to Delta's former USSR refugees.

Concerned about the results of Miša's doctor's visit, I called, but he didn't yet know anything. (At that time calling Yugoslavia was very difficult. It required about nine attempts and usually wasn't successful. The telephone lines were overburdened, antiquated, and damaged. Internet connection in Yugoslavia was just as bad. It was very difficult to get on a dial-up connection and once on, to maintain it.)

The second time when I called Miša, there'd been an emergency. While Majda was preparing

Majda David and Judy Ferguson, Belgrade, 2000. Judy Ferguson photo.

a holiday meal, Miša had lain down. Immediately he'd gone into a grand mal seizure. He struggled to communicate but could not. Majda called an ambulance.

The next time I called, Miša told me that the doctor said, "There are two possibilities. One is okay but the other is very bad." He added, "The seizure was terrifying, awful. I couldn't do anything. I could hear but I could not do anything." I asked if he saw a light or heaven or anything. He said, "No. It was just black. It was awful." With the next phone call, we both knew that the diagnosis was very bad; he just said it: *cancer*. I implored Miša to go to another country for medical help, at least for testing and possibly for therapy. But he refused. He said, "Judy, I don't want to be where it's a foreign language. When I am sick, I want to be with my family, in my country, with my language. No, I want to be here." I had left a gift envelope for him. I said, "Please use that." He said, "I have to have an operation and," he added both reluctantly but realistically, "I'll probably use that." The next time I called, he was in the hospital. A neighbor answered the phone. She said, "Of course, he took his own bedding and bandages, anything the hospital might need that he could provide." [International sanctions had been back in effect since 1998. Medicine and medical supplies were scarce.] The neighbor said, "He went in for the surgery but the tumor was inoperable. They are sending him home." A couple of days later, I talked with Miša. "Is your memory affected? Can you think and remember okay?" I asked. He said, "Yes, I think so. I hope so." I called every couple of weeks. We chatted and sometimes I asked an important question. Once in a while I e-mailed something I couldn't quite say on the phone. After I'd given up trying to persuade him to get outside help and on a day that he was feeling good, he said to me, "When I am well, I will come and see you. I will travel when I am well all over the world. I'll come to Alaska and," he said with special emphasis, "I'll shoot a silver fox." I said very quietly, "Do you promise, Miša? Do you promise to come to Alaska to see me?" "I promise," he said. Miša never lied.

Miro e-mailed me often. He strongly urged me not to attempt to come visit. He said, "This is a time for the family. It would be much better for them to be alone. Don't try to come." Later I happened to talk with Miša's oldest daughter, Mia, on the phone. I dared to ask, "Would it be a consideration for me to come...?" She said, "No, not now, Judy. Not now." I knew how fast brain cancer can kill. I asked Miro to keep in contact with the family. One day he went over to the David's flat. As it happened, I called while Miro was there visiting. Miša was a long time getting to the phone, and slow to speak. When I asked, "Are you worried about your family?" he answered, "Yes, I was but I'm not now." I promised him I'd try to help them when I could. He said pointedly, "I want you to come." "You want me to come to Belgrade, Miša?" I asked. "Yes, I want you to come," he said. Knowing the logistics and that it would be a bad idea for the family, I said, "But that takes time to arrange and... I want to, Miša, but how?" He dropped the phone. When Miro returned, he said that it was very difficult for both of them for him to be there. He said that only family or very close friends visit Miša now. He said, "He couldn't move his limbs or sit easily. He didn't talk much at all."

I talked to the Lord a lot about Miša. At one church service I got a lot of help. Once after the service, I told my concerns to my son, Ben. As I did, someone on TV began singing, "We shall overcome. We shall overcome. We shall overcome some dayyyyy. Deep in my heart, I know that I do believe that we shall overcome some day." "Ben!" I said. "That song is important to Miša and to me!" Ben asked, "Well, do you believe it? Maybe there is something more you don't know."

Once while on the phone with Danilo about Miša, I also mentioned my desire to write about Yugoslavia, to write what I had experienced. Danilo said, "Oh, then you must come

Left to right: Joan Neuberger, unidentified man, unidentified woman, Nenad Miscevic (Croatia), Dita Dauti (Albanian Kosovar), Bogdan Denitch (NYC). Austin, Texas, 2000. Judy Ferguson photo.

to our conference." "What conference?" I asked. He said in April the University of Texas was hosting the first symposium with representatives from the various republics of former Yugoslavia. "A lot of people are expected to be here," he said. It sounded interesting and I made airplane reservations to visit my family in Tulsa and then to swing over to the conference in Austin. Before I left for Texas, I called Miša from my sister's house in Tulsa. (Later Majda told me that Miša hadn't spoken for a long time but that when I called, he not only

Jasminka and Danilo Udovički-Selb, Univ. of Texas, 2000. Judy Ferguson photo.

Veran Matic, Belgrade. Austin, 2000. Judy Ferguson photo.

Stojan Cerović, Belgrade. Austin, Texas, 2000. Judy Ferguson photo.

Gen. Jovan Divjak, Sarajevo. 2000, Austin. Judy Ferguson photo.

Dusan Makaveyev, Belgrade-Paris. Austin, 2000. Judy Ferguson photo.

spoke but he talked to me in English.) I tried to encourage him by telling him about the conference planned in Texas and added there was a big anti-Milošević demonstration today in Belgrade. He said, "I wouldn't know about that." I said, "Miša, is there something you would wish for, something that you'd really like?" He said, "Yes. I'd like to do something for my country." After a few more words, that was the last time I heard Miša. The next time I called in May, Mia answered the phone. She was gentle and not rushed. I asked how Miša was. She said, "It's kind of really bad right now. He can't breathe and we've called an ambulance." I hurriedly hung up. Miša died that day, a month before his fifty-eighth birthday.

In April in Austin, I was a novice at the gathering of well-known persons from former Yugoslavia. The idea had originated with Jasminka's sister, Drinka Gojković, who'd worked hard with Danilo to bring a unique representation together. *The Future of the Past: Ten Years After Yugoslavia* was hosted by the Center for Russian, East European, and Eurasian Studies (CREES), University of Texas at Austin. CREEES associate professor Dr. Danilo Udovički-Selb and director Joan Neuberger were the creators and organizers of the conference. The theme stated, "The conflicts dividing former Yugoslavia have obscured traditions of tolerance and cooperation in the region. This symposium will bring together artists, activists, scholars, and public figures from each of the newly created countries of former Yugoslavia. Our purpose is to explore the complexities of the past and their bearing on the possibilities of a shared future." The topic for the first morning was "Murder, Guilt, and Redemption." Each person spoke about his topic and each theme was opened for discussion. Jasminka was the moderator, and she fielded questions. Avant-garde filmmaker Želimir Žilnik read "Yugoslavia did not die, did not fall apart: it was murdered: Towards the Clarification of a Murder." Drinka Gojković spoke on "The Future of the Region and the Question of Guilt."

Stojan Cerović shared "Debalkanization of the Balkans: The Road to Rehabilitation." Journalist Stojan Cerović wrote for Serbia's *Vreme* magazine and was a Harvard Nieman Fellow. He had amusing remarks about learning from the global mafia who had no ethnic problems. He said that Yugoslavia had died twice and he did not think it would resurrect. General Jovan Divjak presented "The Future of the Future: The Road to Europe." General Divjak, a Serb of Sarajevo, was retired from being a deputy commander in the Bosnian Army from 1992 to 1997. As a Serb during the war, he refused to fire on the Bosniaks but rather he

organized the defense of the (Muslim majority) city of Sarajevo. He became the president
of the Civil Society Foundation. Divjak said,
"The task of present generations is to transi-
tion from the industrial era to the twenty-first
century, an age of information and knowledge.... Obviously the cult of the state, nation
and false myths will be [must be] replaced by
a [true] state with freedom and justice.... We
should change the conscience of the ordinary
citizen and offer him the possibility of being
led by the law instead of by an individual
leader."

That afternoon, the overall topic was
"Media, Democracy, Civil Society" with
University of Texas professor Peter Jelavich
moderating. Veran Matić, originator and head
of B92 radio and TV, independent media in
Belgrade, spoke on "The Independent Media
in Serbia." Veran only spoke Serbian. He
spoke against the bombing, the interference
in another country's sovereignty, and his fight
and persecution by the Milošević regime. He

Juan Fernandez Eloriaga, Belgrade. 2000.
Austin. Judy Ferguson photo.

said the internet can go where other venues cannot. If he got run off the air in Yugoslavia,
which he had, he could just broadcast from outside of the country. He said the internet cuts
across borders, cultures, and languages and is a great unifier. Drinka was a strong supporter
of Veran, saying privately that if he'd run for president, she'd back him, but Veran wasn't
interested in politics but only in journalism.

Dušan Makavejev, the Belgrade-Paris based filmmaker and director of such films as
The Mystery of the Organism, spoke on "Serbia All the Way to Tokyo," a farcical play on
the theory of "Greater Serbia." Dasa Šilovič, the Croat wife of a former Yugoslav ambassador, shared "Civil Society Response to the Wars in FormerYugoslavia: Focus on Women's
Groups." Bogdan Denitch spoke on "Prospects for Democratization in Former Yugoslavia
after the Elections in Croatia."

For dinner, we caravanned over to Danilo's, ordered in and relaxed, enjoying talk in
Danilo's living room and back yard. It was amazing to see these notables from Yugoslavia in
an Austin, Texas, living room, just talking.

The second day Northwestern University Slavic Department head Andrew Wachtel
moderated the discussion on "Language, Identity, Authenticity." Juan Fernandez Eloriaga
read "Yugoslavia: Total Recall." Juan said what was needed was an amnesia of the bad and a
focus on the traditional good values. He stressed the pragmatic reasons for the new Balkan
states to work together. He said, "It may seem a shame but this Yugoslav history has been a
succession of humiliations, vanities, and pride," and all of that passes. He added, "Among

the greatest humiliation a human group can suffer is to be reduced to starvation and to be bombed with no possibility of self-defense.... It is time to dismantle the hatred, to include the Balkans in Europe who must finally understand the Balkans without its former snobbery and condescension."

Velimir Višković of Zagreb shared "Possibilities of Communication Between Cultures of the Former Yugoslav Republics: A Personal View." Nikola Petković of Austin-Rijeka, Croatia got our attention with "In My Father's Mobile Home: Identity Search, Bad Authenticity, and Limits of Essentialism." Nenad Miščević spoke to "Interculturalism and the South-Slavic Territories." Predrag Dojčinović of Amsterdam focused on "Marginalia on the Abolition of 'Our,' i.e., the Serbocroatian Language." Our last session was "Exile and Return," moderated by Bogdan Denitch of New York City. Ivo Slavnić of Austin, an affable man, offered "Triumph of Hope Over Experience." He said, "the whole history of former Yugoslavia from 1918 to 1991 could best be described as a perpetual tug-of-war between those who were pushing for centralization as the only solution to all our problems, and those who were press-

Mitko Panov, Macedonian. Austin, 2000. Judy Ferguson photo.

ing for decentralization as their only safeguard against assimilation and domination." He cited the proposed panacea of the 1985 Memorandum of the Serbian Academy of Arts and Sciences who suggested a massive transfer of decision-making powers from the republics and autonomous regions to the federal government in Belgrade. He described many instances of Milošević's dismantling of multiethnic Yugoslavia and his manipulations that made a Serb-dominated Yugoslavia unacceptable to Slovenia, Croatia, and Kosovo. These critical changes made the way for separatism and the emergence of ultranationalist parties in the other republics. Finally he said, "the constitution of 1974 [which decentralized and gave more power to the individual republics] was evenhanded in its treatment of all ethnic groups in former Yugoslavia." He added that if Serbs could not be accountable to their errors that caused the dismantling of Yugoslavia, getting rid of Milošević would not make much difference. Šalim Kovačević, from Ljubljana, Slovenia, spoke from his heart about "Ten Years of Separation from Our Land: Ten Years of Suffering, Sadness and Pain." Salim, a Muslim, was a villager who organized the escape of his ethnically mixed village from Bosnia to Slovenia. (Danilo and Jasminka met him in a Boston hospital where he was then recovering from wounds he suffered during the escape.)

Andrew Wachtel, an incisive and gifted thinker and speaker, shared "Cosmopolitanism in Contemporary ex-Yugoslav Literature," contrasting East and West through two lovers. Dita Dauti, an Albanian Kosovar, shared her memories growing up as "other" in Kosovo. The highlight for me was Macedonian Mitko Panov's film, *Comrades,* the story of his search through post-war Yugoslavia for his former army comrades, men from every former republic. He took his camera throughout the changed face of Yugoslavia and talked to the people. It demonstrated Yugoslavia for what it had been: a bold and unusual experiment in an intact multiethnic, multireligious, multicultural country. The film received a standing ovation and inspired Žilnik to say, "We don't have to be ashamed of Yugo-nostalgia. We had a beautiful, complex country to be proud of." Many in the audience applauded his sentiments.

At lunch, Juan Fernandez Eloriaga, a syndicated writer for Spain in Belgrade and long-time friend of Danilo's, was searching for a place to develop his film. Jasminka shared that Juan had just lost his wife during Christmas. I walked with Juan to the drug store where he could leave his film for express developing. Once when I asked him if he didn't just love Yugoslavia, he paused and said, "No. Love for nations kills people." That night over his dinner of garbanzo beans, we began to become acquainted. Juan became a very big help to me later in Belgrade and a dear friend.

The second evening, I interviewed Danilo, going over his life's story before I caught my return flight home. On my way home, I reflected that in my travels, I'd heard occasional voices both from Montenegro, Serbia, as well as one at the conference who cited, "The best we can hope for is that the West teaches us how to think, how to live." This was a humble and truly searching admission, one that I rarely heard, but when I did, it stood out.

In late May as I was driving to work in Delta, a silver fox ran across the highway. I didn't think much about it until I

Želimir Žilnik, Slovenia. Austin, 2000. Judy Ferguson photo.

Drinka Gojković (Belgrade) and her brother-in-law, Danilo Udovički-Selb, Austin, 2000. Judy Ferguson photo.

remembered that Miša had talked about a silver fox. In July, Ben and I took our riverboat to our remote home upriver. As we walked from the lower field to the upper pasture, Ben stopped me. "Shhhh," he said, "There's a big silver fox up ahead. Do you know how unusual that is? He's living up here." Reverently, we watched the fox king. In August, we drove to the Yukon Territory to launch Reb and Ben on the Eagle River to motor their canoe down the Eagle, Bell, Porcupine, and Yukon rivers. As I drove on up to Inuvik, Northwest Territories, several times a silver fox crossed the road. I wondered if they were in a high cycle. In Inuvik, I met a Gwich'in Athabascan woman who offered to show me the town's Igloo Church, the Notre Dame of the arctic, Our Lady of Victory. As we sat together in a pew, she began speaking of the loss of her parents, of grief, and of letting go. Then she turned quietly to me and asked, "And you?" I began to tell her about Miša and the fox I kept seeing. She said, "He wants you to know he'll always be there, that he'll never leave you." A little later, she said, "But there is a time after grief has had its way to let them go, to let them ascend, to be free to go on."

On October 5, I was teaching English to the refugees of the former Soviet Union at Delta Mine Training Center. When I returned home, my husband, a trickster, greeted me with the news, "Something happened in Yugoslavia that you're not going to like." I ran upstairs, turned on my computer and on BBC, I saw the headline that there had been a revolution in Belgrade. I was sure it was a mistake. I looked for the real news report but I saw a video clip of flames shooting out the Yugoslav parliament building in Belgrade. Incredulous, I peered at it frame by frame. Finally I realized that it was real, and screamed, "Yes!" The people had finally been able to overthrow Slobodan. I could not believe it. Even though it was late, I called Miro in Belgrade to congratulate him. He, Vesna and Zora had been downtown all day during the demonstrations. He sighed with fatigue over whether this revolution would really achieve its hoped-for results. The burning of the parliament also bothered him. He said, "I hope my people really know what democracy means and that it will take a long time. They may think it will be fast. They may equate democracy with wealth. I hope they are prepared to wait. I don't know."

Through a friend, Zora e-mailed me. She said that when a young person in the crowd saw her at the demonstrations, he turned and said to her, "Thank you, Baba (grandmother) for coming." However, when the Army began dispensing tear gas to disperse the crowd, Zora got it in her mouth, nose, and eyes. Her throat burned and her eyes began to water profusely. She had to leave but public transport was blockaded. Eighty-two years old and suffering from swelling in her legs, she walked for hours with her face in pain, all the way from downtown to her home.

On September 24 Milošević had needlessly scheduled an early round of elections for the presidency and federal parliament. When he lost to Vojislav Koštunica, he rejected the outcome, claiming the results were illegitimate because they were less than the required fifty percent. Later "Maki" Bogoljub Arsenijević, whom I met in 2005 in Montenegro, told me that he'd been part of the conception and organization of the revolution. He'd decided to fight Milošević with his own means, violence. Maki had networked with people in Valjevo and surrounding towns. On October 5, an organized group of men fired up their bulldozers and trucks and headed for Belgrade to block road access to protest the handling of the elections. The question was would the special police and the army open fire on the people? However to Milošević's surprise, the army commanders would not support him. They refused the violent overthrow of the Serbian government. Milošević was forced to accept the election results. On October 6, Milošević met with opposition presidential candidate leader Vojislav Koštunica and publicly accepted his defeat. Koštunica became the president of the Federal Republic of Yugoslavia on October 7. As a nationalist who had not been involved in Serbia's 1990s political tug of war, Vojislav Koštunica had a chance to defeat Milošević. I only wished that Miša had lived to see the day, just four months after his death.

The coup put Democratic Opposition of Serbia (DOS) leader Zoran Đinđić in a strong position. He forced the Serbian parliament to create a new government under his control, with DOS leading and with the SPS (Milošević's party) and SPO (Drašković and Paja's royalist party) as ornamentation. With the media in hand, Đinđić arranged for Serbian parliamentary elections. To trick Serbian voters, Vojislav Koštunica's name, the Federal Republic

The overthrow of Milošević, called the Bulldozer Revolution, Free Serbia postcard, 2000, Belgrade. No credits available.

of Yugoslavia president, headlined the DOS list. DOS swept the vote and Đinđić formalised his power as Serbia's prime minister with a strong coalition.

I prepared to return to Yugoslavia during my Christmas break from my job in late December 2000, planning to return home the third week of January 2001. It was the last time I went to Yugoslavia for personal reasons alone. It was a hard trip both because of facing Miša's death and because Miro, Vesna and I abruptly realized we expected different things of the relationship. We agreed to find a way to be friends but it would take time. For a month, I

stayed at Majda's and slept in Miša's bed with his self portrait from the 1967 era facing me. Majda slept in her bed just across from me. Every day, Majda was forcing herself to put one foot in front of the other. When she took me to Miša's grave, it was a powerful experience for me. Majda took me everywhere; she cooked for me. She was a sister, a little mother, and a friend. Every Sunday, we went to the cemetery and sometimes she went with me to church at a protestant nondenominational church I had found led by Radovan Bogdanović.

On western Christmas, I went with Zora's Catholic friends to Mass, a beautiful experience. By contrast, the Orthodox celebrated Christmas not with a Christmas tree but with newly sprouted wheat grass. A bowl of new green was on display on kitchen tables and lined the altars of their churches. Majda and I attended several *Slavas*, big celebrations of family patron saint days. Sometimes when we entered a home, we were offered a spoon

Majda David tending Miša's grave, temporary marker, Belgrade, 2001. Judy Ferguson photo.

of *slatko*, a thick fruit preserve, followed by *žito*, soaked, sweetened wheat berries. For New Year's we had a resplendent dinner with

Majda's brother Davor and his wife Marija Salom. We walked over to Terazije, the main square, to welcome 2001.

I took a short trip on the bus to visit *Svetlo* church in Leskovac in south Serbia. They have two congregations: Serbian and Roma. I attended the Roma youth service. With joy, I listened to the children come to the microphone and sing their love of Jesus in Serbian with a brass accompaniment. Pastor Miodrag Stanković took me to the tent where they were passing out humanitarian supplies to the Roma as well as to refugees. That evening, I gathered with Stefan Stanković, Saša and Jelena Kocić, and three girls from the congregation for prayer for the country. As we prayed, I saw a land so dry that it was very hard and cracked. Later I read Belgrade pastor Radovan Bogdanović's church motto, "Bringing water to a dry land." When Pastor Mio put me on the bus to return north, he waved to me warmly. He is

Pastor Miodrag Stanković holding Roma girl, Leskovac, Yugoslavia, 2001. Judy Ferguson photo.

a man of great faith and childlike enthusiasm. As I returned, I prayed that God would give me not just a personal relationship with Yugoslavia but a professional one as well, to help balance my view. I believed that some day I might love the nation for itself not based on my variable feelings for it.

One night, Miro and I had a good talk. Besides trying to understand Eastern European culture, I explained how difficult it was to save enough money from my paltry job to print my book on Hajdukovich in the USA. He said, "Why don't you print it here?" That never had occurred to me. I decided to go see Filip David, Miša's brother, who was an author, filmmaker, a leader in former Yugoslavia's literary circles, and a dissident writer. Filip suggested a layout artist with whom he'd worked: Dragan Mišković. I met with Dragan. He was interested in my work. He also mentioned he wanted me to meet his children, Ivan and Ana, so that they might understand how other people thought. I was puzzled but agreed. We agreed to launch our work for *Parallel Destinies* by teaming up through the internet.

Just when I was feeling light-hearted, that the wars were behind us, that my book might happen, that I could speak English freely in the street, and use my camera openly, a crisis hit. January 11, Majda and I were shopping in downtown Belgrade before I flew home the next day. I was buying last-minute gifts. With my pack riding lightly on my back, I followed Majda and her son-in-law, Filip. Suddenly as we shopped, someone "accidentally" stepped on my right foot; a searing pain shot through me. Puzzled, I glanced from side to side but I saw no one. Shortly on my left side, a young girl passed me while hiding her face and murmuring, "Excuse me." Her female companion passed me on my right side; both of them quickly vanished.

I entered a shop and removed my pack. I was stunned to find it unzipped. As my fingers felt for my passport, paralysis slid over me. Like electric lights in my brain, the realization flashed, "No passport, no plane trip, no exit." As I lived through the next days, I felt an inner assurance that all would be okay contrary to all physical evidence and my state of nerves.

I returned to a police station where I had first registered my passport information when I entered the country. A sergeant pounded an ancient typewriter with two fingers to describe the theft on paper wedged with carbon copies. Then he accused Majda of stealing the passport. The other policeman offered me the chair next to him and said to me in Serbian, "You can sit here. I won't infect you with my radiation," referring to NATO's 1999 bombing of Serbia with depleted uranium.

In stark contrast to workaday Belgrade, we entered the very luxurious Hyatt Regency Hotel across the Sava River where the beginnings of an American embassy were in progress. Previously, Serbia had had no diplomatic relations with the United States. The fledgling embassy at the Hyatt could not yet issue American passports. A qualified American embassy was across the border in Budapest; however, without a passport, I could not go there.

At the Belgrade embassy, the only authorized person who could ask Budapest for a passport for me was permanently leaving Yugoslavia in three hours. She petitioned Budapest, who responded that the process could not begin until after the Martin Luther King holiday. Already I had missed one of British Airway's three weekly flights, and now I would miss the next two.

I began the paperwork shuffle. I was told to obtain a passport photo—"American size," not the smaller European format. However, Belgrade had been isolated from foreigners for a decade; we could only approximate the requested photo size. Further, we were told the passport could not be trusted to a local commercial carrier; an American would have to hand-deliver the sealed document from Budapest to Belgrade.

On Tuesday, a new clerk, Svetlana, had found someone to deliver my passport the next day on Wednesday. But suddenly Budapest said they did not know if the document had even been issued yet while my needed courier was leaving in mere hours.

Desperate to catch the Friday flight to ensure that I still had a job in Alaska, I arrived at the American embassy Wednesday morning. I was told I could not have my new passport until I could prove my American citizenship. I called my husband and woke him in the middle of the night pleading, "You must find my birth certificate and fax it. Tomorrow, I have to be at the police station for an exit visa so I can catch the flight on Friday." Reb drove across the frozen river to Whitestone where there was a fax machine. At 3 a.m., Alaska time, my pastor's wife Bette Grier faxed the document to the Belgrade American "embassy." By 7 p.m. in Yugoslavia, I had the precious American passport in my hand. At Majda's suggestion, I slept in my clothes that night so that we might be at the police station first thing in the morning.

At 7 a.m., we were sitting on a hard bench in the cigarette-smoke-filled air waiting for the Serbian police. Four hours later, we were sent to a window, downstairs. By then, the noon traffic had begun to form in the police station's grimy antechamber. Lines of Chinese immigrants and Serbian refugees waited, stalled in the bureaucratic machine. Like a Pinscher on point, Majda paced the line. As soon as an announcement was made, she pounced with my passport and thrust it under the nose of a startled clerk. We were told to return at 3 p.m. At 2:55 p.m., we raced back to the police station. Lying on the clerk's desk was my new American passport with its exit visa.

The next day at the airport over coffee before my flight, Filip looked at me before I boarded and commented, "You are the luckiest person I ever met in my life." I smiled, "It wasn't luck." But Majda admonished, "Next time, Judy will remember where she is. Not on a hike in Alaska but in the Balkans, where anything can happen."

Facetious posters depicting nonaccountability to corruption and war crimes, Majda David, Belgrade, 2001. Judy Ferguson photo.

Chapter 49

New Beginnings: Milošević Arrested; Misha Mihajlov

After I returned from Yugoslavia in January, my new layout artist Dragan Mišković and I began e-mailing, getting acquainted. Dragan's conversation often returned to his desire for his six-foot-eight son Ivan Mišković to play basketball in the states. I tried to help where I could. In Belgrade, Dragan had compiled a number of books for Serbian intellectuals there. I hoped he would help me put my Hajdukovich/Rika research into a readable book. March 31 as we were e-mailing, a news release flashed saying that masked Yugoslav special forces had surrounded Slobodan Milošević's armed villa. That night, Dragan, a curator, was working late at the Museum of African Art; he listened to the radio, monitoring events as they unfolded. Hours later after several crises, Yugoslav federal officials had Milošević in custody on

Susan Brown, Dragan Mišković and Majda David: the birth of Parallel Destinies, *Belgrade, 2002. Judy Ferguson photo.*

suspicion of corruption, abuse of power, and embezzlement. In 1999 during the war in Kosovo, the International Criminal Tribunal for the former Yugoslavia (the ICTY at The Hague) had indicted Milošević for war crimes and crimes against humanity allegedly committed in Kosovo. On June 28 while Yugoslav President Koštunica was out of town on Mitrovdan, the anniversary of the battle of Kosovo Polje, Prime Minister Zoran Đinđić [Djin´djeech] put Milošević on a helicopter to Bosnia. Before he boarded, Milošević muttered, "Such things seem always to happen on June 28." He muttered in irony, "Where are all the others?" He was flown to Bosnia where he was kept under United Nations custody until he was flown to the International War Crimes Tribunal for the Former Yugoslavia at The Hague to stand trial. The Yugoslav Constitution prohibited extradition of Yugoslav citizens; Koštunica later opposed the transfer that Serbian Prime Minister Zoran Đinđić had ordered. The Federal Republic of Yugoslavia (the Yugoslavia that remained only two republics: Serbia and Montenegro, as opposed to the original six) was far from stabilized.

During the summer I worked on my new book, the story of John Hajdukovich and Rika Wallen. However, because the trip in 2000 was so difficult, I wasn't sure I wanted to return to Yugoslavia. Susan Brown, an intercessor of Gospel Outreach/Open Door church, had prayed for Montenegro when I was there in 1998 although she did not yet know me or know about my trip. Between fall 1998 and 2001, Susan and I became good friends. One day when I was in Fairbanks, after I finished my errands I went to the church to look for Susan.

Heleta Press: (back, center) Jagoda with her son, husband, grandson, daughter-in-law, and employee. Front left: Dragan Mišković. Belgrade, 2002. Judy Ferguson photo.

She was upstairs with a friend, Diane, praying for various countries, including Yugoslavia. When I walked in, she began to laugh. In a few moments, she asked, "When do we leave?" A week later, Susan came to my house in Delta where we talked in depth about a possible trip. After she left, I felt we should go together.

Two months before our trip to Yugoslavia, Ivan Mišković arrived in November to Fairbanks to live with the Chris and Joan Stepovich family. At the same time, Dragan wrote the needed letter of invitation for me to get a visa to enter Yugoslavia, and Miro wrote one for Susan to get her visa. (Since late 2000, I'd been able to fly in and out of Surčin international airport in Belgrade. Parts of the international sanctions began to be lifted gradually in layers.) January 2002 with Susan, I hand-carried two laptop computers, a scanner, my text, and a large number of photos for Dragan to scan. I had two enormous bags loaded with gifts.

Although it was snowing heavily, Dragan, Miro, Majda, Mia, and Filip met us at the airport. I introduced Susan to them. Miro and Dragan loaded my huge bags into Miro's Russian Lada station wagon. Dragan's tennis shoes were getting wet with snow.

Miro was in a dither because he running late. He was supposed to be at his institute's New Year's play where he was the lead actor. To complicate everything, my baggage was late and there was a heavy snowstorm outside. Finally all the baggage was loaded. Everyone else went to Majda's flat while Miro, although he tried his best, took the wrong exit on the snow-camouflaged expressway. After losing precious time, he wound up dropping me a couple of blocks from Majda's flat. At Majda's we all gathered and Dragan's wife, Vesna, joined us. It was my first chance to meet Ivan's mother.

A few days later, Dragan and I began working on *Parallel Destinies*. Susan and I stayed in one room while the living room became the office. Inside Serbian apartments, each room has a door to isolate the heat as necessary. Some rooms have stationery heaters but every home has a portable heater. First thing in the morning the Mišković kitchen was really cold. With a few pellets, Dragan made a fire in the wood cook stove to knock the deep chill off. The living room was pretty warm where we did our work.

By e-mail he had said that he and his two partners had a printing press in a building that we would use. However, when we went there nothing was ready. The room was stone cold; the press didn't work. Focused on saving the ship, Dragan went to a small printing press friend, Heleta Press, which was owned by Jagoda, a wonderful woman who spoke only Serbian. Dragan was the translator for all the business transactions there. While Jagoda agreed to take on the job, she fought hard to use better paper to show the photographs well, saying a product from Yugoslavia must be the best. She insisted we use high gloss paper. However, what wasn't clearly explained was that she didn't have the technology to stitch the shiny pages as well as glue them. With only a cold press glue, the binding of the slick glossy paper did not endure normal handling. Each of us: Jagoda, Dragan, and I had great lacks

Dragan Mišković and Nebojša Popov, Belgrade, 2002. Judy Ferguson photo.

and strengths, assorted foibles, and good intentions mixed with the usual human agenda. The miracle was that, against all odds, the book was born. I trusted God for it, and Susan was always praying.

In the living room, Dragan worked on one laptop that I'd brought and I worked on the other. The photos stacked near the scanner kept Dragan busy when he wasn't doing the layout. Concerned, he began setting deadlines. He knew the process and I did not. Always gentle, infinitely patient, he kept his eye on our time. During the day, he took the work with him to the museum where he worked when he was free. In Belgrade, I was cut off from anyone who could edit my English or whom I could readily consult for historical questions.

I was working day and night to finish. Dragan's wife, Vesna, made our dinners. Schedules in Belgrade were quite different from the west. Businesses usually stopped work at 3 p.m. when employees went home for the main meal of the day, *ručak*. Frequently businesses reopened at 7 p.m. and worked until nine or ten. It was strange to catch a bus and go to Jagoda's as late as we did, at 8 or 9 p.m. As we prepared the book covers, Dragan directed while Jagoda's husband hand-mixed the ink shades to get the desired color. I loved smelling the fresh ink when we walked into the shop.

While I worked, Majda entertained Susan. On Sundays, they went to Radovan Bogdanović's church. Vesna arranged a bus ticket for Susan to visit the church at Leskovac, as well as another church in Podgorica. Vlado, the pastor, and his wife took Susan over to another church at Bar on the coast.

As the books finally began to roll off the press in Belgrade, I remembered my promise to save the first one for Dean Wilson, my husband's fur buyer. Jagoda and Dragan both signed it. The three of us were a team, an incredible success! Dragan turned to me, relieved, and said, "Your God did this!" And he was right.

With a little free time, Dragan introduced me to some of his intellectual friends fighting for Democratic change and tolerance in Serbia. Danilo's lifelong friend Nebojša Popov had the highly respected magazine *Republika*. Dragan was part of the staff and attended their meetings twice a week, and he wrote for them periodically. We met and talked with Nebojša at his table at the Medija Centar at Trg Republika, where he conversed with his colleagues. Nebojša explained that throughout the Milošević regime, their journal *Republika* had remained the only consistent and critical voice. He showed me their statement:

> Participant and Witness of the Change, Magazine *Republika* was born March 1989, founded by intellectuals, members of the Union for Yugoslav Democratic Initiative (UYDI). Their goal: democratic transformation of society and the state. Based on common sense and previous experience in the struggle for democracy, the founders saw as their key goal the establishment in law and practice of the basic principles of human rights; this would be done through elections of the constitutional assembly, and to adopt a new, democratic constitution; hence, all problems and issues would be solved in parliaments (of the federation and member states), and not on battlefields.

Pausing, he pointed out, "That is how we understood the concepts of freedom and democracy; that is what this magazine stands for: civil self-liberation." He emphasized, "When political changes led to wars, crime and plundering—as the state regressed to a 'natural state'—we spoke up against the elements of fear, hate and violence. We published my book, *The Road to War in Serbia*. Additionally we have been on the internet since 1999."

After talking with Nebojša as we walked back to the office, Dragan told me about Mihajlo Mihajlov, a dissident from 1964 who for the last twenty years had lived in Washington, D.C. He was in the process of moving back to Belgrade. Dragan said he would arrange an introduction.

After *Parallel Destinies* was printed, I took a train to Bijelo Polje, Montenegro, to meet Susan and to see Branko, Dana, and another Miro and Saša, two Christian teachers of Vasko

Nenad Božanović, Saša Rabrenović, Nina Hajduković (cousin), Branko Hajduković, Susan Brown and Miro Vukojčić, Bijelo Polje, Montenegro, 2002. Judy Ferguson photo.

Hajduković's. When I found Susan waiting in Bijelo Polje, she was freezing in an unheated Montenegrin hotel room waiting for me to arrive. She was very glad to be rescued! We visited with Miro and Saša and then went to Branko's house for a brief visit before I had to return.

In Belgrade, Susan was delighted with the new book, as happy as I. My only regret was that I'd been so busy trying to finish the book that I hadn't had much time with Majda or Zora or to show Susan around.

Susan and I would take nine seventy-five pound bags of books back to Alaska, but the rest had to be shipped. I asked Dragan what to do. He had a friend, Zdravko, who was an importer/exporter. We met with him to discuss how to export the books. At first Zdravko was perplexed. He said that since the wars that shipping to the Croatian coastline had been impossible, so he arranged for his truck to take the books to Germany where they were shipped to me in Alaska.

Throughout the night before we left, I packed everything in the kitchen at Majda's while Susan slept on the living room divan. Once during the night, I heard her crying. She had fallen in love with Yugoslavia and she hated to leave. Miro and his Vesna, Dragan, Vesna, Majda, Filip, and Mia helped us get the bags of books to the airport at Surčin. We were a parade! I was hand-carrying a painting of Dragan's that he'd given me. But it was unwrapped in my carry on, which was a mistake. Yugoslav security saw it, and wouldn't allow it to go through even when the artist, Dragan, explained that it was a gift. I didn't have the proper

Back: Vesna Mišković, unidentified, Vesna Maksimović, Ana Mišković, Dragan Mišković, Filip; Front: Miro Konstantinović, Majda David, Susan Brown, Mia David. Surčin airport, Belgrade, 2002. Judy Ferguson photo.

government documentation for taking artwork out of the country. I gave it back to him and we waved goodbye to our dear friends and caught the flight home.

A couple of months after my return, I arranged to see my family in Oklahoma and to meet Mihajlo "Misha" Mihajlov in Washington, D.C. Misha and his friend Boris picked me up and took me to a presentation where Misha was being honored at the Brookings Institute. Afterward we joined Misha's longtime friend Predrag Pajić, the head of the Eastern European collection at the Library of Congress. The next day, we visited with Misha's sister Maria and her husband, Chris Ivusic, at their home. As we had coffee, Misha told me some of his story:

> As a result of the 1920s civil war in Russia, there were about one hundred thousand Russian émigres living in Serbia. I was born between the two world wars in 1934. My mother tongue was Russian. I only learned Serbian when I started school. We lived in central Serbia but because my father was an agronomist, we traveled a lot throughout Yugoslavia. During World War II, my father fought with Tito's Partisans, which for a Russian émigré was quite remarkable. During the war, most of the émigrés wanted to side with the Nazis against the Bolsheviks. As a result, the majority of them were thrown in jail or exiled. Even after Stalin split with Tito, because of his allegiances, my father wasn't persecuted. I graduated from high school in Sarajevo, Bosnia. In 1959, I began graduate school at Zagreb University; in 1964, I was earning my PhD on Dostoevsky. That summer there was a cultural exchange of students from Yugoslavia to Russia. From 1959 to 1964, I had been writing articles on Soviet literature and culture for Yugoslav newspapers and magazines. So it was easy for me to establish contacts with writers and intellectuals in Leningrad and Moscow.

> Nineteen sixty-four was the summer of Nikita Khrushchev's liberalization reforms. He opened congress addressing Stalin's cult of personality. During this

summer of his power, he got rid of some of Stalin's programs. When I returned to Yugoslavia, I wrote good things about Khrushchev. When the articles were published in October 1964, Khrushchev was already dismissed. Who could know that would happen? Leonid Brezhnev began immediately re-Stalinizing Russia. My book *Moscow Summer* was coming out in monthly installments. In February the second article was published. Boris Puzanov, a member of the KGB and an ambassador, routinely traveled throughout the world, going wherever there was trouble. In Yugoslavia, he made an official Soviet protest with Tito against my work. The second article to be published in the magazine *Delo* was banned. Tito always tried to play the east-west game. In March, he attacked me publicly at the annual conference of Yugoslav prosecutors, demanding, "Is it possible that politicians always have to tell you who is violating criminal law? Look for example at this professor Mihajlov in Zadar. He's slandering our friends, the Soviet Union!" On the same day his speech was published, March 5, 1965, I was arrested and put on trial.

I served twice for three and a half years each, a total of seven years and two and half months. When you are attacked by the father of the nation, there's no going back. You're automatically classified as a dissident. I was transferred and put into jail. But if I'd been arrested by the local Serbian "KGB," I would have been beaten

and tortured in jail. However, because I was accused by Tito no one would have the courage to touch me. I was Titoized. If Tito had said, "Hang him," they would have. But he didn't because of global opinion. Because my arrest was associated with Khrushchev and the aborted liberalizations in the Soviet Union, the West immediately took notice of me and was very supportive. If my arrest had only been connected to conditions in Yugoslavia, no one in the West would've said one word because they supported Tito. What I wrote about Khrushchev was throughout all the Yugoslav newspapers but—who knew he'd lose power, and that the general party line would change: no one. It was destiny.

Yugoslavia claimed to have no "political prisoners," only "political criminals" (which would be for example, a politically motivated murderer). I went on a hunger strike a couple of times. The first time in 1965 was to draw

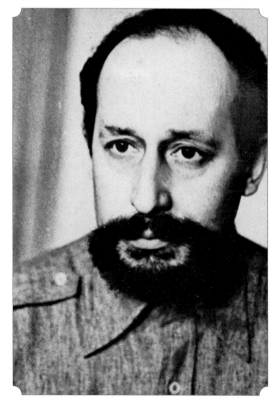

Prisoner Mihajlo Mihajlov, late 1970s, Yugoslavia. Courtesy of Mihajlo Mihajlov.

attention to the fact that Yugoslavia did have political prisoners. They put me in an icebox cell. I almost quit but I felt like I got a sign from God which encouraged me to keep going. The second time was in 1967 after Yugoslavia signed some agreement with the UN regarding political and citizen rights. It was stated that political prisoners have a right not to work but that they can read what they want. Of course, the prison wouldn't recognize my rights as a political prisoner so I went on a hunger strike. The first prison I was in was built sometime before World War I where they did not have a special section for political prisoners, separate from criminals. In 1975 to 1976, I was in a newer prison where they did have a separate section for political prisoners. There were about fifteen of us political prisoners there who had the courage to start a hunger strike asking for the political prisoner section, and to not be forced to work, to have a Bible, books, and newspapers. They locked us in separate cells so we couldn't communicate. Some went a week, some two, but I did more because I didn't know the others had stopped. After the thirty-third day, the prison staff gave me a shot of glucose, probably because they were afraid of public opinion. After the forty-third day, my heart couldn't pump enough fluid to my legs so they said they'd give me everything I wanted. They let me shave and they gave me a Bible and newspapers but they wouldn't give us the political prisoner section because the other prisoners had quit before I had.

Amnesty International had a good idea. Every month, they honored a prisoner of the month but the promotion was never done in the prisoner's own country but in another country, always rotating. That way the prisoner got public attention but not further persecution in his own country.

Senator Robert Dole and Mihajlo Mihajlov, Washington, D.C., 1978. Courtesy of Mihajlo Mihajlov.

While Misha was in prison, his sister Maria translated several of her brother's books into English: *Moscow Summer, Russian Themes, Underground Notes, Unscientific Thoughts,* and *The Homeland is Freedom.* In prison, one of Misha's fellow inmates was Kosovo Albanian leader, Adem Demaci, whose dissident views Misha shared under the Tito regime.

During the seven years Misha spent in Tito's prisons, Maria and their mother Danilova were a lifeline for Misha, helping to keep him before the public and therefore making the prison treat him with better care. After her brother's arrest in Yugoslavia, Maria came to this country seeking asylum, where she was welcomed with open arms. Misha said one of the biggest obstacles that he and others fighting for democracy faced was the New Left in the West. He said, "They think they are helpful, but these liberals undermine intrinsic ground support and erode public credibility for democratic foundations in their search for a utopian society. They feed right into Communism."

Adem Demaci and Mihajlo Mihajlov (Misha), c. 1997, Priština, Kosovo. Courtesy of Mihajlo Mihajlov.

In 1977 when U.S. Senator Robert Dole attended an international human rights conference held in Belgrade, that focus pressured Tito into releasing Misha, but at the same time, he was stripped of his Yugoslav citizenship. When he arrived in the United States in 1978, he hardly spoke English.

For years, Misha spoke on Radio Free Europe/Radio Liberty and Eastern European forums on intellectual and ideological affairs. He filled many posts but at George Washington University, he was a senior associate for Transitions to Democracy at Elliott School of International Affairs.

I knew from Misha's writing that he believed in God, and that he felt a community devoted to God and to human rights could strongly affect society. He said, "Of course personal responsibility is the most important question. To admit sin implies a spiritual rebirth; man can't make that happen—it is a gift from God. And that miracle is exactly what mankind needs and nothing else will do."

When I asked him how he felt about globalization, he said, "There is no going back. Like when tribes in Europe first resisted nationalization, there was war. Today, there may be clanking of swords, but globalization is here to stay." We spoke of the Yugoslav diaspora: Croats, Bosnians, Serbs, Albanians have gone to every corner of the earth. He said, "Perhaps they—like Albanian Adem Demaci and I found in prison—may discover renewal in a new land."

After conferring with her husband, Misha's sister, Maria, came over and gently draped a silk scarf of red, white, and blue around my neck and said, "Appreciate what you have; so few have it." That evening Maria, a naturalized American citizen, and her husband, Chris, showed me, an Alaskan, our nation's capitol, so long a citadel and a refuge for many.

Chapter 50

2003: Assassination; Voices from the Trenches

or seven years, I had been writing my wilderness family's trapline adventures for the *Fairbanks Daily News-Miner.* In February 2003 with the assembled stories, photos, and a slide scanner, I returned to Yugoslavia to print *Blue Hills.* Dragan scanned photos for every page, and we worked around the clock. When I could, I went to church at Radovan and Jelena's New Horizons church at Mileševska 42. Radovan honestly and gently said to me, "Try to come routinely, Judy. Our people here do not understand faithfulness, commitment, and support to a church. They think becoming a Christian means making a decision but not changing your life. They need an example." On Sunday nights then, I dropped what I was doing. I took a taxi to a tall, dark, ominous-looking building where there was a small group of people worshipping and dancing their joy in a Protestant, nondenominational, unregistered church, considered a "sect" in a xenophobic Orthodox society. Over the years, they were a joy and a family to me. When I wasn't there, I could monitor their news at http://www.novihorizont.net

In the evenings, Dragan and I would take a hour break and walk the family dog in Hyde park in Topčider. I wasn't completely comfortable speaking English in public, but the night seemed to cloak us. Once in 2002 we walked past a dark area where a man stood in the shadows holding a rifle at

"In union with NATO" was on posters next to this one of President Bill Clinton with Zoran Djindjic astride his shoulders: a protest of Djindjic's western posture. Belgrade, 2001. Judy Ferguson photo.

attention. I whispered, "Why does that man have a gun?" Dragan said, "He's guarding the military barracks in Topčider." I wondered what else might be hidden. On March 11, 2003, as we walked, Dragan explained that Zoran Djindjić was probably one of the most vulnerable men in Yugoslavia. I was surprised; I thought he was riding a wave of success. He added, "He could be killed at any moment." Several times as we walked, a broad man passed us. Even under the street lamps, there was something noticeable about the man. He seemed to be listening, to be alert. He noticed us as we passed. Once, Dragan whispered, "That man looks like

Slovenia and Croatia independence
Wars in Croatia and Bosnia
KLA & Yu Army in Kosovo
NATO bombing
Bulldozer Revolution
Milošević arrested
Djindjić murdered; end of Federal Republic of Yugoslavia
Three years of Federal of Serbia-Montenegro

1990
2000

Ratko Mladić." (He was the war criminal responsible for the massacre of eight thousand Bosniak men and boys at Srebrenica, Bosnia-Herzegovina, and is still wanted today by the International Criminal Tribunal for the former Yugoslavia.) "No!" I said, "You don't think it could be, do you?" Dragan laughed and said, "No, I don't think so."

The next day about midday, Majda called. "Zoran Djindjić (the Serbian prime minister) has been murdered," she said. Stunned, I thought, "My gosh, no one is safe." In broad daylight, Djindjić was gunned down as he left a government building. When Dragan went out for his nightly walk, I didn't go. I felt that as an American I needed to keep a low profile. Dragan's wife Vesna and I talked while he was gone but Dragan returned soon. On the way, he'd seen a soldier so covered in camouflage that he appeared to have neither a front nor a back, no face at all. On every block there was a soldier, Dragan said. Belgrade was put under martial law for a while.

On March 15, everyone in Belgrade seemed to turn out for the funeral, filling the streets shoulder to shoulder for miles. Hundreds of thousands of people as well as foreign dignitaries filled the downtown boulevard in a solemn procession: all but me. I thought it best to be quiet and keep working. Sunday at the *ručak* meal at her home, Miro's wife Vesna was really concerned, saying that Djindjić was the Serbs' hope of reformation. Parallels were drawn between him and the assassination of John F. Kennedy. Later a trial found organized crime leader Milorad "Legija" Ulemek and his soldier Zvezdan Jovanović guilty. It was also said that Legija helped remove Milošević from power October 5, 2000, at the Bulldozer Revolution and that he also led the operation to arrest Milošević in 2001. Ulemek was one of the leading persons in the "Zemun clan," a major organized crime group in Serbia.

Once Jagoda was printing my book *Blue Hills,* I set up interviews with three of Belgrade's well-known dissidents: Miša's brother Filip David, Sonja Biserko, and Verica Ranković. Later I published the stories in the *Fairbanks Daily News-Miner* as "Democracy: Voices from the Trenches."

Filip met me in the flat where he had grown up, now Majda and Eli's home. He began.

Filip David, c. 1999, Belgrade. Photo by Goranka Matić, Vreme *magazine. Courtesy of Filip David.*

In all my writing there is not one sentence that says that Serbs are bad. Nations are not bad. It's very dangerous to characterize and to use stereotypes. It is a quick step from labeling a nation,

355

to deciding that that people should be eliminated. When times have been bad here in Serbia, the government needed someone to blame. The United States is portrayed here as the enemy; Serbs perceive America as run by the Jews. Consequently, an anti-Semitic document "Protocols of the Elders of Zion" has been published four times in Belgrade in a very short time.

When asked to describe the Milošević years, Filip explained:

Milošević triggered the Serbs' natural emotional mania, fueling their passion for a closed, collectivist society. He told them, "We are the best; that's why everyone hates us." Once peoples' passions were ignited, they could not believe the objective evidence. A hypnotized man will do irrational things.

In Serbia the government's priority was authority and maintaining the political apparatus. The option of a democratic and free society tended to be rhetorical.

In the early 1990s, my friends and I formed a group of activists who had been expelled from TV and Radio Belgrade because they opposed Milošević's politic of war: writers, TV and movie producers, musicians, actors, and editors. They established the Belgrade Circle and met weekly. Later they published the magazine *The Right to Pictures and Words*, which was against Milošević's abuse of the media and presented "a different Serbia," one in which the majority would protect the minorities. Where there would be no fear of having a different political or religious conviction, free from the walls that isolate people. In Milošević's Serbia, the media created a language of hate and paranoia. Critical dissidents were seen as traitors, as a fifth column. The poison disseminated through all of everyday life, into every institution of culture, economy, and policy. In a different Serbia, the great marketplace wouldn't be the monstrous black market of today where the rules of criminals prevail, where the cheapest, most worthless goods are a human life.

This will not be a quick or painless recovery. In any recovery, a ruthless self-examination is critical, evaluating how we think. By becoming resistant to harmful myths, delusions, and lies, Serbia could develop into an

Sonja Biserko, 2003, Belgrade. Judy Ferguson photo.

adjusted, developed country. Being an activist means sacrificing a professional career and personal peace and accepting a life on the edge, a denial of personal security. However, when an effort is made to shape Serbia into this different healthy Serbia, the society calls it a betrayal. Thinking that diverges from the "main line" is seen as interrupting the critical brotherhood and unity with the motherland as expressed in "Only Unity Saves the Serbs." But with a healthy society at stake, being a betrayer to a dysfunctional society is mandated.

Today our country is destroyed, with a ruined economy, isolated from the world, and with a poor outlook for the future. Because of the crimes committed in their name, Serbs have a sense of being muddy, but it's an undefined sense of guilt. The worst result is that many people today have reconciled themselves to the futility of the current Serbia; as a result, they have become apathetic, depressed, and morally callous. However, we have the choice to envision a different Serbia, one that is tolerant and finds its future in Europe, one that stands on the ruins of today's country.

Termed by some the most hated woman in Serbia, Sonja Biserko has a lonely job. When the wars in Yugoslavia began in 1991, Sonja was a high-ranking official in Yugoslavia's Foreign Ministry. Even among some dissidents, it was said that Sonja went too far: advocating that Kosovo should be independent. She responded that if Serbia relinquished Kosovo to its Albanian majority that Serbia's repentance and credibility towards its former republics might be seen as authentic. For that even educated Serbs adamantly claimed that Sonja is paid by the West to betray her own people. The head of the Helsinki Committee for Human Rights in Serbia, Sonja's organization, began trying to educate the ethnically divided population by advocating the safe return home of displaced ethnic groups in the "I want to go home again" campaign. Sonja explained:

> Serbia's cultural model is passing the blame to the next guy. The West's concept of sin and of personal responsibility isn't the norm here. In Eastern Europe, a person is considered an idiot if he plays by the rules. All authority is suspect while cheating is clever, and naïveté is just stupid. To protect themselves, people speak in double-entendre.

> I stay sane by staying in touch with the world through the internet. Even though we are a half a world apart, daily

Dr. Vladimir Stijepović with a photo of his cousin Christopher Stepovich of Fairbanks. Risan, (Serbia)-Montenegro, 2003. Judy Ferguson photo.

contact with like-minded friends softens my reality.

Verica Ranković, a friend of Dragan's who also writes for *Republika* magazine, began:

I don't know why you like my country so much but I am glad that you do.

Recently I was encouraged by the outcome of our elections but still, our people have a long way to go. Serbs must confront what they did during the 1990s wars. The atrocities Serbs committed on their

Vlado Stijepović, Judy Ferguson, Dragan Mišković, Risan, (Serbia)-Montenegro, 2003. Judy Ferguson photo.

neighbors must be acknowledged. Today that repressed violence continues to erupt in unprecedented domestic violence; child abuse has skyrocketed. You can't abuse your neighbor and expect for those emotions to just go away. This is a very immature populace. Honest dialogue with the aim of open friendship is an art we haven't valued at home or in the public forum. Relationship amounts to a cat and mouse game, the conquerer and the conquered, the tribal patriarch and his serfs. Don't expect behavior here based on Christian values. Here there is not the sense of sin or of personal responsibility that there is in the West.

In 2003, the Federal Republic of Yugoslavia ended, replaced by a looser state union named Serbia and Montenegro. A possible referendum on Montenegrin independence was postponed for a minimum of three years.

Before returning home, I wanted to go to Montenegro. I told Dragan that in 1998 I had met a young man in Risan, Montenegro, Vlado Stijepović, who was a relative of the Fairbanks Stepovich family. I told Dragan I'd brought Vlado's phone number from Alaska and would appreciate it if Dragan would call him. Hesitantly, Dragan called. He located Vlado right away and he remembered meeting me. We set up a time to visit him briefly in Risan on the Bay of Kotor. Going as my interpreter, Dragan flew with me to Tivat, where Vlado met us. For two days, Vlado showed us Risan. We climbed the hill to Vuka's home and filmed it as well as the old section of the ancient city. We interviewed with his father concerning the Stijepović history. We met all of Vlado's family. One morning, Branko and Dana Hajduković drove over to Risan so we could visit.

The last evening as we walked by the Bay of Risan, I told Dragan I wanted to do a children's book next. I'd first made a pilot idea thirty years ago after our family's 1974 Yukon River trip. Dragan said, "Hmmm. A children's book is always bright and happy. I have a friend, Rastko Čirić, a very talented art professor at the University of Belgrade faculty of art. When we return, we could ask him about presenting your idea to one of his classes. Rastko thought it was a great idea. The next week, Dragan and I presented the idea as a contest to the students. I showed them my original Yukon River pilot book that I'd brought, some Yukon River photos, and some of my favorite Alaska children's books. The young people listened but one young man was fixed on me, listening with an unswerving intensity. His dark eyes locked in on us. However, after class, no one talked to me about the book. As Dragan and I left, we passed a young man and woman talking on the steps, smoking, and I thought, "These kids can't relate to the Yukon River."

After *Blue Hills* was printed, Dragan, Vesna, Miro, his Vesna, Mia, Filip, and Majda helped me get nine seventy-five pound bags to Surčin. After that, with no Susan there to help me, it was up to me. In Seattle, each bag had to go through U.S. Customs.

Back home, in early June I got an unexpected e-mail from a young man: "Mrs. Ferguson, I am from Rastko Čirić's art class. My name is Nikola Kocić. I was there when you presented your idea for a Yukon River children's book. I am very interested in your book idea. I have some watercolors to show you that I have prepared for you to see please." Nikola was the young man with the riveted brown eyes. It was the beginning of a new era. Neither of us had any idea of the challenges we'd be facing, or of its great rewards.

Jagoda at Heleta Press holding printed cover sheet of Blue Hills, *Belgrade, Serbia-Montenegro 2003. Judy Ferguson photo.*

Chapter 51

2004: Nikola, Bridge Builder

Nikola Kocić painting Alaska's Secret Door, *Belgrade, 2004. Judy Ferguson photo.*

oming into a foreign city that uses a Cyrillic alphabet during a decade of war isn't an easy way for a novice to begin a business. For *Parallel Destinies* and *Blue Hills* in 2002 to 2003, Dragan and I had worked out of an office in his family's flat that belonged to his parents. However, for many years, his parents had lived in their summer house on Hvar in Croatia. Suddenly, with two weeks notice, they sold the house and decided to return to Belgrade. I asked Dragan to find me a flat to rent where Nikola, he, and I could work on the children's book, *Alaska's Secret Door,* but he could not.

In 2000 at the University of Texas conference on Yugoslavia, I had met Juan Fernandez Eloriaga whom I enjoyed. Initially during the years of Belgrade's destroyed economy, he helped me ferry aid to Miro and to Dragan. During the difficult visit to Belgrade in 2000, Juan was an oasis away from home. A fabulous gourmet cook with a small Spanish "villa" overlooking the Sava River, Juan's and his wife's dream home was a wonderful place to laugh, to eat, and to relax. Juan had few prejudices except towards garbanzo beans. He was a veteran of thirty-five years of experience in Yugoslavia; he had spent the war years as an Associated Press writer for Spain in Belgrade and was a good listener. In the spring of 2004, ready to print a book but without an office, I called Juan from Alaska. He said, "Do you want a room or a flat? Do you want someone near to help or to be independent?" "A flat and independence," I quickly replied. "Okay, there are some possibilities," he assured me. I was greatly relieved. I heard back from Juan in a few days. A friend of his sons', a man named Peka, had agreed to rent me a daylight basement with French doors opening to a garden in a very nice section of Belgrade. It was a gift from God; I was extremely thankful.

Since the fall of 2003, Nikola and I had worked by e-mail. Several times a week, I sent him photos and notes while he sent me sketches. When I approved a drawing, he began the painting. In Belgrade, Dragan and Rastko checked Nikola's work in progress. Because most of the time, Nikola was at home in Niš, not in Belgrade, and because he had no laptop, everything was a challenge. At first painting a husky was difficult for Nikola but once he figured it out, he had it. He was very gifted. He was using acrylics although I wanted oils on stretched canvas, but I couldn't beat him from the other side of the earth.

Before I left for Belgrade, I had two large concerns: the book's binding and the capture of Nikola's artwork for publishing. Two people had told me my binding was poor on my first books. When I asked Dragan about it, I got no answers. From Delta, I began research-ing binding technology, trying to learn more before my imminent departure for Belgrade. I asked Dragan if scanning Nikola's paintings on my Epson scanner in Belgrade was adequate for publishing. He assured me that it was. When I arrived in Belgrade, Dragan, Majda, Mia, and Filip met me. We drove to Peka's, my new landlord. I was delighted with the beauty and the size of the apartment. Two hours later, Nikola was due in on the bus from Niš. Dragan and I hurried by cab to meet him. After intensive work by e-mail, it was a delight to meet Nikola in person finally. We returned to Peka's flat and set up Nikola's studio. Dragan brought all my office equipment from his family's flat to mine. Nikola eagerly set up his canvas boards to show me his work, which was magnificent. He had perfectly captured the Yukon River life and our family. His work was fresh, enthusiastic, and alive. However, I was surprised that Nikola had painted on small canvas boards rather than on something more sophisticated. Because he was young and inexperienced, Nikola had not met his deadline; he still had a number of canvases to finish.

Dragan and I arranged to meet Jagoda to discuss the new book *Alaska's Secret Door* and the reprinting of *Blue Hills*, as well as the most critical issue of binding. Dragan interpreted as I tried to delicately handle my friendship with Jagoda while getting some answers about past and future binding. Finally she said she didn't have the technology for what I needed, but she offered to give me a discount and would bind the new children's books with staples.

Predrag (Pedja) Denčić (layout artist) and Zoran Dureinović, interpreter and logistics, Publikum, Belgrade, 2004. Judy Ferguson photo.

Realizing my reality finally, I thanked Jagoda. We hugged and agreed that friend-ship was more important than business. I asked Dragan what ideas he had for getting a new printing company. We called some people but nothing materialized. Juan suggested a layout artist who in turn took me to a publisher but that didn't seem to be the answer. I was in a foreign city; Mia said she thought she remembered such a thing as a telephone book from before the wars. I had no idea how to find a print-ing company and lacked the experience to format a bid. On Sunday, I went to church where I talked to Pedja, the associate pastor and the English interpreter for the services. Pedja worked at a small printing company but said, "We're not big enough for you but try Publikum. It's not close, but it's your best bet. It's also pricey but it's the best printing company in Belgrade!" When I happily told Dragan, he said he was aware of Publikum but he had never mentioned it to me. I made an appointment for the three

Passover service at the synagogue, Belgrade, 2005. Judy Ferguson photo.

of us, Dragan, Nikola, and I, to meet with Publikum. We met in a conference room, laid out all the options on the table, and discussed everything in detailed English: reprinting *Blue Hills* as well as printing the new children's book, *Alaska's Secret Door*. Publikum's specialty was a large, popular calendar of their own; they printed soft drink labels, published textbooks, art books, and academic books. They worked twenty-four/seven. Their large basement was full of Guttenberg printing presses, a bindery, and a packaging department. Upstairs, they maintained a full layout department and a staff of graphic technicians. My relief was boundless. Their printing was not yet digitized but they used chromalins, plastic sheets to separate and test the color. They had a flatbed scanner and a drum scanner. We tried the flatbed but it didn't yield what I wanted. The drum scanner would destroy Nikola's paintings. Probably we should've photographed them with a classical film camera and drum scanned the film, but the film was large and would have to be sent out of country to develop. Publikum's graphic artist, Predrag ("Pedja"), happened to be a good photographer; one of the owners of Publikum let him use his personal digital camera. After photographing, Pedja spent hours adjusting the color of the digital images. We continued prepping the available paintings until Nikola was finished with the last five paintings.

While I was in Belgrade, I wanted to make a short DVD for Alaskans for my planned book, *Bridges to Statehood: The Alaska-Yugoslav Connection*, to feel the Balkan culture. In 2002, I had begun work with Marie Mitchell at Alaska One, University of Alaska Fairbanks. However her funds ran out. After the project fell through, I still had my photos and my script. I talked with Dragan about the film; he referred me to Nebojša Popov's son, Rastko Popov, a videographer. Rastko came over, and we laid the photos on my living room floor. I adjusted my script, and Rastko began work. He felt confidant he could do the narration. I liked the authenticity and music of his accent, but I was concerned if he might be clearly understood by Americans. However a bird in the hand was worth two in the bush, I greatly appreciated Rastko's work, and we proceeded.

While Nikola painted, and Rastko worked at home, I edited *Blue Hills*. A half an hour before printing, Dragan was prepping the layout for the reprinting. For the first edition, he and Jagoda's husband had hand-mixed the color for *Blue Hills* at Heleta Press. However at Publikum Dragan had to approximate the correct color from the first edition cover for the second, selected from the range of the Pantone color inks, which are standards of modern printing.

As spring approached, Majda and I celebrated Passover at the synagogue on April 5. At the communal dinner, I watched fathers explain to their sons the aspects of the meal, symbols of the exodus from ancient Egypt: bitter herbs and lamb. In the sanctuary, we listened to the rabbi as he read the passages for Passover. On the altar, there was a *shofar*, a ram's horn, blown usually at Rosh Hashanah and Yom Kippur. Davor's wife, Marija, and later Davor allowed me to take a photo of the service that I was privileged to attend.

That year, western Easter and Orthodox Easter (*Uskrs*) fell on the same day. Nikola dyed some eggs the Serbian way: boiling them for more than eight hours in water, vinegar, coffee, and spices, cooking them so well that they could be kept throughout the year. From the batch, Serbs would choose one egg to sit on the family's shelf as a protector of the house throughout the coming year.

An hour before the midnight Good Friday church service, Nikola decided we had to go. "Ok," I said, and grabbed an umbrella. We took a cab to two churches but they were closed and dark. We hailed a cab in the dark and the rain and went to Saborna cathedral downtown. When we arrived, however, a large man was guarding the chained gate. As a congregation gathered outside, he declared that because of the rain that day, the traditional ritual of circling the church with the aged Patriarch had been performed eight hours earlier. Without announcing it on radio or TV, the church had made a decision that fit the institution, not the congregation.

Early on Easter Sunday, I heard a cacophony of brass and snare drums moving loudly down the streets. I knew it was the Romani, the gypsies, and I hurried out to my garden to shortcut to the street. "Pot musicians," the men carried their tin pan orchestra, pausing to serenade me while I took in the feast. I turned and went inside to dress to attend the Easter celebration at the Roman Catholic church, a minority left from the old Austro-Hungarian Empire within Orthodox Serbia.

At midnight on Easter Sunday, Nikola and I joined the celebrants at Saborna in Belgrade's city of two million. At a stand in front of the church, Nikola and I searched through the icons, candles, and Orthodox bracelets for sale. I held up a possible purchase to which the young vendor snorted, "Nationalism." I tried to suppress my response. Joining the crowd, we carried two slender candles and began walking with the parade around the church, protecting the fragile flames. "You get your wish," Nikola said, "if you walk three times around the church and your candle isn't extinguished." I didn't notice my musky beeswax candle

Nikola Kocić, Uskrs/Easter midnight service, Saborna cathedral, Belgrade, 2004. Judy Ferguson photo.

Radovan and Jelena Bogdanović, pastors looking in faith to buy Zemun synagogue, Belgrade, 2004. Judy Ferguson photo.

was dripping down my jacket as I kept pace. Suddenly, a caustic voice split the night, "To the right! The Patriarch!" Inadvertently, I stumbled over the marble headstone of the grave of a past patriarch, built into the sidewalk. I glanced over my shoulder and was astonished to see the current Serbian patriarch, Belgrade's equivalent to the pope, tiny and wizened, walking behind me, flanked by archbishops in long, white-brocaded robes.

Since there seem to be no pews or heating in Serbian Orthodox churches, we entered and stood. For the next two to three hours, an archbishop led the liturgy from his nest halfway up the church's left wall. I leaned against a small table and looked at the mixed congregation of heavily made-up women, mendicants, and assorted citizens of the city until, one by one, they began exiting at about 2 a.m. while the bishop continued speaking.

On the way home, Nikola told me about his baptismal experience. Once while he was in Montenegro, he experienced a sudden urgency to be baptized. Having no idea what the protocol was, he hurried to Ostrog monastery and followed the proscribed method. Eager and expecting great things, Nikola lined up with the other supplicants. The priest was in a hurry; he tossed some holy water over them, pronounced a few words, and the newly committed grabbed the last bus back home. "I don't know what it was all about," Nikola said to me, but even so he was also not comfortable with my Protestant church in Belgrade.

With my Belgrade pastor Radovan and his wife, Jelena Bogdanović, I visited the former synagogue of Zemun, now owned by the city. On its facade in Hebrew, there was an inscription, "My House Shall Be a House of Prayer," but in its window, the city had taped a notice reading "Space for sale." The Bogdanovićs dreamed of purchasing the old synagogue for their congregation and renting out space to other churches across Serbia. "Serbia is an unreached land," Radovan said. "In a country ruled by autocratic secular and sacred leaders, people are confused by the curses and pressures that have been accepted as Serbia's so-called fate. The people know nothing of a forgiving and a merciful God in whom they can confide their lives."

In the Balkans, there are many cultural patterns that set the people up for failure. Once, I asked Dr. Dragan Hajduković regarding the crippled daughter of John Hajdukovich, "Could she not have found someone to marry her? Despite her handicap and of being poor and fatherless, could she not have had a real life?" He sighed, looked out, and said with concrete finality, "No, never. Not in this country." As Americans, the values we take for granted are not those of the Balkans or of much of the world. The Balkan culture withdraws into itself, does not seek transparency, communication, truth, or teamwork but rather appearance, an imposing magnificence, intimidation, and victory.

A wonderful Serbian woman of eighty once told me, "We go about our lives, withdrawn from each other, and at the end of the day we crawl back into our holes. We don't know what to do with a love such as yours." Another time, she said, "How we have survived as a people is really impossible. Somehow we mutate, find a way, and miraculously, we survive." Once I gave her a gold cross on a necklace, which she wore proudly. When she wore it to her Orthodox church, however, the priest demanded, "What is that?" She explained that a dear friend from America had given it to her. He reprimanded her, "Well, just don't wear it in here!" Because he was the authority figure in her life, she later asked me, hurt and puzzled, "What is this that you gave me for him to speak so?" Just a garden variety cross, but Protestant. Once I looked at an Orthodox church map of Serbia, Montenegro, and Kosovo. It looked like a thick spider web with bases holding the country in an ancient, tight grip.

Nikola Kocić and Judy Ferguson, holding test proof of Alaska's Secret Door, *Publikum, Belgrade, 2004. Judy Ferguson photo.*

The entrenchments in Yugoslavia are old, deep, and significant.

Since before entering the Balkans in the seventh century, the people have suffered enormously. Their response has not been rugged self-evaluation to attain responsibility: instead they cry victimization, eulogize in epic mythology, and pass the blame, isolating themselves behind an Eastern European wall. Some retreat into academia; many dabble in the occult. What is lacking is a responsibility for others and room for those who reject Serbia's societal norms. In the Balkans what is esteemed is the victor: the proud, egocentric, self-made society. The culture is rich, and like their foods and homemade sweaters, life appears whole, the hospitality overflowing. As the late *Vreme* magazine journalist and Harvard scholar Stojan Cerović said, "The culture of former Yugoslavia was its best part."

When Christianity originally arrived in the Balkans, it was slipped like an outer garment over the existing pagan customs. Frequently the village priests were autocratic and illiterate. After fifty years of communism, the people returned to a veneer of Christianity, a national persona. In 2000, a female scientist, a former hardline Communist whose family I'd helped greatly, challenged me, "*Who is this* God you always speak of anyway?" Communism shaped a generation and its children into austere atheists, today's norm.

I remembered once Ivan asked me, "Judy, are you a Catholic?" "No," I said, "I'm a Protestant." He screwed his face around, puzzled and indignant, and asserted, "If you are not Orthodox, then you are a Catholic!" "No, Ivan, there was a Protestant Reformation." "Humph," he said, indignant and quite sure I was wrong.

Over the last years, I had tried—to my frequent deep disappointment—to make a bridge, a place of understanding between east and west. Nikola and I talked of it often as we worked.

As Publikum prepared to print *Alaska's Secret Door*, with no experience, I had to decide how many children's books to print. After a few quiet moments, I settled on five thousand. I called a friend who was an employee at British Airways. She said, "If you have them packed like luggage, I will give you half of them for free. But," she cautioned, "get them here early and checked in."

Nikola and I were up all night at Publikum doing press checks as they printed the five thousand books. Finally at dawn, we took a cab back to the house. As the rosy sun peeked over the horizon, a subtle suggestive great promise of light and heat, Nikola got up on a post to see better. With his arms outstretched, he proclaimed to heaven and earth, "WE MADE A BRIDGE!" Yes, I mused to myself, by golly we did. Not quite what I had originally figured, but nevertheless it was a real and a solid bridge. And who was I to know how to build a bridge.

Again my parade of friends ferried in eleven bags of books to Surčin. But at the last minute, Ivan's mother, Vesna, gave me a huge bag of candies to give Ivan in Fairbanks. That coupled with another heavy gift from Dragan's mother, my computer, and more made my carryon a backbreaker. I waved goodbye to each dear one and headed through the gate. In London, the eleven bags checked by my friend at Belgrade British Airways were snagged. A British Airways supervisor pulled me aside, tried repeatedly to call Belgrade, couldn't get through, and to my astonishment, finally waved my bags on through. But to survive, I bought an expensive bag in the airport to offload and checked my huge carryon.

SERBIA

Chapter 52

Risan: Little Fairbanks

first met David Salmon, a Gwich'in Athabascan priest from Chalkyitsik, in the early 1990s at the Athabascan Fiddling Festival in Fairbanks. Because of the twinkle in his eye and a certain solidity to his person, David was someone I wanted to know. I asked him if he'd consider doing an interview sometime; he would. I was deeply involved with my first books at the time but made a mental note to find him at the first opportunity.

In the fall of 2003, I felt it was time. I called the Episcopal diocese in Fairbanks to contact David Salmon. After I got his number, I called David's home in Chalkyitsik. Janet Curtiss answered the phone. I explained that I wrote and published books and wanted to interview David. In the background, I could hear

Nikola Kocić and Judy Ferguson, after complet-ing Alaska's Little Chief, *Belgrade, 2005. Judy Ferguson photo.*

singing. David got on the phone with, "Praise the Lord! We're having revival!" The next time he flew to Fairbanks, I interviewed him. Throughout the winter, when David was in, he and Janet usually got together. When I could, I joined them. The more I heard David's story, I realized that with our background as fur trappers and Nikola's art work, we could make a children's book of David's life. A vibrant book of paintings would be a great way to present David's story to everyone. David agreed. With the story in hand in February 2004, I flew to Belgrade. I told Nikola that I had a story to tell him after we finished *Alaska's Secret Door.* After the book was printed and we were exhausted from the push, I still had to pack to go home. Finally I sat on the sofa reeling in fatigue. However, Nikola was eager to hear my idea for the "next" children's book. I said, "Get the tape recorder and tape me because I am too tired to make notes." Nikola eagerly held the recorder to my mouth as I swerved in and out of consciousness trying to tell the story, talking of David's life, of trapping, of Alaska's animals. Nikola, a lover of the out of doors and of critters, loved the story from the start.

In the spring of 2005, Nikola and I were back in the harness again: sending photographs, research data, drawings, and later, acrylic paintings (still, no oil...) but on stretched fine linen canvases! Publikum said we had to find our own prepress. Nikola was in Serbia; I wasn't. I asked him to find a layout artist who could capture the paintings and prep them for printing. He was at a disadvantage; he didn't live in Belgrade, he was trying to do the illustrations, and he was inexperienced at prepress. He tried two or three leads suggested to him. Only one seemed viable to him: a classmate, Sonja Mijajlović. She was a professional

367

photographer and had a calibrated monitor and would flex her schedule to meet ours. She promised Nikola she would take off a week or whatever was necessary.

This time Nikola had the paintings ready. Sonja had a job during the day and a second job in the evening. Nikola and she felt that she could work with us after the second job in the evening at home. I thought it was crazy, but we had no other options. Sonja rented a sixteen megapixel Mamiya digital camera from Belgrade's oldest newspaper, *Politika*, where we set up our studio. Sonya's girlfriend, a makeup artist, cleaned, greased, camouflaged, high-lighted, and colored every square inch of my face and Nikola's to take professional photos of us for the book. Every now and then as fifteen minutes became two hours, I'd suggest, "We need to allow enough time to photograph the paintings...." Finally we set up an easel and began setting lights and photographing Nikola's twenty-four paintings. In a monitor con-nected to the camera, we could see each photo of each painting. It looked excellent. What was very strange was that later when we looked at the photos in Sonja's monitor at home, the photos were nearly black. Each one had to be heavily manipulated. Every night after Sonja got off her second job at about 9 to 10 p.m., we took a cab to her house to prep each photo-graph, painting by painting. Every night, we returned to our flat at 3 to 4 a.m. It was a long and painful work for all three of us.

As it went to press, we were up all night doing press checks at Publikum. With each sheet, Nikola urged some color adjustments. Later when the final product wasn't quite what we'd hoped, he wondered if he had increased the black too much. I didn't complain to Publikum because I thought it was our fault in the prepress. However in 2007, a Publikum owner, a technician, and I looked at Sonja's original Adobe Indesign files in the monitor. The owner looked at the first edition hard copy and then at the files in the monitor and agreed, "There's nothing wrong with those files; it was a bad print run." I was relieved that Sonja had done a good job. We'd tried so hard. But by 2007, Publikum had gone digital; controlling color was near perfect. The second edition of *Alaska's Little Chief* was much better. Later someone said they could see no difference between the two editions, but I could.

Kingsway church conference, Pula, Istria, Croatia. Pastors from former Yugoslavia: Radovan Bogdanovic (Belgrade), Aleksandar "Aca" Mitrovic (Novi Sad), Nebojsa Djuric (Pula, Croatia), and Aleksandar "Sasa" Vuletic (Skopje, Macedonia). Judy Ferguson photo.

Rainbow-filled valley in Istria, Croatia. 2005. Judy Ferguson photo.

Every Sunday, I had *ručak* [ruchak], the day's big meal, with Majda and her family: Mia, Filip, and Eli. Every Sunday evening, I took a cab to church. Kingsway Connection, a ministry from the states, partnered with the Bogdanovićs' church. In 2005, they were organizing a conference in Pula, Istria (Croatia), with several sister churches from former parts of old Yugoslavia: Novi Sad in Vojvodina, Macedonia, Belgrade, and of course, Pula. They asked if I'd like to go. I cleared the deck. I hadn't been to Croatia in thirty-eight years. The focus of the conference would be discipling, a type of reconciliation conference within former Yugoslavia.

As we drove, I was surprised at the contrast between Serbia and the modern, prosperous-looking Croatia. The turnpike looked as good as any in Germany or in the States, complete with gas station/café rest stops. The money was the *kuna*. The cost of living was higher than in Serbia. We arrived at our cottage motel by the sea.

The next day, we met in small groups, each with a pastor, discussing a topic. At the end of the day and a half together, we took communion. A minister said, "This was a beginning, but it was only a beginning." As he spoke, with my eyes closed, I saw an old Roman aqueduct, dry, but an aqueduct. We loaded up in our cars to leave. As I got in, I saw a rainbow over to the right. As we drove through the day of sunshine and storm clouds, there were rainbows everywhere: a chunk on the left, a piece up ahead. Then a full arching rainbow filled the panorama in front of us. For miles as we drove there were rainbows off to the right, filling valleys, short, fat, full rainbows, close rainbows, intense rainbows. God was laughing rainbows! I could feel His pleasure and with it, a promise. As the evening began, we entered a long tunnel that seemed to go on and on. When we came out, the light, the rainbows, all were gone. It was raining, snowing, and dark. It was like leaving the Land of Oz for earth.

Before leaving home in Alaska, the Orthodox Vladyka had arranged for me to meet Father Irinej, a priest in Belgrade. Nikola asked if he might also come. We went downtown to the church. I was a little apprehensive, unsure of what to say to a Serbian priest. To my astonishment, Father Irinej was a Serbian American raised in the States. Charismatic and warm, he was very easy to talk with. I asked a lot of questions and listened closely.

Also before leaving home, I had received an e-mail from a stranger, Gordan Stojović, in Montenegro. He also was an author and one who specialized in the Montenegrin diaspora,

Nikola Kocić, Vlado Stijepović and Gordan Stojović, Vuka Stepovich's front yard, Risan,
Montenegro, 2005. Judy Ferguson photo.

particularly those in Argentina. In many ways, we were parallel: both writer-bloodhounds interested in a tantalizing trail. Gordan was a fun-loving, driven and outgoing person, a poet, the son of two physicians. I said, "If you come to Belgrade, meet me and we'll visit." One afternoon, Gordan and his cousin dropped in. We visited in "my garden" and we hit it off. Vlado Stijepović had invited me to come to Risan, Montenegro, so Gordan and I figured to see each other then.

A week before I had to leave for home, Gordan and Vlado met me and Nikola at the plane in Montenegro. At sunset, I insisted on showing Gordan Vuka's house up the hill. It was getting dark as we climbed and scrambled through fences, but Gordan and Nikola saw the home of the Alaska diaspora matriarch, Vuka Stepovich, overlooking the sea.

During the winter, Vlado had stunned me by sending me an e-mail with a photo of "Maki" Bogoljub Arsenijević reading my book, *Parallel Destinies*. During 1999 on the B92 website, I had read Maki's story, how he had been beaten by Milošević's police. I could not believe this person reading my book was that Maki. Apparently he was in Risan "on retirement," living near Vlado's. When Nikola and I arrived in Risan, "Maki" Bogoljub Arsenijević was living in a building that belonged to the church located on "Wise Mike" Stepovich's old ground. Maki and Vlado had decided that Nikola and I would stay with Maki. Maki was a fine iconographer and painted frescoes in churches across Serbia and

Raymond (son) and Mato Seferović, fifty-year retail distributor in Seward, Alaska, c. 1930. Courtesy of Nataša Seferović Bigović and Vojka Seferović.

Montenegro. His home was perfect for an artist: ascetic for the basics of life with a gourmet kitchen and a very workable studio with ready access to his outdoor table, chairs, and a view of the Bay of Risan and surrounding mountains. The guys gave me the bedroom. Maki slept in his studio and Nikola on the kitchen sofa. Every morning, Maki was first up with a scrumptious breakfast ready: sheep meat, eggs, vegetables, breads, juices, good Montenegrin coffee, making jokes and sounding like a morning canary. With tropical spring weather around us, it was perfect. Vlado arranged for us to meet Mato and Nataša (Seferović) Bigović and Nataša's father, Vojka Seferović. Nataša spoke English well, was a terrific organizer, and was a nice person who made loza with wild roses flavoring the brandy in the sun on her kitchen shelf. One of the elder Bigovićs arrived to tell the story of Fairbanks Blažo "Bob" Bigovich while Nataša translated. Nataša began by saying that Montenegro was the oldest state in the Balkans, first founded in 1494.

They explained that the Austrian Empire conquered the Bay of Kotor in 1815 and held it until 1922. In the mid-1800s, the Austrians were building roads in Montenegro, trying to unite the Croatians and the Montenegrins. Nikola Bigović had seven sons, including Bob, born in 1905, and two daughters. Three of his sons, Nikola, Mico, and Andrija, went to Montana to work in the mines. In 1914, Nikola and another three of his sons were arrested on suspicion of rebellion against the Austro-Hungarian Empire and were taken to Hungary. In 1923 when he was eighteen, Bob Bigovich followed his brothers to Montana to work in the mines. The brothers sent money home, and with it, the Bigović family moved from the village of Zelenika and built the house we were in in Risan. During World War II in the army, Bob served in North Africa and Italy. After World War II, he went to Alaska where he began bartending in Fairbanks. From 1949 to the early 1950s, Bob became a guardian of the Pete Mesich estate, which included the International Hotel. (That story is told in the Joe Jackovich chapter.) By the time Bigovich died, he was a partner in the Nevada and Cottage bars. His pallbearers read like a who's who list of Fairbanks in 1988: Dan Pekich, Duane Albin, George Matusovich, Mike Stepovich, Bud Kelly, and Paul Gavora. His honorary pallbearers were Clyde Geraghty, John Butrovich, Joe Franich, Hap Ryder, Jack Sexton, Drago Mesich, Louis Krize, Billy Vuicich, and Danny Thompson.

Priest Momčilo Glogovac, Risan church built in 1796 and the bell tower in 1805. Risan, 2005. Judy Ferguson photo.

In Risan, the Bigović family owned a bakery on the corner of the main street as well as a small restaurant by the bay.

Nataša's father, Vojka Seferović, decribed his Uncle Mato who'd lived for over fifty years in Seward on the Kenai Peninsula. Born in 1889, eighteen-year-old Mato Seferović went to Seward by ship in 1907, two years after Bob Bigovich was born. For over fifty years, Seferović worked as a retailer in Seward. In 1950, Mato's brother Stefan Seferović fell to his death in Juneau's A-J Mine. Very often, these Montenegrin men sent gold rings with the word Alaska surrounded by Montenegro's grapevines home to their families. The rings symbolized the unity between the families in Montenegro and in Alaska, and they were also a secure investment. Because times were so difficult during World War I, many Montenegrins sold those rings. Fascinated by the story of the gold rings, I was thrilled to discover that the Bigovićs had such a ring. Vlado went to his dental office, returned with some silicone, and made a delicate mold of the Bigović ring. Later in Alaska, my friend Tom Grapengeter, a jeweler, made a beautiful rendition of the ring, pictured on the back cover of *Bridges to Statehood*.

After interviewing with the Bigovićs and Seferovićs, Nikola, Vlado, and I went to the Bigovićs' café where we met with Dr. Mihailo Mihaljević, a neurologist. Mihailo was the cousin of the Mellicks of the Kuskokwim River and resembled Pete Mellick, his relative. I showed him photos of the Mellicks on my laptop.

We stopped by the church and spoke with the priest about the church's records and to see Goyko Stijepović's grave. I was struck by the eloquence of the priest's figure with the church in the background.

I was determined for Gordan to see John Hajdukovich's house in Podgor Utrg. Branko and Dana Hajduković met us and we took Gordan and Nikola to see the house and meet the neighbors. We ate figs and apples and the men had *rakija*.

Neurologist Dr. Mihailo Mihaljevic holds Judy's laptop with photo showing resemblance of the doctor with his cousin, Pete Mellick, of Sleetmute on the Kuskokwim River. Risan, 2005. Judy Ferguson photo.

The next morning Maki talked about his life. He explained that he was a child of an unmarried woman. As an adult, he had finally met his father, who wouldn't have anything to do with him. Repeatedly, Maki said, "I am a self-made man." He said he had three families and seven children. In Serbian but using a little English and with some translation from Nikola, he explained how Milošević's police had beaten him and put him in prison, of his incredible escape, and of his plan that led to the October 5 Bulldozer Revolution. He said before the revolution, he'd decided the only way to fight Milošević was with violence. From surrounding cities, he had organized a network of men who with bulldozers and trucks had rolled into Belgrade, blocked traffic, and demanded that Milošević acknowledge that he had lost the elections. Since I was getting this in a torrent of Serbian, I believe that Maki said he was the one who threw the fire into the Serbian parliament building. Much later I found on the internet a copy of an interview with Maki done by Free Serbia (FS) where he described his plan to overthrow Milošević, published in part here:

Maki: I believe in a similar scenario including previously thoroughly prepared rebellion following the model I've suggested. General uprising articulated through civil resistance movement is fully justified, necessary and the only viable model for a rapid liberation of the country. Civil resistance movements are not political parties or similar entities—they represent the people, they stand for every single citizen of this country. Organized citizens are to surround all the buildings housing municipal and state organs as well as post offices, heating plants, local courts, police stations, prisons, companies, schools, banks, offices of Serbian Revenue Administration, premises of ruling political parties, broadcasters and city assemblies demanding that all the cities and lands be peacefully surrendered to the people. If the dictator does not accept the terms of the people's ultimatum within the specified deadline, then the citizens of the civil resistance groups will take advantage of all means available until the liberation day.

FS: What about the police?

Maki: I leave nothing to chance. I'm well aware of their psychological and physical condition. Milosevic's private army numbers around 120,000 policemen including the civilians working for the police force. The objective of the Civil Resistance is to engage them simultaneously in as many cities and towns throughout the country as possible so that they dissipate their energy and power. We'll show how serious we are when we put them to the test and give them a few days only to withdraw.

FS: Will this foreshadow a civil war in the country?

Maki: Instigators of the civil war have emerged both within the regime's ranks and on the opposition scene for reasons only they have knowledge of. However, every normal man is well aware that it's an artificial warmongering psychosis created for internal use only. Direct conflict in which people might get killed is simply impossible.

Between 30 and 40 per cent of the citizens will take part in general uprising and the same percentage of the police force because they're also the citizens of their hometowns. Milosevic will be forced to deploy local police officers and they're actually our fellow citizens. Will those people of flesh and blood 'courageously' come up against their neighbors, friends and relatives in the name of utter uncertainty without previously asking themselves a simple question: "And what about tomorrow?" They should be aware of the fact that none of their colleagues from neighboring towns would come to

"Maki" Bogoljub Arsenijević, iconographer in his studio, Risan, Montenegro, 2005. Judy Ferguson photo.

their rescue. If the dictator dares deploy local police force in other towns for tactical reasons, then those wretched fellows will be even more confused as they'll find themselves in unfamiliar surroundings. However, there can be no armed conflict in either scenario for quite simple reasons. You'd have around 3,500,000 citizens confronting some 30,000 or 40,000 policemen. As we know that the police would have to stretch their power to cover countless places throughout Serbia, they certainly won't be able to put up any defense against the citizens. And particularly so if we bear in mind that more than a hundred people per one policeman on average have come up against them. For psychological reasons, given that the citizens will have the initiative, it's hard to believe that anyone from the police force will dare spark the conflict. If we further take into account that Milosevic will certainly build around himself at least five lines of defense, which would engage some 10,000 elite police officers, he will have to rely in the field on traffic policemen only. They have to deploy at least 30,000 policemen in 150 municipalities. In each municipality we'll have 5,000 citizens confronting 50 policemen. Could anyone imagine this 'standoff' evolving into a civil war?

FS: What about the army?

Maki: The people are the army and the people will stand up for their families. The people will certainly not defend Milosevic and a couple of his scarecrows—army generals. However, these calculations will turn out to be useless because the citizens gathered in their cities and towns with an articulate idea on how to temporarily take over the reins of power will represent an extremely forceful weapon which will make Milosevic vanish into thin air even before anything actually takes place. I want just to show the citizens by citing these figures that the real power lies in the people and not in Milosevic's hands as his television portrays it. Milica Bjelovuk.

Note: First published in the Belgrade daily Glas javnosti, *available at http://www. xs4all.nl/~freeserb/interviews/e-index.html*

I could hardly believe my host did all that.

The next day was beautiful. I wanted to go to Dubrovnik. In forty-one years of contact with Yugoslavia, I'd never been to historic Dubrovnik. Vlado, Nikola, and I jumped in Maki's car and hoped it would make it okay to Dubrovnik and back. Going through the

Judy Ferguson and Vlado Stijepović, above Dubrovnik, 2005. Judy Ferguson photo.

border was no problem. We were getting a late start, but I figured that seeing the walled city formerly called Ragusa was better than never seeing it at all. As we looked from the hill overlooking the city, the town that paid tribute to the Turks during the Ottoman Empire looked like a gem from our bird's-eye view. About sunset, we entered the walled city where the streets were a smooth, polished stone. Streetlamps lit the plaza, fountain, and bell tower. We walked down alleys where there were intimate restaurants, jewelry shops, and people enjoying a tête-à-tête at candlelit tables. We stopped in an affordable café for pizza. The next morning, it was hard to say goodbye to our chums.

After quickly pulling everything together to return to Alaska, I realized how wonderful it was to no longer have to check eleven bags of books. Air freight was now affordable. No longer did I need a letter of invitation to enter the country or a visa. On entry and exit, I did have to still register and sign out with the police department. My life in Belgrade had become a businesswoman's errand with an enjoyable retreat to Montenegro per visit. I was beginning to enjoy a quieter, less intrusive experience in Serbia. Peka and Nikola took me to Surčin. As always, I gave my friend Ana at British Airways a copy of my new book, this time *Alaska's Little Chief*. As Nikola and I waited for me to board, to my amazement, I looked across the waiting room and I saw someone reading *Alaska's Little Chief*! He must have been a friend of Ana's. I waved goodbye to Nikola, not knowing that the following spring, we'd begin another and this time probably our final book. Nikola was growing up, and there were a lot of things he still wanted to do in life.

Majda David, Judy Ferguson, Zorica Petrović, Belgrade, 2003. Judy Ferguson photo.

Chapter 53

Bridges Running East-West: Parallel Destinies

hen I was selling *Alaska's Little Chief*, the biography of Gwich'in Athabascan First Traditional Chief David Salmon, at the Alaska State Fair in Palmer, it became clear I needed another book with a broader scope to include all of Alaska's indigenous cultures. I made a plan to write *Alaska's First People*. For two years, I'd been writing the "Alaskana" column for the *Anchorage Daily News*; I had featured people representing all of Alaska's cultures. Not only did I learn a lot but I made friends with people who could guide me. Nikola agreed to make a third children's book. I researched and sent pictures and data to Nikola. Once I got his drawings, I submitted them to Native elders to approve. Once we had an okay, Nikola

The Organization of the Montenegrin-American Friends: Gordon Stojović, Vlado Stijepović, Danica Hajduković, Judy Ferguson, Branko Hajduković, Podgorica, Montenegro, 2007. Judy Ferguson photo.

began painting. This time he used oils on stretched canvas, but we decided that he would ship them DHL; I had them scanned in Alaska. For every page, he designed cultural tokens overlaying a color-coded map. He made a master map for the front inside cover. Indigenous educators endorsed the pages relevant to their culture. Doyon Foundation, Alaska Native Knowledge Network, and the University of Alaska Fairbanks' Alaska Native Language Center were a big help. My friend, artist Diane Folaron, designed the back cover. As Nikola and I worked, a retired educator designed lesson plans, based on state performance standards, to sell on an accompanying CD.

After the paintings were scanned here in Alaska using top-of-the-line technology, I was ready. From January 15 to February 14, 2007, I was in Belgrade. I hand-carried my external hard drive with all my files on it. I had some files backed up on CDs as well. On the first day at Publikum, I gave my external hard drive to the graphics lab to extract the files. To my horror, it was empty. The hard drive sounded like broken glass. The map logos were not on my CDs, and so they were gone. I returned to my flat and called my husband and Diane Folaron. I asked Diane if she could go to my house, retrieve the logos, and send them to me by e-mail. My landlord, Peka, took the hard drive to a couple of computer shops to try to retrieve the data, but it was totally destroyed. After three days, I had received all the needed files. As always, Diane, who made the original maps for my two adult Alaska books, had saved me.

Publikum had converted to digital; it was now much easier to control the color printing. All day every day for two weeks, I was at Publikum working with Tanja in prepress. There was another bad surprise; Nikola's map was not saved in its large size but in a small size. Tanja had to build the map all over again based on Nikola's template. Also, Tanja and I improved my first two children's books, *Alaska's Secret Door* and *Alaska's Little Chief,* and we reprinted them.

On the weekend and during the evenings, Zorica and I took walks. We'd start from our homes and meet each other midway on JNA Boulevard. To stock my larder, I walked uphill for half an hour to the C Market a couple of times a week. I cruised the aisles, discussed meat in Serbian with the butcher, weighed the fruit with the produce manager who labeled it, and then glided over to checkout where I used my Alaska Airlines credit card and got a receipt from the register. Life had changed drastically from the days of international sanctions. (During 1998 to 2003, all money had to be hand-carried in. Credit cards were useless. Money changing was done illegally on the street or in a currency exchange, sometimes in a bank. Receipts were handwritten or were generated by an adding machine.) After shopping, I hand-carried my bags of heavy groceries in the dark down the steep hill to my flat. (Taxis in Belgrade won't take a customer to a location near their home, so I walked.) I tried to learn the bus system from Zorica, but it was complicated as well as slow so I paid extra to be taxied. There was no printed intracity bus schedule. It

Aleksandra Stojanović (Nikola Kocić's fiancée) and Nikola's sister, Jelena Kocić, celebrate Nikola's third children's book, Alaska's First People, *Publikum, Belgrade, 2007. Judy Ferguson photo.*

was "the people's bus" and you had to know the stops, the transfer points, the names of the buses, and pay with a chit.

After the pressure was off at Publikum, I scheduled two interviews: the first with Majda's brother, Davor Salom, at the synagogue. Davor and his wife Marija lived in one of the apartments belonging to the synagogue, rented to members of the Jewish community. In former Yugoslavia, Davor was an activist and leader in the Jewish community but when Yugoslavia began to disintegrate, he moved to Israel. When he returned to Belgrade, he became the secretary for the Federation of the Jewish communities in Serbia. Since 2004, he has been a UN adviser to the Parliament of Serbia.

General Peko Dapčević greets Moše Salom, Davor and Majda's father, Ljubljana, Slovenia, Yugoslavia, 1945. Courtesy of Davor Salom and Majda David.

Davor gave me a tour of the synagogue, the Jewish Historical museum, and the old Dorćol Jewish quarter, which included the former Sephardic synagogue and the Oneg Shabat building, a social hall. Davor said his father Moše Salom was born in 1908 in Višegrad and later moved to Sarajevo, Bosnia. The Salom family spoke Ladino, the Sephardic Judeo-Spanish language. During the Holocaust, his grandfather's family was taken to Jasenovac and Djakovo concentration camps where they were killed by the Ustaše. By fighting as a Partisan under Tito, Moše Salom survived World War II. As a member of the Communist party, he could still attend the synagogue and work in the Jewish Community.

As Davor and I toured the Jewish museum, he began teaching me how Jews came to the Balkans in the first place.

Jews began migrating in large numbers to the Ottoman Empire because in the lands of the sultan they found a religious tolerance unimaginable in the Christian Europe of that day. In 1634 in the empire, Jews amounted to fifty million, compared to the five million in England.

The Jews were a very strongly integrated society, and after the French Revolution, they were an emancipated culture. There were strong communities in Croatia, Bosnia, Herzegovina, Serbia, and Macedonia but there were few in Montenegro. The number in each area reflected the attitude of the surrounding population. Slovenia had very strong laws against Jews, with anti-Semitic laws imported from Empress Maria Teresa, the Austro-Hungarian monarch.

Jews were from two derivations: Ashkenazi, whose descendants were from Germany but had come through Poland, Czechoslovakia, and Hungary. These Ashkenazi spoke Yiddish but if they lived in Vojvodina, north of Belgrade, they

The great-great-grandmother of Davor Salom and Majda David, Rifka Salom, Sarajevo,
c. 1890–1900. Courtesy of Davor Salom and Majda David.

The great-great-grandfather of Davor Salom and Majda David, Avraham Salom, Sarajevo, c. 1890. Courtesy of Davor Salom and Majda David.

spoke Hungarian. The Ashkenazi tended to migrate to a Catholic environment: Catholic Croatia. Vojvodina was predominantly Catholic as well as Protestant but later it also became Orthodox. Bosnia-Herzegovina was a mix of Orthodox, Catholic, and Muslim. Both Macedonia and Serbia were Orthodox and Muslim. Macedonia and especially Serbia had been under Muslim rule for over four centuries. The deprecatory word for Serbs was *Raja*, meaning "common people" or "mob." In Turkish times, Jews were in a better position than Serbs. My great-great-grandfather Avraham, who lived in Bosnia was allowed to carry a sword because he was a respected citizen, but he was still not considered an equal citizen with the Turks.

As manufacturing began to develop, Jews were allowed to travel. Having a high level of education, they were used in state offices and in diplomacy. They knew languages and carried out collections. However, their capability created competition. In earlier centuries, Serbs banned Jews from certain activities around Serbia. Jews were allowed to open businesses in large cities, but in small places there were some problems.

The father of Zionism and the forefather of the newborn state of Israel, Theodore Hertzl, was born in the nineteenth century in Vienna. He had a grandfather, Simon

Davor and Majda Salom with their parents, Matilda and Moše Salom, c. 1956, Belgrade. Courtesy of Davor Salom and Majda David.

Davor Salom at the original Sephardic synagogue that was destroyed by the Nazis during World War II. Belgrade, 2007. Judy Ferguson photo.

Loeb Hertzl, who lived in the old city of Zemun. (Today a municipality of Belgrade.) But Zemun used to be an Austro-Hungarian military outpost on the northwest side of the Sava River. Across on the Belgrade side, there were Turkish troops at Kalemegdan fortress. The Danube and the Sava rivers were the borders between the two empires: Vojvodina to the north belonged to the Austro-Hungarian Empire and Belgrade to the south, to the Ottoman Empire. For centuries, the two forts were enemies. To feed the Zemun fortress, there were ten to twelve Jewish families living there during the seventeenth to nineteenth centuries. Simon Loeb Hertzl, the grandfather of Theodore Hertzl, was one of those people.

A significant early rabbi, the former Spanish-speaking chief rabbi of Ottoman Bosnia, Rabbi Yehuda Alkalay (1798 to 1878), was an early writer on Zionism and also lived in Zemun. Hertzl's grandfather, Simon Loeb Hertzl, was a disciple of Rabbi Alkalay. Hertzl's grandfather attended Alkalay's synagogue and the two visited frequently. Simon Hertzl had one of the first copies of Alkalay's 1857 book prescribing the "return of the Jews to the Holy Land and the renewed glory of Jerusalem." Hertzl's own later Zionism was probably influenced by the relationship of his grandfather and the Sephardic rabbi. Alkalay influenced not only Jews of Zemun but Jews all over the world. These two key figures,

Alkalay and Theodore Hertzl, were profound shapers of international Judaism and both lived in Zemun.

Before World War II, Jews were mostly integrated into the south Slavs' multiethnic, multireligious society, which was liberal toward the Jews. There were no ghettos. There was no persecution or pogroms of the Jews as were normal in Eastern Europe, particularly in Poland and Russia. Because of the strong Catholic church in Croatia, local attitudes toward Jews did differ from those in Serbia, even before World War II. But the Serbian Orthodox community was much more open. Jews felt close to the lighthearted Serbs. Serbs weren't as strict as the Croats in Catholic Croatia. In Serbia, people fell in love and it was common to have mixed marriages. It was also accepted in some places in Bosnia, but it was not as prevalent as in Serbia.

Before World War II, there were eighty-six thousand Jews in former Yugoslavia, including Serbia. World War II destroyed up to ninety percent of Yugoslavia's Jewish population. In Macedonia, it was almost one hundred percent. In March 1942, all the Macedonian Jews were taken to the gas chambers in Treblinka. Today Macedonia claims about two hundred Jews. Out of the 15,000 that survived in Yugoslavia, in 1948 over half of them migrated to Israel.

There are ten surviving, reestablished Jewish communities in the province of Vojvodina and in Niš, Serbia. But the Jewish communities in places like Kragujevac—where Miša came from—and in Kraljevo, Shabatz, and Biacher, were completely destroyed. The only Jewish names there today are on street signs and in the cemeteries.

In Serbia, we have about three thousand members in our Jewish community. Of that three thousand, two thousand live in Belgrade. By the state's census, only 1,158 citizens of Serbia claim to be of Jewish origin. Of those members, only about thirty percent are active; about two to three hundred people come to the community meetings. The others orbit in a more distant circle.

The assimilation of Jews into mainstream society is very high here partly due to the level of intermarriage, as well as the decline of traditional and religious life. There is a lack here of Jewish education both within the family and in the schools. In the current, democratic government, there is support to improve the situation. However often leadership and members in the community itself are to be blamed for the inadequate interest. If we Jews were a strong, closed, nonintegrated society, everything would be different, but we are not. We are open and consequently we suffer the same fate as the community at large from the policies in the government, finances, and education. As we are emerging from a Communist country into a privatized one, we in the Jewish community would like to see restitution of our confiscated Jewish properties which would provide a source of income to our community. However almost nothing has been done.

There is a contrast between how a Jew in the States relates to his country and how we do to ours. In America, a Jew would say, "I am an American of Jewish derivation," but here, I would say, "I am a Jew who lives in Serbia."

Just as everywhere in the world, there is anti-Semitism in Serbia. But by nature, Serbs are not anti Semitic. Much of the anti Semitic literature like the *Protocols of the Elders of Zion* (an extreme anti-Semitic pamphlet published during the twentieth century in Russia) is printed in the United States.

However because of America's connection to Israel and due to anti-American feeling resulting from the 1999 NATO aggression, many Serbs equate us with America. They suppose we are rich, or freemasons, maybe controlling the world through a conspiracy. The only way to fight anti-Semitism is through strict laws prohibiting the language of hate, racism, and xenophobia as well as teaching tolerance of minorities. Lately there has been a significant improvement. We invite our non-Jewish friends to our Jewish community to hear lectures, to educate them about the Holocaust, to meet us and to know our history so that we may emulate the prewar atmosphere when they used to like us.

Serbs are xenophobic in a way because they tend to not esteem diversity and they reject a global view. They offer hospitality but it stops there. No other country has hospitality like Serbs. It's a trademark. Some people have mountains, rivers, or volcanoes, but Serbs showcase hospitality.

When you consider all that has happened to Serbs in the last ten to thirty years, they need someone to blame. If they can't find a foreigner, then it's the Jews. If not the Jews, then it's the Masons, or the Roma, or neighbors from other cities. However the guilt should fall on the Communist leaders who were in power until 2000. The Serbs also suspect the superpowers' global interests, perceived by many as the cause for the misfortune of small nations, like Serbia. This problem of myopia and blame is very deep rooted, and it will take a very long effort to change it.

One of my missions is to help children who lost their grandparents during the Holocaust to discover their identity, to be proud of being Jewish

Davor Salom and the Imam, Muhamed Jusufsphahić, Belgrade, 2007. Judy Ferguson photo.

and to respect those who are not. I want them to learn the values of Western civilization. It is very important to love your neighbor, to help the poor.

That is why I have joined a United Nations Development Program (UNDP). For the last five years I have worked as an adviser in the Serbian Parliament to support programs to reduce poverty. By accomplishing Millennium Development Goals, Serbia will reduce poverty among some of society's marginal groups: the unemployed, the disabled, the refugees, Roma, and rural families. We work hard to fight corruption by developing democratic values in our parliament.

We are most grateful to the American Jewish Distribution Committee. Through them, we are developing cultural, religious and social programs to help our needy members, some of whom are Holocaust survivors. Over many years, Jews have established welfare institutions around the world: for the poor in America, Europe but especially in Eastern Europe, and also in Ethiopia and Biafra.

Afterward, Davor drove me over to Sajmište [Siimeeshtuh], one of the main sites of the Holocaust in Nazi-occupied Serbia, called the Semlin Judenlager by the Germans. Together, Davor and I read the story.

Established by the Nazis in December 1941 on the outskirts of Belgrade near the

Davor Salom at the old Sajmište fairgrounds that was once the largest Nazi concentration camp in Serbia. Belgrade, 2007. Judy Ferguson photo.

river, Sajmište, its Serbian name, was one of the first concentration camps in Europe, created specifically for the internment of Jews. Between March and May 1942, approximately seven thousand Jewish women, children, and the elderly (almost half of the total Jewish population of Nazi-occupied Serbia) were systematically murdered there by the use of a mobile gas van. After the Jewish internees were killed, Semlin, as it was called by the Germans, was turned into an *Anhaltelager*, a temporary detention camp. Many were political prisoners, captured Partisans, and forced laborers, most of whom were later transported to various labor camps in Germany. Between May 1942 and July 1944, thirty-two thousand inmates (mainly Serbs) passed through the camp, of whom 10,600 were killed or died of starvation, exposure, or disease. Semlin was the largest concentration camp in Nazi-occupied Serbia.

In spite of its importance in the Holocaust, the Semlin Judenlager played a marginal place in the memorialization of the destruction of Serbian Jewry in post-war Yugoslav/Serbian society. The memory of the destruction of the Jews was assimilated within the dominant symbolic orders, first within multiethnic Yugoslavia—where the heroism of the Partisans, rather than the victimization of the civilian population, constituted the primary memory—and later within the post-Yugoslav ideological milieu, which was dominated by Serbian nationalism and preoccupied with the suffering of Serbs under the Ustasha regime in Croatia during the Second World War.

After reading, Davor showed me the monument down by the river. However very little had been done with Sajmište itself; I greatly hoped more would be memorialized.

I hurried home to meet Nedjo and Teri Spaić of Palmer, Alaska, visiting at the same time as I was in Belgrade.

Two years earlier, I had met Teri at an IDEA homeschooler curriculum fair in Anchorage. I was amazed to learn she was married to a Serb. Afterward we met several times. To our great surprise, we planned to go to Serbia at the exact same time in 2007. We exchanged contact information and when they arrived in Belgrade, they called me.

I stood in front of my flat waiting for them. After awhile, I heard two cars careening around the curve, heading in the opposite direction away from me. A man stuck his head out of his window and yelled at the other driver, "Hey, where is this house?!" I laughed, knowing who it had to be, and yelled loudly, "NEDJOOOOO!" Sure enough, the car slowed down, backed up and came to get me. We went to a nice Serbian restaurant and talked, and Nedjo shared his story.

I was born in a nonfertile, stony country, snake and us, and sun, right on the riverbank in Trebinje in 1955. The river was clear and wide. They show us how to breathe and swim. River's so fast. They threw us in, and it brought us right down to them right away. We came up for air; they pick us up half dead. They do it again

Nedjo Spaić telling his story and that of his people. Belgrade, 2007. Judy Ferguson photo.

Teri, Judy Ferguson, Spaić daughter, Nedjo Spaić, Belgrade, Serbia, 2007. Judy Ferguson photo.

and again until we learn how to float. We learned in one day. I love to swim. That was the first six years of my life with my two sisters. I used to play on the three-hundred-foot cliffs and dive straight down into the river. My mother thought she's going to die, seeing me play there. Ten years later they built two big dams, two big lakes, and this river lost all its identity. The first time I saw the Little Susitna in Alaska, I tell Teri, "It's like my river!"

In our culture, parents are there to help kids to stand on their own feet until they are ready to make their own money. Then when parents are old, the kids return the favor and take care of their parents. I am my parents' only son so when I decided to go to the States that was hard. I deeply love my culture but I made a new life in America. Nobody in my family is like me; they tried to figure where I came from. But they hid from me that I was like my great uncle, Savo Spaić, I call "Grampa" who went to Alaska. Because he was like black sheep: never married, never came back from Alaska.

In 1984 when I was twenty-nine, I went to America on a tourist visa. I really didn't care if they sent me back. I didn't care about legal paperwork. A year after I came I started my own construction company, "*Loza* [brandy] *Konkreton* [concrete]." That was so funny in Serbian community. I wanted at that time to go to Alaska to see where is my "Grampa," but I never made it then.

When I was thirty-two, one day I was in a restaurant drinking and I saw Teri. I'd spent so much time in Serbian restaurants and bars. I was really tired of that lifestyle and wanted to change it. For fifteen years, I never went back to Herzegovina to visit my parents, my family. My parents came to visit me, and they wanted to take me back. I work hard, drink hard, fight hard. I really give Teri credit for marrying me. We married and the kids began coming; things started to slow down. I began building my name in the construction world. Later after we got kids, I want to go visit my parents but I can't without legal paperwork. We worked on getting it, and did. I was one of best construction companies in that part of Chicago; I did houses like for Walgreens, those type people. I knew multimillionaires. They all knew my name.

In 1988 when we got first kid, I tell Teri, "Buy me a ticket. I want to go by myself in February." "Where?" she asked. I said, "Alaska." She almost flipped. I said, "I wanta find my great uncle, Savo Spaić. In 1988 at –37F, I had on a t-shirt and leather jacket; I drove a two-wheel drive, little car, to Homer, Anchorage, Valdez, and Fairbanks by myself. I saw a moose and put my fist out in case it might hit me. That's all I knew then. I came back four times with my kids. I never find great uncle but I push Teri and we move there. My last crazy thing was that with seven kids, I picked up and took my company and left for Alaska where I knew no one and nothing. People in Chicago couldn't believe it when I left. Teri's father asked, "What's this guy going to do next?" Teri was crying, "What are we gonna do? We have seven kids."

When I told Teri we're going to move to Alaska, I started looking at real estate, houses, how to set up my company. On the internet in 2001, I saw "Sheep Mountain Lodge for sale on Glenn Highway. $600,000." I tell Teri, "That's it. We're going to sell our house, go to the bank, no problem cause my house worth much more than that." But when Teri checked the next day, it said, "Sold." So we came to Alaska to get a place. We drove up to Sheep Mountain, I went in and I told owner we almost bought this place. Then I looked down in their glass case and I see *this guy,* dressed like *my* people! And I said, "Who is *this guy*?!" "I dunno," he said. I said, "Give me *this* book. I open it, sonofagun, I cannot believe it's *my* guy!" I start reading about *Hajdukovich!* [*Parallel Destinies.*] He's from *my area*! I take it, show it to Teri, to my kids. I was so proud! I never really knew Serbs were in Alaska except my "Grampa" who was lost in action. (Who knows what happened with him.) And then, I found *Parallel Destinies* and your other books. Over the years, we read your articles about Serbs in the *Anchorage Daily News*! And we kept all that and that really was nice. And I show the book, the articles to Americans and I say, "SEE, we used to rule Alaska!" This history made me feel much comfortable, knowing that my people were much present here. Yeh. Now, I see why my "Grampa" came here. Serbs were here and told him, so more came. Then I find out we used to have church and have cemetery in Juneau! I see pictures of my people at Independence Mine and that was amazing!

When I took my kids hiking, they were scared to go over a mile from the house. I say, "Hey, you got my blood in you. Challenge that bear!"

I continue construction here but at a much slower pace. We've been here four and a half years. I started making wine, *loza* (brandy), *kiseo kupus* (soured cabbage heads), *sarma* (stuffed sour cabbage simmered in a pork broth), and *prsut* (smoked meat).

The border between Montenegro and my country, Herzegovina, has only been there 110 years. Never before was there a border there; it was all Herzegovina. The southwestern area adjoining us in Trebinje, the hills north of the Bay of Kotor, was Old Herzegovina. [I remembered that Vuka Stepovich said that in the old days, the men of Herzegovina came over to help them in Risan fight the Turks.] What they call "Montenegro," today was called Old Herzegovina; it never ever was called Montenegro in that area.

Montenegro then was Cetinje, Podgorica, John Hajdukovich's country of Utrg, and on up to the town of Mojkovac.

We called the Venetians "Mladiks." They came against Risan. From Trebinje, we came down from mountain; they backed up. We backed up, they advanced. There were so many of us that they were scared of us. Then, and now, we in Herzegovina are pure Serb.

Many of the higher-up Turks who occupied us were actually Serb kids who were often kidnapped and forced to convert to Muslim and came back then to rule us. Like this Mehmed Pasha Sokoli in *Bridge Over Drina*. That was Bosnia, old Herzegovina, all this huge viziers, some (not all) of them were Serbs who converted to Muslim, and in their way, they helped their people. That's that people.

Bay of Kotor, Montenegro, 2007. Judy Ferguson photo.

Most serious communists, what we don't like, were from that area. Communism used us and divided families. The best Serbs, the best protectors of the land was from that area. My people have survived in a nonfertile, stony country, snake and us, and sun. We're like America's Apaches. Over us went Turks, Germans, Austro-Hungarians, Croatians, Napoleons, Muslims now; we got bombed by Americans and English. And we are still there in same mountain. We never attack nobody around us. We came there thousand years ago. We still there. We never went over border, or over river. We got our Saint Sava who brought us to Christianity in 1100. He ruled that area: Herzegovina. That's why I'm proud 'cause we never attacked, we never got bigger, never took more territory. We never had a full big law state and we were always defending ourselves against other empires. We resist always others telling us what to do, how to do, and trying to take advantage of us. People think we are ignorant; we are not. Communists tell us to work for one dollar. Why? He take nine dollars and give us one dollar. A lot of people turn bad, turn to gambling, wanna lotta money, imitating how others acted in history. Thank God we're not all like that. If someone push us down, we really react. We're not used to democracy, to freedom. Feels like someone wants to use us again, like the other empires and more recently, Communism. We really resist. We really don't press anybody. Treat others equal, and us too. We got hot blood, yeh. Look at what Grampas had, that was good and keep that. Take what's good in western countries but throw out the bad. Money interests and companies are taking over. What is left? A person only needs a little furniture, food, and good toilets. We got no good toilets. But there are things in life that are much, much more important. There's such a fast pace in Serbia and Herzegovina now. They are tearing down everything. Do we have to go to a restaurant now to see old Serbia?! It should be in our hearts, outside, on the street, between families. We can still have democracy and freedom, perfectly. But it looks like we don't have time. They are going faster, and faster than our life. Where we gonna end up? Nowhere. That's problem here. Listen little bit. Have to go slow, measure things what's coming here, and act appropriately. Otherwise, you're beating your head against a brick wall. Only get bloody head and brick wall is still there. [Later in the November-December 2006 *Serb World USA* magazine, an article "Serbs in Alaska" described the mines of Juneau-Douglas; in the early 1900s, there was a listing for a miner with Nedjo's family name, Spaić.]

In the fall of 2006, reporter Aleksandar Apostolovski from *Politika* contacted Miro regarding the story of his *Radio Mileva*. In the process, Miro told him about my Hajdukovich research. In early March, Apostolovski interviewed me about the Alaska Yugoslav immigrants, then ran the story. Apostolovski wrote the story in an entertaining and ludicrous manner. (*Politika,* which has a fine and old heritage, went through a period of flashy, superficial writing.) Apostolovski was inundated with calls and e-mails regarding his story

Granica Hajduković, using a hand spinner, Cerovo, Bijelo Polje, Montenegro. 1999. Judy Ferguson photo.

on the Alaska families. When families asked Apostolovski how to contact me, Apostolovski freely (with no apologies later) volunteered my telephone number in Belgrade and my e-mail to anyone and everyone who called. Consequently I had many calls (and e-mails) from excited callers speaking in fast Serbian to me, urging, even requiring me to meet with them. I had to juggle manners, keep up with their language and not make a faux-pas, then ease out of the call. However, a good result was a call from a refined Serbian woman with excellent English, Mary Dapčević. Very politely, she asked me if I'd consider coming to a family reunion hosted by her cousin Branka. Since Stalin's break with Tito in 1948, the family had been split down the middle because two brothers, both military generals, Peko and Vlado, chose separate, critical allegiances. Vlado stayed loyal to Stalin while Peko sided with Tito. Simply because of blood relation, sev-

Jovo Dapčević, Belgrade, 2007. Judy Ferguson photo.

eral family members were sent to Goli Otok, Tito's concentration camp. However, since the death of Peko in 1999 and Vlado in 2001, the family have begun having family reunions and trying to heal. This was the second and the largest reunion. Mary said her son could pick me up and bring me to the party. Careful at first, I soon relaxed and was glad to accept.

Mary's six-foot-eight son picked me up in a beautiful new Toyota, spoke perfect English, and was very well mannered. We had to go across the river to the new Slovenian-owned shopping mall, Merkator. I was amazed. As we entered through the electric-operated glass sliding doors, I felt like I was in Walmart. We rode an escalator and entered a megastore. From 1998 to 2000 during the sanctions, I had gotten used to closed and half filled department stores but out on the street, kiosks of very active illegal vendors. At Merkator, we bought some soda pop and left. We drove to the party. Branka welcomed us and introduced me to Stefan's fine parents, Mary and Jovo, as well as to the Belgian widow of Vlado and the adult children of Peko. I met Ljubo, a Belgrade nightclub owner, and his very similar cousin from Montenegro. I passed around pages with text and photos of the Alaska Dapceviches and told Ljubo how much he reminded me of his cousin John in Juneau. When I sat with Peko's children, Vuk and his sister, Danica, Vuk said, "I don't know half these people. Family—what a situation." Then of Serbs, he made a point, "We're not good people. No, I mean it; we're not. I mean, in what other land with each change of regime, does a country, every fifty years, change the names of 482 streets? 482!" Vuk was nice and his sister, Danica, beamed with strength.

Jovo and I retreated to another room and began an interview. He explained that both his father and Branka had been sent to Goli Otok. While his father was emprisoned, his mother and he, a young boy, were thrown out of their flat with nothing. In 2007, Jovo had a successful business selling and repairing outboard motors. He was a big bear of a man with penetrating blue eyes. Too soon the party was over. I had intended to get together with Jovo and Mary again, but I was leaving the next day for Montenegro and then for home. I was out of time. I was encouraged to contact a well informed matriarch of the family in Montenegro and an older man in Cetinje, near the Dapčević family village. I wanted to, but for that I needed a ride and an interpreter in Montenegro and another free day.

In the year that I didn't visit Serbia-Montenegro, in 2006 Montenegro became independent. In 2007, I flew to Montenegro where Vlado met me. I stayed in a small rental unit his brother owned. I visited with his dear mother, Bosa, a paralyzed woman with a radiant heart.

In 2005 after Gordan Stojović and Branko Hajduković met each other, Branko formed the Montenegrin-American Friendship (MAF) organization. In 2007, Branko scheduled a television press conference. The government of Montenegro had given John Hajdukovich's original Montenegrin home to our new MAF organization. The day after I arrived in Risan, Vlado drove us to a meeting spot by the Bay of Kotor to wait for Gordan Stojović, who would meet us coming from Herceg Novi. We were running late. Worried we might miss the ferry, Gordan drove us pedal to the metal to catch the ferry. We just made it. We arrived in Podgorica at the press conference on time. Miro Vukojčić's father was there waiting for me with his painting of John Hajdukovich's valley of Rijeka Crnojevića to give me.

Branko said the American consulate had said they would help in reconstructing John Hajdukovich's home, creating a parallel "roadhouse" similar to Rika's Roadhouse, a museum saluting the Yugoslavian diaspora who had so greatly shaped Alaska.

Jovo Hajduković pionir Aljaske

Džudi Ferguson

Jovo (u Americi nazvan Džon) Hajduković potiče iz crmničkog sela Utrg. Početkom dvadesetog vijeka pošao je u pečalbu rukovođen snom da se kao bogat čovjek vrati svojoj ženi i nerođenoj ćerki. Nije našao zlato, niti uspio da ispuni svoj zavjet, ali je proživio jedan izuzetno uzbudljiv život. Aljaska je postala njegova druga domovina, u čijem je preobražaju bio aktivni učesnik. Bio je prijatelj Indijanaca, njihov zaštitinik i zastupnik. Tragao je zlatom, lovio irvase, medede, losose, trasirao puteve, gradio otkupne stanice za kože, kafane, trgovine. Nije mu se dalo da se obogati. Njegov rođak Milo

Parallel Destines *now* Jovo Hajduković, Alaskan Pioneer, *published in Montenegrin in Podgorica, Montenegro, 2008. Judy Ferguson photo.*

Gordan said that Matica crnogorska, a nongovernmental cultural institution that promotes Montenegrin identity and language, had published several of his books on the Argentinian diaspora. Gordan suggested to them translating and publishing *Parallel Destinies*. To my deep satisfaction in fall 2008, they published the book, *Jovo Hajduković pionir Aljaske* (Alaska Pioneer) in Montenegrin. John, who along with Alaska's prominent pioneer families—Stepovich, Butrovich, Dapcevich, Begich, Jackovich, Bigovich, Mellick, Agbaba, Paskvan, Krize, Miscovich, Jankovich, Raykovich, Miller/Milaich, Garbin, Peratrovich, Glavinovich, Banic,

Babic, Borovich—who had shaped Alaska, had finally returned to the land of his forefathers in a book about him that was printed in his own language: a *Paralelne sudbine, Parallel Destinies.* As Nedjo Spaić of Palmer said, "From the eighth century, we're still the same people there, top-standing, and we never got kicked out. And we are still there in same mountain. And I tell my people, we have nothing to protect us, only stone, but we love that stone. Our heritage, our culture. After all this unbelievable story, this heritage, we are still there." With the addition, "I like the freedom, the landscape and the attitude of most people in Alaska. I'm making five times less here than in Chicago. But I like Alaska five times more. Alaska has so much sense of freedom and the nature is so beautiful."

And here, those people found the land where east meets west, a land of opportunity, equality, space, and freedom, a land free of war. Like a transplanted wild plant, they took root and they flourished.

Neda, Ivan and Jelena "Duda" Konstantinović, Trebješa hill, Nikšić, Montenegro, c. 1995. Miroslav Konstantinović photo.